Human Monsters
The Definitive Edition

An Expanded Companion Volume
to the Forgotten Horrors Collection

Human Monsters
The Definitive Edition

An Expanded Companion Volume to the Forgotten Horrors Collection

by *Michael H. Price*
with
George E. Turner

Foreword by Fay Wray
Afterword by Vincent Price

Luminary Press
Baltimore, Maryland

Copyright © 2004 Michael H. Price
Cover Design/Layout Design: Susan Svehla

This book is a thorough revision and expansion—*overhaul* is more like it—of a volume published in 1995 by Kitchen Sink Press as *Human Monsters: The Bizarre Psychology of Movie Villains*. Portions have appeared, in markedly different form, in *The Cinema of Adventure, Romance & Terror* (A.S.C. Press; 1989) and *Michael H. Price's Hollywood Horrors* (Shel-Tone Publ.; 1993); in the magazines *Mad About Movies, Midnight Marquee, The American Cinematographer, Monsters from the Vault* and *The Spider*; in the *Business Press* of Fort Worth, Texas, *The New York Times* and the *Fort Worth Star-Telegram* and as dispatches of the New York Times News Service; in M.H. Price's Texas State Network radio broadcasts; and as program notes of the Amarillo (Texas) Film Society, the American Society of Cinematographers and the Lone Star Film Festival. The original *Human Monsters* has, in turn, has been selectively excerpted, not necessarily to say cannibalized, for the collections *Forgotten Horrors 2: Beyond the Horror Ban* and *Forgotten Horrors 3: Dr. Turner's House of Horrors*. The section on *The Big Country* is drawn from M.H.P.'s original typescript for a book accompanying that film's 1990 soundtrack-CD album from Screen Archives/Screen Classics Entertainment. Extensive new material here was composed for a hitherto unpublished critical survey of the work of Boris Karloff and, expressly, for this Luminary Press edition.

Without limiting the rights reserved under the copyright above, no part of this publication whatsoever may be reproduced, stored in or introduced into a retrieval system, or transmitted, in any form, or by any means (electronic, mechanical, photocopying, recording, or otherwise), without the prior written permission of the copyright owner or the publishers of this book.

ISBN 1-887664-50-5
Library of Congress Catalog Card Number 2004105733
Manufactured in the United States of America
Printed by King Printing, Lowell, MA
First Printing by Luminary Press, a division of Midnight Marquee Press, Inc.,
   May 2004

Dedication

In Memory of

Linwood Dunn
and
Vincent Price

Whose Mastery at Transforming the
Unbelievable into the Believable
Has Left Us with Any Number of
Entertainments to Cherish—
Some of Which Are Even
Accounted for within These Pages

CONTENTS

11	Foreword by Fay Wray
12	Author's Preface: In Search of That Motiveless Malignity
19	Acknowledgments

The 1920s & '30s

20	Two Versions of Jekyll & Hyde (1920)
26	The Unholy Three-Times-Two (1925 & 1930)
29	The Ancient Mariner (1925)
32	The Charlatan (1929)
35	The Great Gabbo (1929)
40	Svengali (1931)
45	Murder by the Clock (1931)
48	Guilty Hands (1931)
51	The Spider (1931)
59	The Unholy Garden (1931)
62	The Mad Genius (1931)
65	The Hatchet Man (1932)
68	Behind the Mask (1932)
70	Mystery Ranch (1932)
72	Almost Married (1932)
75	The Old Dark House (1932)
81	The Mask of Fu Manchu (1932)
87	Secrets of the French Police (1932)
90	Murders in the Zoo (1933)
93	I Cover the Waterfront (1933)

95	Cross Country Cruise (1934)
98	The Mystery of Mr. X (1934)
101	The Black Cat (1934)
110	The Love Captive (1934)
114	Smoking Guns (1934)
117	The Man with Two Faces (1934)
121	The Man Who Reclaimed His Head (1934)
124	Mystery of Edwin Drood (1935)
129	Mark of the Vampire (1935)
134	Let 'Em Have It (1935)
136	The Black Room (1935)
138	The Eagle's Brood (1935)
141	Show Them No Mercy! (1935)
144	Uncivilized (1936) a.k.a.: Pituri; Pituri (It Makes Them Uncivilized)
147	Sweeney Todd, the Demon Barber of Fleet Street (1936)
150	The Walking Dead (1936)
154	Broken Blossoms (1936)
156	Trouble for Two (1936)
168	Juggernaut (1936) a.k.a.: The Demon Doctor
160	The Man Who Changed His Mind (1936) a.k.a.: The Man Who Lived Again; Dr. Maniac; The Brain Snatcher
164	Night Key (1937)

166	The Attic of Terror *et Seq.* (1937-39)
170	The Spider's Web (1938)
176	The Man They Could Not Hang (1939)
179	Dark Eyes of London (1939)
	a.k.a.: The Human Monster
183	Tower of London (1939)

The 1940s & '50s

188	Black Friday (1940)
192	The Man with Nine Lives (1940)
196	Island of Doomed Men (1940)
198	Stranger on The Third Floor (1940)
201	Before I Hang (1940)
203	You'll Find Out (1940)
206	The Tell-Tale Heart (1941)
213	The Devil Commands (1941)
216	The Mad Doctor (1941)
220	Among the Living (1941)
223	The Night Has Eyes (1942)
	a.k.a.: Terror House
225	Who Is Hope Schuyler? (1942)
227	The Man Who Wouldn't Die (1942)
229	Moontide (1942)
232	The Boogie Man Will Get You (1942)
235	The Leopard Man (1943)
239	The Seventh Victim (1943)
243	The Mad Ghoul (1944)
246	The Soul of a Monster (1944)
248	Dark Waters (1944)

259	The Missing Juror (1944)
252	Guest in the House (1944)
	a.k.a.: Satan in Skirts
255	Dragonwyck (1946)
259	So Dark the Night (1946)
262	The Dark Mirror (1946)
264	The Locket (1946)
266	Ivy (1947)
268	A Woman's Vengeance (1948)
270	The Sign of the Ram (1948)
272	The Queen of Spades (1949)
277	Obsession (1949)
	a.k.a.: The Hidden Room
277	In a Lonely Place (1950)
283	M (1951)
287	Nightfall (1957)
289	The Tattered Dress (1957)
291	Touch of Evil (1958)
302	The Big Country (1958)
306	Afterword: Vincent Price and the Villains That Still Pursued Him
311	About the Authors
313	Index

Foreword by Fay Wray

What station I may hold in the history of Hollywood shall, I suppose, forever be identified with films of the ilk that George Turner and Mike Price have assembled for discussion in this book. The "ilkiest" of the lot, of course, is *King Kong*. But that one has been amply discussed elsewhere—and examined in especially satisfying detail in a book called *The Making of King Kong*, which Mr. Turner and my friend Orville Goldner wrote. [That book has been revised as Luminary Press' *Spawn of Skull Island*.]

I am most appreciative that Mr. Turner has seen fit not to limit his attention to *King Kong* in his continuing survey of my career. He and Mr. Price devoted considerable effort to the rediscovery of one assignment—a movie I did with Melvyn Douglas and Lionel Atwill, *The Vampire Bat*, in 1933—for their first book, *Forgotten Horrors*. And true to their title, even *I* had practically forgotten *The Vampire Bat*! Their researches served to correct my mistaken belief that it had been a Universal Pictures production. While my memory of shooting *The Vampire Bat* at Universal proved accurate, it took *Forgotten Horrors* to bring back to me that this film had been an independent production by Majestic Pictures on rented Universal sets.

So long as I am digressing, I must take modest issue with the title of that first book of Mr. Turner's and Mr. Price's: Such pictures may well have been *Forgotten*—but *Horrors*? I do so wish that a gentler term, like *Fantasies*, perhaps, could come into popular usage.

Now, I was glad to see Mr. Turner and Mr. Price soften the punch somewhat with a more dignified title for their later collection of essays, *The Cinema of Adventure, Romance, & Terror*, where they devoted a chapter to *The Most Dangerous Game*, a picture on which I worked with many of the people who would become our *King Kong* "family." But then, Mr. Price tells me he and Mr. Turner are planning to call this new book *Human Monsters*—a return to the sensational after a brush with dignity!

Well, it *is* their book, after all.

And once again, I am proud to be a part of a Turner & Price book, particularly in the company of some distinguished pictures—as well as, I suppose, some *not* so distinguished. The picture of mine they have selected is *The Unholy Garden*, an adventurous fantasy (and I emphasize *fantasy*), which I had believed to have been thoroughly forgotten.

As ever, I find it reassuring and pleasantly surprising to find writers so concerned with investigating the bigger picture of film history.
—Fay Wray
New York

The Definitive Edition

Author's Preface: In Search of That Motiveless Malignity

The strange profession of journalism takes its name and its very cue from the same root that gives the language *soup du jour* and *journeyman*, as in day laborer. George E. Turner and I long labored as newspaper journalists and often wound up in the soup as a consequence, but inasmuch as our assignments commonly found us prowling the city by night, we figured we might more fittingly be called *nocturnalists*. Now, the after-dark denizens whose activities we used to chronicle—they're an unstable lot who are as likely as not to turn on you and knock you down. Hence the term *nocturnal*.

We promoted ourselves out of that police-reporting sector of the racket none too soon to suit us, provoked by one case too many of Murder Mo' Foulest, another orchestrated drug-buster pageant that never quite managed to tap the root of the problem, one more head-on flesh-scrambler along the two-lane Death Alley that used to connect Northwest Texas with New Mexico. Give us the Entertainment Desk any day—emphasis on *day*—and the freedom to tackle subject matter that would take somewhat less of a toll upon the human spirit.

Our crime-journalist days seemed safely behind us when George and I first knuckled down to the research end of this book called *Human Monsters*, an inquiry into the essence of Hollywood villainy. Which is to say, fictional and/or allegorical, and explicitly *cinematic*, villainy. This, as opposed to the Real World variety of criminal malice, in uncomfortably close quarters with which we had both grown up, in distinct generations, and pursued much of our kindred careers.

We recognized, of course, the affinity between the fiction of evil and the fact of evil, and we said as much in the notes we had begun compiling. We had taken to heart, more from experience than from passive assent, Joseph Conrad's Socratic argument that "Men alone are quite capable of all wickedness," and we had made due note that many of the movies we had chosen to study had taken explicit cues from the bad people of history and the headlines, from ruthless bluebloods to derelict sociopaths. Still, there was the safe-distance factor of fictionalized storytelling, with the added sanitizing effect of that pure-white beam from the projector-lamp.

George and I were more or less comfortably ensconced during the 1970s at a Texas newspaper, where we held forth as editorial art director and film critic (George) and business/financial editor, show-business columnist and cartoonist and, at length, newsroom boss (my own self). Our assignments ranged agreeably far from our backgrounds in cop-shop reporting, suspect-sketching and courtroom portraiture.

George's pen-and-ink drawings from witnesses' accounts had brought about the nabbing of several murder suspects and any number of rawboned Texas Plains grotesques wanted for assorted deeds of hateful violence. I had covered a ghastly variety of police cases, including the abduction and murder of a state legislator's teen-aged daughter—whose killer owed his capture to a Turner sketch.

All of which plays out impressively enough on the Front Page, but it also is sandpaper to the soul unless the reporter is the classic Frustrated Cop of journalistic legend. Even then, one is not necessarily safe from the Abyss: One Frustrated Cop Journalist who taught me the ropes turned out to be a miscreant in his own right, and at one point a key suspect in the slaying of his wife. One must enjoy looking for trouble and finding same to get much of a charge out of front-lines crime reportage. George and I had seen so much concentrated malfeasance, at inadvertently close range, since our respective childhoods that we knew better than to perceive police work as a glamour gig.

George's first such encounter had come in 1930, when as a preschooler roaming his own neighborhood in Amarillo, Texas, he chanced upon the grisly immediate results of the notorious A.D. Payne automobile-bombing case. Thirty-odd years later, George retold that harrowing tale for the historical journal *Southwest Heritage*, and then in 1992 he and I and fellow illustrator

Lamberto Alvarez developed a graphic-novella version for *Heavy Metal* magazine and our own *Southern-Fried Homicide* series of anthologies.

I was born in 1947, by which time George had seen a genial roommate from his college days lapse into a brief career of extortion and murder-by-torture and, elsewhere, observed a sweet-natured neighbor lady fall into a lethal rage. As a new journalist during those postwar years, George helped to cover the mutilation slaying of Tex Thornton, the grandstanding explosives expert whose choice of drinking companions left fatally much to be desired.

My own childhood years in Amarillo—an extraordinarily violent burg, which even today retains both the nihilistic lawlessness and the fascist vigilante spirit that characterized the oil-and-cattle booms of the early 20th Century—were overshadowed by an ominous Shunned House just down the street: This was a cottage that once had belonged to my paternal grandparents, but now it was ill-reputationed as the last abode short of Death Row of the despicable Sam Gasway, executed for the ravishment of a neighbor girl. Sam Gasway, once regarded as the most chivalrous of citizens, had been turned over to the police by another neighbor, a hard-shell Baptist minister whose son was a playmate of mine. This playmate grew up to become a horse thief and bank robber.

And they say suchlike only happens in the movies. Whoever "they" are.

The Solace of Cinema and
Real-World Intrusions upon Same

Both George's childhood and mine were leavened by a fascination with motion pictures. We would spend hours at a stretch in my uncle Grady L. Wilson's moving-picture theaters, taking notes, screening favorite films repeatedly, and looking forward to the day when a career might be forged from this interest.

When finally we wound up as fellow news-hacks in 1968, it developed that we might as well have been brothers born a generation apart. The interest in movies was still more a pastime than a trade, but we determined to intensify that concern.

We began finding a right direction with the 1975 publication of the George Turner-Orville Goldner book, *The Making of King Kong*, on which I had apprenticed as a proofreader and research assistant. The Turner & Price book called *Forgotten Horrors* had wrapped by 1977 and awaited release, and with this prompt follow-through called *Human Monsters* we felt grateful to begin writing of crime as merely a function of the cinema. Our police-reporting dues seemed paid in full.

But no sooner had we decided upon the basic contents of this project, than one of our editors, a Junior G-Man-type with crackpot sanctimonious/adventurous delusions, decided that I should tackle a couple of investigative projects that would prove to involve some Human Monsters of the real world. All of a sudden, the menacing souls of *Guilty Hands*, *I Cover the Waterfront*, and even *The Man Who Reclaimed His Head*—to name-drop a few of the pictures herein—became more identifiably real for their resemblance to the low-lifes whose activities these assignments involved.

There was the New Mexico-based pornographer whose forays into Texas were taken as a personal affront by our church-deacon editor (who expense-accounted a large private collection of the offending materials in the name of research). My small team of reporters and photographers, deployed to the field while our editor held court in the office he had christened his War Room, wound up having our lives threatened, 'way off in the backroads of the Sangre de Cristo Mountains, unless we backed away from a story that wasn't all that much of a story to begin with. (We stuck with it, out of plain bull-headedness. The Big Scoop proved to be a bust by the Texas Comptroller of Public Accounts—bureaucrats, playing at cops-and-robbers—on the mere grounds that the sleaze-mongering entrepreneur had neglected to register as an out-of-state corporation.)

And then there was the Matter of the Misappropriated Petroleum Leases—reams of documents, hinted at in a vaguely tantalizing tip, that I found myself under orders to locate in a hicktown courthouse, then to pore over until they yielded the revelation that a locally prominent lawyer/politico/philanthropist had helped himself to a hefty sum in some struggling farmer-family's oil-well royalties.

My crusading editor had bragged it about that our daily sheet was on the point of nailing a Big Shot—before simple arithmetic demonstrated that the statute of limitations had long since passed. No story here, just the sad understanding that fountain-pen banditry had been committed with impunity. In orchestrating this non-news extravaganza, of course, Ye Ed. had conveniently attached my name to the boast, paving the way for a couple of years' worth of threatening harassments: anonymous, naturally, but hardly a mystery as to the source.

Journalism was growing less pleasurable a calling by the moment. My advancement to City Editor in 1977 seemed a safe enough holding pattern—if only it had not coincided with the selection of our burg as the trial venue for a relentlessly sleazy blood-and-money fiasco known as the Cullen Davis Murder Case.

George and I toughed that one out as a team: I supervised the field-reporter scene, George produced a portfolio of widely published courtroom drawings—and we decided to jump ship as soon as we had wrapped the coverage. Not that the calming came easily, but finally the mock-aristocratic defendant met with the same outcome that had proved such a relief to Teddy Kennedy: "This chap's acquitted." Our teamwork won us an Associated Press Managing Editors Award that was meant to encourage us to devote even more time and energy to a dehumanizing profession. But instead, George lit a shuck out of Texas, bound for more soul-satisfying prospects within the movie industry. I stayed put but began planting greener pastures that finally took root around 1980.

The Book Takes Shape, With Internal Complications

Is every film-history book so intimidatingly intertwined with real-world parallels? Or is it just us?

We had called *Human Monsters* a Done Deal on several occasions since the first manuscript was completed, late in 1978. By which time, our paths had diverged drastically—George to a new career in Hollywood, myself to a holding pattern in public relations and college administration, then back to the newspaper grind—and we kept tampering with this book until the time felt right to publish. George's hiring in 1980 of a prominent denizen of Beverly Hills as our literary agent had some curiously awkward repercussions: The gent casually informed us in 1982 that he had "lost, or at least misplaced" the manuscript. There were copies, of course, and we had retained the appropriate photographs, but a great deal can happen in only two years. Our representative, for example, had used the lag time to bring into print a similarly concerned book of his own making, while holding George and me to an exclusive agentry agreement. Jeeze Louise.

That debacle also found George and me re-thinking our own book, whose eventual revamp for a Kitchen Sink Press edition proved immeasurably better than the manuscript we had entrusted to the wrong hands. "I'm actually grateful to the old yob," George said, years later. "Whatever his machinations, he caused us to wind up with an improved product, while that little scrapbook of his own yammerings was forgotten within a year of its publication."

Human Monsters' 1995-96 edition, in turn, has been rendered irrelevant by the present presentation, a thorough revision and enrichment. Upon George's death in 1999, I stepped up the process we had recently begun on sequels to the original *Forgotten Horrors* and found that certain chapters of *Human Monsters* would better serve if cannibalized for the second and third *Forgotten* collections. These have been replaced with such selections as these:

- The John Barrymore and Sheldon Lewis versions of *Dr. Jekyll & Mr. Hyde*, both from 1920, in perspective with that tale's numerous other turns upon the screen.
- Both versions of *The Unholy Three*, from 1925 and 1930, starring Lon Chaney.
- Fox's since-mislaid *The Ancient Mariner* (1925), a curious attempt to weave Coleridge's souls-in-torment poem together with a modern-day tale of lustful intrigues. It is Coleridge, after all, who lends this book its overriding concern with Very Bad Things Occurring for No Good Reason at All.
- The silent and soundtracked versions of 1929's *The Charlatan*, a forerunner of Universal Pictures' celebrated cycle of talkie horror films.
- 1931's *Murder by the Clock*, with its household full of skulking murderers and its nerve-wracking wail-from-the-crypt sequences.
- The fascinating *Almost Married* (1932) and *Cross Country Cruise* (1934), whose very titles have long camouflaged their horrific essence.
- A reappraisal of a sustained series of short-subject hair-raisers from Warner Bros., centering upon 1937's "The Attic of Terror."
- A survey of the many filmings of E.A. Poe's "The Tell-Tale Heart," centered upon MGM's splendid short-subject adaptation from 1941 and placing the story itself in context with Poe's troublesome dealings with a parasitic editor.
- Detailed studies of the Nicholas Ray-Humphrey Bogart production of *In a Lonely Place* (1950) and Orson Welles' *Touch of Evil* (the 1958 version vs. the 1998-99 re-edit).
- A distillation of my long-out-of-print book accompanying a soundtrack-CD album on 1959's *The Big Country*, with a restoration of the players' candid observations on the tyrannies of William Wyler—remarks that had been censored by the album project's underwriter, the director's daughter, Margaret Wyler.
- And the entire text of a study that George and I had intended to devote to Boris Karloff's long sequence of so-called mad-doctor pictures.

Fortunate connections have given us Fay Wray's Foreword and an entire Afterword's worth of enhancements from Vincent Price, who proved during visits spanning almost 20 years to be not only a generous source but also a distant cousin of mine.

And inevitably, True Crime intrudes upon our discussions of cinematic trespasses. Just as George and I were wrapping our chapter-by-chapter revisions for the 1995 edition, a New Jersey publisher hired me to develop an encyclopedia of serial-murder cases to be published in portfolio form. This assignment resulted in the *Bloody Visions* series of trading-card folios, a three-volume collection whose key impact upon my other work has been to serve the reminder that fiction is not half so malicious or debauched as fact. If Peter Kurten, the despised Vampire of Dusseldorf, was *not* the inspiration for Fritz Lang's masterpiece *M*, then certainly Kurten's murderous debaucheries anticipated that breakthrough picture in many particulars.

M figures significantly in this book, by the way, though not in the form of the famous Lang original. It is Joseph Losey's Americanized remake that George and I would choose to discuss—a mid-century production that is by turns forgotten and unfairly dismissed as a mere copy.

For that matter, *all* the films here are long overdue for fresh consideration. Their binding concern is a general avoidance of the fantastic—even 1935's *Mark of the Vampire* and Boris Karloff's healer-turned-heel escapades are rooted in mundane urgencies—and yet each movie has its monster, a creature that either is or once must have been as unremarkably human as a down-the-street neighbor.

Selecting the Selections

This demon within the mind—Mr. Poe's Imp of the Perverse—gave literature such choice Human Monsters as Iago, who laid his creation to an evil god; Emily Bronte's haunted Gypsy, Heathcliff, of *Wuthering Heights*; Richard Connell's man-stalking Zaroff of "The Most Dangerous Game" and quite a few moving-picture adaptations and knockoffs; ruthless arch-criminals epitomized by Conan Doyle's Prof. Moriarty and Sax Rohmer's Dr. Fu Manchu; Danny, the baby-faced guardian of the ominous hatbox in Emlyn Williams' *Night Must Fall*—and many another master at holding the populace in the thrall of unease.

But such boons to literature become curses when imposed upon life itself. Extravagant and far-removed from reality though some of these characters seem, the most effective of them are traced from Real World counterparts; often, in fact, dictates of taste and even dramatic license have required that they be toned down. Few such fictitious exploits are half so depraved or bizarre as the deeds of Gilles de Rais, Vlad Tepes, Countess Erzebet Bathory, the Axeman of New Orleans, Jack-the-Ripper, David Berkowitz, the Boston Strangler, Dr. Cream, Scorpio, Burke & Hare, the Texarkana Sniper, Kate Bender or Alastair Crowley. In a world that has spawned and spread the Inquisition, Lyndon Johnson's own private Veet Nayum, the Third Reich, and Murder, Inc.—to say nothing of those benighted Payne and Gasway households in whose neighborhoods George Turner and I grew up—most Human Monsters of fiction are safely within the bounds of realism.

Our selection of these showcases for fiendishness hinges as vitally upon the genres the films represent and the cinematic history they reflect as upon their central characterizations. In the choosing, we have sought to display both the acclaimed and the neglected. To illustrate:

Behind the Mask and *Island of Doomed Men*—ignored in their time by the critics, except as convenient objects of stylish sneers—examine sadistic abuses of official authority with remarkable insight. *Svengali* is the defining study of mesmerism applied for cruel purposes, run a close second and third by *The Love Captive* and *The Man with Two Faces*. A spellbinding Australian production called *Uncivilized* comments profoundly upon the unexpected civility of savagery; we find, conversely, the savagery of civilization in James Cruze's *I Cover the Waterfront*. Brutish behavior appears all the more so in contrast with innocent beauty in both *Moontide* and the little-known remake of *Broken Blossoms*. A touching yet chilling portrayal of haunted genius informs *The Soul of a Monster*, a film that illustrates by imitative example the powerful influence of Val Lewton's formula for conveying terror via understatement. Moral outrage, as a rule mishandled on film as mere tantrum-throwing, is given dignity and genuine shock value in *The Hatchet Man*.

Show Them No Mercy! and *Let 'Em Have It* are gangster films—but gangster films of distinction, demonstrating the horror engendered by the public enemy, rather than the fun-and-games of outlawry. Bruce Cabot's portrayals in both are, we insist, the equal of anything set forth by such more celebrated crime stars as Edward G. Robinson, James Cagney, Humphrey Bogart and Richard Widmark.

Sympathy for the Human Monster seems justified at times because the victim is hardly so worthy as the one plotting his demise. The deserving object of the afflictions in *Obsession* is a wife-stealer; in *Guilty Hands*, a scoundrel whose doom is desirable to the end of improving the species. A scorecard would prove useful now and again to help distinguish malicious heroes from righteously indignant villains: Lionel Atwill in *The Man Who Reclaimed His Head* deserves to lose his to Claude Rains' bayonet, and Boris Karloff's insults and injuries to Bela Lugosi in *The Black Cat* earn him nothing as much as the privilege of being skinned alive. The title vigilante of *The Spider's Web* is as fearsome as the criminals he torments. Even the psychopaths of *Murders in the Zoo* and *The Missing Juror* are right in their own minds, for nobody wants to be perceived as the bad guy.

The female miscreant, relatively rare in the Jazz Age and Depression Era selections, becomes dominant in the wartime batch—representative of the fundamental tone of the psychological-thriller genre that flourished during and following the Second World War. The likes of *Guest in the House*, *Sign of the Ram*, *Ivy* and *The Night Has Eyes* both derived from and paced this segment of the industry.

Bela Lugosi puts the bite on Elizabeth Allen in a staged publicity shot for *Mark of the Vampire* (1935).

In sum, this grouping amounts to the makings of a splendid extended festival for the movie buff intrigued by vamps, scamps, schemers, outright evildoers and villains in spite of themselves. George and I had made obscurity and low-budget origins a requisite for inclusion in our inaugural volume, *Forgotten Horrors*. No such conditions necessarily apply here, for we cannot resist the temptation to cast additional light onto such well-known items as *The Old Dark House*, *The Black Cat*, *Svengali* and two of Val Lewton's justly revered productions, *The Seventh Victim* and *The Leopard Man*.

The Rediscovery Imperative

Among our lesser-known choices—the likes of *The Hatchet Man* and *Trouble for Two* and *Secrets of the French Police*—many are in excellent positions now to find a wide and appreciative audience: These three examples represent, respectively, the legacies of Old Hollywood's Warner Bros., MGM, and RKO-Radio studios. An MGM nitrate-conversion program, begun during the 1960s, has seen the transfer of every surviving MGM title from chemically unstable nitrate film stock to virtually imperishable safety stock, with a second tier of digital preservation in many cases. In an under-acknowledged follow-through development, modeled after the MGM preservation project and picking up where it left off, Turner Entertainment Co. (no kin to George) has generated definitive safety-film editions of such MGM finery as *Gone with the Wind* and *The*

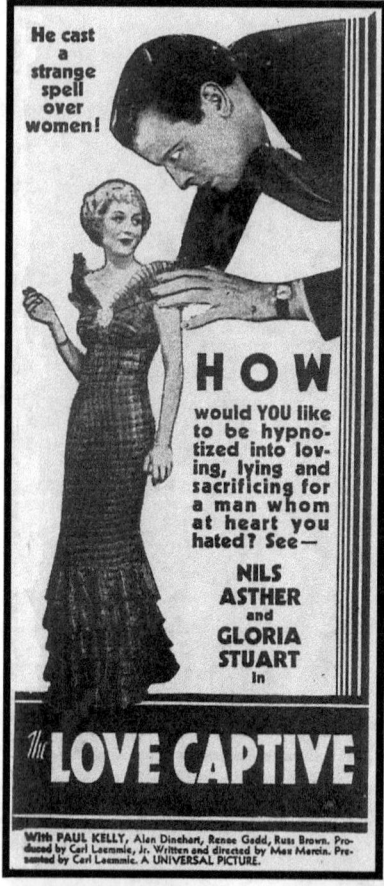

Wizard of Oz—recapturing the grandeur of those pictures' 1939 release prints, invoking the period's very *style* of print-making—and meanwhile enabled the transfer to safety stock of much of the surviving pre-1948 Warner Bros. library.

Then with its purchase of the RKO library in 1988, Turner Entertainment continued that formidable task of rescuing the master elements from the inexorable decay of nitrocellulose film stock. This costly archival commitment has been conveniently ignored in a once-fevered controversy involving the role of Turner Entertainment in the computer-coloring of video-source masters struck from various recognized classic motion pictures. We'll invoke a Sam Goldwynism here and include ourselves out of that argument—except to suggest that preservation carries more weight than Colorization. The archival proprietorship has since shifted to Warner Bros., but it is Ted Turner's interests that bear recognizing for rendering many historic properties safe, sound and accessible.

In this gallery of seminal and transcendent portrayals can be found the ancestors of such enduring latter-day performances as Angela Lansbury's show of vicious mom-ism in *The Manchurian Candidate* (1962); Bill Paxton's deceptively amusing sadist in *Weird Science* (1985); Michael Berryman's cannibalistic desert rat in *The Hills Have Eyes* (1977); Joe Spinell's deadly big-city recluse in *Maniac* (1980); J.T. Walsh's ostensibly helpful predators in *Black Day, Blue Night* (1995) and *Breakdown* (1997); and Rod Steiger's evil-eye surgeon in *The Kindred* (1987). Much as these more recent examples distinguish motion pictures that range wildly in terms of artistry and entertainment value, our entries following are chosen more for their vivid performances than for any categorically high merits on any arthritically reverent scale of filmmaking artistry.

Some of these films will bear regard as excellent in every respect; some, as merely good; some, as seriously flawed. But even the lesser entries contain elements that set them quite apart from the run-of-the-mill (or the run-of-DeMille, for that matter). And all are noteworthy for their explorations of what Coleridge called "the motive-hunting of a motiveless malignity."

—Michael H. Price
North-by-Northwest of the Divide

Boris Karloff in *The Black Cat*

Acknowledgments

Thanx and a tip of the Price pith helmet to John Wooley, screenwriter, novelist and playwright, cultural historian, songwriter and journalist-with-a-soul; and to Jan Alan Henderson, that most loyal of George Turner's Hollywood protégés, for helping this project to sustain a crucial momentum. And our gratitude to these additional sources of motivating information, encouragement and assistance, in varying degrees:

Carroll Baker; Billy Barty; John Belushi; Robert Bloch; DeWitt Bodeen; Peter Bogdanovich; Ron Borst; William "Hoppy" Boyd; Ryan Brennan; Steve Brigati; Mel Brooks; T. Sumter Bruton III; Larry Buchanan; Bob "Tracy" Burns; Bruce Cabot; Nicolas Cage; Sam Calvin; Charles Clarke; Jim & Susan Colegrove; Edward Colman; Richard L. Connor; Chuck Connors; Francis Ford Coppola; Robert Crumb; Guillermo del Toro; August W. Derleth; G. Michael Dobbs; Linwood Dunn; William K. Everson; Claire Eyrich; Leonard Feather; Joan Fontaine; Morgan Freeman; David F. Friedman; Josh Alan Friedman; Kinky Friedman; Kerry Gammill; Lee C. Garmes; Whoopi Goldberg; Ron Green; Charlton Heston; Rose Hobart; Tobé Hooper; James Wong Howe; Burl Ives; Greg Jackson; James Earl Jones; Joan Fontaine; Lee Garmes; Boris Karloff; Larry King; Leonard J. Kohl; Nan Grey Laine; Mark Lamberti; Janet Leigh; Joseph Losey; Bela G. Lugosi [Jr.]; Scott MacQueen; Taj Mahal; Henry Mancini; Miles Mander; Mark Martin; Russell Metty; Walter Murch; John Murphy; Edwin Neal; Bob O'Neal; John E. Parnum; Bill Paxton; Gregory Peck; Samuel A. Peeples; Robin Pen; Lou Diamond Phillips; John Pierson; Vincent Price; Bruce Raben; Basil Rathbone; Carl Reiner; Gary Don Rhodes; Fred "Sardo" Richards; Alan Rickman; Paul T. Riddell; Heinz Roemheld; Roy & Dale Evans Rogers; César Romero; George A. Romero; Angelo Rossitto; Mickey Rourke; James Sallis; Hans J. Salter; Rick Schmidlin; Martin Scorsese; Rod Serling; Jean Simmons; Andrew Solt; Larry D. Springer; Frank Stack; James Stewart; Patrick Stewart; Oliver Stone; John Sturges; Grady Sutton; John Sutton; Gary & Susan Svehla; Tony Todd; Edgar G. Ulmer; George Waggner; Mark Evan Walker; Rich Wannen; David Wayne; Michael Weldon; Orson Welles; Ian Whitcomb; Don Williams; Grady L. Wilson; Grant Withers; Fay Wray; Frank Zappa; Albert Zugsmith; and Terry Zwigoff

And on the Institutional & Corporate Fronts: The Academy of Motion Picture Arts & Sciences; the American Film Institute; the American Society of Cinematographers; the American Society of Composers, Authors & Publishers; the Billy Barty Foundation; the British Film Institute; the Dallas-Fort Worth Film Commission; the Fort Worth Film Festival, Inc., and its Lone Star Film Society offshoot; the Hoblitzelle Theatre Arts Library at the University of Texas; the Library of Congress; Little People of America; the National Association of Theatre Owners; the Screen Directors Guild; the Screen Writers Guild; Southwest Film & Video Archive at Southern Methodist University, Fort Worth; the Sundance Institute; the Tandy Archive, Texas Christian University; and the USA Film Festival of Dallas

The 1920s & '30s

TWO VERSIONS OF JEKYLL & HYDE
(Famous Players-Lasky Corp./Paramount-Artcraft Pictures
and Pioneer Film Corp.; 1920)

The movies' first generation—that so-called silent-film era—is commonly acknowledged as the most inventive and important stage of the medium, and not merely because it is the wellhead. The gradual coming of sound as a component of filmmaking, during the 1920s, proved revolutionary, of course, and might even be considered the last true technological revolution to affect the process. But sound proved more a setback than any advancement of picture-making for several tense years, there, and it is always fascinating to compare the confident sophistication of the silents' last decade with the awkwardness of the early talking pictures. (About which, more later, in our entry on 1929's *The Great Gabbo*.) Sound, after all, served at first to reduce many pictures to scarcely more than photographed stage-plays, while the generally accomplished silents of the '20s convey a literalized essence of the concept of *cinema*, with the camera serving more than a passive observational function.

Sound, of course, had been a component of cinema all along—nobody called these pictures "silents" until after talking pictures had caught on—but that quality amounted to musical accompaniment, applied externally, as opposed to the integral technology of synchronized sound recording. The eyes meant more than the ears. A film could not rely upon the spoken word or the emphasis of sound effects or synchronized music to tell its story, and the cinema in its first generation required an intimate collaboration between actors and camera operators, with the director as a sight-savvy conduit. Acting for the silent screen called for more of a Grand Manner approach, which may seem overwrought to a present-day audience; it helps to put oneself in a 1920s state of mind.

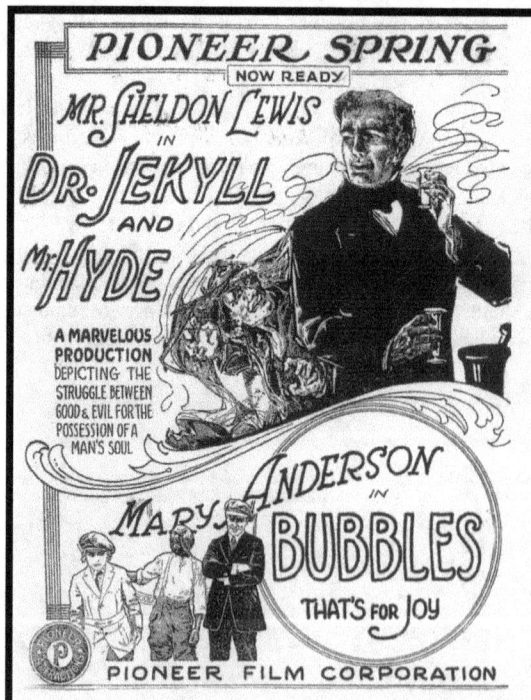

As a consequence of this imperative, even many of the lesser silent films will yield a profound wealth of evocative visual detail when rediscovered today. Practically all the creative energies (apart from the talent necessary to write concise dialogue-and-narration cards, as required) went into the pictorial values of dramatized storytelling.

Such a film is John Stuart Robertson's 1920 adaptation of Robert Louis Stevenson's celebrated novella, *The Strange Case of Dr. Jekyll & Mr.*

Hyde, a film that stands out from a horde of *Jekyll & Hyde* adaptations, takeoffs, parodies, homages and so forth, dating from as early as 1908.

John Barrymore's title-role portrayal is merely the most conspicuous reason for the staying power of this particular version, which holds up well by comparison with not only its immediate competition—the Louis Meyer-Charles J. Hayden production of *J&H*, starring that villain-among-villains, Sheldon Lewis—but also with the more ostentatious versions of 1931-32 (starring Fredric March) and 1941 (starring Spencer Tracy).

For one thing, a rediscovery of the Robertson-Barrymore edition will restore the story's truer meaning to the popular consciousness. Stevenson's thrilling narrative gimmick—the transformation of a man into a monster—has long since overwhelmed the author's essential concern with *everybody's* potential for monstrousness, the personalization of a perpetual struggle between Good and Evil. So successful was the prototypical High Concept with which Stevenson triggered his story, that the massed conception of *Jekyll & Hyde* has become that of a tale of transformation, or degeneration, for its own sake.

Much as Stevenson's 1886 novella was more a moral argument, more a polemic with the head-in-the-sand repressiveness of Victorian England, than a tale of horror, so this film uses the ghastly plight of a good man at war (and in collusion) with his inner demons as merely a vehicle for ideas larger than commonplace shock value. Barrymore's performance(s) as the doctor, Henry Jekyll, and his brutal *alter ego*, Edward Hyde, are haunting in their directness and simplicity: The film proves itself less a star vehicle than a showcase for striving artistry and immersion in character. Barrymore's audacious facial expressions warp Jekyll into Hyde without extravagant makeup or technical-effects work beyond rudimentary dissolves: False teeth, a skull-cap and elongated fingers (plus strategic lighting and stagecraft) are the only cosmetic enhancements. The absorbed and experienced viewer will recognize the transformation as it relates to many other such movies (even Mark Blankfield, in the 1982 doper comedy *Jekyll & Hyde... Together Again*, gave a nod or two in Barrymore's direction), but this instance remains definitive. Barrymore's profile is iconic within the popular culture, and the sight of its transformation here is nothing short of astonishing.

The story finds Dr. Henry Jekyll (Barrymore), a scientist and all-'round good citizen, at a hard-earned plateau of a fine career. But Jekyll is troubled by a need to plumb the depths of his very being, and the temptations posed by a profligate acquaintance, Sir George Carew (Brandon Hurst), lead Jekyll to delve deeper into the forbidden impulse via scientific methods. To this end, Jekyll concocts a potion that will reveal some hidden nature that may prove itself beyond control.

The Robertson-Barrymore version hews loyally to Stevenson's insistence that all people harbor a lust for sensations beyond the realm of common decency. The scenes of happy normalcy have a lilting quality quite at odds with the sense of doom and decay that asserts itself upon the arrival of Hyde. Barrymore's conflicted interpretation of Jekyll seems almost impossibly saintly on the one hand—so much so, that it becomes too easy to blame the lurking Hyde for every last atrocity—but so dedicated to the exploration of his hidden nature that Hyde presents himself as merely a logical extension of the respected healer. Jekyll cannot have comprehended his potential for inflicting damage, and his presumptuous insistence upon attempting the experiment proves itself an act more damnable than any of Hyde's deeds. In this portrayal, more so than any other, it becomes patent that Hyde would eventually come bursting forth, potion or no potion.

The Robertson-Barrymore *Dr. Jekyll & Mr. Hyde* is more than just a tale of the Dark Side, unleashed. It also suggests a workable scenario for the persistence of civilized normalcy. A benchmark in the development of the art and science of moviemaking, the film also demonstrates many of the greatest strengths of the silent-picture age, in which the success of any such story depended upon an intimate communion between the screen and the audience.

Both Adolph Zukor's Paramount-Artcraft Pictures and Louis Meyer's Pioneer Film Corp. launched their respective *Jekyll & Hyde* adaptations during the spring of 1920—Paramount with the aggressive head-start of a March copyright date and a massed release in April. Pioneer, which

had announced its *J&H* in 1919 as *The Monster and the Man*, managed an April 1920 copyright filing and settled for piecemeal states'-rights distribution, which relied on territorial bookings, gradually deployed, to the exclusion of a formal release date nationwide.

Both studios, too, touted a basis that lay as much in a famous stage play as in Stevenson's tale. Paramount's advertising campaign cited its version's pedigree as related to "the play which Richard Mansfield immortalized," while Pioneer's assigned director-screenwriter, Charles J. Hayden, announced in advance of production that his inspiration lay in Mansfield's interpretation, as first staged in Boston in May 1887—the year following publication in London of Stevenson's novella. Mansfield received acclaim for his rapid-fire illusions of transformation, "and a generation of playgoers recalled the green face of Hyde as the ultimate in terror," as a theatrical journal once appraised Mansfield's portrayal.

Where Barrymore (1882-1942) came to *Jekyll & Hyde* as an all-'round leading man with impeccable stage credentials and a distinguished literary, artistic and dramatic lineage, Sheldon Lewis (1868-1958) tackled his version of the dual role as more a logical extension of a career in sensationalized villainy, including a well-received *Jekyll & Hyde* on stage. Hollywood had yet to codify the horror film as a genre *per se*—such a categorizing tactic would not emerge until the early 1930s—but such pictures were nonetheless plentiful during the years before talking pictures, and Lewis might even bear consideration more so than Lon Chaney as a living prototype for the notion of a horror-movie star. (Certainly, Lewis would distinguish a handful of the early talking pictures in such a capacity, delivering showy turns in *The Phantom*, *The Monster Walks* and *Tombstone Canyon* during 1931-32.)

Lewis' *Jekyll & Hyde* trades strikingly upon the actor's ability to seem, by turns, pious and suave and gleefully degenerate. Lewis' is less subtle a portrayal than Barrymore's, but Lewis achieves the dichotomy of selves with zeal and intensity. Where the Barrymore version climaxes with Jekyll's attempted suicide and a scoundrel's death for Hyde, the Lewis interpretation allows Hyde an unspectacular arrest and trial; as the moment of execution nears, Jekyll awakes to find the ordeal has been a fevered dream.

While preparing for *Jekyll & Hyde*, Lewis granted an interview to a reporter named Rose Cummings, who published the result in the June 1919 issue of *Theatre Magazine*. The first-person authorship is essentially inane, but Lewis' tolerant remarks bear repeating, in a selective

Behind the scenes on the set of the 1920 *Dr. Jekyll and Mr. Hyde*.

context. The *Iron Claw* reference concerns a famous serialized adventure-film from 1916, still in international distribution at the time of this article:

> Sheldon Lewis has been kind enough to grant me an interview—and I must confess that the prospect of meeting the hero-villain of Iron Claw fame left me as excited and flustered as a schoolgirl. For a villain is meant to be cordially hated… any admiration one feels for his superb acting must be fought out in the privacy of one's home—and not openly expressed. Anyway, that's the dictum handed down from grandmother's time.
>
> Now I kept watching the passive, finely chiseled face as Mr. Lewis talked of his books, his home, and above all his treasures—his wife. Somehow, he didn't fit my conception of what a "reg'lar" villain should look and act like. He was too sympathetic, too sensitive and fine in his details…
>
> "Don't think for one moment that I've lost my great enthusiasm and high regard for the legitimate drama," he added. "Some day I expect to go back—but right now, the motion-picture field appeals to me strongly. It gives me a greater opportunity for real character work, and enables me to reach thousands of people who are constructive in their criticisms and appreciative of the hard work such acting requires. These people haven't

the means or the opportunity to get to the theatre—but moving pictures keep them enlightened, and entertain them as nothing else can."

I asked Mr. Lewis if he was fond of athletics, to which he replied:

"My present work requires a supple, active body, and so I spend two hours every day in my gymnasium…"

Rose Cummings' brief article is what a modern-day editor might characterize as a puff-piece, and it is a pity that she put more about herself than about Lewis into the writing. Even so, the opportunity to consider an actor in light of his own words is rare and valuable.

By the 1950s, Jekyll & Hyde had proved its staying power through sheer numbers of radio adaptations, animated cartoons, comic-book condensations and recurring editions of the actual book, and of course feature films both earnest and silly, with even Bud Abbott & Lou Costello weighing in on the issue during their waning span as a ticket-selling comedy team. Sheldon Lewis' version had been by-and-large forgotten—deservedly so, perhaps, given its retreat to the trivializing resolution of a just-a-dream finale—but Barrymore's nuanced reading remained a touchstone. And by the 1950s, too, Fredric March's essence-of-horror version had been eclipsed by the Freudian pretentiousness of Spencer Tracy's portrayal, which served little greater purpose than to encourage yet more outlandish psychiatric hogwash in 1953's *Son of Dr. Jekyll*, starring Louis Hayward. A more responsible bit of revisionism would come along in 1957, with Edgar G. Ulmer's utterly cheap but intellectually ambitious *Daughter of Dr. Jekyll*.

Outcroppings of *Jekyll & Hyde* over the long term also include a 1912 short, which parcels out the title roles between director-in-waiting James Cruze (as Jekyll) and Harry Benham (as Hyde); a 1913 two-reeler, directed by Herbert Brenon and starring King Baggot; F.W. Murnau's German production of *Der Januskopf* (1920), with Conrad Veidt; the 1959 French production of *Le Testament du Docteur Cordelier*, directed by Jean Renoir and starring Louis Barrault; Terence Fisher's *The Two Faces of Dr. Jekyll* (England; 1960), with Paul Massie; and remarkable television-movie entries of 1968 and 1981, respectively starring Jack Palance and David Hemmings. Among others too humorous to mention.

CREDITS, PARAMOUNT VERSION: Presented by: Adolph Zukor; Directed by John Stuart Robertson; Assistant Director: Shaw Lovett; Scenario: Clara S. Beranger, from Robert Louis Stevenson's Novella; Photographed by: Roy Overbaugh; Art Directors (Sets): Robert M. Haas and Clark Robertson; Art Director (Décor): Charles O. Seessel; Length: Seven Reels; Released during April of 1920

CAST, PARAMOUNT VERSION: John Barrymore (Dr. Henry Jekyll and Edward Hyde); Martha Mansfield (Millicent Carew); Brandon Hurst (Sir George Carew); Charles Lane (Dr. Richard Lanyon); J. Malcolm Dunn (John Utterson); Cecil Clovelly (Edward Enfield); Nita Naldi (Gina); George Stevens (Poole); and Louis Wolheim

CREDITS, PIONEER VERSION: Producer: Louis Meyer; Scenarist and Director: Charles J. Hayden; Based upon the Stevenson Novella; Length: Five Reels; Released: On a Region-by-Region Basis Beginning in April of 1920

CAST, PIONEER VERSION: Sheldon Lewis (Dr. Jekyll and Mr. Hyde); Alexander Shannon (Dr. Lanyon); Dora Mills Adams (Mrs. Lanyon); Gladys Field (Bernice Lanyon); Harold Forshay (Edward Utterson); Leslie Austin (Danvers Carew)

THE UNHOLY THREE-TIMES-TWO
(Metro-Goldwyn-Mayer Pictures, Inc.; 1925 and 1930)

Once as a silent, once as a talkie—and each time, a triumph for the mighty Lon Chaney. *The Unholy Three*, in either incarnation, is no less a triumph for the intense actor Harry Earles, and in fact the original story had belonged more rightly to the evil-midget character whom Earles would play—until MGM re-tailored it as a Chaney showcase. Chaney's prominence notwithstanding, it is Earles who accounts for the crucial element of sadistic menace in *The Unholy Three*.

Small wonder, you should pardon the expression, that midgets and dwarves have often found themselves predisposed to antisocial behavior, and even to the suicidal bitterness that has cost the culture two extraordinary actors: Michael Dunn, of *Ship of Fools* and network television's *The Wild Wild West*, during the 1970s; and David Rapaport, of Franc Roddam's *The Bride* and television's *L.A. Law*, in times more recent. The little guy of *The Unholy Three* must go through life under the demeaning name of Tweedledee, much as Earles himself (*né* Kurt Schneider) half-tolerated and half-exploited his own carnival billing for many years as Harry Doll, a partner with his sisters in a crowd-pleasing troupe called the Doll Family, with the Ringling Bros./Barnum & Bailey Circus.

The bigotry persists, though it is confronted today with an increasing resistance from an entrenched civil-rights lobbying group called Little People of America. Even *midget* is no longer a preferred term; we employ the word here because historically it has differentiated a tiny person, of more-or-less conventional proportions, from a *dwarf*, a person of distinct physiognomy. Which is a polite way of saying, as our dwarf-actor pal Joe Gieb (of *Weird Science* and *Under the Rainbow*, among others) has put it more frankly: "Midgets are like a miniature of a so-called normal adult—*normal* being a relative word, don'tcha know?—while dwarves have bigger heads, shorter trunks and limbs and bigger backsides." Among the important Little People of Old Hollywood, Harry Earles and his sister, Daisy Earles, were midgets and Angelo Rossitto (all three seen in Tod Browning's 1932 benchmark *Freaks*) was a dwarf.

From the historical vantage, it proves simply the mettle to stand against the slights and slurs of self-professed normal folk that has kept Little People from losing altogether too much ground in the struggle for equality. In 19th Century Louisiana, a dwarf aristocrat named Bernard de Marigny became a powerful politician whose response to any perceived insult was to demand a duel-to-the-death. Few risked Marigny's ill temper because he was a crack-shot marksman. In Clarence Aaron "Tod" Robbins' rancorously lifelike source-novel *The Unholy Three*, the pivotal midget deals with the disappointments dealt him by turning to crime.

There is nothing fanciful about the concept. When Harry Earles, as the movies' Tweedledee, lashes out at an abusive child in the sideshow audience, he is more or less crystallizing experiences of his own from carnival life. Little People seldom grace that midway circuit nowadays; although popular interest abides, the show-business tactic of inviting a mass audience to gawk at fellow human beings of aspect remarkable has become a socially incorrect practice. But even within the confines of mundane reality, folks can be alarmingly rude in their approach to individuals who stand out from the reeking herd.

We are reminded here of a Real World episode from the early 1990s: A citizen and his preschool-age son are strolling through a Southwestern shopping mall when they encounter a dwarf. The kid breaks free from his father and rushes toward the Little Person. "Hey!" he demands. "Are you a puppet?"

"Why, no, sonny," replies the dwarf. "I'm just a very small grown-up human guy-type individual." Words to that effect, in any event.

"Don't gimme that crap!" says the child, quote/unquote. "You're a *puppet*!"

It can only be reckoned fortunate that the boy's father intervened at this point with an apologetic shushing. More fortunate yet that the affronted Little Person proved somewhat more easygoing than *The Unholy Three*'s Tweedledee.

Which is chiefly the point of *The Unholy Three*. The trio consists of Prof. Echo (Lon Chaney), a ventriloquist; Hercules (Victor McLaglen in 1925, Ivan Linow in 1930), a muscleman; and Tweedledee (Earles), who share star billing in a carney sideshow. They provide the entertainment while Echo's mistress, Rosie O'Grady (Mae Busch in 1925, Lila Lee in 1930), meanders through the distracted crowd, picking pockets. Echo and Hercules figure that there are bigger heists worth committing. Tweedledee pitches in, less because he is greedy than because he wants vengeance on a society that has denied him any semblance of manly dignity, save for the occasional cigar.

The gang's front is a pet store, where Echo, in granny-lady drag, uses his voice-throwing abilities to make untrained parrots appear to talk—assuring the birds' sale to wealthy customers.

Chaney and Earles make a brisk exit in *The Unholy Three*.

Tweedledee pretends to be an infant. Rosie and Hercules pose as family members. A complaint from a dissatisfied buyer brings the disguised crooks on a house-call; Hercules and Tweedledee scope out the premises while Echo distracts the householder by putting words into the bird's beak. They return as burglars. Murder is inevitable, and an innocent clerk named Hector (Matt Moore in 1925, Elliott Nugent in 1930) is framed for the deed. Rosie, who has fallen in love with Hector, promises she will remain with Echo if only the ventriloquist will clear Hector's name. A courtroom appearance by the disguised Echo vindicates Hector, and Echo releases Rosie from her vow. Tweedledee and Hercules are killed by the carnival's ill-treated ape. (The ape is the genuine article in the 1925 version—an indignant-by-nature adult chimpanzee. The creature becomes a gorilla in the remake, impersonated by the great Charlie Gemora in one of his earliest such outfits.)

The 1925 version has the advantage in Tod Browning's directorial sense of foreboding and ferocity (plus the meaner of Earles' portrayals of Tweedledee), but it is Jack Conway's remake that proves Chaney to have as many voices as he has faces. In temporary recovery at the time from the throat cancer that would soon claim his life, Chaney utilizes the Depression Era's newly added dimension of sound to establish his natural voice on a par with his genial-tough-guy looks. He utilizes a distinctive falsetto for Echo's dummy in the sideshow routines; gives the pet-shop proprietor a convincingly reedy voice with the right feminine inflection; speaks for the parrots; and supplies the remake with a plot-gimmick twist beyond the technological grasp of the silent cinema.

It is in the climactic courtroom scene, while testifying as the woman, that Chaney's Echo gives in to the pressures of the moment and allows his voice to crack. The lapse in speech betrays Echo, and he delivers a confession on the spot. Upon Echo's departure for prison, Chaney delivers an unforgettable closing line: "I'll send ya a postal card."

The addition of sound also cinches Harry Earles' credential as something more than a physically suited player. The primitive recording equipment was hardly attuned to Earles' high-pitched voice. Earles complicated matters further with a heavy-duty Germanic accent. But his passionately felt declamatory style overcomes such obstacles. Even in lesser-grade television-syndicate prints from the 1950s, Earles accomplishes with *tone*-of-voice what is lacking in clear articulation. The articulation is much more precise in a 1995 restoration by Turner Entertainment. Earles' make-believe baby-talk is at once creepy and humorous. Particularly chilling is the tiny madman's fond reminiscence about how a murder victim had begged for mercy.

Earles belonged more to the carnival world than to the movies, and after a vastly more sympathetic leading role in *Freaks*, he resettled in the circus-folk Mecca of Sarasota, Florida—returning to Hollywood, and to MGM, to accept a prominent Munchkin part in 1939's *The Wizard of Oz*. Earles died in Sarasota at age 83 in 1985.

CREDITS, SILENT VERSION: Presented by: Louis B. Mayer; Director: Tod Browning; Screenplay: Waldemar Young; Based upon: Clarence Aaron "Tod" Robbins' 1917 Novel; Photographed by: David Kesson; Settings: Cedric Gibbons and Joseph Wright; Editor: Daniel J. Gray; Length, Seven Reels; Released: August 16, 1925

CAST, SILENT VERSION: Lon Chaney (Echo); Mae Busch (Rosie O'Grady); Matt Moore (Hector McDonald); Victor McLaglen (Hercules); Harry Earles [Kurt Schneider] (Tweedledee); Harry Betz (Regan); Edward Connelly (Judge); William Humphreys (Attorney); A.E. Warren (Prosecutor); John Merkyl (Jeweler); Charles Wellesley (John Arlington)

A bit of horseplay on **The Unholy Three** set.

CREDITS, TALKING VERSION: Director: Jack Conway; Continuity and Dialogue: J.C. Nugent and Elliott Nugent; Based upon: Waldemar Young's 1925 Screenplay and Tod Robbins' Novel; Photographed by: Percy Hilburn; Art Director: Cedric Gibbons; Editor: Frank Sullivan; Sound: Anstruther MacDonald and Douglas Shearer; Wardrobe: David Cox; Running Time: 72 Minutes; Released: Following New York Premiere on July 4, 1930

CAST, TALKING VERSION: Lon Chaney (Echo); Lila Lee (Rosie); Elliott Nugent (Hector); Harry Earles (Tweedledee); John Miljan (Prosecuting Attorney); Ivan Linow (Hercules); Clarence Burton (Regan); Crauford Kent (Defense Attorney); Charlie Gemora (Gorilla)

THE ANCIENT MARINER
(Fox Film Corp.; 1925)

William Fox's big holiday-season picture of 1925 was *The Ancient Mariner*, a hybrid modern-dress/costume-fantasy melodrama calculated to preach a moral lesson by literalizing Coleridge's epic narrative poem as a warning to a wanton scoundrel. Anything to lend the musty old literary realm a sheen of relevance—and Fox Film Corp. spent a bundle to promote the picture with a direct appeal to 30,000 high schools and an essay contest in 100 newspapers.

Memory serves to qualify the film as a beauty of sorts, passionately enacted if conspicuously ragged in the production-values department. *The Ancient Mariner* has become by all accounts a lost item somewhere along the way since we cast eyes on the thing in 1968. The rental exchange that supplied our provincial Texas film society with a 16-millimeter nitrate print—already a perishable antique by that time—is long defunct, its inventories scattered if not self-immolated. The impression of two screenings remains vivid enough. But not as vivid as the wish that we'd reported the print mislaid and scraped together a replacement fee. Yes, and the historian William K. Everson often said the same of his one encounter with the since-lost *London after Midnight* (1927).

The Ancient Mariner figures here in part because of Leslie Fenton's supporting presence—a nice-guy prelude to that versatile actor's more hate-worthy presence in *The Hatchet Man*, later on in this volume—but also because the stills and commercial images we've preserved are too worthy to stay hidden, and too fragile to entrust to dead storage for much longer. A great deal of this book's overall complement of illustrations comes from well-kept glossy photos and painstakingly restored advertising materials, but our surviving *Mariner* photos are newspaper half-tones that were close to crumbling when retrieved in 1999 from a file drawer in George Turner's Pasadena archive.

In *The Rime of the Ancient Mariner* (1797-98), Samuel Taylor Coleridge tells of a wedding guest detained to listen to a tale of a seafaring voyage doomed by an act of wanton destruction. Human souls become the stakes in a game of dice between the mated specters of Death and Life-in-Death.

In her quaintly melodramatic framing story for *The Ancient Mariner*, Eve Unsell tells of a wealthy rounder named Victor Brant (Earle Williams), who is detained on the eve of his wedding by a sea captain (Nigel De Brulier) with a story that wants telling. That story is Coleridge's narrative poem, and its presentation takes on a baleful context as the captain drugs Brant with a potion to render him more susceptible. Brant deserves such rough handling, of course, having stolen innocent Doris Matthews (Clara Bow) away from her perfectly wholesome sweetheart, Joel Barlowe (Fenton). The film leaves no question but that her marriage to Brant will mean Doris' downfall. (Such a plight also figures in our chapter on *Guilty Hands*.)

The captain's recitation of Coleridge tracks the high points of the misadventure with an emphasis on the ghastlier aspects: The Mariner (played by Paul Panzer) impulsively kills an albatross that has been accepted as an omen of smooth sailing. Thirst and famine assail the now-stalled vessel, and the men are tormented by hallucinations of servants bearing fresh water.

As the urge to commit self-cannibalism takes hold ("I bit my arm, I sucked the blood..."), the promise of a rescue surfaces with an approaching ship. But no such luck. The craft advances "without a breeze, without a tide," bearing only Death and Life-in-Death:

> Are those her ribs through which the Sun
> Did peer, as through a grate?
> And is that Woman all her crew?
> And is that Death? And are there two?
> Is Death that Woman's mate?

Gladys Brockwell and Robert Klein serve impressively as the agents of doom, particularly in fidelity to Coleridge's description of "the Nightmare Life-in-Death":

> Her locks were yellow as gold
> Her skin, as white as leprosy.

The casting of the dice leaves the Mariner's shipmates dropping lifelessly, their souls passing as if launched from the crossbow with which the Mariner had slain the albatross. Too late to serve any purpose beyond caution, the Mariner comes to the realization that:

> He prayéth best, who lovéth best
> All things both great and small...

And much as the Mariner's tale leaves his impatient listener "a sadder and a wiser man," the film's recounting of the poem proves so sobering to Victor Brant that he abandons his plan to elope with Doris Matthews. An epilogue discloses that Doris has patched things up with Joel Barlowe.

As a star vehicle for the luminous Clara Bow, *The Ancient Mariner* calls upon her to do little more than radiate innocence. Earle Williams portrays the playboy suitor in broad strokes, and Leslie Fenton matches Miss Bow in terms of providing a convenient target for Williams' manipulative scheming. Fenton would find his truer level as one of the more memorable villains of the talking-picture era. Nigel De Brulier seems appropriately sinister as the skipper who shanghais Williams for no greater purpose than to teach the rascal a thing or two about common decency.

The framing story is of course secondary to the staging of the Coleridge fable, which though smartly condensed and well played suffers from Fox's characteristic attention to cost-cutting, even at the sacrifice of necessary spectacle. Only the ghost-ship—whose decrepit condition is a foregone conclusion—looks precisely right for the situation. The Mariner's ship, though skimpy in the crew department, provides an adequate setting as the voyage degenerates into a struggle for survival. Co-directors Henry Otto and

The mated spectres of Death and Life-in-Death.

Chester Bennett pace the crewmen's ordeal with the right air of desperation. Otto's work prior to *Mariner* had included the 1924 *Dante's Inferno*.

William Fox, who ran the company from New York, left the day-to-day Hollywood operations in the hands of chief assistant Sol M. Wurtzel, with standing orders to slash production values at every opportunity. The investment in promotion was an unusual extravagance—"We've shot the whole works and are confident of the result," Fox's chief of sales, James R. Grainger, told *The Exhibitors Herald*—but the film played well and widely on into 1926 despite mixed critical notices.

CREDITS: Presented by: William Fox; Directors: Henry Otto and Chester Bennett; Based upon: Samuel Taylor Coleridge's *The Rime of the Ancient Mariner*; Scenario: Chester Barnett; Narrative Title Cards Written by: Tom Miranda; Modern-Day Story: Eve Unsell; Photographed by: Joseph H. August; Assistant Director: James Tinling; Length: 6 Reels (Approx. 60 Minutes); Released: December 27, 1925

CAST: Clara Bow (Doris Matthews); Earle Williams (Victor Brant); Leslie Fenton (Joel Barlowe); Nigel De Brulier (the Skipper); Paul Panzer (the Mariner); Gladys Brockwell (Life-in-Death); Robert Klein (Death)

THE CHARLATAN
(Jewel Productions/Universal Pictures/Movietone Sound System; 1929)

"The old hocus-pocus about crystal gazers, swamis with midget assistants, cabinets in which women alternately disappear or are murdered, is revived in the film, *The Charlatan*, a story of the revenge which a one-time circus clown seeks on his wife for deserting him for another." So grumbled the New York *Times* in a desultory, pure-hackwork review that is remarkable nevertheless for its passive so-what? response to the film's strategic use of newfangled talking-picture technology. "The photoplay is further complicated by a dialogue sequence during which the murderer is apprehended," quoth the unsigned and unappreciative critic, very late in the article.

The Charlatan was presented in both wholly silent and part-talking, fully scored versions. The finished product(s) veered far afield from the plans of studio chief Carl Laemmle, but the replacement of the intended leading man, Conrad Veidt, with the distinguished English actor Holmes Herbert proved an inspired touch, born of necessity.

While Veidt was making *The Man Who Laughs* (1927-28), Laemmle kept his story department on the *qui vive* for properties that might provide suitable showcases for Veidt's genius at sinister characterizations. In December of 1927, a play by Leonard Praskins and Ernest Pascal, *The Charlatan*, was purchased for Veidt. Produced originally in 1922, the play bears more than a passing resemblance to Andreyev's *He Who Gets Slapped*, which had opened on Broadway just the year previous and would become the basis of one of Lon Chaney's better MGM pictures. The title role of *The Charlatan*—which demands three distinct characterizations, each in its own challenging makeup, would have been ideal for Veidt and the studio's paint-and-putty genius, Jack Pierce.

Although *The Charlatan* was announced as Veidt's next picture, it was postponed in favor of *The Last Warning* and *The Last Performance*. But then, Veidt returned to Europe—suffering from a bad case of microphone anxiety brought on by the advent of talking pictures. In February of 1929, *The Charlatan* was at last put into production with Holmes Herbert. (Veidt recovered his gumption in Germany and reasserted himself as an important talent for the talkies. As a fugitive from the Third Reich, he became a British citizen and ended his career back in Hollywood, from 1940 until his death following a heart attack in 1943.)

Herbert serves *The Charlatan* as a circus clown named Peter Dwight, who is devoted to his glamorous wife, Florence (Margaret Livingston), and their little daughter, Ann. When Florence leaves him for the wealthy Richard Talbot (Rockcliffe Fellows) and takes Ann with her, Dwight swears vengeance.

Years later, disguised as a Hindu crystal-gazer known as Count Merlin, Dwight arrives as a hired entertainer at the Talbot mansion. Unrecognized, Dwight learns that Florence plans to leave Talbot. As a thunderstorm rages, Florence playfully takes part in a vanishing trick involving a sealed cabinet. When the cabinet is opened, Florence is found murdered.

The district attorney pegs Dwight as the likeliest suspect. Dwight imprisons the lawman, then impersonates him and pursues the case to a solution: Talbot killed Florence, for reasons that should be fairly obvious to just about anybody with half a brain. Exonerated, and with his revenge exacted by convenient proxy, Dwight takes his daughter (Dorothy Gould) away from the murder house.

Herbert makes a convincing transformation from mild-mannered entertainer to saturnine mystic. Veidt undoubtedly would have endowed the character with a demonic emotional core, but Herbert offers a sufficient hint of such shadings. Herbert receives good support from Margaret Livingston and Rockcliffe Fellows.

George Melford's direction has pace and atmosphere, and camera boss George Robinson provides unusual lighting and strong radial compositions. The principal set conveys to perfection the impression of a palatial residence.

And about that part-talking version: The selectively loquacious edition of *The Charlatan* was issued a week after the silent film. The closing reel was re-shot with dialogue, and an elaborate orchestral score was assembled for the first six reels. Sound effects also were employed, notably during a thunderstorm; the noises were artificially created in the manner of stage effects. The voice of Holmes Herbert registers quite well on the Movietone soundtrack. Herbert was a veteran of the stages of London and Broadway, silent films and the second all-talking Vitaphone picture, *The Terror* (1928). Tough luck that English accents only alienated American audiences in those days—the conspicuous exception of Ronald Colman notwithstanding—a fact that would consign Herbert to the ranks of backup character actors for the longer term.

Musical director Josef Cherniavsky prepared the scoring in the same way he had built what he called "musical settings" for the bigger silent films, utilizing dramatic works published for theatre orchestras. He also composed a pleasingly weird theme song called "Caucasian Love" in the style of his mentor, Erno Rapée. This motif serves both as a romantic vocal and as orchestral mood-building music.

CREDITS: Presented by: Carl Laemmle; Director: George Melford; Scenario: J.G. Hawks; Based upon the Play by: Ernest Pascal and Leonard Praskins; Title Writer: Tom Reed; Adaptation: Robert N. Lee; Photographed by: George R. Robinson; Editors: Robert Jahns and Maurice Pivar; Art and Technical Effects: Max Cohen and John P. Fulton: Makeup: Jack Pierce; Length: 5,972 Feet; Released: April 7, 1929

ADDITIONAL CREDITS, PART-TALKING VERSION: Dialogue: Jacques Rollens and Tom Reed; Music Synchronized by: Josef Cherniavsky; Song: "Caucasian Love," by Lloyd Fry & Josef Cherniavsky; Compositions by: Maurice Baron, Otto Langley, Elizabeth C. Knox, Emil Bierman, H. Maurice Jacquet, J. Savasta, L. Sonek, Charles Huerter, Hugo Frey, J.S. Howgill,

Happier times for a doomed household in *The Charlatan*.

Holmes Herbert turns doomsayer in *The Charlatan*.

Justin Elie, Paul Perrier, Frances Popy, Irenee Berghon, Gaston Borch, Jean Beghon, William Axt, Bruno Hilse, Gabriel-Marie and J.S. Zamecnik; Recording Supervisor: C. Roy Hunter; Running Time: 68 Minutes; Released: April 14, 1929

CAST: Holmes Herbert (Peter Dwight and Count Merlin); Rockcliffe Fellows (Richard Talbot); Margaret Livingston (Florence); Fred Mackaye (Jerry Starke); Philo McCullough (Dr. Paynter); Anita Garvin (Mrs. Paynter); Crauford Kent (Frank Deering); Rose Tapley (Mrs. Deering); Dorothy Gould (Ann Talbot)

THE GREAT GABBO
(James Cruze, Inc./Sono Art-World Wide Pictures; 1929)

Talkies proved an apt and not entirely charitable term for motion pictures made during the early days of the industry's plunge into audio synchronization. Top-heavy with sound over sight, the new technology promised a great deal more than it had come prepared to deliver. The novelty that talking pictures afforded moviegoers of 1927-1930 was paltry compensation for the restraints the microphone placed on the camera. Talk, as it developed, was practically all that most of the early sound pictures had going for them: If a story lacked emotional impact or intellectual stimulus, then neither camera nor cutting room could do much to help.

One musically charged melodrama from the period, James Cruze's *The Great Gabbo*, bears up strikingly well in terms of story and bravura performance. It also reveals much about how filmmakers, hobbled by microphone cables, sought to overcome the documentary function to which sound had temporarily reduced the camera.

Although the yarn is gripping enough to have worked as merely a photographed stage play, it is clear that cinematographer Ira H. "Joe" Morgan held still only when there was no other choice. And although lengthy takes of exposition rely on actor-director strengths, there are still evident a willingness to experiment and an impatience with the injunctions demanded by sound. The insertion of footage depicting laughter and applause is more interruption than complement, serving chiefly to demonstrate a forced compatibility between lens and microphone. More effective is the use of superimposition, heralding the climax with a chaotic mingling of visual imagery underscored by shouts and orchestral dissonances.

Gabbo's greater appeal today lies in its station as Erich von Stroheim's talking-picture début—a seething portrayal of gathering madness, foreshadowing the greater thrust of Stroheim's career from here on out.

Gabbo (Stroheim) is a coldly perfectionistic, self-absorbed ventriloquist who performs on the lesser Vaudeville circuits with his dummy, Otto, and a pretty assistant, Mary (Betty Compson). Mary loves Gabbo and understands that he is capable of expressing tenderness only through Otto. Gabbo finally drives her away with his eternal kvetching.

Gabbo finally has become a star on Broadway, where he encounters Mary and her new song-and-dance partner, Frank (Donald Douglas). Comprehending at last his love for Mary, Gabbo woos her through Otto and assumes that she will return to him. When he learns that Mary and Frank are man-and-wife, his mind snaps. He rushes onstage during a musical number in which he has no part, raving insanely, and smashes Otto. When Mary attempts to comfort him, he cannot recognize her. Dragging Otto, Gabbo wanders aimlessly into the street.

No longer considered affordable as a director, his bull-headed extravagances having alienated the studios, Stroheim plainly contributed more to *Gabbo* than the depiction of a haunted artist. The Stroheim-style exposition, complete with integrated sub-plot, makes patent the star's influence upon producer-director James Cruze, who practiced a similarly deliberate approach and solicited suggestions from what he called "a community council" of cast and crew members following the first recitation of the script. It has long been rumored that Stroheim ghost-directed the picture; there remains no room for doubt that Stroheim—a frustrated experimenter with ideas unaffordably big—at least took advantage of Cruze's receptiveness.

Cruze (1884-1942) entered the movies as an actor, his roles ranging from a 1912 *Dr. Jekyll and Mr. Hyde* to heroes in the Thanhauser company's serials. He became a director of remarkable versatility, as adept at showcasing Fatty Arbuckle's slapstick style as at handling epic spectacle (1923's *The Covered Wagon*), and fluent in sophisticated humor (*Ruggles of Red Gap* and the picture-biz parody *Hollywood*, both from 1925). Upon completion of his Paramount contract in 1928, Cruze organized his own company in Hollywood on Santa Monica Boulevard. By March of 1929 he had acquired the I.E. Chadwick Studios on North Gower Street, whose spacious sound-film facilities enabled Cruze to turn out several short subjects as a prelude to an ambitious lineup starting with *The Great Gabbo*. Cruze adapted readily to sound, which had caused an intimidating if fleeting de-evolution of moviemaking to a primitive state. After *Gabbo*, Cruze was responsible for such strong efforts as *I Cover the Waterfront* (1933), *David Harum* and *Helldorado* (both 1934), and *Sutter's Gold* (1937). His career suffered from a chronic appetite for booze.

None of *Gabbo*'s weaknesses—most stemming from the microphone's undermining of pictorial confidence—is crippling. An understanding of the technology explains why the players often appear self-conscious, with muffled voices and long exchanges unrelieved by close-ups. Cameras were confined to soundproofed, windowed Celotex booths known as iceboxes, which kept the motor's whir from registering on the soundtrack—but of course sacrificed maneuverability. A centrally positioned, hidden microphone (boom-miking out of camera range had yet to be perfected) could capture voices faithfully only if the players spoke directly into it. The fear of botching synchronization with post-production intercutting evidently discouraged Cruze from blocking drawn-out conversations into shorter takes.

One such sequence illustrates both the awe in which the artisans held the new technology and Stroheim's professed distaste for memorizing dialogue: The actor scrambles the words *now* and *more* into a muttered "nor," then recovers his line and proceeds. Why Cruze allowed such blot upon his reputation as a perfectionist defies an answer, although a retake would have demanded more work by far than a simple patch.

Near-lavish production numbers, incorporating the Gershwinesque orchestral jazz that was all the rage in 1929, impart welcome motion and propel the story. One of the tunesmiths, identified in the formal credits as King Zany, is the great slapstick comedian and writer-director Charley Chase. A pivotal song, "I'm Laughing," explores the value of hilarity as anesthesia for the ventriloquist's emotional pain, but then is distorted into a cruel self-contradiction as Gabbo, his depression decayed into mania, charges off-cue into the finale of his own show, screaming, "I can laugh!" Ziegfeld-style spectacle merges with Expressionism in a sequence for which the stage is strung with a vast spider web. This dominant prop, a metaphor for the tangled emotions of Gabbo's love interest, is as important dramatically as it is scenically: Between stanzas of a duet, Betty Compson and Donald Douglas argue violently about her feelings for Gabbo. To compound the participatory feeling, there are realistic scenes of backstage hustle-and-bustle as the performers grumble about Gabbo's pomposity while hurrying to change costumes.

The narrative hinges on the secondary tale of a struggling show-business couple, who had known Gabbo as a small-timer and now track his rise and fall by eavesdropping, reading trade paper accounts, and at last observing his breakdown from the audience. Here is a Stroheim trademark, one he had used in *Blind Husbands* (1919) and *Greed* (1925). Ben Hecht, a world-class journalist-gone-Hollywood, had originated Gabbo as a Stroheim-like character in a short story called "The Rival Dummy," a flashback yarn framed by a description of Gabbo as a down-and-out eccentric. The film invests Gabbo with Stroheim's own superstitious nature as well as his fragile self-esteem and militaristic formality. He is a tyrant who drives away his lover, but then lets surface an excitably childlike tenderness that deteriorates to violence and finally withdrawn apathy. In depicting this loss of control, the camerawork contributes as much as the acting and the direction through the expert superimposition of stage-revue excerpts alongside a close-up of Stroheim's contorted face. Happy Expressionist-deco sets become nightmarish as their setting darkens and closes in upon itself; the sense of a deepening storm is intensified by the aural blurring of musical fragments and dialogue. One fixture, a huge revolving spiral of the sort used in the silent German Expressionist films to signify chaos or madness, dominates this passage.

The use of Gabbo's dummy, Otto, as an outlet for suppressed feelings anticipates Ealing Studios' acclaimed portmanteau film, *Dead of Night* (Great Britain; 1945); an Alfred Hitchcock teleseries episode called "The Glass Eye"; Lindsay Shonteff's American-British production of *The Devil Doll* (1963); and Sir Richard Attenborough's *Magic* (1978). Unlike these descendants,

Stroheim bestows a continental *hommage* upon Betty Compson in *The Great Gabbo*.

which all were calculated to shock or horrify, *The Great Gabbo* is purely a tragic study of a deteriorating mind.

Otto's falsetto voice, supplied by George Grandee, is given a Viennese accent that nearly matches Stroheim's own, but there is a significant discrepancy: Otto addresses Betty Compson's character as "Mary," but Stroheim pronounces the name as "Muh-*ree*"—in much the same way that he would lend an unintentionally laughable note to *As You Desire Me* (1932) by referring to Greta Garbo's Maria as "Muh-*rear*." The ventriloqual routines are entertaining in their broadly cornball way; these include a homage to the famed act of Marshall Montgomery in which Otto speaks while Gabbo smokes, drinks and dines.

Joe Morgan (1889-1960) had become a cameraman in 1911. He spent the 1920s on glossy, expensive productions but by the 1930s found himself relegated to the quick-and-cheap Poverty Row companies. He spent much of the 1940s as a portrait photographer, then shot numerous Sam Katzman serials and *Jungle Jim* features. A heart attack forced Morgan's retirement in 1956.

Gabbo does not showcase Morgan's skills at their best; the new technology was too restrictive. Generalized lighting thwarts the dramatic possibilities, and the static camera misses many opportunities for enhancement of the spoken situations. The stage-production sequences were shot in Multicolor, a process that rendered the screen garish in a film of otherwise subdued visual effect. The bipack two-color system yielded a surprising range of tones from the basic hues of orange and blue, resembling the later and better-known Cinecolor. (Even Technicolor was a two-color process at that time, deriving from red and green elements.) Other manifestations of Multicolor include *Fox Movietone Follies of 1929* and the animated cartoon "Goofy Goat" (1931). The company's chief owner and vice president was Howard Hughes, who used the

Stroheim's crack-up scene in *The Great Gabbo*.

Multicolor plant as his California headquarters after the process was discontinued in 1932. (The surviving prints we have found of *The Great Gabbo* are entirely in black-and-white.)

Stroheim dominates the cast with brusque ease and moments of surprising affability. Betty Compson's bittersweet portrayal provides a realistic counterweight to Gabbo's paranoia; her displays of affection, mother-hennish concern and unwitting cruelty are uniformly convincing. Pauline Starke had been announced for the role, but Miss Compson applied the pressure to Cruze—her husband during 1927-29—and landed it instead. Miss Compson's voice recorded rather stridently, and her stardom in the talkies proved brief; she carried on gamely as a backup player. (A lovely portrait of Miss Compson in better days figures as a significant prop in *Invisible Ghost* [1941], where she plays a haggard intruder whose nocturnal rambles drive Bela Lugosi to a murderous rage.) As Miss Compson's sorehead husband in *Gabbo*, light-opera veteran Donald Douglas proves a better singer than an actor.

Though initially appealing today as a curiosity, *The Great Gabbo* delivers a fascinating story and characterizations to match. The mostly stock-still camerawork must be accepted as a matter of historical reality. Audiences of the time, spoiled to the fluid photography of the thoroughly well-evolved silents, would have faced a similar caveat, if not for the distracting novelty of sound. What the camera could not capture through motion, however, is sometimes brought to life through the art of composition. In a poignant closing scene that comes near reconciling sight with sound, the lens has the last word: As the microphone picks up Stroheim's receding footfalls, the camera captures a scene of horrid desolation. At ground level, Gabbo meanders past the scene of his last hurrah while, above, a handyman removes, letter by letter, the suddenly lapsed star's billing from the marquee.

CREDITS: Presented by: Henry D. Meyer and Nat Cordish; by Arrangement with: Harry H. Thomas and Samuel Zierler; Director: James Cruze; Continuity and Dialogue: F. Hugh Herbert; Story: Ben Hecht; Photographed by: Ira H. Morgan; Color Sequences: Multicolor Process; Art Director: Robert E. Lee; Musical Director: Howard Jackson; Songs: "The New Step," "I'm in Love with You," "The Web of Love," "I'm Laughing," "The Ga-Ga Bird," "Ickey," and "Ev'ry Now and Then," by Paul Titsworth, Lynn Cowan, Donald McNamee and King Zany (Charley Chase); Dance Director: Maurice L. Kusell; Sound Supervisor: Helmar Bergman; Costumes: André-Ani; Production Manager: Vernon Keays; Running Time: 90 minutes; Released: September 12, 1929

CAST: Erich von Stroheim (Gabbo); George Grandee (Voice of Otto); Betty Compson (Mary); Donald Douglas (Frank); Margie "Babe" Kane (Comedienne); Harry Ross (Performer)

SVENGALI
(Warner Bros. Pictures, Inc./The Vitaphone Corp.; 1931)

> Although the book [George du Maurier's *Trilby*] is almost forgotten, its most interesting character, Svengali, lives on, king of the mountebanks, hypnotist par excellence, and seducer of helpless victims, female variety, through the Mephistophelean force of his animal magnetism.
> —David Carroll *The Matinée Idols* (1972)

Surpassing even his work in *Dr. Jekyll and Mr. Hyde* (1920), two versions of *Moby Dick* (1925 and 1930) and *Romeo and Juliet* (1936), *Svengali* represents John Barrymore's finest contribution to motion pictures. The role of the predatory, self-destroying mesmerist sparkles with an enthusiasm Barrymore seldom applied to his more usual matinee-idol portrayals; his transformation of Maestro Svengali avoids the brutal degeneration of an Edward Hyde or an Ahab and plants the nagging worry of how such an amusing rogue could change so abruptly into a brooding menace. Barrymore had insisted that Svengali must be so laughable, so almost likable, at first as to confront audiences with a moral question of whether to sympathize with him upon disclosure of the sinister side. Thus did Barrymore become the most distinctive Svengali since Wilton Lackaye's defining portrayal in the original stage presentation of 1895, and thus does Barrymore's interpretation remain the standard.

The picture opens with Svengali's absurdly formal entrance from his piano studio when Mme. Honori (Carmel Myers), a flighty young matron, arrives for her lesson in voice. Their conversation makes it plain he is more to her than a tutor. Svengali is delighted at her news: "I've left my husband—for good!" He inquires, "And how much has he left *you*?" His warmth fades as she explains, "I've come to you just as I am." Svengali fixes his eyes upon the woman; she begs him to avert his gaze, then flees in terror. Later, upon learning that Honori's body has been found adrift, Svengali is philosophical: "She was very, very sweet—but a bad businesswoman."

Up to this cruel juncture, Svengali has seemed an affable (if unsanitary) rogue, but he soon reasserts that roguishness to disarming effect: He and his helper, Gecko (Luis Alberni), impose upon two acquaintances from Scotland, Taffy (Lumsden Hare) and the Laird (Donald Crisp), and chance to meet Trilby O'Farrell (Marian Marsh), a model whose untutored but powerful voice awes Svengali. He turns ever more menacing when he learns that Billee (Bramwell Fletcher), a young English painter, and Trilby are engaged. Placing Trilby in a hypnotic thrall, he plants the suggestion that she "will think of nothing but Svengali—Svengali—Svengali." Trilby vanishes, leaving a note that hints at suicide. Svengali has departed.

Years later, Paris is soon to hear a concert by La Svengali, toast of the continent and wife of the long-absent Maestro. Recognizing La Svengali to be a mesmerized Trilby, Billee comprehends that Svengali is running from "fear of the day when his spell... will be broken." Billee tracks the couple to Cairo, where they are performing under diminished circumstances. During Trilby's performance, Svengali clutches his chest and pitches forward. Trilby's voice veers off-key, and she collapses. Svengali, dying, prays: "Oh, God, grant me in death what you have denied me in life—the woman I love!" Trilby utters the name of Svengali and expires.

So great is the spell cast here that Barrymore actually elicits pity for this scabrous creature. An especially poignant moment occurs in the bedchamber, where Svengali caresses Trilby longingly. Under his gaze, she becomes a creature of passion. Appalled at his own power, Svengali snarls, "*Ach!*... [I]t is only Svengali, talking to himself again." The physical acting here is as powerful as the hissed condemnation-of-self: Barrymore turns his back to the audience, and yet he is thoroughly in control of the viewer's response.

Though Barrymore had a near-absolute say-so over *Svengali*, the film is the vividly realized result of collaboration and compromise—faithful to the novel that inspired it, and yet freehanded enough to accommodate the inventiveness of director Archie Mayo; designer Anton Grot; camera chief Barney McGill; effects masters Fred Jackman and Hans Koenekamp; and the personally troubled but still magical Barrymore.

Scenarist J. Grubb Alexander modified George Du Maurier's charming account of Parisian student life in the 19th Century to a Gothic study heavily influenced by the German cinema. The changes are realized profoundly well, thanks to Barrymore's penchant for the bizarre, Mayo's pragmatic admiration of the German art films, McGill's gift for evocative lighting and Grot's mastery of the Expressionist setting. Some scenes could be paintings sprung to life, with a richness of chiaroscuro.

This blend of scenic values and motion is most striking in an amazing sequence engineered by Koenekamp: Svengali's eyes glaze as he projects his will across the jagged rooftops. The camera withdraws until Svengali is a distant shape, then makes a right-face in a headlong swoop, capturing shadowplay and gusts of wind. Miles away, the camera pivots again and races to Trilby's bedside as she wakes in terror. The scene ends with a masterful flourish: Svengali laughs as he watches a black cat pawing at a mouse's nest. So dazzling a job would be remarkable in a film of the present day; it is far more so for 1931, when mobile camerawork had become the exception.

Koenekamp told us in 1989 how he pulled off that scene: The sets of the two apartments were built full-scale at opposite ends of Warners' huge Stage No. 5. The cityscape was a large-scale miniature that ran the length of the stage. The camera simply pulled away from Barrymore's eyes and traveled over the rooftops.

Mayo, strictly a big-timer among directors, addressed the *Svengali* motif again in Warners' *The Man With Two Faces*. *Svengali* marks the first stab at a Germanic style for Mayo, whose numerous pictures include *The Petrified Forest* (1936), the film that made Humphrey Bogart famous; *Crash Dive* (1943); and *A Night in Casablanca* (1946), with the Marx Brothers.

Svengali surrounded Mayo with players whose response to his incisive direction is as true as their physical similarities to Du Maurier's written and sketched descriptions. Lumsden Hare and Donald Crisp are older than Du Maurier had envisioned the Scots, but their maturity anchors Bramwell Fletcher's impulsive young Englishman. As Svengali's worried sidekick, Luis Alberni captures the novelist's description of unimposing stature and Spaniel-eyed loyalty—Gecko is assertive toward all but Svengali—but eliminates the youthful aspect and the scarred countenance.

John Barrymore contemplates his *Svengali* get-up in a full-length mirror.

The Definitive Edition

Barrymore glares as romance blossoms between Marian Marsh and Bramwell Fletcher.

Of Trilby, du Maurier wrote that she "could hardly be called beautiful at first sight" but added that "you can never tell how beautiful—or how ugly—a face may be 'til you have tried to draw it." The film's Trilby, teen-aged Marian Marsh, is—need we say?—an angelic knockout, and yet her resemblance to the du Maurier drawings is remarkably close. Warners touted Miss Marsh as a Barrymore discovery. Other accounts hold, however, that Barrymore had asked Warners for a more seasoned actress, Evelyn Laye, but that, when assigned instead to work with the relatively inexperienced Miss Marsh, he proved a patient tutor, seeing to it that she felt sufficiently comfortable around his Satanic makeup that no unconscious reaction would register on film.

Music for *Svengali* is eclectic European, dominated by a sentimental ballad from the mid-19th Century, "Ben Bolt." Sinister underscoring is employed at just the right times, and there are classical selections from Chopin and Donizetti. For the sequence involving La Svengali's big performance, Warners borrowed Universal's Stage No. 28, site of the Paris Opera House interiors from 1925's *The Phantom of the Opera*.

Svengali, or more properly *Trilby*, has been brought to the screen in other versions, including Biograph's 1896 "Trilby and Little Billee," a prompt follow-up to the runaway-hit stage version. This one is a brief and self-contained romantic scene, without the character of Svengali, from back in the day when *all* films were short subjects. Then have come such outcroppings as these:

- The 1915 *Trilby*, starring Clara Kimball Young with the stage's original Svengali, Wilton Lackaye.

Svengali reasserts his hypnotic control over Trilby.

- The 1923 *Trilby*, starring Andrée Lafayette with Arthur Edmund Carew as Svengali.
- The 1955 British-made *Svengali*, with Sir Donald Wolfit and Hildegarde Neff.
- Al Adamson and Paul Aratow's *Doctor Dracula* (1981), also known as *Svengali* and owing more to Du Maurier than to Bram Stoker.
- And a 1983 telefeature *Svengali*, which plants Peter O'Toole and Jodie Foster in a modern-day pop-music setting.

A tense almost-reunion in *Svengali*.

•To say nothing of the *Mighty Mouse* cartoon-series entry, "Svengali's Cat," from 1946.

The 1931 production holds up as the most artistically adventurous and frightening version of the lot, with full due given the romantic, the melodramatic, the tragic and the comic—thanks largely to John Barrymore's unequaled gift for covering all such bases in a swoop, and for inspiring the colleagues in his orbit.

CREDITS: Director: Archie Mayo; Based upon: George Du Maurier's 1894 novel, *Trilby*; Screenplay: J. Grubb Alexander; Photographed by: Barney McGill; Art Director, Anton Grot; Editor: William Holmes; Gowns: Edward Luick; Technical Effects: Fred W. Jackman and Hans F. Koenekamp; Composer, Arranger and Conductor: David Mendoza, with the Vitaphone Orchestra; Song, "Ben Bolt," by Dr. Thomas Dunn and Nelson Kneass; Additional Music: Arthur Franklin, Wesly, Naggiar and Robert Emmett Dolan; Assistant Director: Gordon Hollingshead; Makeup: Johnny Wallis; Running Time: 93 Minutes; Released: May 22, 1931

CAST: John Barrymore (Svengali); Marian Marsh (Trilby O'Farrell); Donald Crisp (The Laird); Bramwell Fletcher (Billee); Carmel Myers (Mme. Honori); Luis Alberni (Gecko); Lumsden Hare (Taffy); Paul Porcasi (Signor Bonelli); Ferike Boros (Marta); Adrienne D'Ambricourt (Madame Vinard); Yola D'Avril (Maid); Henry Otto (Man With Opera Glasses)

MURDER BY THE CLOCK
(Paramount Publix Corp.; 1931)

More a lifelike horror movie than a bizarre crime yarn—but a great deal of both, in carefully intertwined proportion—Edward Sloman's *Murder by the Clock* provided in its day a helpful early counterweight to the more purely outlandish fantastical monstrosities of *Dracula, Frankenstein* and *Dr. Jekyll & Mr. Hyde*. The nerve-wrenching *Murder by the Clock* abounds with Human Monsters and exhibits the gumption—rather like Tod Browning's once-scandalous *Freaks*—to invest its greater share of repellence in a not-quite-right individual who might more politely be considered pitiable.

Irving Pichel's hideous leading-man-by-default has long reminded us of a village-idiot type who ranged at large in the town we called home for too many years. This Real World character, as a schoolkid riding the narrow margin between normalcy and Special Education, was especially fond of tormenting and brutalizing his classmates, only to be nabbed and reprimanded time and again by this or that Authority Figure. His stock rebuttal: "You can't spank *me*! I'm ree-*tor*-ded!" Later on, as an adult regarded variously with fear, compassion and revulsion, he developed a fascination with the handiwork of the Charles Manson mob and broke into several (blessedly vacant) dwellings to adorn their walls with vile graffiti. An overdue institutionalization followed, lest the Manson fixation escalate.

Pichel has already escalated by the time *Murder by the Clock* gets down to business, and the film is all the stronger, all the more abrasive, for it. The fine actor, who was edging gradually toward a fully fledged directing career, contributes an irresistibly repugnant depiction of a gleefully uninhibited menace-to-society ("a lecherous giant of a half-wit," as our pal Bill Everson once put it), who derives his richer delights from terrorizing people who would be more comfortable just feeling sorry for the pathetic nincompoop.

Actually, conniving Laura Endicott (Lilyan Tashman) is more comfortable with provoking dimwit Phillip Endicott (Pichel), her cousin-by-marriage, to commit mayhem. Phillip is already under suspicion, being a violent oaf with reason to despise his wealthy mother, Julia Endicott (Blanche Friderici), because she had written him out of her will. The new heir is Julia's drunken socialite nephew, Herbert Endicott (Walter McGrail), who in fact becomes Julia's strangler—moved to the deed by Laura, his wife. So Phillip is arrested, even though Police Lt. Valcour (William "Stage" Boyd) considers him innocent, believing Phillip too much the brute to have committed the comparatively dainty strangulation murder.

Laura manipulates her partner-in-adultery, sculptor Tom Hollander (Lester Vail), supposedly a devoted friend to her husband, into an attack on Herbert. Herbert rallies, and Tom tries again to kill him without the desired result. A fleeting apparition resembling Julia frightens Herbert to death. Laura appeals to Phillip's lustful nature to inspire him to break out of jail. Phillip discombobulates Tom, then abducts Laura and holds her captive in Julia's burial vault. In a hidden chamber, Lt. Valcour has found the body of Julia, along with more genuinely incriminating evidence. Laura activates the crypt's alarm system—one of Julia's paranoia-driven amenities. Valcour rescues Laura, who attempts to use her seductive wiles on the cop, to no avail. The evidence proves to be a death-mask, bearing Laura's fingerprints.

The villainy belongs more properly to Lilyan Tashman's cold-eyed, ultra-bourgeois Lady Macbeth, but it is Pichel's grinning-idiot strongman presence that dominates the generous running time. No one in this snakebit household is particularly admirable, of course, what with the self-indulgent, social-climbing, bitterly wedded couple of Miss Tashman and Walter McGrail; her two-faced lover Lester Vail; and dour Blanche Friderici as the eccentric old bat whose distrustful nature triggers crises before and after her death. Tough-talking William Boyd, not to be confused with his namesake contemporary William "Hopalong Cassidy" Boyd, accounts for the role-model quotient, boasting enough good horse sense to place duty ahead of

Lilyan Tashman appeals to Irving Pichel's animalistic desires in *Murder by the Clock*.

Miss Tashman's formidable temptations. Regis Toomey supplies recurring comedy relief as a blarney-spouting cop who must be scarcely a generation removed from Ireland; it is Toomey who provides the story with its touchstone to the film's cryptic title.

An unforgettable gimmick—and especially so, during that transitional early-Depression period when *any* noise was a novelty to moviegoers—is a hoarse, wracking shriek that blares forth at precisely the right moments to unnerve all concerned. This hair-raising honk issues from an alarm in the family crypt, so planted just in case the Widow Endicott should find herself entombed alive. Even for the encore viewer who knows just when to expect the ghastly blast, the effect still can generate a cringing response.

Director Edward Sloman was a silent-screen veteran who leapt wholeheartedly into the new challenges of the talkers but proved less prolific as the decade wore on, retiring by the late '30s. Sloman moves *Clock* along at a precipitous clip, with welcome pauses to let the viewer admire the gloomily evocative camerawork and set décor, and he dwells rewardingly on the sardonic humor and smoldering sexuality of the intrigues behind the mayhem.

A chunk of *Murder by the Clock* also can be seen in Paramount's autobiography-of-a-studio feature, *The House That Shadows Built*, issued that same year.

CREDITS: Director: Edward Sloman; Adaptation: Henry Myers; Based upon: Rufus King's 1929 Novel, *Double Murder*, as serialized in *Redbook* magazine and collected as *Murder by the Clock*, and Charles Beahan's 1929 play, *Dangerously Yours*; Photographed by: Karl Struss; Operative Cameramen: George Clemens and Cliff Blackstone; Assistant Cameramen: Fleet Southcott and Al Smalley; Stills: Frank Bjerring; Running Time: 75 Minutes; Released: August 8, 1931

CAST: William "Stage" Boyd (Lt. Valcour); Lilyan Tashman (Laura Endicott); Irving Pichel (Phillip Endicott); Regis Toomey (Officer Cassidy); Sally O'Neal (Jane); Blanche Friderici

(Julia Endicott); Walter McGrail (Herbert Endicott); Lester Vail (Tom Hollander); Martha Mattox (Miss Roberts); Frank Sheridan (Police Chief); Frederick Sullivan (Medical Examiner); Willard Robertson (Police Captain); Charles D. Brown (O'Brien); John Rogers (Butler); Lenita Lane (Nurse); Harry Burgess (Coroner); Guy Oliver (Caretaker)

"I swear, I'll put you in the electric chair!"—Lionel Barrymore to Kay Francis in *Guilty Hands*.

GUILTY HANDS
(Metro-Goldwyn-Mayer Corp./Loew's, Inc.; 1931)

In 10 years as District Attorney of New York, Richard Grant (Lionel Barrymore) sent more than 50 men to the electric chair. "I didn't like it," avers Grant. "Now that I've returned to private practice, I've kept a hundred of 'em *out* of it... A clever man in such a case could commit a murder so skillfully... that he could get away with it."

Hired by a notorious womanizer named Gordon Rich (Alan Mowbray), Grant learns to his horror that Rich is intent upon marrying Grant's daughter, Barbara (Madge Evans). Grant impulsively states his intention to kill Rich.

On the eve of the wedding, while the servants see Grant's pacing shadow on the drawn shade of his room, Grant invades Rich's quarters and kills the lecher, then arranges the appearance of suicide.

Marjorie West (Kay Francis), Rich's mistress, finds that Grant had rigged a paper silhouette to a phonograph turntable. When she threatens Grant, he counters with an oath to frame her. The police examine Rich's body, which still clutches the revolver Grant had used. As the muscles contract, the gun fires. Grant falls, mortally wounded.

So striking was Lionel Barrymore's performance as a doomed alcoholic lawyer in MGM's *A Free Soul* (1931), that producer Hunt Stromberg was quick to cast him as another star-crossed counselor in *Guilty Hands*, filmed about two months later. The eldest member of the celebrated acting clan received an Academy Award for *A Free Soul* and widespread acclaim for *Guilty Hands*.

A contemplative moment from *Guilty Hands*.

One of the better perfect-crime yarns, *Guilty Hands* was written by the playwright Bayard Vieller to suit the Barrymore personality. More stable and dependable than his erratic brother, John, Lionel was an important figure at MGM, being a director, dramatic coach and casting advisor as well as a leading player. He was an accomplished etcher and a serious composer as well—as close as any 20th Century artist has come to being a Complete Renaissance Man.

The script permits the star to be almost entirely sympathetic despite his crime—a devoted father who does away with a pervert who sorely wants killing. The absorbed viewer instinctively roots for Barrymore, who nevertheless becomes somewhat the demon as he intimidates a woman who had been loyal to Barrymore's victim. This shift renders the finale more ironic than tragic.

The difficult role of compatible perversion, the woman who has been tolerant until now of her lover's lustful indulgences, is set forth with an appropriate intensity by Kay Francis, a fast-rising star of the day. The victim, a thoroughgoing blackguard, is well performed—while he lasts—by Alan Mowbray, a hard-drinking *compadre* of John Barrymore's. His character is described by Lionel to Madge Evans as "...a beast about women... so that your wedding night... will be a horror and a shame." Mowbray later became more keenly identified with comic-eccentric portrayals.

The big set-piece is Miss Francis' confrontation of Barrymore, who proceeds to enact for her a courtroom scene in which she is convicted of his crime: "Have you ever seen a murder trial?" he begins. "Sit down, and I'll show you *yours*... [The victim] was on the eve of his marriage to a beautiful, innocent girl who adored him. Life stretched out before him happily, but this woman couldn't bear the thought... " He pauses emphatically, then: "I swear, I'll put you in the electric chair!"

The tension goes practically unrelieved, what with the tautly sarcastic exchanges, the ominous engagement party with its veneer of cordiality, the murder during the obligatory thunderstorm and the shock-value climax. Norbert Brodine's photography matches the impact of all these.

The ambiguity of the protagonists amply reflects that of W.S. Van Dyke II, MGM's most dependable director. He was well loved by many, but considered a bully by others. He was a rugged and adventurous outdoorsman, but also a writer of poetry. A former assistant to D.W. Griffith, Van Dyke began directing in 1917 as a specialist in outdoor actioners. He joined MGM in 1926 and delivered one box-office hit after another—nearly 50 pictures, with only the rare flop. With few exceptions—1931's *Trader Horn* being the most conspicuous—Van Dyke brought in his films within budget and ahead of schedule.

Guilty Hands marked Van Dyke's first pure crime drama, but it was far from the last. *Penthouse* (1933), *The Thin Man* (1934) and *Rage in Heaven* (1941) proved equally fine examples. Van Dyke's versatility may be gauged by a random selection of titles: *Tarzan, the Ape Man* (1932), *Naughty Marietta* (1935), *San Francisco* (1936), *Marie Antoinette* (1938), *Andy Hardy Gets Spring Fever* (1939), and *Journey for Margaret* (1942). The last-named was completed shortly before his death.

CREDITS: Producer: Hunt Stromberg; Director: W.S. Van Dyke II; Story and Dialogue: Bayard Vieller; Photographed by: Merritt Gerstad; Settings: Cedric Gibbons; Recording Supervisor: Douglas Shearer; Recording Engineer: Paul Neal; Editor: Anne Bauchens; Musical Director: Dr. William Axt; Music: L. Andrieu and Domenico Savino; Song, "Kiddie Kapers," by: Nathaniel Shilkret, Al Sherman & Lew Pollack; Western Electric Sound; Running time, 68 minutes; Released: August 22, 1931

CAST: Lionel Barrymore (Richard Grant); Kay Francis (Marjorie West); Madge Evans (Barbara Grant); William Bakewell (Tommy Osgood); C. Aubrey Smith (Rev. Mr. Hastings); Polly Moran (Aunt Maggie); Alan Mowbray (Gordon Rich); Forrester Harvey (Spencer Wilson); Charles Crockett (H.G. Smith); Henry Barrows (Harvey Scott); Blue Washington (Johnny)

THE SPIDER
(Fox Film Corp.; 1931)

Nobody is to leave this theatre!
—A Command Issued Early On in *The Spider*

"Barnum was right—Herrmann was wrong," declared Edmund Lowe, cryptically stating a case for his new starring picture. The year was 1931, and *The Spider* was strategically well positioned to become a significant broadside in the launching of a genre complete unto itself, the wired-for-sound horror film.

Lowe was speaking not of P.T. Barnum's famous line about "a sucker born every minute"—although that might apply, too—but rather of a lesser-known philosophy of entertainment from the pioneering impresario.

"I mean," Lowe explained, "that Barnum was right when he said that slow, natural motion [in the performance of magic] deceives the spectator, and that Herrmann's theory of the hand being quicker than the eye is incorrect.

"I refer, of course, to Herrmann the Great, the magician, not Babe Herman, the outfielder," Lowe added.

The occasion was an interview contrived by the publicity department of Fox Film Corp., and so Lowe was as much in charge of the Q&A process as his character—a magician embroiled in amnesia, murder and the violent Haves vs. Have-Nots conflicts of the Great Depression—would prove himself in charge of the weirdness at large in *The Spider*. The actor proceeded to mystify the anonymous interviewer with a vanishing-card trick at a leisurely pace, then: "You see, Barnum was right."

"I must inform the public at once!" the interviewer quoted himself, facetiously. "Where is my portable typewriter?"

"Where you left it," replied Lowe, pretending to retrieve the machine from under the writer's coat. "And here's your watch. And your wallet. Careless, *aren't* you?"

This was an unusual promotional stance, and particularly so by comparison with campaigns for kindred films of the day as a bandwagon slowly began rolling along.

In its promotion of *Dracula*, the watershed film of this talkie-terror movement, Universal Pictures had promised forbidden romance and underscored that intention audaciously with a St. Valentine's Day opening in 1931. For its later-in-1931 follow-through, *Frankenstein*, Universal had taken a similar tack—but only for so long as Bela Lugosi, the exotic leading man of *Dracula*, had been attached to *Frankenstein*'s pivotal role of a humanlike creation of renegade science. Upon Lugosi's rejection of the part and Boris Karloff's ascent to the career-cinching assignment, Universal let the publicity campaign find its own level of terrified anticipation. Universal's *East of Borneo*, from the autumn of 1931, bears regard as a horror picture but was marketed more as a hard-bitten adventurous entry, and perceived accordingly by the public.

Paramount, with its 1931 opening of *Murder by the Clock*, touted the novelty of sound, in the form of a horrendous mechanical wail that issues from a mausoleum with a nerve-wracking unpredictability. For its 1931-32 opening of *Dr. Jekyll and Mr. Hyde*, Paramount took a sensationalistic, star-driven approach to selling the horrific appeal of the material.

Warner Bros. brought to the table *Svengali*, a haunting tale of mesmerism in the service of evil, but marketed this film more in terms of the snob appeal of star player John Barrymore and the innocent beauty of Barrymore's chosen leading lady, Marian Marsh. The studio allowed a prompt follow-up from the same unit, *The Mad Genius*, to glide by on the coattails of *Svengali*. Although *The Mad Genius* is not without its charms, it served chiefly as a means for Barrymore to fulfill a contract for one last Warners assignment. For that matter, *The Mad Genius* might not exist without *Svengali* as its springboard.

In the case of *The Spider*, which gives a procedural detective yarn a generous garnish of eerie menace and the illusion of audience participation, Fox couched its fall-of-1931 pitch to the public in terms of antic wit, a whiff of the supernatural and an ambiguity as to whether Edmund Lowe might turn out to be a threatening character. The comic-relief shenanigans of El Brendel, a popular Swedish-dialect goof, provided a key selling point. There is a residue of the Broadway-derived mystery-farce, and indeed *The Spider* had its own Broadway origins, however distinctive. But this quality is merely a touchstone to the familiar—helpfully placed alongside the film's bolder use of depth-of-field and sound itself in an attempt to involve the audience beyond absorbed observation.

Where the audience attending a conventional mystery-farce could witness at a comfortable distance the mayhem threatening the inmates of some confining mansion, the audiences for *The Spider* were themselves situated in theaters not unlike the venue shown on screen, the physical reality of an auditorium becoming a telescopic extension of the picture at the appropriate moments. This was a calculated strategy on the part of co-director William Cameron Menzies, a championship set designer and art director who fancied a fuller involvement of the audience to be a logical next phase in the evolution of filmmaking. He was quite ahead of his time, as usual: In this respect, *The Spider* proves itself a foreshadowing of Menzies' more striking experiments in depth design of a generation later, including *The Maze* (shot in a three-dimensional process) and *Invaders from Mars* (which could scarcely have seemed more three-dimensional if it *had* been shot in 3-D).

This array of films from 1931, though patently the new foundation of a genre, constituted not so much the beginning of a trend—for staged terrors, even though not quite designated a genre as such or as yet, had been crucial to the cinema since its early outcroppings—as it marked a turning point geared to the emerging technology of synchronized sound.

The second all-talking feature film had been Warners' *The Terror*, from 1928, a farcical maniac-at-large piece that did scarcely more than carry on the Broadway-derived traditions of such Jazz Age silent-movie hits as *The Cat and the Canary*, *The Bat* and *The Gorilla*, all reprised sooner or later as talking pictures. The surviving soundtrack elements of *The Terror*—

the film itself can be presumed lost beyond recovery—play out almost like a self-contained radio melodrama, as if underscoring but not necessarily adding anything to the images that graced the screen.

But 1931 would become the year of the Big Detour, serving emphatic, crowd-pleasing proof in a handful of pictures from only four major studios that a uniquely cinematic genre, beholden to no style handed down from the silent screen, was ripe for development and exploitation. Of this formidable lot, *The Spider* has suffered the most damnable long-term obscurity. If the larger history of cinema were a Top 40 Oldies radio station, then *Dracula* and *Frankenstein* would be Motown and The Beach Boys and *The Spider* would be some seldom-played deep-cuts act like The Thirteenth Floor Elevators or The Vejtables. Even Rouben Mamoulian's 1932 *Jekyll & Hyde*, acquired outright by MGM as the basis for a more pretentious but ultimately lesser 1941 remake, finally returned to prominence after years of dog-in-the-manger suppression by MGM.

The prevailing school of thought holds that obscurity is usually deserved—that the cream rises and the inferior content settles unnoticed. A truer understanding, however, lies in the realization that the Popular Culture procreates so prolifically that most of its progeny, whether brilliant or tarnished, hasn't a chance of getting recognized without exhaustive promotion and over-merchandising. Mass man must be served by mass means, as the satirist Roger Price once averred, hammering this chillingly self-evident truth about the culture: "If everybody doesn't want it, then nobody gets it." For everybody to want it, then, it becomes necessary that everybody be *told* (by the advertising and marketing industries) that they must have it.

Outbreaks of mass-marketing over the long haul have kept *Frankenstein* and *Dracula* as familiar now as they were when unspooled fresh. The 1932 *Jekyll & Hyde* was kept forcibly obscure for generations, lest anyone get wise to its superiority in comparison with the remake. But when MGM mounted a big-screen reissue during the early 1970s, the big studio set aside its own version and released its long-hidden acquisition from Paramount, with a bombastic publicity campaign. *Svengali* is better known today as folklore than by its literary and cinematic outcroppings; a lapsed copyright has made the Warners version a perennial among the off-brand video labels. That curious companion-film, *The Mad Genius*, has become a forgotten picture despite the boon of copyright maintenance for television syndication.

Fox's *The Spider*, on the other hand, enjoyed its day in the glare of the carbon-arc projector beam. It made back its investment, and then some. It helped to bolster Edmund Lowe in an extended career of playing suave, often mysterious chaps—including, a year later, the title role in Fox's *Chandu the Magician*, with Menzies and Marcel Varnel co-directing.

Whereupon *The Spider* found itself retired to the vaults. Its resurrection for early-day television came without fanfare, and when seldom the film resurfaces today it is heralded by the finest of fine print in the night-owl TV listings. To the viewer willing to regard it as more than an antique or a curiosity, *The Spider* rewards the most eager attention. Here is the story it tells:

A magician known as Chatrand the Great (Lowe) announces via a radio broadcast that he seeks to find the true identity of a victim of amnesia—his assistant, who answers for now to the name of Alexander. Alexander (Howard Phillips) was found, wounded and unconscious, two years ago in Washington. He has become a mind reader in Chatrand's routine, but Alexander cannot read his own mind sufficiently to dredge up any memories of his previous self.

Listening intently to the announcement is Beverly Lane (Lois Moran), whose brother, Paul Lane, has been missing for two years. Beverly's uncle, big-shot businessman John Carrington (Earle Fox), dismisses Chatrand's announcement as a publicity hoax. Beverly insists upon attending Chatrand's next performance, and Carrington goes along with her.

Surveying the audience from behind the curtains, Chatrand recognizes Beverly from a photograph in a locket that Alexander carries. As the performance progresses, Chatrand blindfolds Alexander and calls upon the youth to describe objects carried by various patrons. When Alexander is asked to describe Beverly's locket, identical to his own, Carrington objects and resorts to violence to halt the routine.

Directors Menzies and MacKenna determined that they must retain the witty dialogue and the intimacy of the play. Their success not only overcame the talk-over-action imperative but brought to the project some purely cinematic inventions.

Chatrand's second assistant (Manya Roberti) cuts the lights. A hand, wearing a ring bearing the likeness of a spider, fires a gun. Carrington drops. The police arrive to corral the audience and staff while one showgoer, Dr. Blackstone (George E. Stone), attends to Carrington.

Inspector Riley (Purnell Pratt) finds a gun behind Alexander, who is unconscious. Beverly embraces Alexander and identifies him as her brother. Snapped out of his trance, Alexander, recognizing his sister, declares: "He tried to kill me! I *had* to do it!"

Riley orders Alexander and Beverly sequestered in an office. Chatrand steals away through a trap door. Alexander recalls the circumstances that brought on his amnesia: Carrington had tried to take control of the siblings' fortune, and Alexander suffered a head injury while dodging an attack from Carrington.

Chatrand learns that Carrington has been under threat from a disgruntled investor. Carrington is pronounced dead, and Alexander is arrested for murder. Chatrand persuades the law to allow him to conduct a séance, the better to smoke out the true killer. As a ghostly voice appears to speak through Chatrand, another shot is fired. Chatrand takes this development as a hopeful sign and orders Alexander, in mind-reader mode, to track down the killer. After several false starts involving various embarrassing secrets among the audience, Alexander mentions the spider-ring and prepares to reveal the killer. Again comes gunfire, followed by Dr. Blackstone's unveiling as the killer. The physician declares that Carrington deserved to die for his financial racketeering, which had betrayed the trust of Blackstone and many other investors.

Chatrand, wounded in the last outburst, is comforted by Beverly. She seems to have become infatuated with the magician.

When it débuted on Broadway in March 1927, *The Spider* impressed the theatergoing public as a galvanic novelty: Playwrights Fulton Oursler and Lowell Brentano, breaking severely with stage tradition, shattered the footlights' barrier between the performance and its customers to make the entire auditorium the setting of the play. An extended run was the play's reward.

For the movie version, directors Menzies and Kenneth MacKenna determined that they must retain both the witty dialogue and the tornadic intimacy of the play. Their success not only overcame the talk-over-action imperative that generally afflicted the early talking pictures, but they brought to the project some purely cinematic inventions, especially in the smooth editing and great variety of camera angles, that were beyond the capabilities of the stage. Shrunken today to fill the video screen, *The Spider* loses much of this gripping presence—but the imaginative viewer can summon the atmosphere of an early-'30s movie palace and thus embrace the film on a level nearer its original presentation.

Much of the film's charm still fares nicely in a living-room situation, where the interest might be compounded by the chance discovery of a low-profile telecast. James Wong Howe's photography is a marvel of confining vastness, conveying at once the high-ceilinged spaciousness of the locale and the sense of enthralled imprisonment. Howe's cameras range unimprisoned—conveying the excitement of a festive theatrical event, establishing the immensity of  the setting and the occasion, and darting about more freely than most other pictures of the age were accustomed to doing. The lighting is often of portrait quality, the better to emphasize the anxieties of leading lady Lois Moran and the dashing urgency of Lowe's maverick investigation.

Menzies' involvement is more that of a supervising art director, granted additional control of the (melo)dramatic thrust of the piece. MacKenna, an actor-turned-director, concentrates upon the more conventional functions of directing, the pacing of dialogue and motion and the relative placements of the players. Gordon Wiles, formally credited as art director on *The Spider*, said he drew inspiration from Menzies' conception of the aisles of an auditorium as strands of some gigantic spider web.

Lois Moran, a stage-trained player, told the press that one of her greater annoyances was a recurring question as to what differences she found between acting for the screen and acting in person before an audience.

On stage in *The Spider*

"There is a difference, of course," said Miss Moran, "and it affects theatrical people who have played in both mediums in different ways. In my own case, it is the audience. In the theater, one feels the response of the spectator to one's work. It is personal. In the studio, this contact is gone. One's work becomes abstract." (It is significant that Miss Moran quit the screen altogether after 1931 to concentrate on stage work, then formally retired in 1935 after marrying well.)

"However," she added, "when we were making *The Spider*… I felt all the glamour of the theater again. For the whole [sound stage] had been turned into a theater for the production.

"I was seated [among the audience] for my part, in which I am the ward of a designing uncle, Earle Foxe, who is keeping me from my brother… Suddenly, I recognize my brother on the stage… When Edmund Lowe brings him down to me, and Mr. Foxe interferes and there is a struggle, I could feel the thrill of the audience's response, even though they were my fellow players. Then, when the lights go out and a flash and a gunshot pierce the pitch-blackness, you could feel that whole crowd throb with excitement."

That same crowd had ample reason to throb with laughter, as well, thanks to the broad-stroke buffoonery of El Brendel (*née* Elmer Goodfellow Brendle), who plays a talkative, put-upon member of the audience. The comedian fairly well steals the show during its opening moments, employing a self-effacing brand of gentle humor that would be amusing even without the broad Scandahoovian dialect that had been a trademark since Brendel's days in Vaudeville as "The Synthetic Swede." Kendall McComas, a smart-aleck child player, lends a wisecracking edge to Brendel's gentle tomfoolery.

George E. Stone, a dignified but emotional character man, conveys well the tensions driving the doctor-in-the-house who proves to be a vengeful killer. He appears nervous but game at first, then makes a show of refusing to let Edmund Lowe's Chatrand put him on the spot for the sake of a stage routine. Stone seems almost too eager to rush to the aid of the fallen big shot, but then manages to redirect suspicion onto various other characters. The revelation of the murderer notwithstanding, the truer villainous presence belongs to Earle Foxe, as the grasping Wall Street wolf who precipitates the immediate crimes by presenting himself as a ready victim. By Foxe's reckoning, *The Spider* marked "my 43rd death in films, I believe." He added: "I also think it is the seventh or eighth time Edmund Lowe and myself have been pictured as bitter enemies."

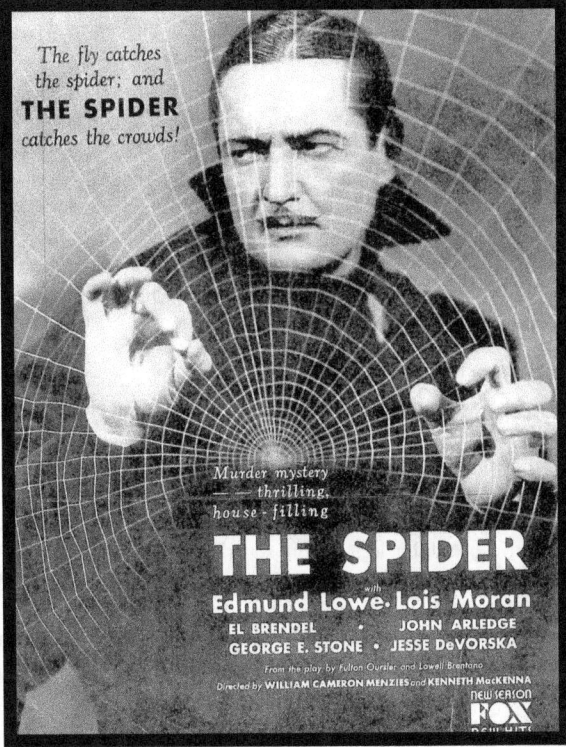

Lowe said his rehearsals for the picture involved as much magical stagecraft as dramatic exercise.

"The mind-reading and spiritualistic séances are easy for me," Lowe told the press, "because they only call for acting and the reading of lines... But the sleight-of-hand and other tricks requiring dexterity, those are something else. For one thing, I've mastered the tricks called for in this picture. I certainly should be an expert at parlor games..." The film's choicest example of staged magic is a presentation of the classic Hindu Decapitation Illusion, with Manya Roberti as Lowe's beheaded helper.

Fox Film Corp. took especial pains to show *The Spider* to an invited audience of magicians. This was presumably an acid test, although the resulting endorsements suggest something more along the lines of a publicity ploy. The artists involved included Howard Thurston, whose name by 1931 had become synonymous with magic; Mme. Adelaide Herrmann, widow of Herrmann the Great; and such well-established prestidigitators as Nate Leipzig, John Mulholland, Louis Zingone, Elmer P. Ransome, Ernest Davids and Julian J. Proskauer. All pronounced the magical pivot of the film well done—according to Fox's publicity department, at any rate.

Fox—or its forced-merger descendant, 20th Century-Fox—returned to the 1927 play in 1945 for another film called *The Spider*, which is not so much a remake as it is a radical reworking of an idea along the lines of film noir. Gone is the ever-present theatrical setting, and the magician character is now known as the Great Garonne (played by Kurt Krueger), who finds himself under suspicion in a series of murders dating back several years. The heroic presence belongs to Richard Conte, as a private eye. The great black comedian, Mantan Moreland, plays a valet who has a quip ready for every desperate occasion.

The Definitive Edition 57

And while we're about it: Two serials from Columbia Pictures, *The Spider's Web* (1938) and *The Spider Returns* (1941), have no bearing here—being derivatives from the pulp-magazine exploits of a masked crimestomper known as The Spider. About whom more later, incidentally.

CREDITS: Associate Producer: William Sistrom; Directors: William Cameron Menzies and Kenneth MacKenna; Assistant Director: R.L. Selander; Based upon: *The Spider*, a 1927 Broadway Play by Charles Fulton Oursler and Lowell Brentano, and "The Man with the Miracle Mind," a Story by Samri Finkelle [Pseudonym of Fulton Oursler]; Continuity and Dialogue: Barry Conners and Philip Klein; Contributing Screenwriters: Albert Lewis and Leon Gordon; Photographed by: James Wong Howe; Art Director: Gordon Wiles; Western Electric Sound Engineered by: Albert Protzman; Sound Recording: Alfred Bruzlin; Editor: Alfred De Gaetano; Costumer: Dolly Tree; Musical Score: Carli Elinor; Running Time: 65 Minutes; Released: Following New York Opening on September 4, 1931

CAST: Edmund Lowe (Chatrand the Great); Lois Moran (Beverly Lane); El Brendel (Ole); John Arledge (Tommy); George E. Stone (Dr. Blackstone); Earle Fox (John Carrington); Manya Roberti (Sonya); Howard Phillips (Alexander); Purnell Pratt (Inspector Riley); Jesse De Vorska (Goldberg); Kendall McComas (Willy); Ruth Donnelly (Mrs. Wimbleton); William Pawley (Butch); Warren Hymer (Schmidt); Ward Bond, C.A. Bachman and Anders von Haden (Cops); Raymonda Brown, Marguerite Caverly, Doris Morton and Lee Kinney (Usherettes); Pat Haley (Electrician); John Lester Johnson (Nubian); Robert Kerr (Stagehand); Charles Wheelocjk, Anita Wilson, Doris Campbell, Bond Davis, Irene Dale, June De Vaney, Eleanor Frances, Mel S. Forrester, Baldy Belmont, Violet Bird, Marie Stapleton, Morris Selvage, Jerry Storm, Margaret Mayo, Dorothy McLaughlin, James McPherson, Ruth Magden, George Milo, Walter Lawrence, Helen Long, Helen Lambert, Richard French, Rupert Franklin, Peggy Graham, Jimmy Gray, Jenny Gray, Beauregard Bonifacio, Frank Henry, Charles Hammond, Samuel E. Hines, Caryl Lincoln and Charline Burt (Audience Members)

THE UNHOLY GARDEN
(Samuel Goldwyn, Inc./George Fitzmaurice Productions/United Artists Corp.; 1931)

"It was an interesting kind of tension we felt, working on *The Unholy Garden*," Fay Wray told us in 1989. "For all the importance that each had to the other, Ronnie [Ronald] Colman and Samuel Goldwyn were at odds on this particular project—not on speaking terms, for reasons that neither would explain—and Ronnie had this standing order that Mr. Goldwyn not intrude upon the set. I met with Mr. Goldwyn when I was hired, and then never heard from him again until after we had completed the principal photography."

As a team, the self-made plutocrat producer Goldwyn and the dashing matinee idol Colman had proved early in the game that talking pictures could be more than merely photographed stage plays. The proof they offered was *Bulldog Drummond* (1929), a droll high-adventure thriller whose blending of words and pictures is so nearly perfect as to seem the very reason talking pictures were invented. (See the *Drummond* chapter in our 1989 book, *The Cinema of Adventure, Romance & Terror*.) In silent-era Hollywood, Goldwyn had developed a reputation as a calculating businessman with fairly discriminating middlebrow tastes. He surrounded himself with creative people and inspired their best efforts. Ronald Colman was among this select group. Moderately significant as a silent player, Colman learned early on how to utilize the added dimension of sound and thus assured his stardom of longevity.

Bulldog Drummond had established Colman as Goldwyn's chief player. Anxious to build upon this bonanza, Goldwyn cast Colman in *Condemned* (1929), a grim tale of Devil's Island; *Raffles* (1930), a comedy-melodrama about a suave crook; and *The Devil To Pay* (1930), another light melodrama. All were successful, but none as spectacularly so as *Drummond*. Goldwyn determined he must make a Colman vehicle that would exploit the same elements that had worked so ideally in his first talkie: chilling horror, comedy, romance and artistic appeal. Goldwyn hired the eccentric but efficient team of Ben Hecht and Charles MacArthur (of the hit play, *The Front Page*) to concoct an original script, *The Unholy Garden*. The great pictorial stylist, George Fitzmaurice, was signed to direct. The famed Hungarian illustrator-architect-muralist, Willy Pogany, made the production designs.

As work on *Garden* was beginning, Joseph M. Schenck decided he would step down as chief production executive of United Artists (of which Goldwyn was a member-owner) and asked Goldwyn to take over. Goldwyn accordingly cranked his annual schedule from four to eight productions, leading off with *Garden*. The picture was produced with Goldwyn's usual care, but the critics lambasted it so cruelly following its previews that Goldwyn yanked it for extensive retakes and editing, finally releasing a modified version in October.

Fay Wray recalled: "I left for New York on a vacation after we had wrapped *The Unholy Garden*, and that was when I finally had direct contact again with Mr. Goldwyn. He caught up with me by telephone and demanded that I must come back immediately to begin retakes. So I cut my vacation short, thanks to whatever problems Mr. Goldwyn was having with the early responses to our picture.

"The opportunity to work with Ronnie Colman was a pleasure, of course, whatever the tensions may have been at the time," added Miss Wray. "He was a wonderfully skilled actor, and a man of genuine modesty. We became fast friends during the shooting, and we maintained that friendship over the years. A very shielded man, Ronnie was—didn't let out a great deal of information about himself—genial, but never garrulous. If he was outgoing toward you, that meant a great deal more than it would have meant from somebody else. He was a figure of special quality."

Colman plays the fugitive Barrington Hunt. Believing Hunt bound for Palais Royale, a desert sanctuary, the Algerian police arrange for the notorious Mrs. Mowbry (Estelle Taylor) to set a trap. But Hunt commandeers the woman's car and takes her to the once-grand establishment—now in decay. The guests include the scholarly Dr. Shayne (Lawrence Grant),

Romance amidst treachery: *The Unholy Garden*.

who murdered three wives and uses the skull of the first as a tobacco jar; Prince Nicolai Poliakoff (Mischa Auer), a Hussar captain who killed his sweetheart for her pearls; Colonel von Axt (Ulric Haupt) of the Prussian Guards, who swindled his government out of millions; Kid Twist (Kit Guard), a strangler; Nick-the-Goose (Henry Armetta), an international thief; and Smiley Corbin (Warren Hymer), an American hoodlum. The elderly Mme. Villars (Lucille LaVerne) runs the establishment.

Aloof from the others are the aged Baron de Jonghe (Tully Marshall) and his lovely granddaughter, Camille (Miss Wray). The cutthroats plot to dispatch the Baron, who has been promised immunity if he will return a stolen fortune in negotiable securities. Hunt is greeted meanwhile by Smiley (Warren Hymer), his now-and-again accomplice.

When asked about the proceeds from their last job, Smiley admits, "In Tunis, you see, I met a dame." It is decided that Hunt, as a stranger, may be able to pry the secret of the securities from de Jonghe. Gaining the old man's friendship, Hunt falls in love with Camille but feels unworthy of her affections. Mrs. Mowbry suspects a double-cross. Smiley seduces Mrs. Mowbry and learns that the others mean to kill Hunt and the Baron, and to torture Camille. Hunt finds the securities. The Baron is slain. Believing Hunt the killer, Camille starts to turn him over to the plotters but, swayed by love, hides him instead.

Hunt hands Camille the securities and tells her to hurry away: "And someday, when your eyes are shining and you meet an honest man, look at Paris for me and think of it as my wedding present." Hunt and Smiley escape in a hail of bullets. Smiley asks if Hunt got as much loot as expected. "Much more, Smiley, and here's your share," Hunt replies, handing over the petals from a rose Camille had given him. "I'm sorry, Smiley, but you see—I met a dame."

History's consensus holds that *The Unholy Garden* must be the least of Colman's pictures. This simplistic dismissal takes into account some rather predictable elements of plotting and perhaps an overabundance of bizarre touches, but neglects to acknowledge that the production shimmers with high artistry. Not to mention that the cast in support serves up some of the most intriguing vamps and scamps any lover of melodrama could desire. *Garden* does sink deep into the *outré*, an excess that the viewer will find either charming or offensive. The skull-as-tobacco-jar is one such example, but the most effectively disturbing touch is a Christmas scene where the criminals sing carols in clashing keys and languages.

The dialogue sparkles with romance and wit. Pogany's evocative sets are magnificently lighted and photographed to generously eerie effect. Colman's rakish sophistication is complemented beautifully by the innocence of Miss Wray; by the crudeness of his sidekick, Warren Hymer; and by the brashness of the *femme fatale*, Estelle Taylor. The villains are a grand crew of seriocomic fiends under the menacing guidance of Lawrence Grant, who had provided a similarly depraved characterization for *Bulldog Drummond*.

CREDITS: Producer and Director: George Fitzmaurice; Screenplay: Ben Hecht and Charles MacArthur; Photographed by: George Barnes and Gregg Toland; Art Director: Willy Pogany; Musical Director: Alfred Newman; Supervising Editor: Stuart Heisler; Costumes: Bridgehouse; Makeup: Blagoe Stephanoff; Running Time: 75 minutes; Released: October 10, 1931

CAST: Ronald Colman (Barrington Hunt); Fay Wray (Camille de Jonghe); Estelle Taylor (Elize Mowbry); Tully Marshall (Baron de Jonghe); Warren Hymer (Smiley Corbin); Ulric Haupt (Col. von Axt); Mischa Auer (Prince Nicolai Poliakoff); Morgan Wallace (Capt. Kruger); Lawrence Grant (Dr. Shayne); Henry Armetta (Nick-the-Goose); Kit Guard (Kid Twist); Lucille La Verne (Lucie Villars); Henry Kolker (Col. Lautrac); Arnold Korff (Col. Lautrac in Unreleased Version); Charles Hill Mailes (Alfred de Jonghe); Nadja (Native Dancer)

Once again, John Barrymore casts a menacing gaze upon Marian Marsh—this time, in *The Mad Genius*.

THE MAD GENIUS
(Warner Bros. Pictures, Inc.; 1931)

Considered here for the sake of context within an emerging genre, *The Mad Genius* is more an exercise in marking time than any breakthrough in itself, a clever variation upon themes and techniques defined slightly earlier in the superior *Svengali*. In the greater scheme of John Barrymore's career, *The Mad Genius* also provided the actor with a graceful exit from his Warner Bros. contract, allowing in the process encores from *Svengali* for Marian Marsh and Luis Alberni. And *Genius* reunited most of the behind-the-scenes artisans who had given *Svengali*, a profoundly personal picture for Barrymore, such a palpable atmospheric depth and a headlong momentum.

Michael Curtiz, that versatile workhorse-plus-tyrant among the Warners directors, takes up *Genius* where Archie Mayo had left off on *Svengali*. The artists' shared affinity for Gothic Expressionism proves evenly matched via immediate comparison of these close-kin pictures.

Some sources have cited *The Mad Genius* as a sequel to *Svengali*—no such thing. If anything beyond merely a follow-through, *Genius* seems almost an alternate-reality twist upon *Svengali*, a transplant from a Parisian art-colony setting to the ballet. In such a light, the film might be said to transform the defiantly helpless, counterfeit diva of *Svengali* into a young man, a dancer conditioned to advance his master's ambitions.

Genius' story, from a more recent source than *Svengali*, begins as Ivan Tsarakov (Barrymore), the club-footed proprietor of a traveling marionette show, shelters a runaway named Fedor Ivanoff

(Frankie Darro) from the child's abusive father (Boris Karloff, just then on the cusp of stardom). Tsarakov impulsively abducts the boy to raise as his own. Tsarakov perceives in Fedor's agility a means "to create my own being... I will make him the greatest dancer of all time!"

Fifteen years have passed, now, and Tsarakov has built around Fedor a fine ballet company. The maestro manipulates all his artists with extravagant rewards and extreme penalties. The company's director, Serge Bankeff (Luis Alberni), seems brilliant enough to strike out on his own, but Tsarakov keeps him in tow with a painstakingly controlled addiction to dope. Tsarakov's scheme to reward Fedor (now played by Donald Cook) with a procession of women backfires when the dancer falls in love with the ballerina Nana Karalova (Miss Marsh).

Marian Marsh poses for a studio portrait to publicize *The Mad Genius*.

Bent upon protecting his investment in Fedor, Tsarakov prevents the youth from finding work with other companies and persuades Nana to halt the romance. She takes up with a wealthy count (André Luguet). Fedor, who has become as temperamental as his mentor, rebels on the eve of a crucial production. Tsarakov resorts to threats: "I've poured my soul... into you... If you fail me now, I'll *kill* you!" Fedor relents.

Serge's descent into madness begins in earnest as the ballet progresses before a packed house. He attacks Tsarakov behind a curtain that is soon to rise for the climax. The raising of the curtain reveals Tsarakov's body, which falls from atop a huge piece of plaster statuary. Nana rushes to a tender reunion with Fedor.

The figurative resemblance to *Frankenstein* is patent enough, and Barrymore plays the title role with all the godly conceit one could ask—although Tsarakov's madness is less a matter of derangement than of taxing his controlling energies beyond reasonable limits. "I made that magnificent specimen," he says of Fedor, "... just as surely as God made the world."

The photography is particularly beautiful, and the record should show here that art director Anton Grot and cinematographer Barney McGill were among the first to master diffused set lighting by means of gauze-draped ceilings. Open ceilings were the norm, for they made lighting easier. By topping the sets with muslin, however, Grot filtered the illumination onto the players with a rippling, shimmering effect. This technique was revived and modified by

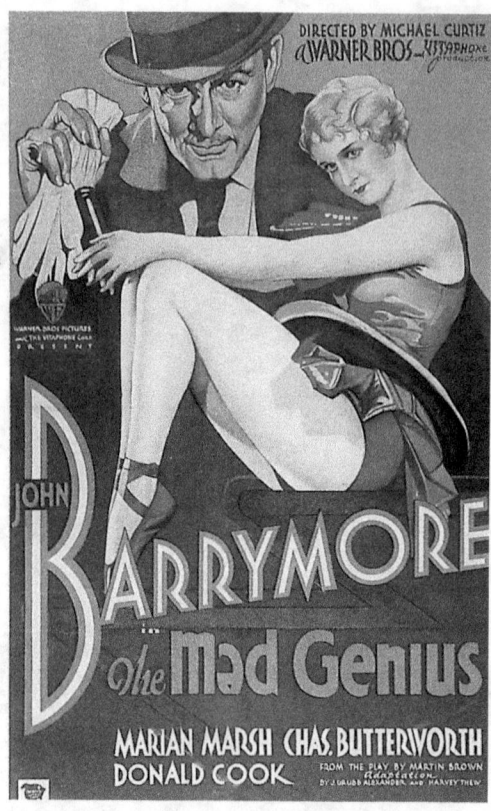

the camera artist Gregg Toland for Orson Welles' *Citizen Kane* (1941)—a picture that owes its purportedly unique style to a good many films long conveniently ignored and/or forgotten.

CREDITS: Director: Michael Curtiz; Screenplay: J. Grubb Alexander and Harvey F. Thew; Based upon: Martin Brown's 1929 play *The Idol*; Photographed by: Barney McGill; Film Editor: Ralph Dawson; Art Director: Anton Grot; Costumer: Earl Luick; Choreographer: Adolph Bolm; Music Director; David Mendoza; Conductor: Leo F. Forbstein, with the Vitaphone Orchestra; Selected Compositions: Tchaikovsky's "Danse Russe Trépak," from *The Nutcracker Suite, Op. 71a* and "First Movement," from the *Symphony No. 4 in F Minor, Op. 36*; Running Time: 75 minutes; Released: October 10, 1931

CAST: John Barrymore (Vladimar Ivan Tsarakov); Marian Marsh (Nana Carlova); Charles Butterworth (Karimsky); Donald Cook (Fedor Ivanoff); Luis Alberni (Sergei Bankieff); Carmel Myers (Sonya Preskoya); André Luguet (Count Robert Renaud); Frankie Darro (Fedor as a Boy); Boris Karloff (Fedor's Father); Mae Madison (Olga Chekova); Lee Moran (Montmartre Cabaret Director)

THE HATCHET MAN
(First National Pictures, Inc./Warner Bros. Pictures, Inc./Vitaphone Corp.; 1932)

The song and the movie are not to be confused with one another, but in fact The Robins' (later, The Coasters) Spark Records hit of 1955, "The Hatchet Man," owes its inspiration to a boyhood viewing of the film by tunesmiths Jerry Leiber and Mike Stoller. Or so Leiber told us, 'way back during the 1960s. The resemblance begins and ends with the title, of course, but it is nonetheless fascinating to note that the song's thinly veneered erotic metaphor ("I've been swingin' so long, they call me the Hatchet Man") derives from a film so dead-earnestly concerned with possessive jealousies and blood vengeance.

The Hatchet Man finds the uncompromisingly tough director "Wild Bill" Wellman transforming an outmoded and quaintly mannered stage play into an unusual and exciting entertainment. J. Grubb Alexander's screenplay takes lurid liberties with the source, boasting a shock ending that cannot help but elicit gasps.

Edward G. Robinson, who had succeeded John Barrymore as First National's top character star, manages a compelling characterization of a sympathetic fellow who is nonetheless frightening. Robinson handles well the transformation from Tong executioner to Americanized businessman, making his reversion to ancestral ways all the more remarkable. Loretta Young does fine work as the disloyal girl whom Robinson cannot help but love, as does Leslie Fenton as a dissolute young miscreant and seducer. Briefly seen but memorable as a victim of Tong vengeance is J. Carrol Naish. A grand assortment of Western character actors proves entirely convincing in Asian roles, especially Dudley Digges, Charles Middleton, Edmund Breese and Tully Marshall. Even that consummately sinister highfalutin' grouch of numerous pictures, Blanche Friderici, is effective as the hard-boiled madam of a Chinese brothel. These enactments are helped along immeasurably by the young Perc Westmore's makeup artistry.

The story begins in 1916 in San Francisco's Chinatown, where the honorable hatchet man Wong Low Get (Robinson) goes in sorrow to kill his best friend, Sun Yat Sen (Naish), who has been adjudged guilty of murder. Wong swears that his victim's daughter, 6-year-old Toya San, will know only happiness.

Fifteen years later, Chinatown has changed: Wong has become an Americanized merchant, and Toya San (Loretta Young) is a beautiful woman. Wong is deeply in love with his ward, and when she reaches the proper age they marry. But Toya San longs for the company of people of her own age. The Tong leaders, still more of East than of West, are displeased that Wong has retired his ceremonial hatchet.

American gangsters muscle in on Chinatown. The Tong hires Harry En Hai (Fenton), a Westernized punk, to guard Wong, and prevails upon Wong to dispose of Big Jim Malone (Ralph Ince), a rackets boss. Peaceful overtures prove useless, and Wong must resort to lethal tradition.

Toya San and Harry have fallen in love. Wong permits them to leave intact, warning Harry that Toya San must never come to grief. The Tong, appalled that Wong has not killed the illicit lovers, precipitates Wong's downfall.

Upon learning that Harry has sold Toya San into slavery in China, Wong takes up his hatchet and tracks his errant wife to a brothel. The madam (Miss Friderici) bars his path. In an adjoining barroom, Harry leans against a wall, in a stupor. Wong draws his weapon—his proof to the madam of high authority—and hurls it with breathtaking accuracy at the glass eye of a dragon adorning a distant wall. Wong finds the contrite Toya San and leaves with her.

In the bar, the madam angrily app-roaches Harry, who only shakes his head. On the other side, servants struggle to remove Wong's hatchet. They find its blade bloodied. Even the hardened madam is horrified to see Harry's body slide downward, leaving a trail of gore.

Leslie Fenton puts the moves on Loretta Young in *The Hatchet Man*.

The production is handsomely designed by Anton Grot, who with *Svengali* had proved himself one of the screen's more inventive architects. Sid Hickox's photography artfully combines diffused, soft-lighted shots (necessary for Old Chinatown) with the starkly illuminated naturalism of his more celebrated Warners gangster pictures. The story belongs to two worlds, and so does the camerawork.

The musical score is more elaborate than most others of this period. It incorporates venerable Tin Pan Alley tunes (including the schmaltz-laden "Poor Butterfly," as a romantic theme); traditional Chinese music; and original works by Leo Forbstein, the West Coast musical director for Warners. Forbstein wrote two additional compositions for an elaborate coming-attractions trailer—trailers in those days being somewhat more original, evocative works than the flash-fried jump-cut messes we know today.

CREDITS: Director: William A. Wellman; Screenplay: J. Grubb Alexander; Based upon: the Play, *The Honorable Mr. Wong*, by Achmed Abdullah and David Belasco; Photographed by: Sid Hickox; Art Director: Anton Grot; Editor: Owen Marks; Gowns: Earl Luick; Music: Leo F. Forbstein (Conducting the Vitaphone Orchestra) and Otto Langley; Songs: "Poor Butterfly," by Raymond Hubbell, and "When It's Sleepy Time Down South," by Léon T. René & Clarence Muse; Makeup: Perc Westmore; Special Effects: Fred Jackman; Sound Recording: Robert Lee; Second Cameraman: Wesley Anderson; Stills: John Ellis; Running Time: 74 Minutes; Released: February 6, 1932

CAST: Edward G. Robinson (Wong Low Get); Loretta Young (Toya San); Dudley Digges (Nog Hong Fa); Leslie Fenton (Harry En Hai); Edmund Breese (Yu Chang); Tully Marshall

(Long Sen Yat); Noel Madison (Charles Kee); Blanche Friderici (Madame Si-Si); J. Carrol Naish (Sun Yat Sen); Toschia Mori (Miss Ling); Charles Middleton (Lip Hop Fat); Ralph Ince (Big Jim Malone); Otto Yamoka (Chung Ho); Evelyn Selbie (Wah Lee); E. Allyn Warren (Soo Lat); Edward Piel (Bing Foo); Willlie Fung (Fung Loo); Anna Chang (Sing Girl); and James B. Leong

Edward Van Sloan and Boris Karloff in *Behind the Mask*

BEHIND THE MASK
(Columbia Pictures Corp.; 1932)

Jack Holt spent the early 1930s as Columbia's top star, having helped propel the onetime (silent-era) Poverty Row company into the major leagues via the Frank Capra trilogy *Submarine* (1928), *Flight* (1929) and *Dirigible* (1931). A true-to-form Holt action vehicle, called *In the Secret Service*, was begun in November of 1931—but in light of the success of Universal's very recent *Frankenstein*, the story was amended with gruesome touches that would justify its marketing as a horror film. The title became *Behind the Mask*.

The advertising campaign touted the presence of Boris Karloff, who had been swept suddenly to fame by *Frankenstein*. The irony here is that Karloff, seen in support as a somewhat helpful heavy, is subordinate to a sadistic manipulator played by Edward Van Sloan—the kindly, tragic professor of *Frankenstein*.

In *Behind the Mask*, Van Sloan portrays one of the most fiendish Human Monsters ever beheld on screen. Especially memorable is his prelude to surgery: "Has it ever occurred to you... that you can commit almost any crime if you select the proper environment?... If I were to stick a knife into you in the street... I might have to answer embarrassing questions. Here... nothing will happen"—*a grave pause*—"to me." He explains further, "Wasn't it Nietzsche who said that unendurable pain merges into ecstasy? We shall find out whether that is an epigram or a fact..."

Leading up to this masterful cringe-inducer is a campaign to track down one Mr. X, narcotics racketeer deluxe. Not even his own gangsters know who the boss is, for when a henchman comes too near the truth, Mr. X arranges for him to visit a hospital run by one Dr.

August Steiner, whose knife also claims nosy Secret Service agents. The authorities are under pressure from a civic reformer, Dr. Munsell (Van Sloan).

Agent Jack Hart (Holt) poses as a convict in order to meet a gang member, Henderson (Karloff). When Hart is freed, Henderson refers him to an X henchman named Arnold (Claude King), who expects to be purged for talking too much. Hart falls in love with Arnold's daughter, Julie (Constance Cummings). Arnold and Julie are taken to Steiner's hospital, where Arnold is slain under the guise of emergency surgery.

Hart reaches the hospital but is overpowered. Steiner, a burly, bearded man with thick spectacles, looms over Hart, who now comprehends that Steiner not only is Mr. X, but also has another identity. A shot is heard, and the surgeon falls dead: Julie has escaped to avenge her father and save her lover. Hart reveals that Steiner had posed as the do-gooder Munsell.

Jack Dillon, whose directing career had begun in 1917, whipped the midcourse changes of *In the Secret Service/Behind the Mask* into a surprising coherence. Dillon made only three more films, including Clara Bow's comeback effort, *Call Her Savage* (1932), then died in 1934. Ted Tetzlaff, a leading glamour photographer and later director of (among others) the suspense classic *The Window* (1949), sets the right tone throughout *Behind the Mask*, mingling an almost documentary realism with appropriate shadowplay.

Jack Holt is squarely in his heroic element, and Constance Cummings is excellent as the tragic heroine. Karloff (British accent notwithstanding) does well as the cigar-smoking gangster, although he is considerably less monstrous than the advertising campaign suggested. Bertha Mann is properly grim as Van Sloan's granite-faced assistant.

CREDITS: Producer: Harry Cohn; Director: John Francis Dillon; Story, Adaptation and Dialogue: Jo Swerling; Continuity: Dorothy Howell; Assistant Director: Edward Sloman; Photographed by: Ted Tetzlaff; RCA Photophone Sound: Glenn Rominger; Editor: Otis Garrett; Musical Director: Louis Silvers; Music: Milan Roder and Dan Dougherty; Running Time, 68 minutes; Released: February 25, 1932

CAST: Jack Holt (Jack Hart); Constance Cummings (Julie Arnold); Boris Karloff (Jim Henderson); Claude King (Arnold); Bertha Mann (Edwards); Edward Van Sloan (Dr. Munsell); Willard Robertson (Hawkes); Thomas Jackson (Agent); and Clarence Burton, John Ince, Charles Meacham

MYSTERY RANCH
(Fox Film Corp.; 1932)

Arizona Rangers Agent Bob Sanborn (George O'Brien) heads into a remote valley to put down a reign of terror instigated by rancher Henry Steele (Charles Middleton). Mudo (Noble Johnson), Steele's Apache servant, is a mute giant as deadly as his master. Circumstances can only get more vicious from here, so watch out.

Stewart Edward White's novella, *The Killer*, tells of a rancher driven to destroy any creature that crosses his path. White based the character upon a predatory stockman who lived in Arizona during the late 19th Century. In 1921, scarcely a year after the yarn's publication, Benjamin Hampton produced a striking movie version called *The Killer*, with Frank Campeau as the madman and Jack Conway as his nemesis. Then Fox adapted the property in 1932 for *Mystery Ranch*, one of several high-grade Westerns starring George O'Brien. O'Brien was an actor-athlete who had done outstanding work for John Ford, and for F.W. Murnau in *Sunrise* (1927).

Mystery Ranch is the very definition of an unusual genre—*sub*-genre, if you prefer—the Western horror story. The free-rein adaptation is by Al Cohn, whose thrillers include *The Cat and the Canary* (1927) and *The Last Warning* (1928). *Mystery Ranch* is beautifully—and sparsely—dialogued, and its construction allows for rapid pacing and dramatic pictorial effects. These qualities are served well by director David Howard, who had done eight Spanish-language filmings of Fox pictures during 1930-31, including *The Big Trail* and *Charlie Chan Carries On* (as *Eran Tréce*, a distinctive film that George Turner single-handedly rescued from becoming lost for keeps). Howard's first English-language film was a highly popular O'Brien version of Zane Grey's *The Rainbow Trail* (1932), followed by *Mystery Ranch*. Although he never acquired a place in the Pantheon of Celebrated Big-Deal Directors, Howard was nonetheless a master of the outdoor action film. *Mystery Ranch* suggests he could have done as well with psychological drama.

The story complicates itself as Bob encounters beautiful Jane Emory (Cecilia Parker), who has been thrown from her horse. Bob brings Jane to Steele's hacienda, where the owner invites him to stay the night. Steele warns Bob not to leave lest he run afoul of marauders. Jane reveals that she is the daughter of Steele's defunct—and probably murdered—business partner. Steele has lured her here with a promise of a share of the estate.

Promising help, Bob leaves, escaping an Indian ambush and telegraphing headquarters. Artie Brower (Forrester Harvey), a messenger, informs Bob that Steele will force Jane into marriage the next morning. Bob learns too late that Steele is awaiting him. Steele kills Artie, who had sought to cover Bob and Jane's escape.

Bob and Jane climb into a towering formation of rocks. Steele and Mudo gain the summit, but Bob topples the giant to his death. Bob shows Steele a warrant for his arrest. "If you want to serve that warrant, you will have to do it in hell," Steele says, and with a grim chuckle he steps over the edge.

Most of *Mystery Ranch* was filmed on location in Arizona, with additional work near Los Angeles and at the old Fox Western lot, where many of the Tom Mix and Buck Jones silents were made. A comparatively leisurely schedule of about five weeks allowed for stunning photography by Joseph August, who would shoot *The Informer* (1934) and *Gunga Din* (1938); and by mystery specialist John Schneiderman. Few other outdoor films have been so exquisitely photographed. Much of *Mystery Ranch* has a pictorial style reminiscent of the German Expressionist films of the 1920s.

Nor can many other actionful pictures of the period claim such elaborate and intelligent musical scoring. Dramatic passages were especially composed, for the most part, by such influential talents as Hugo Friedhofer, Rex Bassett, Louis deFrancesco, Arthur Kay, J.S.

Zamecnik and William Kernell. Ballads commonly associated with the West abound—but so do classical themes.

O'Brien's breezy acting suits the heroics, and Cecilia Parker is a lovely ingénue. This is one of the few star-driven Westerns, however, in which the villains take the palm. Charles Middleton is best remembered for his serial roles, especially as Emperor Ming in the three *Flash Gordon* serials. It is in *Mystery Ranch*, though, that Middleton gives his most polished performance, creating a character both subtly and flamboyantly mad. There is no maniacal cackling as Middleton trains his gun on O'Brien in the heroine's bedroom and says, "My dear, would you mind stepping aside a foot or so? I don't want to injure my bride-to-be." Middleton's chilling smile as he plunges to his doom is unforgettable. His depravity is abetted ably by the fascinating black actor, Noble Johnson (in a role similar to his Cossack torturer of 1932's *The Most Dangerous Game*), and by Charles Stevens, the gaunt grandson of the famed Apache war chief, Geronimo. Forrester Harvey, better known as the pubkeeper in *The Invisible Man* (1933), contributes elements of Cockney humor that make his slaying at Middleton's hands all the more bewildering.

CREDITS: In Charge of Production: Sol M. Wurtzel; Director: David Howard; Based upon: Stewart Edward White's 1920 Novella, *The Killer*; Screenplay: Alfred A. Cohn; Photographed by: Joseph August; Art Director: Joseph Wright; Editor: Paul Weatherwax; Wardrobe: David Cox; Assistant Director: Walter Mayo; Western Electric Sound by: Albert Protzman; Music: Hugo Friedhofer, Rex Bassett, Louis deFrancesco, Arthur Kay, J.S. Zamecnik and William Kernell; Songs, "Cowboy Dan," by Cliff Friend, "Blue Bell," by T. Morse & Edward Madden, "Cheyenne," by Egbert Van Alstyne, "She Was Only a Bird in a Gilded Cage," by Harry von Tilzer, and "On a Bicycle Built for Two," by Dacré; Classical Themes: "Finlandia," by Jan Sibelius, "Why Are the Roses So Pale?" by P.I. Tschaikowsky, "Wedding March," by Felix Mendelssohn, and *Concert Etude No. 3 in D Flat*, by Franz Liszt; Additional Photography: John Schneiderman; Second Cameramen: C. Curt Fetters and Irving Rosenthal; Assistant Cameramen: Harry Webb, Jack Epstein, Lou Kunkel and James Gordon; Stills: Bert Lynch; Running Time: 65 Minutes; Released: June 12, 1932

CAST: George O'Brien (Bob Sanborn); Cecilia Parker (Jane Emory); Charles Middleton (Henry Steele); Noble Johnson (Mudo); Charles Stevens (Tonto); Forrester Harvey (Artie Brower); Roy Stewart (Buck); Virginia Herdman (Homesteader's Wife); Betty Francisco (Mae); Russ Powell (Sheriff).

ALMOST MARRIED
(Fox Film Corp.; 1932)

Almost Married was a troubled production during 1931-32—a collaboration-by-default, in fact, and afflicted with such extensive post-production tampering as almost to have been rewritten and re-shot. It seems in hindsight a remarkably coherent and near-seamless picture, and its patchwork essence comes as rather a surprise. An under-an-hour running time helps the pace considerably, although it is tantalizing to wonder how a lengthier preview cut must have played out. The point of the film is an unnerving show of predatory madness from Alexander Kirkland, as a deranged maestro intent upon doing away with his estranged wife from an unconsummated union.

Somewhere along the path toward a delayed opening, *Almost Married* found itself shorn of nearly two reels despite its belated additions: Premature reviews, published as early as December of 1931, cite a running time of 67 minutes. Later notices clocked the film at 51 minutes, the length of a surviving print unearthed by Price & Turner in a television-syndication warehouse during the 1980s. It is a cram-packed 51 minutes, at that—propelled by a sense of foreboding, with outbursts of headlong terror that the bland title scarcely would suggest. (The source-novel's London edition of 1931 bears the title *The Devil's Triangle*; it surfaced in America as *Almost Married*, serving as a merchandising tie-in with the movie. The film's work-in-progress titles were *Circumstance* and, later, *Circumstances*.)

Variety misspoke in citing this one as a remake of a like-titled picture from 1919—that silent-era *Almost Married* is a Metro romantic farce—and also in declaring it to be a directing début for William Cameron Menzies; the acclaimed designer and favored contender of the Academy Awards had served already as co-director on the maudlin *Always Goodbye* and the extraordinary mystery-thriller *The Spider*, both from 1931.

Menzies' co-director status on *Almost Married* came as more an imposition than a collaboration, although Fox's enlistment of Marcel Varnel to direct retakes and additional footage worked out so well that the artists were assigned formally as co-directors on Fox's summer-of-1932 filming of *Chandu the Magician*.

Menzies had completed *Almost Married* during October-November of 1931, with a team including John Mescall in charge of photography and Wallace Smith as screenwriter. In mid-December, having announced a January-of-'32 opening, Fox began tampering with what was for all practical purposes a finished product and assigned scenarist Guy Bolton to write a new opening sequence. Studio documents trace the revisions but do not state explicitly what faults the brass had found in the Menzies version. The process dragged on into March of 1932, when an officially designated "final script with revisions" went back before the cameras—with Varnel directing and George Schneiderman as cinematographer. Fox did not revise its tradepaper advertising, which had given Menzies sole directing credit, but the on-screen credits give collaborative billing to Menzies and Varnel; to Mescall and Schneiderman as directors of photography; to Smith and Bolton for the screenplay; and to W.W. Lindsay, Jr., and Eugene Grossman as sound-recording engineers.

Another significant substitution had taken place shortly before Menzies got cracking on the project on October 26, 1931: Paul Cavanagh, a Cambridge-educated leading man of the London stage, had come to Hollywood in 1930 and soon found himself pursuing a busy agenda of screen jobs, including the Kenneth McKenna-William Menzies *Always Goodbye*. Cavanagh was announced for *Almost Married*'s dapper heroic role of a British statesman but bowed out with only three days' notice. His replacement was Chigagoan Ralph Bellamy, a stock-theater circuit veteran who had only recently launched a film-acting career. Cavanagh would have been a natural for the role, but Bellamy summoned a suitably English presence on abrupt notice. His leading lady, Violet Heming, was an occasional screen player with but one silent-era credit, on 1922's *When the Desert Calls*; her follow-through to *Almost Married*, 1932's *The Man Who*

Played God, also would be her final picture.

The story goes that Anita Mellikovna (Miss Heming), an exiled Russian aristocrat, and diplomat Deene Maxwell (Bellamy) had met in passing some time ago in Scotland. Maxwell fell in love with Anita and has cursed himself ever since for neglecting to declare his affections. When they meet again, in Russia, Anita is dodging the Soviet authorities—for she has returned with a forged passport and has gained possession of jewels that her father had hidden years before while fleeing the Bolsheviks. Maxwell is en route to Moscow on a trade mission. He suggests that they get married at the British Embassy, for his diplomatic immunity will allow her safe passage out of Russia; they can always secure an annulment if she so wishes.

After the ceremony, Anita reveals that Maxwell has made her a bigamist: Five years past, while studying in Paris, she had

married an erratic composer named Louis Capristi—but abandoned him on their wedding night in fear of his violent behavior. She has no idea what might have become of Capristi. Maxwell only grows more enamored of Anita, and they travel safely to England.

Meanwhile, in London, Capristi (Kirkland) cools his heels in an asylum under an alias, Charles Pringle. Seems he had strangled a woman but cheated the hangman with an insanity defense. A newspaper account of Maxwell's marriage provokes Capristi to escape from custody, and he confronts Maxwell and Anita in their own home—threatening to have them arrested for bigamy unless they grant him house-guest privileges until he can skip the country.

Maxwell receives a visit from a friend, Scotland Yard Inspector Slante (Allan Dinehart), whose psycho alarms are triggered by Capristi's peculiar behavior. The authorities, already searching for the fugitive Charles Pringle, are alerted to watch Capristi. A young Frenchwoman (Maria Alba) is strangled after she recognizes Capristi as Pringle. Capristi lures Maxwell to the victim's apartment, then invades the Maxwell residence, kills the butler (Herbert Mundin) and attacks Anita. Capristi has cornered Anita on a high ledge when Maxwell returns, just in time to gun down the interloper. Slante, suitably sensitive to Anita's concerns about a scandal, agrees to identify the corpse only as Charles Pringle.

The film is probably needlessly compact, but the breakneck pace is an asset nonetheless, serving at least to obscure the outlandish coincidences that cause the paths of the spouses-by-technicality to cross anew. It promptly introduces the thrall of terror that Alexander Kirkland's Capristi, even in long absence, exerts over Miss Heming, and thus his predictable return becomes an eagerly awaited inevitability. A busy stage-and-screen leading man and future television producer, Kirkland hardly looked the part of an ill-balanced menace, but his fair-haired and blue-eyed aspect proved an asset to the role, which calls for a soothing and deceitful approach. Particularly gripping is Kirkland's lethal encounter with Maria Alba, whom he calmly escorts to private quarters—the better to discuss her recognition of him as a wanted killer. His low-key confession to Miss Alba, followed by Miss Alba's forcible demise, is a moment worthy of a Peter Lorre.

Among the leading players, only Bellamy was bound for a larger stardom: He promptly registered as both a B-picture leading man and a scene-stealing secondary lead in bigger movies, landing an Oscar nomination for 1937's *The Awful Truth* and taking the title role in the *Ellery Queen* detective series of the early 1940s. A flop on Broadway during the late 1920s, Bellamy returned in triumph to the New York stage during the '40s, and in 1958 he earned the Tony Award and the New York Drama Critics Award for his portrayal of Franklin D. Roosevelt in *Sunrise at Campobello*; he repeated the role in the movie version of 1960. Bellamy followed through with a lasting prominence on television, returning occasionally to the big screen with such rewarding results as *Rosemary's Baby* (1968), *Cancel My Reservation* (1972) and *Oh, God!* (1977). He died in 1991.

Menzies (1896-1957) found consistently greater respect as an art director, "one of the most visually gifted artists of the American cinema," as the historian Ephraim Katz put it. Menzies was already an Oscar winner (for *The Dove* and *Tempest*, both from 1928) by the time he undertook to direct his own pictures, and he would take another Academy Award as art director on 1939's *Gone with the Wind*. Menzies continued as a co-director into the middle 1930s, and his most fondly remembered solo-director jobs of the 1950s—*Drums in the Deep South*, *The Whip Hand*, *Invaders from Mars* and *The Maze*—also boast his nightmarishly Baroque sets-and-lighting designs.

Marcel Varnel (1894-1947), a diminutive Frenchman, had come to America in 1925 as a Broadway director, then worked briefly in Hollywood. As a filmmaker in England during 1934-46, Varnel specialized in earthy and fanciful comedies, turning out such gems of droll buffoonery as *Alf's Button Afloat* (1938), *Get Cracking* (1943) and *He Snoops To Conquer* (1944).

CREDITS: Associate Producer: William Sistrom; Directors: William Cameron Menzies and Marcel Varnel; Screenplay: Wallace Smith and Guy Bolton; Based upon: Andrew Soutar's 1931 Novel, *The Devil's Triangle*; Additional Dialogue: Alexander Kirkland; Contributing Writers: Doris Malloy, Kathryn Scola, Edith Ellis and William Cameron Menzies; Photographed by: John Mescall and George Schneiderman; Assistant Directors: Walter Mayo and Horace Hough; Art Director: Gordon Wiles; Editor: Harold Schuster; Costumer: Dolly Tree; Music: George Lipschultz; Sound Recording: W.W. Lindsay, Jr., and Eugene Grossman; Unit Manager: Archie Buchanan; Casting Director: J.E. Gardner; Running Time: 51 Minutes; Released: July 17, 1932

CAST: Violet Heming (Anita Mellikovna); Ralph Bellamy (Deene Maxwell); Alexander Kirkland (Louis Capristi); Allan Dinehart (Inspector Slante); Herbert Mundin (Jenkins); Maria Alba (Mariette); Eva Dennison (Lady Lavering); Grace Hampton (Aunt Mathilda); Herbert Bunston (Lord Lavering); Mary Gordon (Cook); Harrington Reynolds (Inspector); and Gustav von Seyffertitz, Tempe Pigott

Boris Karloff and Gloria Stuart in *The Old Dark House*

THE OLD DARK HOUSE
(Universal Pictures Corp.; 1932)

A cloudburst maroons a touring party in the mountains of Wales. Phillip Waverton (Raymond Massey) and his wife, Margaret (Gloria Stuart), are undecided whether to try to forge on through or to seek shelter. Their bored passenger, Roger Penderel (Melvyn Douglas), suggests they approach a stone mansion looming nearby because, "Something might happen here...."

"Something," indeed! *The Old Dark House* is a veritable pageant of dire happenstance. Its combination of eventfulness and atmosphere (to the near-exclusion of plot) proved, in its turn, a wellhead of inspiration for any number of films to come along in both rapid and long-term order. Pictures from *The Rogues Tavern* and *Murder by Invitation* during the 1930s and '40s, on through *The Texas Chain Saw Massacre* and its descendants, owe volumes to *The Old Dark House*. Even the 1962 *Cabinet of Caligari* is closer kin to *The Old Dark House* than to the silent-screen watershed *The Cabinet of Dr. Caligari*.

A mountainous butler, Morgan (Boris Karloff), scarred and bearded, answers the travelers' knock and mutters unintelligibly. Tall, thin Horace Femm (Ernest Thesiger) descends from a precipitous staircase. Horace's sister, Rebecca (Eva Moore), is next to come forth—squat, semi-deaf and anything but friendly. Two other stranded motorists arrive: Sir William Porterhouse (Charles Laughton), a good-natured businessman, and his companion, Gladys DuCane (Lillian Bond), a dancer.

Upon discovering the bedridden father of the clan (Elspeth Dudgeon, in a bit of gimmick casting as "John Dudgeon"), Phillip and Margaret learn the house's dread secret: "Morgan is a

Karloff heralds an ominous entrance in *The Old Dark House*.

savage... We wouldn't keep him if it weren't for *Saul*... Poor Saul, he just wants to destroy, to kill... If Morgan gets very bad, he will certainly let him out." Naturally, Morgan frees the feared Saul—who proves to be a harmless-looking oldster.

"Don't let them shut me up again!" pleads Saul (Brember Wills). "I'm not mad—I swear..." Suddenly, Saul grabs a carving knife. "I want to talk about flames," he continues, now posing an earnest threat.

Mayhem breaks out, and Saul and Penderel crash through a railing to the stone floor. Morgan charges into the room, but his fury dissolves as he looks upon the pitiful corpse of Saul. He lifts the body of his friend and, moaning in despair, trudges upstairs. Penderel, thought dead at first, wakes in Gladys' embrace. Sir William seems philosophical about losing Gladys to Penderel. Next morning, the sun is shining and Horace Femm genially bids his guests farewell while Rebecca snarls at them from her window.

Following *Frankenstein* late in 1931, Boris Karloff handled several supporting roles until his Monster's great popular impact became evident to Universal's president, Carl Laemmle, and his son, Carl, Jr., general manager of the studio. The British director James Whale was promoted via *Frankenstein*—his fourth film—into the top echelon. The Laemmles in 1932 considered Karloff one of their two most valuable talents (the other being the Austrian actress Tala Birell) and sought stories to fit the perceived successor to Lon Chaney. Early that year, Junior Laemmle acquired numerous properties: H.G. Wells' *The Invisible Man*, J.B. Priestley's *Benighted*, Abner J. Geluka's *Automaton*, Ted Fithian's *The Wizard*, Robert Louis Stevenson's *The Suicide Club*, Tom Buckingham's *Destination Unknown*, Gordon Morris' *Bluebeard*, Nina Wilcox Putnam's *Cagliostro*, Gustav Meyerinck's *The Golem* and Philip Wylie's *Murderer Invisible*—all of which were announced as starring vehicles for Karloff. Of the four that were eventually made at Universal, Karloff took part in only two: *Benighted* became *The Old Dark House*, and *Cagliostro* became *The Mummy* (1933).

Ernest Thesiger keeps his house guests on edge.

Benn W. Levy and James Whale were assigned as writer and director of *The Old Dark House*. Levy, a successful British playwright who specialized in society dramas, had taken a recent fling at film-directing in England in association with Alfred Hitchcock. R.C. Sheriff, a friend of Whale's and author of the hit play *Journey's End*, also arrived from England in answer to a summons to write the adaptation for Whale's proposed film of Erich Maria Remarque's *The Road Back*. Instead, he was set to work writing dialogue for *The Old Dark House*.

Shooting began in mid-April on the finest such set of them all, a cavernous crazy-quilt designed by Charles Hall to include some of the most terrifying stairway angles imaginable. Top-billed now for the first time, Karloff headed a distinguished cast composed for the most part of English imports—Walter Byron, Lillian Bond, Charles Laughton, Ernest Thesiger, Eva Moore, Brember Wills and one fabled "John Dudgeon, 102-year-old English actor," as a publicity handout stated. The last-named was in actuality Elspeth Dudgeon, an English *actress* several decades younger. Jack Pierce altered her looks to suit the role. Thesiger, a former painter and longtime friend of Whale's, had come to the States as a player in Levy's *The Devil Passes* on Broadway. Laughton also was well known in the legitimate theater but new to Hollywood. The American quotient was to be filled by Gloria Stuart, a lovely blonde newcomer discovered at the Pasadena Playhouse; and Russell Hopton, a wry-faced Broadway actor with a penchant for playing world-weary types.

Jack Pierce had almost as much latitude in creating the makeup for Karloff's mute, crazed giant as he had known with the Frankenstein Monster, for Priestley had described the butler as "a lump." Karloff's guise at first included a mass of curly, greasy hair, a bulging forehead,

A tense encounter—one of many—in *The Old Dark House*.

beetling eyebrows and a matted beard. The early rushes displeased Junior Laemmle. The picture was shut down while exhaustive makeup tests were undertaken.

Walter Byron meanwhile was replaced by a lanky Canadian-English stage actor, Raymond Massey. When shooting resumed, Karloff had been built up and padded out as massively as he had been for *Frankenstein*. Pierce gave him straight, black hair and wiry whiskers, a built-out nose and a variety of deep collodion scars. After a few days' shooting, Hopton was replaced by a young stage actor from Georgia, Melvyn Douglas. (Douglas had made his film début the year before as Gloria Swanson's leading man in *Tonight or Never*, in which Karloff handled a brief comic role.)

Sheriff and Levy had the good grace to follow the Priestley book closely, though the film is shorn of much of the author's digressive philosophizing. The only storytelling change of consequence is that Penderel survives the climactic fall. Happy endings were essential in Laemmle-land.

The Old Dark House is prime Whale—and one of the most sophisticated of horror films. As satisfying in its way as *Frankenstein*, it surpasses even *The Cat and the Canary* (1927) in terms of claustrophobic melodrama. Its restraint is impeccable, with only one on-screen death and little gruesomeness aside from the atmosphere and Karloff's makeup. Deft bits of dark humor artfully dispel the viewer's tendency to laugh nervously at the wrong moments, and the romantic scenes—like the comic touches—are handled with somewhat more assurance than in *Frankenstein*.

Most of the story is disclosed through Gloria Stuart. It is she who is menaced first, and her perceptions reveal the secrets of Femm House—or rather, what secrets we are allowed to learn; there remains at the close a *residuum* of puzzlement. We never know why Horace fancies himself a fugitive or whether Rebecca murdered a sister of whom she speaks hatefully. With Miss Stuart, we gain an appreciation of the heroism of her outwardly commonplace husband and the annoyingly jaded Penderel, and we learn that the flashy Gladys is just a plain country girl named Perkins.

The terror commences to grow early on until at last the hand of Saul is perceived on the stair railing. Inasmuch as the Femms are more fearful of Saul than of Karloff's Morgan, the audience is conned into fancying Saul a monster of the most horrendous sort. On seeing a frail and frightened old man, the viewer might chuckle, relax, and half-believe Saul's plea for protection. Then, while the hero's attention is diverted, Saul's bland face contorts into a mask of cunning hatred. The effect is not unlike that of the unmasking scene in *The Phantom of the Opera* (1925), but it is more subtle. Saul spouts Biblical lore and talks softly about his fascination with fire, but when he attacks, biting and giggling, he is a wild beast.

Arthur Edeson's cameras poke about the angular sets, peering anxiously into the shadows and gazing up at the towering figures of Thesiger and Karloff. The same interiors were used often in later films, both by Universal and by independent companies that rented facilities at the studio, but never again with such high artistry. (Prominent examples of subsequent use: *Secret of the Blue Room*, *Secret of the Chateau*, *The Great Impersonation*, Chesterfield's *Strange People* and Majestic's *The Vampire Bat*.)

Karloff is a marvel, a brute who nonetheless commands sympathy in a single touching scene. A foreword signed by Carl Laemmle assures the audience that, yes, the man who plays Morgan is indeed the actor from *Frankenstein*. Massey and Douglas are fine as unlikely heroes. Laughton, in his first American film (he took the supporting part while awaiting his MGM star vehicle, *Payment Deferred*), is most winning as comedy relief, though the buffoonish character is hardly without his private sorrows. Lillian Bond and Gloria Stuart, physically opposites but equally attractive, are entirely capable.

The show really belongs, though, to the horrible Femms. Thesiger, who owned the most expressively sinister nose imaginable, makes a superb Horace, a gaunt, effeminate and thoroughly frightened scoundrel, his shabby gentility masking some horrid bygone indiscretion—one of the more winning grotesque characterizations extant. In his opening moments, he picks up a bundle of flowers, snuffling, "My sister was on the point of arranging these," before throwing them into the fireplace. Likely no other actor could have done as much with the dinner scene, in which Thesiger forcibly urges his guests to "have a potato" every time the conversation veers toward forbidden areas. In his long career, he topped this performance but once—in Whale's *Bride of Frankenstein* (1935).

Eva Moore conveys to perfection the character of a guilt-ridden lesbian driven by conscience into a morass of religious fanaticism and shrieking near-idiocy. In one memorable shot, she pauses to admire her distorted reflection in a mirror after carping at Margaret for being interested only in "your long white legs and how to please your man." To Brember Wills falls the most terrifying moment, when the innocent-looking Saul suddenly reveals his uglier fixations.

The Old Dark House went to the cutting room in the second week of June 1932 and saw release the following October. Although it never captured the popular fancy to the extent of *Frankenstein*, it developed a devoted following despite many subsequent years of general unavailability. William Castle delivered a rather heavy-handed, slapstick-heavy remake in 1963. The authentic *Old Dark House* film attracted an unprecedented rush of renewed attention during 1997-98, when Gloria Stuart proved resurgent in James Cameron's epic Oscar-baiter, *Titanic*.

CREDITS: Producer: Carl Laemmle, Jr.; Director: James Whale; Based upon: J.B. Priestley's Novel, *Benighted*; Adaptation and Screenplay: Benn W. Levy; Added Dialogue: R.C. Sheriff; Art Director: Charles D. Hall; Photographed by: Arthur Edeson; Editor: Clarence Kolster; Editorial Supervision: Maurice Pivar; Special Effects: John P. Fulton; Music: Bernhard Kaun; Makeup:

Behind the scenes during principal photography for *The Old Dark House*.

Jack P. Pierce; Set Décor: R.A. Gausman; Assistant Director: Joseph McDonough; Recording Supervisor: C. Roy Hunter; Western Electric Sound Recording by: William Hedgcock; Camera Operator: King Gray; Assistant Cameraman: Jack Eagan; Stills: Roman Freulich; Running Time, 71 minutes; Released: October 20, 1932

CAST: Boris Karloff (Morgan); Gloria Stuart (Margaret Waverton); Melvyn Douglas (Roger Penderel); Charles Laughton (Sir William Porterhouse); Raymond Massey (Phillip Waverton); Lillian Bond (Gladys DuCane); Ernest Thesiger (Horace Femm); Eva Moore (Rebecca Femm); John (Elspeth) Dudgeon (Sir Roderick Femm); Brember Wills (Saul Femm)

THE MASK OF FU MANCHU
(Cosmopolitan Productions/Metro-Goldwyn-Mayer Corp./Loew's, Inc.; 1932)

MGM, largest and richest of the movie companies, generally shied away from horror films. The brass preferred to put its vast array of star power into the more politely acceptable arenas of drama, romance and comedy. Whenever MGM did veer into the macabre, however, it did so with a vengeance, piling on the atrocities more densely than the less powerful studios ever dared. Hence such harrowing fare as *Kongo*, *Freaks*, *Mad Love* and a handful of others that were widely condemned in their day.

Such a curiosity is *The Mask of Fu Manchu*, which at surface is a glossy action piece about that dreaded Yellow Peril that used to drive otherwise reasonable denizens of the civilized Occident to a paranoid frenzy. A deeper look reveals perverse layers, indeed, beyond the simplistic Them-vs.-Us fantasy: Here lie reciprocal ethnic hatreds, religious frenzies, addictions both chemical and sexual, sado-masochism and emotional torments, incest, and an unbridled glee in mutilation and dismemberment. It is as though a *Rover Boys* novel had became interleaved among the pages of a Kraft-Ebing report. The film also can be seen as one of the more pressing influences upon the delightful—and often shocking—*Indiana Jones* franchise of George Lucas and Steven Spielberg.

Mask appalled the critics but delighted a large public and brought in respectable grosses. However, it caused the studio a great deal of trouble, with costs running 'way beyond reason.

The basis is a novel by the British author Sax Rohmer (*née* Arthur Sarsfield Ward), which was serialized weekly in *Collier's* magazine from May 7 through July 23 of 1932 and then published in book form by Doubleday-Doran in October. MGM had a production/distribution agreement with Cosmopolitan Productions, the motion-picture branch of the Hearst publishing empire. Intrigued by Boris Karloff's success in *Frankenstein*, Cosmopolitan-MGM bought the *Fu* rights early in August and borrowed Universal's newly minted horror star just as he was finishing *The Old Dark House* and awaiting *The Mummy* and a proposed star turn in *The Invisible Man*.

Dr. Fu Manchu had a pre-sold marquee value. He had been portrayed on film by Harry Agar Lyons in 23 silent two-reelers made in England during 1923-24, and he was impersonated by Warner Oland in three dandy Paramount talking features during 1929-31: *The Mysterious Dr. Fu Manchu, The Return of Fu Manchu* and *Daughter of the Dragon*.

By the beginning of September, *Mask* had already survived a false start under director Charles Vidor, a gifted but temperamental Hungarian. Gaetano "Tony" Gaudio was the cinematographer. Supporting Karloff was a wonderful cast: Myrna Loy as Fu Manchu's daughter, Fah Lo See; Lewis Stone as his arch-enemy, Sir Nayland Smith; Gertrude Michaels and Charles Starrett as the juvenile leads; and Lawrence Grant, Jean Hersholt and David Torrence as Smith's archeologist allies. Almost simultaneously, *Rasputin and the Empress* began shooting at MGM, with John, Lionel and Ethel Barrymore and a huge supporting cast under direction of the British-born veteran Charles Brabin.

Karloff holds court in *The Mask of Fu Manchu*.

Both pictures had begun prematurely, with tentative screenplays and other unresolved problems—a break with MGM's policy of having scripts thoroughly polished *before* production and demanding that directors stick to the written word. Before the end of August, the studio halted the troubled shoots, removing both Vidor and Brabin. Richard Boleslavski took over *Rasputin*, which the insiders were now calling *Disputin'*. Vidor was put at liberty, and Brabin was transferred to *Mask*. All available staff writers were assigned to the two pictures.

After two weeks, a new story plan for *Mask* was cautiously agreed upon. Indecision reigned all through September, which saw numerous rewrites and retakes. Karen Morley replaced Miss Michaels, and some minor roles were recast. On October 9, a tradepaper reported that both *Rasputin* and *Mask* were "still in the throes of story trouble, with no satisfactory ending yet written for either." *Mask* finally wrapped late in October. Only Irene Kuhn, Edgar Allan Woolf and John Willard (playwright of *The Cat and the Canary* and *Fog*, which had been filmed in 1929 as *Dark Waters*) received screen credit.

Karloff comes close to being *the* Fu Manchu, even though this conception omits the better side of Fu's nature. (Per Rohmer, Fu had been wholly admirable, and a pacifist to boot, before the destruction of his family during the Boxer Rebellion.) Oland had captured both conflicted traits of the Insidious One, but the portly Swedish actor bore no resemblance to the tall, slender Mandarin of Rohmer's imagination. Physically, Karloff is perfectly cast. The script, however, permits nothing of pathos or understanding for Fu—too bad, that, for Karloff's greatest talent lay in the sympathetic portrayal of menacing characters.

Karloff is matched all the way by Myrna Loy's beguiling performance as a sadistic nymphomaniac, equally bereft of pity. Her unusual beauty lent itself well to Oriental characterizations, of which *Mask* is the last of quite a few. Her later stardom would hinge upon Miss Loy's zestful approach to sophisticated comedy and romantic drama.

The story finds Sir Nayland Smith (Lewis Stone), of the British Secret Service, determined to beat Fu to the tomb of Genghis Khan. Should Fu obtain the mask and sword therein, he can lead Asia against the world-at-large. Fu's agents seize Sir Lionel Barton (Lawrence Grant), an archaeologist who has learned the tomb's location.

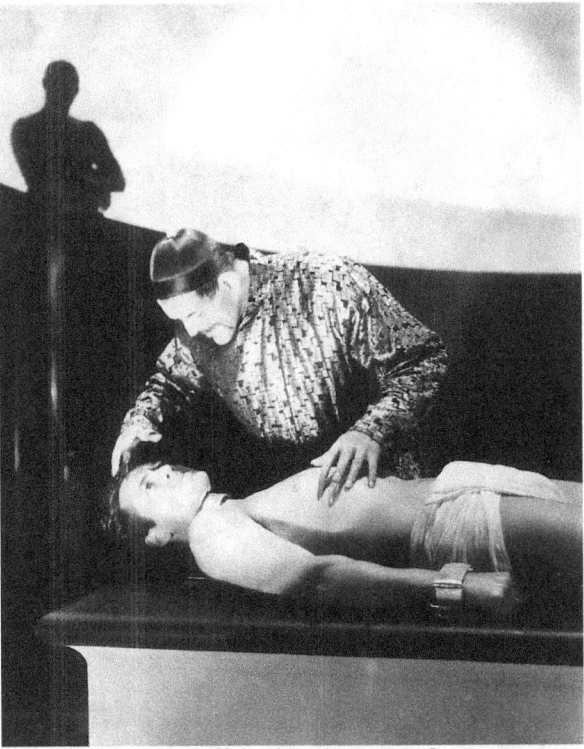

Karloff, in charge—as usual.

Sir Lionel's daughter, Sheila (Karen Morley), and her fiancé, Terrence Granville (Charles Starrett), join the expedition. Sir Lionel's severed hand drops from the darkness. Fu demands the mask and sword lest other such trinkets be forthcoming. Sheila and Terrence decide to deliver the relics as instructed. But when Fu tests the sword in an electrical arc, it melts—Smith has substituted a replica. Fah Lo See has Terrence lashed unmercifully, then ravishes the unconscious youth. Sir Lionel's corpse is delivered to expedition headquarters.

Terrence, under Fu's will, leads his comrades into a trap. Now Fu has the genuine sword and mask. Terrence regains his wits and spurns Fah Lo See. Smith is placed at the mercy of crocodiles. Von Borg (Jean Hersholt) is imprisoned in a room of moving, spiked walls. Sheila is designated the source of blood that will anoint the sword. Smith escapes, then takes charge of Fu's death ray. Terrence seizes the sword, fells Fu Manchu, and carries Sheila to safety. Smith flings the sword into the sea.

Makeup artist Cecil Holland, in an article called "Orientals Made to Order" in the December 1932 issue of *The American Cinematographer*, said that in transforming Karloff he filled in the area between eyelid and brow because Chinese eyes are set in the head differently from those of Europeans. This was done with thin layers of cotton saturated with collodion and shaped to fit, then surfaced with nose putty and blended into the natural contours. He drew the eyebrows up and shaved off their ends to give "the Mephisto effect necessary." He distended Karloff's nose with plugs and putty. The ears were built up and pointed. Teeth caps, a coarse black wig with forelock, a plunging mustache, long fingernails and 'specially formulated greasepaint completed the illusion. It took three hours each day to get Karloff ready to face the cameras over a long schedule.

One of Dr. Fu's more elaborate gizmos

Myrna Loy was much easier, Holland said, because her round face and high cheekbones made her look more nearly Asian in the first place. Tapes under a wig drew her eyes into an angle, and her lips were painted to an artificial fullness. "Such character makeup is certainly no game for amateurs," Holland averred.

Stern and authoritative, Lewis Stone is the best of the screen's many Nayland Smiths, and the usually villainous Lawrence Grant is the Stoic Briton incarnate as the tragic Sir Lionel. Karen Morley, one of the more interesting young actresses of the time, lends grace to the ingénue role. The classically handsome Charles Starrett, later to become a popular Western star at Columbia, does well as the dashing adventurer and delivers a chilling scene in which, under Fu's control, he laughs maniacally at having betrayed his colleagues. Jean Hersholt, David Torrence and E. Allyn Warren (as a minion of Fu) lend sturdy support.

Visually eloquent, the big sets (augmented by Warren Newcombe's fine matte paintings) are filled with gigantic golden idols. A museum's exhibition hall is replete with dinosaur skeletons, mummies, a pterodactyl and other imposing props, including a crocodile and the gorilla from *Tarzan, the Ape Man*. The tomb features ornately carved golden doors and the enthroned, jewel-bedecked skeleton of the great Khan. Fantastic pseudo-scientific electrical equipment was supplied by Kenneth Strickfaden, who also created the machinery of Universal's *Frankenstein* and *Flash Gordon* productions. Strickfaden stood in for Karloff in some of the pyrotechnical scenes; the artisan was almost electrocuted in the process. (The substitution is obvious because Strickfaden stood much shorter.)

The costuming is spectacular. For Fu's banquet scene with hundreds of chieftains, MGM ordered some 200 brocaded garments in addition to many rented from the Chinatowns of Los Angeles and San Francisco. A museum loaned the costumes of six Samurai warriors.

Among the pre-Code, censor-baiting delights is one of the most unabashedly erotic sequences this side of some stag movie, where the gorgeous Fah Lo See orders Terrence flogged by two muscular black men. Myrna Loy's placid features become contorted with lust as she cries, "*Aiee!* Faster! Faster! Faster! Faster! Faster! Faster!" She orders the unconscious youth placed on her bed and sends the slaves away. Panting heavily, she kisses his lips and runs her hands over his body. When her father walks in, she says, coyly: "He is not entirely unhandsome, is he, my father?" Karloff doesn't miss a beat: "For a white man, no."

Bigoted slurs and condescensions are hurled without restraint. The insults begin when Fu and Sir Lionel meet: "You're Fu Manchu, aren't you?"

Myrna Loy and Boris Karloff

"I'm a Doctor of Philosophy from Edinburgh, I'm a Doctor of Law from Christ's College, I'm a Doctor of Medicine from Harvard. My friends, out of courtesy, call me 'Doctor.'"

"Oh, I beg your pardon! Well, *three*-times-Doctor, what do you want from *me*?"

When an offer of $1 million to reveal the location of the tomb fails to sway Sir Lionel, Dr. Fu turns to Fah Lo See: "Even my daughter, even that, for you!"

Sir Lionel's daughter regales Fu: "You hideous yellow monster!" Sir Nayland also gets in a dig: "Is this a friend of your family?" he asks Fu as a snake slithers past. The aristocratic Dr. Fu meets such insults with more of the same but retains his dignity. He calls Terrence a

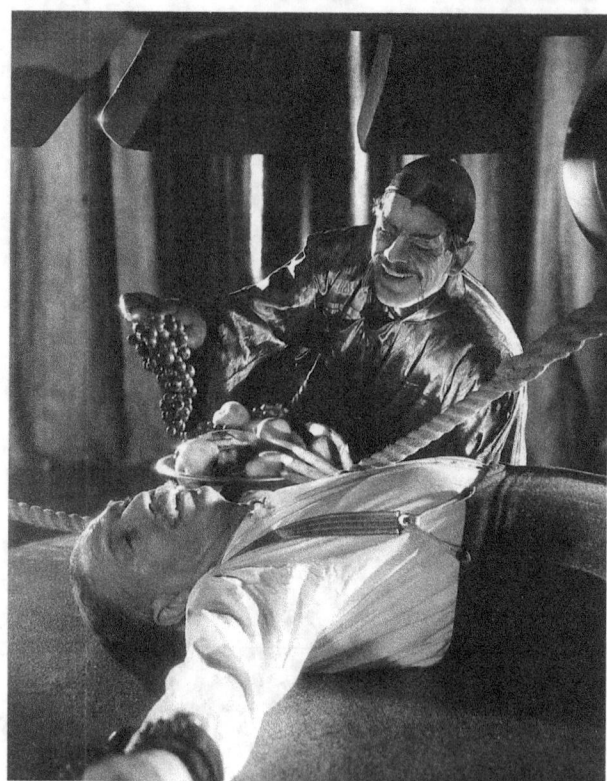

Dr. Fu offers a spot of temptation.

"cursed son of a white dog" and warns Smith that "the slightest move will send a bullet crashing through your stiff British spine." When Smith invokes the authority of the Crown, Dr. Fu resorts to a higher volume: "British government! I'll wipe them and the whole accursed white race off the face of the Earth!" Introducing the blonde, diaphanously gowned Sheila to his hordes, Fu exults: "[C]onquer and *breed*! *Kill* the white man and take his women!"

The Mandarin describes the enslavement of Terrence: "[H]e becomes a reflection of my will... So much better than hypnotism!" That the same hellish drugging procedure is used to make Terrence a suitable lover for Fah Lo See, adds a bracing *lagniappe* of depravity.

CREDITS: Director: Charles Brabin; Screenplay: Irene Kuhn: Edgar Allan Woolf and John Willard; Novel: Sax Rohmer; Sound Director: Douglas Shearer; Art Director: Cedric Gibbons; Editor: Ben Lewis; Photographed by: Tony Gaudio; Gowns: Adrian; Special Effects: Warren Newcombe; Musical Score: Dr. William Axt; Makeup: Cecil Holland; Electrical Properties: Kenneth Strickfaden; Recording: Andrew MacDonald; Assistant Director: John Waters; Set Décor: Edwin B. Willis; Animal Supervision: Jack Allman. Running time: 72 minutes; Released: November 5, 1932

CAST: Boris Karloff (Dr. Fu Manchu); Lewis Stone (Nayland Smith); Karen Morley (Sheila); Charles Starrett (Terrence Granville); Myrna Loy (Fah Lo See); Jean Hersholt (Von Berg); Lawrence Grant (Sir Lionel Barton); David Torrence (McLeod); E. Allyn Warren (Goy Lo Sung); Ferdinand Gottschalk (Dr. Nicholson); C. Montague Shaw (Dr. Fairgyle); Steve Clemente (Knife Thrower); Edward Peil, Sr. (Coolie Spy); Lal Chand Mehra (Indian Prince); Tetsu Komai (Swordsman); Everett Brown (Slave); Willie Fung (Steward); Chris-Pin Martin (Potentate); James B. Léong (Guest); Allen Jung (Coolie); Clinton Rosemond (Slave); Victor Wong (Opium Attendant); Ray Benard (Corrigan) (Stuntman); and in Deleted Scenes Directed by Charles Vidor: Gertrude Michael (Sheila) and Herbert Bunston (Dr. Fairgyle)

SECRETS OF THE FRENCH POLICE
(RKO-Radio Pictures, Inc.; 1932)

The most popular series in the Hearst newspapers' *The American Weekly* was *Secrets of the Sûreté, the French Police Detectives* by H. Ashton-Wolfe, an operative associated with the celebrated Bertillon. The movie version's script—also containing portions of *The Lost Empress*, by the influential Old Left author Samuel Ornitz—represented the work of a large team of writers including Ornitz, mystery novelist Rufus King and director A. Edward Sutherland, with Robert Tasker, Robert Benchley, Frank Moss and Aubrey Wisberg. L.E. Ansélme, a former Sûreté operative who had sent six murderers to the guillotine, was found working as a watchmaker in Los Angeles and hired as technical director.

David O. Selznick, then chief of production at RKO-Radio, intended the picture as a showcase for his glamorous Danish import, Gwili André, whom he hoped to fashion into a rival to Garbo and Dietrich. Like most other European actresses of the day, Miss André failed to catch on with us Yanks. Frank Morgan was cast as the Ashton-Wolfe surrogate and proved a capable dramatic player in this respite from whimsical roles. Even more uncharacteristic is the chilling performance of the Russian Gregory Ratoff, usually cast as a dialect comedian but fascinating here as a reptilian murderer.

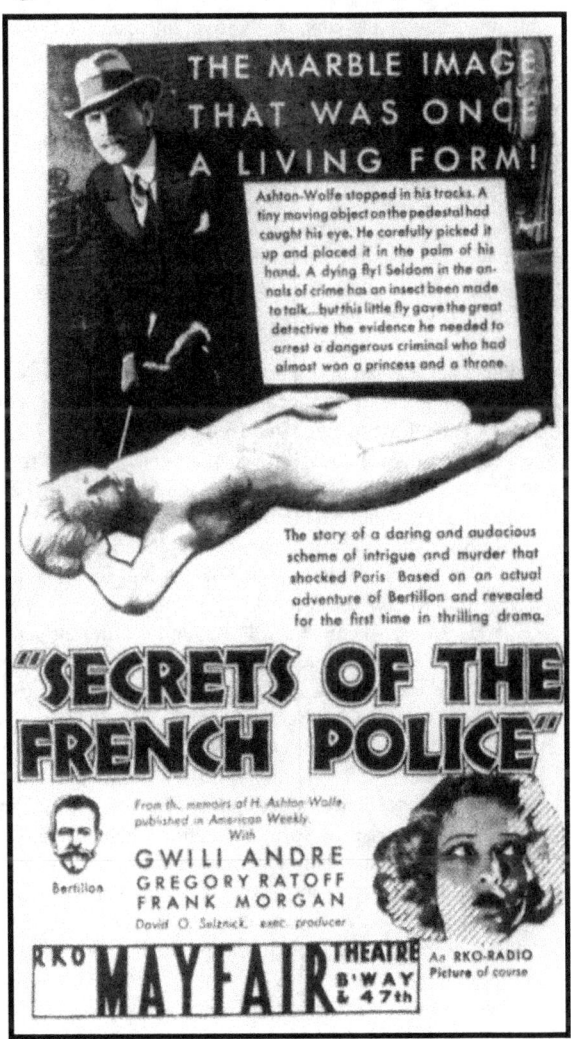

The principal photography coincided with a near-epidemic of influenza. Rod LaRocque was set for the romantic lead, and then Nils Asther was borrowed from Walter Wanger Productions as a last-moment substitute. When Asther fell ill, a likable Britisher named John Warburton stepped into the role and thus made his American début. Gwili André became ill, and the company had to shoot around her for a week. Ratoff, too, was sidelined for several days.

The story hangs on Léon Renault (Warburton), a handsome pickpocket at large in Paris. Léon is betrothed to Eugénie Dorain (Miss André), a flower vendor. Her foster father, Anton (Christian Rub), is bitterly opposed to the marriage. General Han Moloff (Ratoff), late of the White Russian Army, schemes to find a ringer for the missing Princess Anastasia and claim the estate of the Czar. Accomplices are his mistress, Rena (Kendall Lee), and another fallen nobleman, Baron Feodor Lomzoi (Lucien Prival).

Frank Morgan as St. Cyr

Lomzoi finds Eugénie suited to Moloff's purposes. Eugénie is abducted, and her father is slain. Lomzoi, who has learned too much, is fished out of the Seine.

Clearing himself of suspicion, Léon becomes allied with Francois St. Cyr (Morgan) of the Sûreté. Léon stakes out an isolated mansion and sees Moloff spreading plaster over the corpse of Rena. He learns that Eugénie is in the house, but he must escape before he can find her. The exiled Russian Grand Duke (Arnold Korff) questions Eugénie but has misgivings about her supposedly royal lineage. The Duke and a diplomatic escort die in an auto crash. St. Cyr, using the wreck as an excuse, calls upon Moloff. St. Cyr notices a fly drop dead from a statue; he has seen flies die of formaldehyde poisoning in the morgue. Cutting a small hole in the statue, he reaches inside and blanches in horror: He has found the missing Rena.

Finally, Eugénie is rescued from Moloff's embalming room. Moloff slams his handcuffed wrists into a power panel, electrocuting himself. Eugénie is reunited with Léon, who promises to reform.

Secrets of the French Police was photographed during August-September 1932. Sets included a Paris street, tenements and a sidewalk cafe, all constructed at the RKO ranch in Encino, and café and tenement interiors and a standing castle set at the Pathé Culver City lot—the same one used for 1932's *The Most Dangerous Game*. Selznick rode herd on the picture, bringing in *The New Yorker* magazine's ace humorist, Robert Benchley, to add sparkle to the dialogue and demanding many retakes to accentuate Miss André. At the same time, Selznick took the company to task because by September 9 the shoot had gone $15,000 over its $172,646 budget. Part of the overage involved the wrecking of a Rolls limousine—a futile extravagance, because the full-scale crash proved unacceptable; it was remade with one of Don Jahrous' flawless miniatures. About the only thing Selznick *didn't* growl about (the producer was notorious for firing off confrontational memoranda) was *Secrets*' photography: "I approve highly of Al Gilks' work," Selznick writes in one surviving document.

After principal photography had wrapped on September 14, Selznick ordered further changes. Among other nit-pickings, Ashton-Wolfe was renamed Francois St. Cyr, villainess Zenia Harka was rechristened Rena, and a different setting was demanded for a sequence in which White Russian exiles sing their anthem. The picture reached the scoring stage in October. Max Steiner conducted a full orchestra for the titles and dramatic passages; Dudley Chambers directed an 11-voice Russian choir; and Steiner led an eight-piece *musette* for the café scenes. Final negative cost (literally, the cost of everything required to make the finished negative) was $195,805. Editing left a running time of 59 minutes—a slick and fast-moving picture.

Ratoff's excellence, in a role that ordinarily would have gone to, say, Bela Lugosi, comes as a pleasant surprise. Moloff's depravities include a passion for surrounding himself with dead cats. He embalms his slain mistress, then plasters her over as a piece of statuary. In one neatly underplayed scene, that mistress complains that too many people know about his scheme; he replies casually, "Several have died." (And so: Guess who's next.) Later on during the 1930s, Ratoff detoured into directing and producing and piloted some 30 movies until his death in 1960. Some are memorable: *Intermezzo* (1939), *Adam Had Four Sons* (1941), *The Corsican Brothers* (1941), *Moss Rose* (1947) and *Black Magic* (1949).

Secrets of the French Police would have been highly censorable within only two years. The 1934 incarnation of the Motion Picture Producers & Distributors' Production Code Administration would have nixed a nude shot of Kendall Lee; a scene in which Morgan jams a finger into a statue containing a corpse; a close-up of Ratoff's hands turning black with an electrical surge; and a wrap-up in which the dashing thief-turned-hero gets gracefully off the hook for his own crimes.

The lighter touches that keep the grimness at bay can be traced largely to director Sutherland, whose *fortissimo* was comedy. His pacing and the performances wear especially well, for a movie of so long ago. The realism of the sets and the delicately diffused lighting add to the make-believe French ambiance. In a lengthy career, Sutherland walked that fine line between humor and horror only one other time, in the following year's *Murders in the Zoo*.

CREDITS: Executive Producer: David O. Selznick; Associate Producer: Willis Goldbeck; Director: A. Edward Sutherland; Screenplay: Samuel Ornitz, Robert Tasker and Edward Sutherland; Added Dialogue: Robert Benchley; Based upon: H. Ashton Wolfe's *American Weekly* serial, *Secrets of the Sûreté, the French Police Detectives*, and Samuel Ornitz' *The Lost Empress*; Musical Director: Max Steiner; Art Director: Carroll Clark; Photographed by: Alfred L. Gilks; RCA Photophone Sound by: George D. Ellis; Assistant Directors: Jo von Ronkel and Dewey Starkey; Technical Adviser: L.E. Ansélme; Editor: Arthur Roberts; Adaptation: Rufus King, Aubrey Wisberg and Frank Moss; Unit Manager: Fred Fleck; Dialogue Director: Gene Lewis; Special Effects: Vernon L. Walker, Linwood Dunn and Donald Jahrous; Set Décor: Thomas Little and D. Burke; Makeup: Sam Kaufman; Hairdresser: Gwen Holden; Script Clerk: Adele Cannon; Second Cameramen: Harry Wild and Joseph Biroc; Assistant Cameramen: Harold Wellman and Jimmy Daley; Chorus Master: Dudley Chambers; Songs: "Beau Ideal," "Chi Chi," "Valse Lente," "Ninette" and "Serenade," by Max Steiner, and "Berceuse," by Rudolph Friml; Orchestrations: Joseph Mueller and Léonid Raab; Music and Effects Recording: Murray Spivack; Marionettes: Dorothy Goldner; Stills: Edward Cronenweth and P. MacKenzie; Running Time: 59 minutes; Released: December 2, 1932

CAST: Gwili André (Eugénie Dorain); Gregory Ratoff (General Han Moloff); Frank Morgan (St. Cyr); John Warburton (Léon Renault); Murray Kinnell (Bertillon); Lucien Prival (Baron Feodor Lomzoi); Julia Swayne Gordon (Madame Amienes); Kendall Lee (Rena); Christian Rub (Anton Dorain); Arnold Korff (Grand Duke Maxim); Guido Trento (Count de Marsay); Rochelle Hudson (Agent K-31); Evelyn Carter Carrington (Madame La Prop); Michael Visaroff (German); Kate Lawson (Concierge); Dina Smirnova (Russian); Reginald Barlow (Prefect); Harry Cording, Arthur Thalasso, Sam Appel and Malcolm Waite (Detectives); Gertrude Pilar and Eleanor Vandevier (Ladies-in-Waiting); Cyril Ring (Gendarme); Virginia Thomas (Model); Wong Chung, Ming Woy, Wong Haye and Chester Gan (Tartar Servants); Capt. Girardo Garcia, Al Garcia, Gilbert Sanchez and Octavio Gerard (Policemen); Chic Collins, Wesley Hopper and Helen Lambert (Stunts); and H. Koontz, Wells Blanton, Mark McFee, Jean Girard, Betty Rome, Eugene Beday, Jimmy Coleman, Ray Cooper, Major Nichols, H.A. Perline, Fay Holderness, Nick Shaid, William Lally, Gino Corrado, Harry Cornbleth

MURDERS IN THE ZOO
(Paramount Productions, Inc.; 1933)

A splendid set of unusual optical-process images gets A. Edward Sutherland's *Murders in the Zoo* off to a fine start: The main title and credits are superimposed over animals. An applauding seal, in a striking anticipation of the much later technique of digital morphing, dissolves into comical leading man Charlie Ruggles. A bear becomes crusty old Harry Beresford. A dove and an owl become romantically involved scientists Gail Patrick and Randolph Scott. A pair of sleek pumas dissolves to the handsome-but-hungry Kathleen Burke and John Lodge. Finally, a snarling tiger introduces Lionel Atwill.

As a portrayer of mad scientists, Atwill was without peer. No other actor could convey with comparable eloquence a man so monomaniacal as to regard human life as worthless compared with his schemes. Atwill is at his best in *Murders in the Zoo*, wherein he not only removes anybody who displeases him but also takes an unholy glee in utilizing the most gruesome and agonizing means at hand. It is also made explicit that murder represents his idea of sexual arousal.

In a remote jungle, zoologist Eric Gorman (Atwill) gloats over a helpless visitor who had put the moves on Gorman's wife. Trussed and with his lips sewn together, the young man is left to predators. Says Gorman: "Now, you'll never lie to a friend again—and you'll never again kiss another man's wife." Evelyn Gorman (Miss Burke) asks Gorman if her admirer left a message. "He didn't say anything," comes the reply. Returning to America with a cargo for a municipal zoo, Gorman senses an affair developing between Evelyn and a passenger, Roger Hewitt (Lodge).

The zoo, run by Prof. Evans (Beresford) and Dr. Jack Woodford (Scott), faces financial ruin. Press agent Peter Yates (Ruggles) is hired to stir up popular interest. When Gorman delivers the animals, Woodford seems particularly interested in a rare green mamba in light of his antitoxin research.

Hewitt dies in agony during a banquet. The fang marks of a mamba are found on his leg, and it is discovered that the snake has escaped. Later, Evelyn sees Gorman working on some strange device. She finds it to be an artificial snake-head. Gorman disposes of his wife in a crocodile-pit.

Yates must double as a workman to keep his job. He captures the mamba, collapses, and afterwards inquires whether there is a laundry nearby. (A variant on this creaky vulgarian gag would resurface 61 years later in *Ace Ventura: Pet Detective*.) Woodford and his fiancée, Jerry Evans (Miss Patrick), take the reptile to his laboratory. Woodford discovers that the fangs are spaced differently from Hewitt's wounds. Woodford summons Gorman, who sinks the bogus fangs into Woodford. Gorman releases several animals to create a diversion while he hides in a cage—where a python makes short work of the madman. Woodford recovers, saved by his own serum.

Top-billed Charlie Ruggles adds some (arguably) welcome comedy of the flustered, lowbrow variety, and romance is supplied by the unusually handsome couple of Miss Patrick and the long-reigning Western star Scott, who seems not the least bit out of his element in this citified setting. Miss Burke is her usual sultry and sloe-eyed self as Atwill's faithless wife, with Lodge (later to become governor of Connecticut) as a doomed lover. Beresford is a delight as the befuddled zoo director, and likewise for Edward McWade as a cranky keeper. Not even all their capable work can keep Atwill from stealing the show.

Early on, Atwill speaks of the animals, like some hellborn Dr. Doolittle: "I love them! Their honesty, their simplicity, their primitive emotions. They love, they hate, and they kill." He calls his wife's marked-for-death paramour "just a veddy good friend... like one of the family." Later, he tells the victim-to-be: "On the boat, you and I seemed to have a mutual interest. *I* was

A murder in the zoo—hence the film title

referring to my animals." When his wife accuses him of murder, Atwill snorts: "You don't think I sat there all evening with an eight-foot mamba in my pocket, do you? It would be an injustice to my tailor!"

Atwill's passion is heightened enormously by the killing urge. "I know—you're going to make love to me," Miss Burke cries in disgust. He pants: "I've never wanted you *more... I'm* not going to kiss you—*you're* going to kiss me!" Later, trying to reason with her on the bridge, he argues: "If I lacked the courage to kill for you, I couldn't expect you to go on loving me."

The crocodile feast is a shocker: The saurians converge on the struggling woman, seizing her in their jaws and gyrating to tear their prey apart, pausing only to lift their heads as they gorge themselves on her flesh.

The zoo, especially in night scenes suggestive of the jungle, is as frightening as any Gothic castle. Ernest Haller's distinctive photographic style makes each shadow a potential menace. There is effective dramatic scoring during the jungle scenes and, later, a tour of the zoo, with a distinct motif for each animal, plus incidental music and low-denominator comic passages for Ruggles. The sparseness of orchestral scoring during later action passes unnoticed, for the animals' furor keeps the soundtrack sufficiently well occupied.

English-born Edward Sutherland's follow-through to *Secrets of the French Police* marks his second and final run at such a heady mixture of wit and terror. Each has its charms, but *Murders in the Zoo* has the cut-and-dried advantage in the magnificent Lionel Atwill.

In a press kit for a mid-1990s video edition of *Murders in the Zoo*, MCA-Universal (which had acquired a number of the Paramount properties) mis-identified Ruggles as Atwill. Yes, and without such brilliant contributions to Cultural Literacy, none of our labors would be necessa—... *uhm*, possible.

Atwill, energized by the act of murder

CREDITS: Associate Producer: E. Lloyd Sheldon; Director: A. Edward Sutherland; Screenplay: Philip Wylie and Seton I. Miller; Photographed by: Ernest Haller; Art Director: Hans Dreier; Musical: Nat W. Finston; Musical Cues by: Rudolph G. Kopp, Karl Hajos, John M. Leipold and Sigmund Krumgold; Songs: "Please," by Leo Robin & Ralph Rainger, "Look Who's Here," by Harold Adamson & Burton Lane, "At the Bow-Wow Ball," by Edward Heyman & Boyd Bunch, and "Roses from the South," by Johann Strauss; Stills: Sherman Clark; Sound System: Western Electric; Running Time: 66 minutes; Released: March 31, 1933

CAST: Charlie Ruggles (Peter Yates); Lionel Atwill (Eric Gorman); Gail Patrick (Jerry Evans); Randolph Scott (Dr. Woodford); John Lodge (Roger Hewitt); Kathleen Burke (Evelyn Gorman); Harry Beresford (Prof. Evans); Edward McWade (Dan); Walter Walke and Edwin Stanley (Doctors); Syd Saylor, Lee Phelps, Stanley Blystone, Syd D'Albrook and Eddie Boland (Reporters); Ethan Laidlaw (Reardon); Duke Green (Stevedore); John Rogers (Steward); Jane Darwell, Samuel Hinds and Cyril Ring (Zoo Patrons)

I COVER THE WATERFRONT
(Reliance Pictures, Inc./United Artists Corp.; 1933)

James Cruze—like such other successful silent-era directors as D.W. Griffith, William Nigh, Fred Newmeyer, Marshall "Mickey" Neilan and Erich von Stroheim—found his talking-pictures career a succession of exhilarating highs and demeaning lows. The collapse of Cruze's producing company and a dizzying plunge into alcoholism blighted a decade in which his great talents veered only occasionally in a productive direction. Cruze was hired by Reliance early in 1933 to direct its first picture, *I Cover the Waterfront*. Reliance was established by Edward Small and Harry Goetz with the partial backing of Joseph M. Schenck, of United Artists. *Waterfront*, based loosely on a memoir by reporter Max Miller of the San Diego *Sun*, is a bright spot of Cruze's career, mingling lurid fact with lurid fiction in a virile mixture of near-documentary realism and chilling melodrama.

Julie Kirk (Claudette Colbert) knows that her father, Eli Kirk (Ernest Torrence), is troubled, but she cannot fathom why. Fact is, the Coast Guard is closing in on Eli's Chinese-smuggling operations. A reporter, Joseph Miller (Ben Lyon), has vowed to expose the seafaring crook. Old Chris (Harry Beresford), a harbor bum, dredges up the corpse of a Chinese, bound in a chain from Eli's fishing shack. Eli goes on a binge at a waterfront dive, where Miller and a colleague, McCoy (Hobart Cavanaugh), also show up. Julie comes to seek her father, and Miller helps her trundle him home. Julie and Miller have a rendezvous the next day on the waterfront.

Miller and federal agents meet the next arrival of Eli's boat, which appears to contain only gigantic sharks. Miller slashes open a shark—and a Chinese is found inside. Eli strikes Miller down but is wounded and escapes after a struggle. Julie turns against Miller. Miller tracks Eli to a partially sunken barge, where the smuggler shoots the snoop. As he is about to do away with Miller, Julie arrives. Sensing his daughter's affection for the reporter, Eli helps her take him a speedboat. Eli dies before he can make a getaway. Miller survives, and he and Julie are reunited.

In addition to its United Artists Studios work, the production involved locations at San Pedro and in the Pacific off San Pedro, San Diego and Monterey. A harpooning expedition brought in several 20-foot sharks for scenes in which undocumented immigrants are hidden in the carcasses. Snorkels enabled the hardy Chinese extras to survive the ordeal; today, such a scene would involve digital fakery or sculpted imitation sharks.

The San Pedro Harbor provides a colorful backdrop. The U.S.S. *Constitution*, the Pacific Fleet, and the *Carma* (the very

Ernest Torrence, Claudette Colbert and Ben Lyon

yacht on which Capt. Walter Wanderwell had recently been murdered), lend authenticity. The company was at work at the United Artists facilities when an earthquake struck, dumping Ben Lyon out of the bed in which he was emoting and killing the lights and power.

The nominal stars, Claudette Colbert and Lyon, do fine work as a waterfront waif and her boyfriend. The real star, however, is Ernest Torrence, a former concert pianist and operatic baritone from Edinburgh who became famous as an actor after portraying the degenerate Luke Hatburn in *Tol'able David* (1921), Henry King's celebrated rustic tragedy. Six-foot-four, lantern-jawed and muscular, Torrence created in Eli Kirk what must be his finest characterization. It is difficult to imagine a more cruel or fearsome villain than this tobacco-chawing and scenery-gnawing smuggler and killer, and yet Torrence invests the man with enough humanity to impart a deep poignancy to his passing. His bumbling fondness for his daughter, his loyalty to his murderous colleagues and even his drunken bout are curiously affecting. Few actors have accomplished this feat (Karloff in the *Frankenstein* films comes to mind, as do Brian Donlevy in the 1939 *Beau Geste* and James Cagney in 1931's *Public Enemy*). Torrence died shortly after the completion of *Waterfront*. Other notables on view here are Harry Beresford as a harbor scavenger and Hobart Cavanaugh as a happily inebriated journalist.

Ray June, a real master of the camera, managed somewhat to overcome Cruze's usual talkie-era reluctance to vary the shooting angles; the result imparts an eerie sense of prowling through forbidden places, suffusing both on-location and in-the-studio settings. This is a somber picture, and yet it avoids being depressing. Miss Colbert even has some playfully erotic banter with Lyon and a discreet pre-Code nude swimming scene—which probably helped to provoke the toughening of the Production Code that following year.

CREDITS: Presented by: Joseph M. Schenck; Executive Producers: Harry M. Goetz and Edward Small; Producer: Edward Small; Director: James Cruze; Based upon the Journalistic Memoir by: Max Miller; Screenplay: Wells Root; Additional Dialogue: Jack Jevne; Music Composed and Conducted by: Alfred Newman; Themes: "Weiner Maederlin," by Ziehrer and "Love Song," by Minnie Wright; Assistant Director: Vernon Keays; Art Director: Albert S. D'Agostino; Photographed by: Ray June; Sound: Oscar Lagerstrom; Editor: Grant Whytock; Operative Cameraman: Stuart Thompson; Assistant Cameramen: Hal Carney and Ellis Carter; Second Unit Photography: Harry Perry, Assisted by Jimmy Hackett; Produced at: United Artists Studios; Running Time: 70 minutes; Released: May 17, 1933

CAST: Claudette Colbert (Julie Kirk); Ben Lyon (Joseph Miller); Ernest Torrence (Eli Kirk); Hobart Cavanaugh (McCoy); Maurice Black (Ortegus); Harry Beresford (Old Chris); Purnell Pratt (John Phelps); George Humbert (Silva); Rosita Marstini (Mrs. Silva); Claudia Coleman (Mother Morgan); Wilfred Lucas (Randall); Florence Dudley (Blonde); Al Hill (Thug); Burr McIntosh (Old Man)

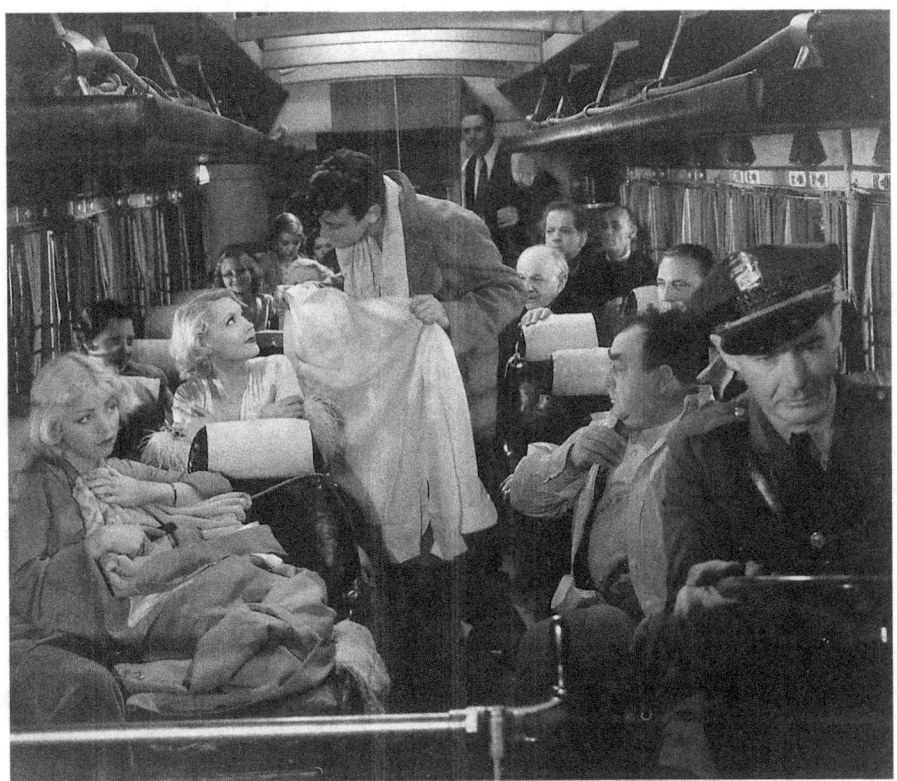

Aboard the doomed bus

CROSS COUNTRY CRUISE
(Universal Pictures Corp.; 1934)

Sue (June Knight), a beautiful young model, waits at a bus station in New York for her lover, Steve (Alan Dinehart). He arrives in the company of his possessive wife, Nita (Minna Gombell). Sue, who had been unaware of any wife, rebuffs the jerk's efforts to explain. The bus pulls out with all aboard. Norman (Lew Ayres), a wealthy playboy en route to a California logging camp owned by his father, finds himself fascinated by Sue.

From such soap-operatic narrative cloth, the forgotten director Eddie Buzzell and writers Elmer Harris and Stanley Rauh fashion one of the most striking murder thrillers in long memory. The story begins deceptively as a light romantic affair, but its development into a freakish crime yarn is entirely logical. Most of the action transpires in transit. Extensive location work lends momentum and a sense of frenzied disorientation.

Aboard the bus, Norman gets chummy with Sue. Steve, sitting in back with Nita, seethes with rage. When the bus lays over in Denver, Steve trails Sue to a department store, overtaking her in the sporting-goods section. Nita arrives unexpectedly. Sue tries vainly to explain, finally absenting herself while Nita berates Steve. Alone with his wife, Steve impulsively skewers her with an arrow.

Steve remains hidden until the store closes. He substitutes the corpse for a mannequin on display. He returns to the bus, explaining that Nita is staying in Denver with relatives. A window-trimmer discovers the body. The police trace the bus from Nita's ticket. Steve tries to frame

The Definitive Edition

June Knight and Lew Ayres in *Cross Country Cruise*

Sue. Norman, who knows that Sue is an experienced archer, learns that the arrow point had been broken off in Nita's body. He argues that anyone familiar with archery would have removed the arrow by pushing it through, rather than by trying to pull it free.

Steve kidnaps Sue and pulls a getaway in the bus. The airborne police land just ahead. Steve swerves into the plane, and the bus tumbles over a cliff and into a stream. Norman rescues Sue. Steve drowns.

Lew Ayres was known as "the king of Universal" at the time, what with his can't-miss heroic appeal. Ayres' versatility is as great an asset here as the charm of his leading lady, June Knight, a Ziegfeld Follies standout who became famous when it was revealed that she had doubled Greta Garbo for the celebrated dance sequence in *Mara Hari* (1931). The petite Alice White is fine as a flashy chorine, and there are good small-part character vignettes by such scene-stealers as Eugene Pallette, Henry Armetta, Robert McWade and Jane Darwell.

The strongest performances, however, belong to Alan Dinehart as the cad who becomes a killer and Minna Gombell as his hated and hateful better half. Dinehart—a cultured intellectual who was not only an actor but also a theatrical producer and a zoologist—gives the role just the right touch of shifty charm and plays the mad-scene business for vividly seething contrast. Miss Gombell, also of the stage and a rather extreme beauty with high cheekbones and a wide-eyed glare, followed this role with many similarly bitchy studies.

Although the picture plays out a bit choppily because of its overabundance of characters, it is impossible not to find a fascinated focus in the machinations of the murderer. Most gripping is the scene in which Dinehart plants his victim as a window-display prop—an early exploration of the terrifying possibilities of a big retail space after hours. Camera chief George Robinson keeps the visuals interesting with smooth matching of the location and studio work, despite the difficulties of shooting so much of the yarn within the constricted setting of the bus. John Fulton's composites, process photography and miniature work are convincing.

Cross Country Cruise marks a distinctly different sort of assignment for the diminutive Eddie Buzzell (1895-1985), a former musical-comedy performer who had entered films early in the talkie era as a Vitaphone comedy star. Buzzell's usual realm as a director lay in musicals and romantic comedies. Here, the festering intrigues, the ghastly slaying and the desperate chase are handled with the same skill and attention to detail that Buzzell applied to his more characteristic work. Later, during a long tenure with MGM, Buzzell turned out numerous tuneful hits, including *Best Foot Forward* (1943), *Neptune's Daughter* (1949), *A Woman of Distinction* (1950) and *Ain't Misbehavin'* (1955). His one return to the crime-thriller genre came with *Song of the Thin Man* (1947), last of the William Powell-Myrna Loy series.

CREDITS: Executive Producer: Carl Laemmle, Jr.; Producer: Sam Jacobson; Director: Edward Buzzell; Screenplay: Elmer Harris; Story: Stanley Rauh; Photographed by: George Robinson; Editor: Philip Cahn; Settings: Harrison Wiley; Sound: Gilbert Kurland; Running Time: 78 Minutes; Released: January 12, 1934

CAST: Lew Ayres (Norman); June Knight (Sue); Alice White (May); Alan Dinehart (Steve); Minna Gombell (Nita); Eugene Pallette (Bronson); Robert McWade (Grouch); Henry Armetta (Italian); Arthur Vinton (Murphy); James Conlin (Sid); Ara Haswell (Old Maid); Dick Stevens (Sick Man); Peggy Terry (Toots); Herta Lind (German Girl); Jean Fenwick (Schoolteacher); Kay La Velle (Henpecking Wife)

THE MYSTERY OF MR. X
(Metro-Goldwyn-Mayer Corp./Loew's, Inc.; 1934)

The Mystery of Mr. X started a lasting movement: the murder mystery in which urbane, romantic comedy replaced heavy-handed humor (as in the brash witticisms of, for instance, 1931's *Murder by the Clock* and 1932's *The Thirteenth Guest*). With the release of the even more popular *The Thin Man*—about two months later, from the same company—this approach began to inspire many imitations. The mixture requires a difficult balance, with extraordinary directorial finesse and leading players possessed of great charm.

Mr. X handily matches *The Thin Man* for wit and surpasses it in atmosphere and suspense. Scripting and dialogue are as sophisticated as some British drawing-room farce, but the prevailing tides of romanticism and cleverness yield at all the right times to the basic mood of gathering horror. The straight-mystery source-novel had been a Crime Club selection in July of 1933, well before the launching of Universal's low-budget *Crime Club* series. Author Philip MacDonald (who used the pseudonym of Martin Porlock on the novel) helped with the screen version.

A prowling Mr. X has stabbed five London policemen to death. The commissioner, Sir Herbert Frensham (Henry Stephenson), hurries back from a rest cure with his daughter, Jane (Elizabeth Allan). They are met by Sir Christopher Marche (Ralph Forbes), Jane's fiancé, a pleasant but irresponsible sort.

Victim No. 6 dies outside a house where Nicholas Revel (Robert Montgomery), a gentlemanly burglar, is stealing a fabulous diamond. Marche, on a drunken wager, knocks out a bobby and steals his helmet as a trophy. Mr. X finds the fallen policeman and kills him. The police theorize that whoever took the diamond killed the bobby. Marche is charged with murder. Revel steps forward to clear Marche. Sir Herbert is impressed with Revel's theories for capturing X, but Inspector Connor (Lewis Stone) is distrustful. Marche finds Jane at Revel's apartment and, misunderstanding, breaks the engagement. Jane and Revel realize they have fallen in love.

To help Sir Herbert, Revel forges a letter in the style of Mr. X. Complications place Revel at risk of having framed himself. Jane is stunned to learn that Revel is a thief. Disguised as a bobby, Revel almost becomes the next victim. After a desperate chase, Revel corners X in an abandoned warehouse. They fight on an upper story, and X falls just as Connor and the police arrive. The dying Mr. X (Leonard Mudie), laughing, declares: "Squared it, Connor, with your blasted p'lice... I hate you. *Hate* you." Sir Herbert decides that the man who ended X's spree should be allied with Scotland Yard.

Now, one camp of mystery fans feels that *The Mystery of Mr. X* cheats the armchair detective of the opportunity to identify the culprit: The dreaded X proves to be a character not recognizably introduced until the end—and even then, left a mystery man. Director Edgar Selwyn, untroubled by this consideration, stated his opinion to the press:

"The most mysterious of all mysteries is the one which tells the least. This is not a conundrum, but a tenet of all mystery-story creation. The most dire feeling of dread is instilled by keeping the menace a secret. Its effect is felt, but it must not be seen. This is an iron-clad formula in the creation of eeriness.

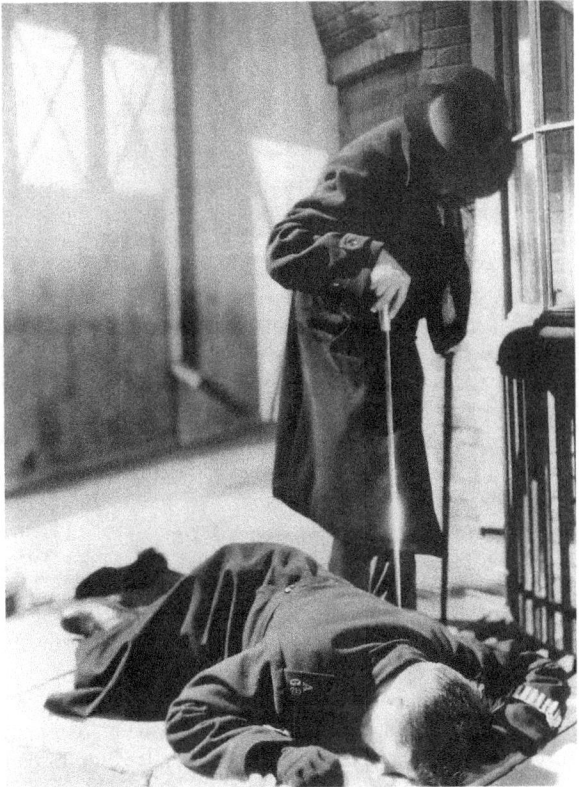

Mr. X counts coup.

"... The horror is known only as 'X,' whose shadow is seen passing over the inert bodies of his victims," continued Selwyn. "The snatch of song he whistles is heard. His living quarters are seen, even part of his shoulder. But not until the final exciting sequence does he appear. The underlying psychology is based on the world-old recognition that fear of an unknown assailant is more terrible than fear of a tangible object, no matter how imposing. Strong men have been known to break down as a result of imagined adversaries.

"Fear is instinctive. It is strongly allied with superstition and lurks in even the most sophisticated human mind. Thus mystery stories are always popular."

The director lives up to his words in *The Mystery of Mr. X*. Selwyn, in addition to being a film pioneer, was a successful writer, actor, director and producer on Broadway. His production of *Within the Law* in 1912 was one of the first plays to net $1,000,000. He and his younger brother, Arch, had founded the All Star Feature Films Corp. in 1912. The names of Selwyn and Samuel Goldfish, *née* Schmuel Gelbfisz, were combined upon the founding in 1917 of the Goldwyn Pictures Corp., *Goldwyn* sounding somehow more dignified than the other possible combination, *Selfish*. (Sam Goldfish liked the coined name so well that he changed his own to match.) From 1929 until shortly before his death at 68 in 1944, Edgar Selwyn worked for MGM, first as a writer-director—his *The Sin of Madelon Claudet* won an Academy Award for Helen Hayes in 1932—and later as a producer and executive.

Selwyn had the right partners on *X*. Merrill Pye's settings, superbly lighted and photographed and draped in studio fog, provide the ideal milieu for menace. The killer's whistling—an idea that may have been purloined from Fritz Lang's *M* (1930), but which had yet to become a cliché—adds to the eeriness. The atmosphere of terror is all the more pronounced because of the contrast with the cheerful romantic scenes and the shenanigans of a gang of likable crooks. The role of thief-detective-lover is tailor-made for Robert Montgomery, who as a dashing rogue was the closest rival to Ronald Colman. English actress Elizabeth Allan projects an innocence that makes her the ideal reformer for such a scoundrel.

Montgomery's chicanery finds fitting foils in Lewis Stone's taciturn and suspicious inspector and Henry Stephenson's cranky but gullible commissioner. Forrester Harvey, as an unscrupulous Cockney hack-driver, and Ivan Simpson, as a grouchy insurance agent, make the partners-in-crime antically true-to-life. As the killer, veteran English character actor Leonard Mudie provides a chilling glimpse of implacable hatred.

The story was remade with very few changes in 1952 by MGM British Studios as *The Hour of 13*, with Peter Lawford and Dawn Addams.

CREDITS: Producer: Lawrence Weingarten; Director: Edgar Selwyn; Screenplay: Howard Emmett Rogers; Adaptation: Philip MacDonald, from His 1933 Novel *The Mystery of the Dead Police*, a.k.a. *X vs. Rex*; Additional Dialogue: Monckton Hoffe; Art Director: Merrill Pye; Décor: Edwin B. Willis; Gowns: Adrian; Photographed by: Oliver T. Marsh; Music: Dr. William Axt; Songs: "This Is the Night" and "We'll Make Hay While the Sun Shines," by Nacio Herb Brown & Arthur Freed; Editor: Hugh Wynn; Western Electric Sound: Douglas Shearer; Special Effects: James Basevi and Robert T. Layton; Running Time: 84 minutes; Released: February 23, 1934

CAST: Robert Montgomery (Nicholas Revel); Elizabeth Allan (Jane Frensham); Lewis Stone (Inspector Connor); Henry Stephenson (Sir Herbert Frensham); Ralph Forbes (Sir Christopher Marche); Forrester Harvey (Palmer); Ivan Simpson (Hutchinson); Leonard Mudie (Mr. X); Alec B. Francis (Judge Malpas); Charles Irwin (Willis); Lumsden Hare (Officer); Claude King (Crown Prosecutor); Olaf Hytten (Reporter); Barlowe Borland (Waiter); Ted Billings (Drinker)

THE BLACK CAT
(Universal Pictures Corp.; 1934)

On honeymoon in Europe are Peter Alison (David Manners), an author of outlandish crime yarns, and his bride, Joan (Jacqueline Wells). A mix-up in train reservations obliges the couple to share a compartment with the debonair but vaguely sinister Dr. Vitus Werdegast (Bela Lugosi). Werdegast is bound for Vizhegrad "to visit... an old friend." Peter is disturbed by the stranger's piercing scrutiny of Joan. Werdegast explains that she reminds him of his wife, whom he has not seen since he went to the battlefront—"Kaiser and country, you know"—18 years ago. He has survived imprisonment in Siberia. "Many men went... and few have returned," Werdegast snarls. "*I* have returned."

Thus opens Edgar G. Ulmer's *The Black Cat*, a recognized and still-provocative classic of not merely its genre, but also of the cinema of visionary pictorial design, and of provocative subversion as a class. In its day, however, *The Black Cat* was an albatross for some key participants, and a red flag for the censors—a film that can only have caused Universal Pictures honcho Carl Laemmle, Sr., to wonder why he had helped to launch the talkie-era horror-movie bandwagon in the first place.

Laemmle, a family man who took pride in purveying wholesome entertainment, was a founder of the Motion Pictures Producers & Distributors Association, which originated in 1922 as a self-regulatory agency to help allay censorship problems at the state and local levels. Its Production Code of 1930, which the member-studios took as gospel, discouraged material that might be construed as profane or salacious or an encouragement to criminal misconduct or licentious behavior. The Code was lenient enough to pose few problems, and there was little worry over occasional nudity or profanity.

The honeymoon ended in the spring of 1934, when a committee of Jesuit bishops formed the National Legion of Decency, a strong-arm group that urged all right-minded Catholics to boycott theaters showing films deemed immoral, lest there be the devil to pay. An alarming tightening of the Production Code resulted. For reasons that defy understanding,

An accident, then shelter—or not!

The Definitive Edition

Lugosi and Karloff match wits.

horror films were a prime target; the Legion automatically classed them as objectionable, sight unseen. A corresponding attitude surfaced among the British censors, who barred minors from seeing the chillers even after the pictures had been scissored beyond recognition. Some such films were refused permits to enter the U.K. countries on grounds that they were "against nature." Several Continental European countries were equally intolerant.

The pressure hurt most, of course, at the box office. It is hardly surprising, then, that Universal released only one purebred horror film during 1934: *The Black Cat*, which is a benchmark on the face of it as the first film to co-star Boris Karloff and Bela Lugosi—if one ignores a cornball meeting-of-bogeymen staged for the *Universal Newsreel*. (The stars' token appearances in *Gift of Gab* occurred a few months later.) After a long gestation and many false starts, *The Black Cat* went before the cameras late in February.

Plans had begun germinating in December 1932, when stories were being bought right-and-left for Karloff. Universal's scenario editor, Richard Schrayer, made a tentative adaptation. A treatment, "The Brain Never Dies," by Jack Cunningham and Stanley Bergerman, utilized ideas from two stories by Edgar Allan Poe, "The Black Cat" and "The Fall of the House of Usher," and created for Karloff the role of Dr. Metta, a mad scientist. When this was rejected, Cunningham fattened up Schayer's version—Karloff's role being that of Edgar Doe, who seals his wife behind a basement wall. This version also failed to pass muster, and another treatment was developed by Tom Kilpatrick and Dale Van Every. E.A. Dupont, of the German masterpiece *Variety*, was docketed as director, but the project was abandoned when Universal suspended operations temporarily in a seizure of Depression-choked cash flow.

Edgar G. Ulmer, assigned to direct in late 1933, decided to write his own scenario. He concocted a plot suggested by the newsmaking escapades of an English Satanist leader, Alastair

Crowley. Crowley had inspired W. Somerset Maugham's novel, *The Magician*, which Rex Ingram filmed as a silent. The Ulmer script was completed by a young detective-story writer, Peter Ruric (known in the pulp magazines as Paul Cain), with input from Tom Kilpatrick and Ulmer's future wife, Shirley Kassel. This rendition was approved in February of 1934—on condition that a black cat be worked in. (And so one was, but only just.) Revisions continued even after filming had started. Principal photography began on February 28, 1934, and finished 19 days later at a cost of only $95,745. This span includes two days and nights of retakes, which served to make Lugosi's role less menacing.

The Black Cat was the first film to co-star Lugosi and Karloff.

The hard-won final version, amazingly coherent for all its internal and external problems, goes a whole lot like this:

As the Alisons board a bus, they are joined by Werdegast and a mute giant, Thamal (Harry Cording). The driver (George Davis) explains they are traversing one of the war's great battlefields: "The house of Engineer Poelzig now stands... on the very foundations of the... greatest graveyard in the world!"

The bus crashes. Reaching the Poelzig mansion, the survivors are confronted by the evil-faced Andreas (Egon Brecher), the majordomo. Werdegast orders the man to wake his master, then dresses Joan's wounds. Poelzig (Karloff) regards Werdegast silently as the latter accuses him of bygone treacheries. Peter enters, and the enemies become smilingly cordial. Peter remarks that the house has an atmosphere difficult to describe. "It may be an atmosphere of death," replies Werdegast. Poelzig agrees, adding that the onetime fortress still is undermined with dynamite.

Poelzig's black cat wanders in. Werdegast cries out in horror, hurls a knife that kills the cat, and collapses. Joan enters, and Peter observes a change in her. Poelzig explains: "You must be indulgent with Dr. Werdegast. He is the victim of... an intense and all-consuming horror of cats." Werdegast suggests that Joan may have become "mediumistic, a vehicle for all the intangible forces in operation around us."

In a subterranean hiding-place, Poelzig surveys glass cases containing the bodies of young women. Later, he resumes his conversation with Werdegast, who demands to be taken to his wife. Poelzig escorts him to one of the corpses. "You see, Vitus? I have cared for her tenderly and well." Poelzig adds that Werdegast's daughter also has died. Werdegast draws a revolver but drops it on seeing the shadow of a cat.

Poelzig lies down beside his slumbering wife, who exactly resembles the dead Karen. She is Werdegast's daughter. "You are the very core and meaning of my life," he says. From a book, *The Rites of Lucifer*, Poelzig reads: "[I]n the dark of the moon, the High Priest assembles his followers for the sacrifice. The chosen maiden..."

Werdegast accuses Poelzig of planning to keep Joan. "Do you dare play chess for her?" asks Poelzig.

"...an intense and all-consuming horror of cats."

Peter and Joan find themselves unable to depart. Peter tries to telephone. "Did you hear that, Vitus?" Poelzig asks. "Even the *'phone* is dead." He redirects his attention to a chessboard and a moment later adds, "Check. Mate." Joan is locked in her room, and Peter is imprisoned.

After Werdegast delivers a warning to Joan and then leaves, Karen (Lucille Lund) enters. Joan realizes who the girl must be and tells her that her father has come for her. Poelzig enters and forces Karen away.

The worshippers gather. Joan is taken to an altar. Werdegast and Thamal hide and watch as Poelzig calls upon Satan. A woman in the congregation faints. Werdegast and Thamal take advantage of the diversion and carry Joan down a stair. Werdegast finds the body of his daughter in Poelzig's embalming room.

Werdegast subdues Poelzig. "Did you ever see an animal skinned, Hjalamar?" Werdegast asks. "That's what I'm going to do to you... " Peter escapes, takes the fallen Andreas' pistol, and is drawn by screams. Misreading the situation, he shoots Werdegast.

"You poor *fool!* I only wanted to *help*," says Werdegast. "Now go—please, *go!*" As the couple flees, Werdegast reminds Poelzig of the undermining explosives: "In five minutes, Marmaros, you and I, and your rotten *cult* will be *no more*." He slams the lever into place and waits in suicidal triumph: "It has been a *good* game."

Later, on the train to Budapest, Peter finds a newspaper review of his latest mystery novel. The article chides him for writing about perils so fantastic they couldn't possibly happen.

No sooner had shooting been completed, than the Legion of Decency dispatched its Fun Police, who administered the worst mauling any Universal film had suffered since 1922-23, when Erich von Stroheim's *Foolish Wives* ran afoul of the New York State censors. Among the casualties were scenes making it explicit that the bride had been possessed by the soul of a cat. Also cut were details of the Black Mass, including a dance performed by Anna Duncan, cousin of the famed Isadora. The well-advertised dancer was left with brief scenes as a servant.

Even this shadow of the original was denounced. It remains today a focus of controversy. Some present-day kvetchers mimic the beratement that was common among critics of the day: a confusing hodgepodge of morbidity and bad taste. Others consider it finery of the highest Art Deco order, as well as the *meisterverk* of the erratic but highly individualistic and forward-thinking Ulmer. The director told us that *The Black Cat* was his own favorite. It is easy to see why: Seldom in commercial

Lugosi, Karloff and Lucille Lund in the chamber of death.

cinema has a film so reflected the personal vision of its principal creator. Ulmer took a hand in set and costume design and encouraged his brilliant but alcoholic cameraman, John Mescall, to provide photography markedly different from most other work of the period.

There was tension on the set because Karloff had the juicier role and a much larger salary than Lugosi, who began here to perceive a rivalry that was, in fact, more perception than reality; Lugosi carried the bitterness to his grave, although he and Karloff would continue to work beneficially together and even find moments of camaraderie. Certainly, Ulmer pampered Karloff, who remembered the role fondly in our conversations of the 1960s: "Such a magnificently sybaritic array of costuming," Karloff said. Macked out to the nines in robes, black silk pajamas, and a smoking jacket that fashion designers were quick to copy, and made up by Jack Pierce with a plunging widow's peak that caused him to look sinister but fascinating, Karloff reveled in the air of suave monstrosity. Here is one of Karloff's few 100-percent villains, one in which even he could find little humanity—but here, too, is his most glamorous characterization.

For Lugosi, Ulmer provided no less interesting a change of pace—a tailor-made role that is one of the best of a checkered career. Lugosi is mysterious, balanced precariously upon the brink of madness, and yet he is wholly sympathetic. It has often been suggested that the roles should have been reversed, but Lugosi ultimately admitted he was pleased to play a tragic hero. Wholly himself, Lugosi plays it straightforwardly, enhancing the script's indulgences in rich self-mockery. When David Manners suggests that Lugosi's talk of Satanism is "a lot of supernatural baloney," Lugosi replies with droll *misterioso*: "Supernatural, perhaps. Baloney—perhaps *not*. There are *many* things under the sun." After Karloff has had David Manners beaten unconscious and ordered Jacqueline Wells imprisoned, Lugosi sternly tells him, "I hope you won't carry this too *far*, Hjalamar!"

Lugosi and Karloff in a relaxed moment backstage

Some of the dialogue is almost poetic, such as Lugosi's accusations against Karloff: "You left the *rest* of us to *die*. It is not to be wondered at, that you chose *this* place to build your home? A masterpiece of construction, built upon the ruins of the masterpiece of des*truc*tion—the masterpiece of *murder*. The murderer of 10,000 men returns to the scene of his *crime*. Those who died were *for*tunate... Fifteen years, I've rotted in darkness... *Now*, I've come *back*, not to kill *you*, but to kill your *soul*."

The sets are far removed from the Medieval gloom of most other Universal chillers. Action is concentrated in luxurious, futuristic surroundings. Some of the super-house's appointments—a digital clock, for example—are familiar today, having been assimilated by designers during the intervening decades, but the overall effect remains one of ultra-Bauhaus modernity.

Stunning visuals justify fully the languorous unfolding. This gradual building process terminates abruptly in a savage climax that is all the more dramatic for its unexpectedness. The dominant tone is one of hovering, impatient evil. Early on, we learn that the house is mined for destruction. This oppressive aura is made more so by Karloff's necrophilia and his prurient interest in the young bride, and by Lugosi's smoldering hatred.

The camera performs with a distinctive virtuosity. Mescall provides deep-focus shots in the best James Wong Howe manner, but the focus shifts artfully from background to foreground and back again when Karloff's hand tightens upon a statuette of a nude woman as the possessed bride passionately kisses her bewildered husband. Carefully composed stationary shots are juxtaposed with scenes in which the camera moves alongside Karloff and Lugosi within the underground domain. Here, the lens becomes subjective, roaming the shadowy corridors as Karloff's voice comes over softly and almost free of emotion: "Come, Vitus... Are we not both as much victims of the war as those whose bodies were torn asunder?... Did we not *both* die here...? We under*stand* each other. We know too much of life. We shall play a little game—a game of *death*, if you like."

A dreamlike passage is handled much differently. In seven curiously angled shots linked by slow dissolves, Karloff walks these same corridors, absently stroking a black cat. Five times, he halts before the encased corpses, gazing inscrutably at these sacrifices. This sequence anticipates by a dozen years the celebrated journey of Josette Day through the chateau in Cocteau's *La Belle et la Bete/Beauty and the Beast* (France; 1946), but without resort to the artifice of slowed motion. Such a blending of the horrific and the delicate, needless to say, annoyed critics and customers alike.

Music is as important as dialogue, settings and camerawork. Heinz Roemheld's score is among the decade's most elaborate, a far cry from the forcible silences of 1931's *Dracula* and *Frankenstein* and more sophisticated than the bravura music for *The Mummy* and *The Invisible Man* of 1933. In later years, Roemheld would term it the most technically challenging of his works.

The main title is accompanied by a free-form orchestral adaptation of the opening to Liszt's *Piano Sonata in B Minor*, followed by a sensuously beautiful original theme, "Cat Love," which bespeaks Roemheld's idolization of Tschaikowski. Early in the film, Karloff turns a dial and the house is flooded with the strains of Schubert's *Symphony No. 8*, which underscores Lugosi's betrayal of his fear of cats. Excerpts from other Euro-classical works are similarly woven in, but the score is not at all like the pastiches used by cue-sheet arrangers as accompaniment for silent pictures; rather, it is a superbly unified fantasia upon classical and original themes.

The appropriately melodramatic music of Liszt predominates, with portions of the *Sonata in B Minor*, "Les Preludes," "The Rakoczy March," "Tasso," and the *Hungarian Rhapsody No. 3*. The second movement of Beethoven's *Seventh Symphony* forms an ominous accompaniment to a speech by Karloff. Dramatic use is made of a Chopin prelude, Brahms' "Sapphic Ode," and Schumann's *Piano Quintet*. Bach's *Doric Toccata* and *Adagio in A Minor* are played on screen (Karloff and John Carradine appear at the organ, although of course they are not performing the music) as celebrants gather for the Black Mass. Interwoven with the Old Masters are seven variations on "Cat Love" (designated in the score as "Scream," "Neutral," "Foreboding," "Suspense," "Crawl," "Interlude" and "Threat") as well as 14 self-contained compositions bearing such manuscript titles as "Hungarian Train," "Fantasy," "Introduction and Religioso," "Karloff," and "Hungarian Burlesque." Much of this music gained additional popularity in the *Flash Gordon* serials of later years. "Cat Love" is particularly remembered as Queen Azura's theme in *Flash Gordon's Trip to Mars* (1938) and continually is mistaken for Tschaikowski's Overture to *Romeo and Juliet*.

Grim as it all is, the picture has some leavening of humor. The best such bit is provided by two comical gendarmes, played by Albert Conti and Henry Armetta. David Manners and Jacqueline Wells, at another point, belabor the mispronunciation of Karloff's character name to breezy effect. (Miss Wells, who had come to film as a child player, was just seven years away from her transformation to Julie Bishop at Warner Bros.)

Edgar George Ulmer was educated at the Academy of Arts & Sciences of his native Vienna, then went to Berlin to study. By age 18, he had sufficient experience as a stage actor and set designer to land an art director's berth at Decla-Bioscop. He served as production assistant to two of Germany's most celebrated directors, Paul Wegener and F.W. Murnau. He also worked on several of Max Reinhardt's stage spectacles, coming to America with Reinhardt in 1923. During the next 10 years, he designed sets for Universal, Fox, MGM, Universum Film Aktien (UFA) in Berlin, and the Philadelphia Grand Opera. Once again, he worked with Murnau, this time at Fox.

Like Erich von Stroheim, Ulmer tended to place himself at loggerheads with the studio bosses, and consequently most of his pictures were made cheaply for independent companies. Ulmer's reckless sin while at Universal was to woo and win the wife of an in-house producer,

Lugosi trips the switch.

Max Alexander, a nepotistically situated nephew of Carl Laemmle, Sr. The sacrificial scissoring of *The Black Cat* was clearly more a matter of appeasement to the outside forces of censorship, but Universal's suits-in-power can only have considered the film's mangling a comeuppance for Ulmer. Later on, Ulmer made sex-exploitation films; seminal film noir entries; Polish-, Ukrainian- and Yiddish-dialogue films; and black-ensemble pictures for very limited markets. On occasion, he managed to indulge his gifts with respectable budgets on such visually lavish projects as *The Strange Woman* (1946), *Carnegie Hall* (1947) and *Ruthless* (1948). Some of his more intriguing work occurred late in life, including a color remake of *L'Atlantide* (1961) and—his last project—the unusual Italian-German production of *The Cavern* (1965). Ulmer died in 1972.

Quite a cult-of-personality following has developed around Ulmer, largely on the basis of his impoverished but often brilliant pictures for Producers Releasing Corp. during the middle 1940s—especially *Bluebeard* and *Detour*. As a result, the often-maligned *The Black Cat* has received belated recognition as the remarkable work it has been all along. The film is not to be confused with Universal's 1941 *The Black Cat*, which despite a common inspiration in Poe is a distinct, and distinctly inferior, job.

CREDITS: Producer: Carl Laemmle, Jr.; Associate Producer, E.M. Asher; Director: Edgar G. Ulmer; Suggested by: Edgar Allan Poe's Story; Screenplay: Peter Ruric; Story: Edgar Ulmer and Peter Ruric; Added Dialogue and Script Clerk: Shirley Kassel; Continuity: Tom Kilpatrick; Art Director: Charles D. Hall; Music: Heinz Roemheld; Photographed by: John Mescall; Editor: Ray Curtiss; Special Effects: John P. Fulton; Effects Camera: David S. Horsley; Makeup: Jack P. Pierce; Matte Paintings: Jack Cosgrove and Russell Lawson; Set Décor: R.A. Gausman; Assistant Directors: William Reiger and Sam Rosenthal; Western Electric Sound: Gilbert Kurland; Music Recording: Lawrence Aicholtz; Costumes: Edgar G. Ulmer, Vera West and Ed Ware; Art Titles: Max Cohen; Additional Script Clerk: Moree Herring; Running Time: 64 minutes; Released: May 7, 1934

CAST: Boris Karloff (Hjalamar Poelzig); Bela Lugosi (Vitus Werdegast); David Manners (Peter Alison); Jacqueline Wells (Joan Alison); Lucille Lund (Karen); Egon Brecher (Majordomo); Harry Cording (Thamal); Henry Armetta (Gendarme); Albert Conti (Lieutenant); Anna Duncan (Maid); Andre Cheron (Conductor); George Davis (Bus Driver); Tony Marlow (Border Patrolman); Paul Weigel (Stationmaster); Rodney Hildebrand (Brakeman); John Carradine (Organist); Michael Mark, Paul Panzer, Symona Boniface, Frazer Acosta, King Baggot, Louis

Behind the scenes on the soundstage.

January, Peggy Terry, Virginia Ainsworth, Duskal Blaine and Harry Walker (Cultists). Players Cut from Released Version: Andy Devine, Lenore Kingston, Herman Bing, Alphonse Martel, Luis Alberni, Albert Poulet

Nils Asther and Renee Gadd star in *The Love Captive*.

THE LOVE CAPTIVE
(Universal Pictures Corp.; 1934)

Virtually forgotten, even by devotees of the Universal chillers, is an oddity called *The Love Captive*. This variation on *Svengali* deals effectively in weirdness without any of the expected dark shadings. Even as a fresh release, the picture failed to attract much attention. Which is the moviegoers' loss, for *The Love Captive* is a creditable perfect-crime yarn with a movingly loathsome Human Monster and a soul-satisfying jolt of a surprise ending.

Dr. Alexis Collender (Nils Asther), an unscrupulous hypnotist, influences his office nurse, Alice Trask (Gloria Stuart), to set up housekeeping with him and break her engagement to Dr. Norman Ware (Paul Kelly). When a reporter, Larry Chapman (Russ Brown), publicizes Collender's healing gifts, the quack becomes sufficiently well known to move into luxurious quarters. Ware wants to kill Collender but is dissuaded by his lawyer, Roger Loft (Alan Dinehart). Ware does, however, prompt charges of lapsed ethics against Collender from the local medical society. Mary Williams (Virginia Kami), a prior victim, promises to testify. Collender brings Mary once more under his power, and she retracts her accusations.

The medical society is meeting at Loft's estate. Collender demands an opportunity to demonstrate his powers, proposing an experiment in which a person under his influence cannot fire a hair-trigger pistol. Barred from the meeting, Collender encounters Loft's beautiful young wife, Valerie (Renee Gadd), and entrances her. Loft and Ware see that Valerie has fallen under

Asther enthralls Renee Gadd.

a strange influence: She becomes increasingly restless when kept away from Collender. At last, Collender is granted a hearing. Loft volunteers himself as a subject. Collender stares into Loft's eyes and makes with the mesmeric gestures: "You will try to shoot me but will be unable to do so." Loft aims at Collender's heart and squeezes the trigger. The hypnotist is killed, and the lawyer is exonerated.

Playwright Max Marcin, onetime New York newspaperman and magazine writer, came to Hollywood during the early-talkie period after creating a string of successful Broadway plays including *House of Glass*, *Cheating Cheaters*, *See My Lawyer*, *Three Live Ghosts*, *The Woman in Room 13*, *Silence* and *The Humbug*—all of which were purchased by various movie studios.

The climactic encounter

Marcin helmed several features for Paramount. Early in 1934, he was brought to Universal to direct *The Humbug*, under which title *The Love Captive* was produced.

Marcin avoided Gothic trappings and frightful makeups in this amply mounted production, which was filmed during April and May with the assistance of movie veteran Edward Venturini. Marcin intended a sophisticated, up-to-date look with a glamorous villain, lavish settings, clever dialogue and characters from the upper crust of big-city society. Much of the action takes place in a palatial mansion; the climactic scenes are enacted in a medical observatory where hundreds of scientists have gathered. Gil Warrenton, former cinematographer to the German master, Paul Leni, lighted most of the scenes in a sparkling style usually reserved for the top-shelf romantic dramas.

Nils Asther, that darkly handsome Swede who specialized in Valentino-like romantic heroes, was chosen as the mesmerist. Marcin even had Asther shave off his well-known mustache so he would have none of the distinguishing affectations of the typical movie villain. The actor's almost Oriental eyes, shown in close-up during the scenes involving hypnosis, are Marcin's only concession to a horror-movie style. Alan Dinehart and Paul Kelly bring dynamism to the more straightforward roles. Gloria Stuart, one of Old Hollywood's more nearly perfect ingénues, and Renee Gadd, an English musical-comedy star, are charming and sympathetic as innocent victims.

Marcin, needless to say, was appalled when Universal's New York office, in a last-moment indulgence of sensationalism, rechristened *The Humbug*—first as *Enemy of Women* (a title that appears on premature promotional materials) and at length as *The Love Captive*.

CREDITS: Producer: Carl Laemmle, Jr.; Associate Producer: E.M. Asher; Director: Max Marcin; Associate Director: Edward Dan Venturini; Based upon: Max Marcin's Play, *The Humbug*; Dialogue and Continuity: Karen DeWolf; Photographed by: Gilbert Warrenton; Art

Director: Charles D. Hall; Editor: Ted Kent; Special Effects: John P. Fulton; Musical Score: Bernhard Kaun, Howard Jackson, Sam A. Perry and Cecil Arnold; Set Décor: R.A. Gausman; Makeup: Jack P. Pierce; Sound System: Western Electric; Running Time: 65 minutes; Released: May 21, 1934

CAST: Nils Asther (Dr. Alexis Collender); Gloria Stuart (Alice Trask); Paul Kelly (Dr. Norman Ware); Alan Dinehart (Roger Loft); Renee Gadd (Valerie Loft); Virginia Kami (Mary Williams); Russ Brown (Larry Chapman); Addison Richards (Dr. Collins); John Wray (Jules Glass); Robert Grieg (Butler); Jane Meredith (Mrs. Fordyce); Ellalee Ruby (Annie Nolan); Franklyn Ardell (Peter Nolan); Sam Godfrey (Dr. Blake); Demetrius Alexis (Dr. Freund)

SMOKING GUNS
(Ken Maynard Productions/Universal Pictures Corp.; 1934)

Recipe for an exercise in mind-boggling cockamamie horrifical lunacy: Take a Saturday-matinee cowboy shoot-'em-up, then stage most of its action on a Halloween night in a haunted house, replete with hidden panels and portraits with peep-hole eyes. Add a spooky graveyard, a lost mine, a jungle manhunt, malaria and murder, gangrene and alligators, parenticide and suicide and insanity, amnesia and abundant leading-lady cleavage and mistaken identity and Southern-fried backwater superstition. Keep the standard Western ingredients—brawls, hard-riding chases, gunplay and dutiful-unto-death Texas Rangers—in generous proportion, and you'll have some idea of what strange places *Smoking Guns* is coming from.

The weirdest horse opera in a century-and-change of the filmmaking art stars Ken Maynard, in a story concocted by Ken Maynard, produced by Ken Maynard Productions, Inc. The official credits neglect to mention that Maynard also did the second-unit location photography (in the sweltering Yucatan, where he traveled in his own airplane) and arranged the music performed for a dance sequence by his own string band, Ken Maynard's Buckaroos. Had the situation demanded, Maynard also could have composed the theme music and handled the singing and fiddle-playing, as he had done in some of his earlier films. He didn't direct—his close associate, Alan James (professional name of Alvin J. Neitz), handled that chore—but *Smoking Guns* is as intensely personal a film as anything by Chaplin or von Stroheim, and every bit as eccentric.

It is most remarkable that this blessedly harebrained nightmare of a Texas Gothic also manages to supply the traditional slam-bang action demanded by the Western-movie fans. The staged mayhem resulted in a broken foot and lacerations for Harold Goodwin, two loosened teeth for Eddie Cobb, a black eye for Cliff Lyons, a severed thumb-tip for Tom Summerville and multiple injuries for Benny Corbett. Maynard displays his brilliant riding and rope-climbing stunts. The youngsters who made up a large portion of Maynard's audience can only have been puzzled by a gag in which black comedian Martin Turner retrieves a mislaid good luck charm from inside the dress of his buxom sweetheart (Etta McDaniel, sister of the more famous Hattie), as well as the ending where Ken snuggles up to his bosomy leading lady (Gloria Shea) in a wagon bed instead of riding away on his famed Palomino, Tarzan. Likewise not for the kids are the ravings of a crazed law enforcer (Walter Miller) when he realizes he has contracted gangrene:

"Rotting like carrion in the sun! Eating its way up, *up*, UP!... To lay here and die by inches, to rot away like something un*clean*...!"

It all starts with Ken Masters (Maynard) accusing Silas Stone (William Gould) of framing Ken's father for murder. Silas' son, Hank (Harold Goodwin), in attempting to conk Ken with a chunk of ore, kills Silas. The Texas Rangers arrive to arrest Ken, who escapes.

Three years later, Ranger Dick Logan (Miller) tracks Ken to a desolate swamp in the Yucatan. Ken surrenders willingly, for he has decided he must clear his name and that of

Ken Maynard and Walter Miller find themselves swamped.

his father. Logan collapses with malaria. Ken's boat is capsized by alligators, one of which mangles Logan's leg. Ken takes the lawman to an abandoned cabin. Ken prepares to perform an emergency amputation. (As if to explain his surgical skills, Ken says: "[O]n the dodge, I learned a lot of things—I lived among strange people.") Logan commits suicide before Ken can start sawing. He leaves a note that Ken must deliver to Alice Adams (Miss Shea), daughter of Logan's boss, Capt. Adams (Jack Rockwell, that perfect Western authority figure).

On Halloween, Ken returns to town and impersonates Logan. He fools everybody except Alice and Hank Stone. Ken gives Alice the note, which declares a belief in Ken's innocence. Hank, who is in love with Alice, orders his henchmen to kill Ken during a barn dance. Adams' servant, Cinders (Turner), takes his girlfriend, Clementine (Miss McDaniel), spooning in the graveyard. The purported ghost of Ken's father appears at the reputedly haunted Masters house.

Ken and Cinders find themselves tormented by make-believe ghosts, actually Stone's thugs. Alice overhears Stone ordering an ambush. Her father summons the Rangers. The apparition of Bob Masters (Ed Coxen) is the man himself, tormented to distraction by the Stone mob. One of the heavies beats the oldster, inadvertently restoring his memory. Ken and Cinders learn the reason for Stone's actions: A gold mine lies under the house. Stone abducts Alice in a buckboard. Ken pursues astride Tarzan, snatching Alice to safety and leaping into the wagon, which plunges over a cliff.

Maynard's productions invariably cost more than Universal wanted to spend. This 16th and last of his pictures for Universal, which was shot under the un-Westernlike title *Doomed To Die*, went well past a three-week shooting schedule while costs soared beyond the $125,000 ceiling. Carl Laemmle, Jr., production chief and son of the president, considered the script outlandish—

an opinion not entirely unjustified—and ordered portions remade along more conventional lines, thus triggering Maynard's famously hotheaded temperament.

Already seething because he suspected the Laemmles were planning to replace him with Buck Jones—which they were—Maynard gave Junior a royal cussing-out and left for Europe without altering so much as a frame. Junior wanted to axe the film but could not do so because it had been pre-sold. The strange opus was previewed in April of 1934 as *Doomed To Die*, but then it was recalled and finally released under the generically upbeat name, *Smoking Guns*. (Which is precisely the kind of matinee-Western title that Mel Brooks spoofed with *Blazing Saddles* in 1974.) Maynard was kaput at Universal, and the most popular Western series of the early 1930s came to an end. Maynard's later films for Columbia and other, lesser, companies were not produced by him and are but pale shadows of his Universals.

Maynard was a unique star with a fanatical following. At Universal, he received from $40,000 to $60,000 per picture plus a hefty percentage. Whatever his shortcomings as an actor and however preposterous his story sense, his films are so Promethean in their defiance of formula and so permeated with the artist's zest for living as to stand apart.

It must have infuriated Junior Laemmle that *Smoking Guns* proved immensely popular. The picture boasts beautiful photography by Ted McCord, vivid settings by Ralph Berger and some spirited, authentically Western (*not* Country & Western) music. The dramatic scoring is that of a weird mystery film, rather than the jazzy rodeo-styled martial cues of the typical oat opera.

Maynard's do-it-yourself footage of real 'gators in the Yucatan is interspersed with backlot action involving several scary but patently bogus saurians left over from *East of Borneo* (1931). Interiors and scenes in the swamp, the town, the graveyard and the old house were made at the studio. The climactic chase was photographed on Dark Canyon Road, running through the mountains just southeast of the backlot.

Gloria Shea plays the ingénue with real grit and more voluptuosity than the Westerns usually required; but then, Maynard was a breed apart. There are colorful performances from Walter Miller (Pathé's former serial star), Harold Goodwin, Bob Kortman, Jack Rockwell, Martin Turner, Etta McDaniel and the stock company of horseback heavies. Tarzan, as always, is magnificent.

CREDITS: Producer and Original Scenarist: Ken Maynard; Director: Alan James (Alvin J. Neitz); Screenplay and Dialogue: Nate Gatzert; Photography: Ted McCord; Art Director: Ralph Berger; RCA Photophone Sound: Earl Crane; Editor: Charles Harris; Properties: Tom Summerville; Musical Score: Ken Maynard, Louis de Francesco, Sam A. Perry, Heinz Roemheld and David Broekman; Titles: Max Cohen; Second Unit Photography: Ken Maynard; Running Time: 65 minutes; Released: June 11, 1934

CAST: Ken Maynard (Ken Masters); Gloria Shea (Alice Adams); Walter Miller (Dick Logan); Harold Goodwin (Hank Stone); William Gould (Silas Stone); Bob Kortman (Bill); Jack Rockwell (Capt. Adams); Ed Coxen (Bob Masters); Charles "Slim" Whitaker (Slim); Martin Turner (Cinders); Etta McDaniel (Clementine); Ken Maynard's Buckaroos (Musicians); and Wally Wales, Frank S. Hagney, Ben Corbett, Edmund Cobb, Cliff Lyons, Cliff Smith, Fred McKaye, Bill Stone, Charles Murphy, Ted Billings, Jim Corey, Hank Bell, Bob Reeves, Blackjack Ward, Dick Dickenson

THE MAN WITH TWO FACES
(First National Pictures, Inc./Warner Bros. Pictures, Inc.; 1934)

Damon Wells (Edward G. Robinson) is the most brilliant director-actor of the Broadway stage. His beautiful sister, Jessica Vance (Mary Astor), is one of the theater's brightest stars. Recovering from a breakdown, Jessica is about to return to Broadway. Weston (Ricardo Cortez), Jessica's sweetheart, feels certain that Jessica's illness was caused by her presumed-dead husband, Stanley Vance (Louis Calhern), who maintained a mesmeric influence over her.

And now Vance returns, cheerfully admitting that he has been in San Quentin for a crime committed under another name. Jessica lapses into decline. How to dispose of the rotter for good? Enter the mysterious Chautard, whom no one seems to recognize as Edward G. Robinson—the dual-role performance is that convincing.

A faithful adaptation of *Dark Tower*, a then-fresh play by two of Broadway's favorite gadabouts, Alexander Woolcott and George S. Kaufman, the film was abruptly rechristened *The Man with Two Faces*, a title that along with a blatant advertising campaign provided a sure tip-off of a mystery angle that the play and the film themselves would save until the last. The picture surmounts such promotional gaucherie, though, and it remains one of the better twists on *Svengali*. Dialogue sparkles with wit despite the prevailing grimness, and the theatrical background is vividly realized.

The loathsome Vance seems unstoppable. Then Chautard, purportedly a wealthy producer from France, approaches Vance about purchasing foreign rights for Jessica's current play. For the right price, Vance is willing to sell both Jessica's rights and her honor. Whereupon Chautard croaks Vance, then watches his victim's death throes with immense pleasure.

Chautard has disappeared. All the police except one investigator, Curtis (David Landau), a theater buff, give up in bafflement. In Damon's dressing room, Curtis hands the actor a blond mustache. He found it, he explains, in the Gideon Bible in the room where Vance was murdered. Curtis tells Wells that the district attorney is a very understanding man.

Robinson dominates the proceedings with forceful and distinct performances. Makeup artist Perc Westmore transformed the star into Chautard by utilizing a false nose, blond hair, mustache and goatee, teeth caps, and pince-nez glasses. He rounded Robinson's naturally slanted eyes and angular eyebrows.

Mary Astor is equally adept as the Trilby of the piece. The tall, high-nosed Louis Calhern makes Vance completely despicable, described by one character as "the lowest form of animal life." As if to illustrate, Calhern is shown as being fond of a pair of caged mice, but he regards his

Louis Calhern and Edward G. Robinson in *The Man with Two Faces*

fellow humans with an arrogance that inspires dislike at once. A servant takes scornful notice of the mice and remarks, "I'd like to know when the three of you are leaving." Calhern replies with a sneer: "If you hurt these mice, I shall have the extreme pleasure of knocking you down and kicking your brains out."

Henry O'Neil is convincing as the stage-struck detective. Such notables as Mae Clarke, Ricardo Cortez, and Arthur Byron perform lesser roles with the customary skill.

Archie Mayo, director of the purebred Gothic *Svengali*, does an equally good job here of presenting a similar idea in a modern, glamorous setting. The scenes of theatrical life, both on- and off-stage, have realism and depth, being handled much differently from those pictured so glamorously in the many backstage musicals filmed on the same Warners sets. Tony Gaudio's manipulation of lights and camera angles is vital to the blending of sophistication with the sinister.

The picture originally ended differently from the released version. It had to be reshot on orders from the newly strengthened Production Code Administration. In the original finale, after Curtis confronts Wells with the telltale mustache, Wells is certain he will be nabbed for murder, but the cop merely advises him to be more careful. The world is better off without Vance, Curtis muses, and as far as he is concerned the case is unsolved. The replacement scene, suggesting that Wells can expect a lenient sentence, really compromises nothing.

In 1939, the same studio scheduled a new version from a script by Anthony Coldewey, projecting Claude Rains and Boris Karloff for the respective Robinson and Calhern roles. It was aborted because of objections from the Legion of Decency. Later, the property was passed on to Warners' British company, which produced it in 1943 as *Dark Tower*, with Ben Lyon and Herbert Lom—this time, in a circus setting.

CREDITS: Producer: Robert Lord; Director: Archie Mayo; Based upon: the Woolcott & Kaufman Play *Dark Tower*, as Produced by Sam H. Harris Theatrical Enterprises, Inc.; Screenplay: Tom Reed and Niven Busch; Photographed by: Tony Gaudio; Editor: William Holmes; Art Director: John Hughes; Musical Score: Leo F. Forbstein, Conducting the Vitaphone Orchestra; Songs: "Stormy Weather," by Ted Koehler & Harold Arlen, and "Am I Blue?" by Harry Akst; Makeup: Perc Westmore; Special Effects: Fred Jackman; Sound Effects: Hal R. Shaw; Sound System: RCA Photophone; Running Time: 72 minutes; Released: August 4, 1934

CAST: Edward G. Robinson (Damon Wells and Jules Chautard); Mary Astor (Jessica Vance); Ricardo Cortez (Weston); Mae Clarke (Daphne); Louis Calhern (Stanley Vance); Arthur Byron (Dr. Kendall); John Eldredge (Barry); David Landau (Curtis); Emily Fitzroy (Hattie); Henry O'Neill (Inspector); Arthur Aylesworth (Morgue Keeper); Margaret Dale (Martha); Virginia Sale (Peabody); Wade Boteler (Detective); Guy Usher (Weeks); Joseph Crehan (Editor); Dorothy Tree (Patsy); Mary Russell (Debutante); Milton Kibbee (Rewrite Man); Howard Hickman (Jones); Maude Turner Gordon (Mrs. Jones); Frank Darien (Doorman); Douglas Cosgrove (Lieutenant); Ray Cooke (Bellhop); Dick Winslow (Call Boy); Bert Moorhouse (Driver); Mrs. Wilfred North (Society Matron); and Leni Stengel, Harry Tyler, Barbara Blair

Lionel Atwill and Joan Bennett star in *The Man Who Reclaimed His Head*

THE MAN WHO RECLAIMED HIS HEAD
(Universal Pictures Corp.; 1934)

Sirens herald a German raid over Paris on a snowy night in 1915. As the populace seeks shelter, a single light gleams from an isolated villa. There is the sound of breaking glass, followed by a scream. A moment later, Army Cpl. Paul Verin (Claude Rains) emerges, carrying his child (played by Baby Jane Quigley), and a valise. Verin hurries to the home of Fernandé de Marnay (Henry O'Neill), a lawyer, who perceives that his friend is agitated. As Verin stammers out his story, de Marnay notices that the soldier clutches the valise protectively.

"I was shy. It's been my curse," Verin says. "You were the only one who was kind to me, respected me."

"Come, come, you had a brilliant mind," de Marnay reassures him. "What have you *done* with it?"

"What have I done with it?" Verin cries. He opens the valise. De Marnay blanches in horror. Verin babbles meaninglessly, then calms himself and tells his story.

Having completed his first film, *The Invisible Man* (1933), Claude Rains returned to New York for *Crime Without Passion* (see our 1989 book, *The Cinema of Adventure, Romance and Terror*). Rains was summoned back to Universal in September 1934 and contracted for two pictures, *The Man Who Reclaimed His Head* and *The Return of Frankenstein* (which became

Human Monsters

Prelude to a confession...

Bride of Frankenstein, without Rains). Rains and Jean Arthur had starred in the 1932 Broadway production of *The Man Who Reclaimed His Head*, an antiwar play by Jean Bart (professional name of Marie Antoinette Sarlabous). Lowell Sherman was supposed to direct the movie version, but a chronic respiratory ailment sidelined him. Sherman died of pneumonia in December while working on the first three-color Technicolor feature, *Becky Sharp* (1935).

The Man Who Reclaimed His Head was filmed during September and October under the Russian-born director Edward Ludwig. Substantial production values were applied, for bossman Carl Laemmle hoped to match the appeal of the studio's previous pacifist epic, *All Quiet on the Western Front* (1930). Miss Bart and Samuel Ornitz wrote the screenplay. This sobering drama was quite a change for Ludwig, whose specialty had been comedy with such high points as *They Just Had To Get Married* (1932) and *Friends of Mr. Sweeney* (1934). Throughout a long career, Ludwig handled many comedies, but he also was associated with mysteries (1935's *Fatal Lady*), musicals (1935's *Old Man Rhythm*), John Wayne vehicles (1948's *Wake of the Red Witch*), and science-fantasy (1957's *The Black Scorpion*).

Direction and photography of *The Man Who...* are unusual for their avoidance of the trappings of both horror and war cinema. Even such Grand Manner performers as Rains and Lionel Atwill apply restraint. The snow-draped night scenes are more beautiful than ominous. The framing sequence is strange but not gruesome. The lawyer's home is lighted by candles—that is, cameraman Merritt Gerstad and art director Albert D'Agostino make it appear so—that flicker gigantically. Rains' close-ups in the murder scene are handled in the manner of glamour portraiture, with diffusion and soft lighting; the effect is stunning. Heinz Roemheld's very European-styled music is similarly restrained, with none of the expected strings or crescendos.

Atwill stalks his prey.

The larger story is a sustained flashback: Verin and his young wife, Adele (Joan Bennett), live in a poverty born of Verin's idealism. Adele longs for wealth and excitement. Henry Dumont (Atwill), a grandstanding publisher, urges Verin to work for him. "I lack the one thing you have: your mind. Give me that, Verin. I'll *pay* you for it!" Failing at a direct approach, Dumont charms Adele. At her urging, Verin agrees to ghostwrite Dumont's articles. These antiwar pieces make Dumont famous. Someone tells Verin he should be more like Dumont, who "has a real head on his shoulders."

The military-industrial complex—and yes, that shadow-cabinet thrived long before Dwight D. Eisenhower pretended to have discovered it—bullies Dumont into revising his policy. When Archduke Ferdinand is assassinated, Verin writes a plea that Dumont revises as a pro-war tract. Dumont has Verin sent to the battlefront. Unhinged, Verin deserts. He finds Adele fighting off Dumont's advances. "My wife was not included in our bargain, Dumont," Verin snarls, drawing his bayonet. Verin works grimly in the darkness.

The flashback has come full-circle. Verin explains: "I wanted back what was *me*, what was *mine*..." He gestures meaningfully to the valise. "You are not the accused, you're the accuser," de Marnay assures Verin.

An epic sensibility prevails. The large-scale crowd scenes include a Bastille Day celebration with hordes of costumed extras. A concert-hall sequence, filmed on the set built in 1924 for *The Phantom of the Opera*, also employs vast numbers of dress extras. The unusual handling suggests that the director, whom history has ignored, might merit a closer look.

The Big Message, though subtler by far than the Broadway version, is still a bit thick. Warmongering Lawrence Grant contributes a bit of real prophecy: "Sometimes, I think I'm a better pacifist than you," he tells Atwill. "If we could release the energy in one atom, two armies could destroy each other in an instant. *Then*, we would have seen our last war." Rains' use of a valise as a trophy case looks ahead to Emyln Williams' *Night Must Fall*, whose MGM version came along two years later.

Universal tried two advertising angles—one emphasizing the antiwar stance and the other touting a horror picture. The exhibitors, well aware that Depression-era audiences would reject any solemn pitch, preferred the shock-value campaign. The horror fans, expecting a follow-through to *The Invisible Man*, were disappointed. When Realart Pictures mounted a reissue in 1949, an all-out horror campaign alienated a new generation. Now, on living-room video, the picture fares somewhat better because audiences are more tolerant of social-problem dramas.

The property was remade in 1945 as *Strange Confession*, part of Universal's six-picture *Inner Sanctum* series, with Lon Chaney, Jr., wielding a machete to reclaim his head from J. Carrol Naish. This, too, was reissued by Realart with a blood-and-horror campaign and a new title: *The Missing Head*. They never learn.

CREDITS: Producer: Carl Laemmle, Jr.; Associate Producer: Henry Henigson; Director: Edward Ludwig; Screenplay: Jean Bart (from Her Play) and Samuel Ornitz; Photographed by: Merritt Gerstad; Music: Heinz Roemheld; Art Director: Albert S. D'Agostino; Editor: Murray Seldeen; Supervising Editor: Maurice Pivar; Special Effects: John P. Fulton; Assistant Directors: W.J. Reiter and Fred Frank; Set Décor:: R.A. Gausman; Matte Art: Jack Cosgrove and Russell Lawson; Music Recording: Lawrence Aicholtz; Sound System: Western Electric; Running Time: 82 Minutes; Released: December 24, 1934

CAST: Claude Rains (Paul Verin); Joan Bennett (Adele Verin); Lionel Atwill (Henri Dumont); Baby Jane Quigley (Linette Verin); Henry O'Neill (de Marnay); Wallace Ford (Curly); Lawrence Grant (Marchand); William B. Davidson (Charlus); Henry Armetta (Laurent); Gilbert Emery (Excellency); Hugh O'Connell (Danglas); Rollo Lloyd (Jean); Bessie Barriscale (Louise); Ferdinand Gottschalk (Baron); Lloyd Hughes (Andre); Noel Francis (Chon-Chon); Valerie Hobson (Mimi); Lois January (Girl); Carol Coombe (Clerk); Doris Lloyd (Baroness); Edward Van Sloan, Walter Walker and Crauford Kent (Magnates); Emerson Treacy (Peace Speaker); Ted Billings (Newsboy); Boyd Irwin (Steward); George Davis (Private); Russ Powell (Railway Conductor); Harry Cording (Burly Man); G.P. Huntley, Jr. (Pierre); William Ruhl (Angry Man); Charles Meacham (Older Man); and Phyllis Brooks, C. Montague Shaw, Purnell Pratt, Crauford Kent, Jameson Thomas, Judith Wood, John Ince, James Donlan, Anderson Lawler, Bryant Washburn, Will Stanton, Lionel Belmore, Wilfred North, Margaret Mann, John Rutherford, Grace Cunard, Nell Craig, William Worthington, Rudy Cameron, Hyram Hoover, Lee Phelps, Rudy Cameron, Norman Ainslee, Harry Cording, Lilyan Irene, Rolfe Sedan, Ben F. Hendricks, Maurice Murphy, William Gould, Carl Stockdale, Ted Billings, Tom Ricketts, Josef Swickard, William West, Colin Kenney, Russ Clark

MYSTERY OF EDWIN DROOD
(Universal Pictures Corp.; 1935)

England, 1864: A handsome young couple marries in the cathedral at Cloisterham. The church spire dissolves into a bedpost, and it becomes evident that John Jasper (Claude Rains) is waking from a dream in an opium den. Jasper returns to work as choirmaster at Cloisterham. His friends fear his health is worsening, even though "he has been going to London twice a week for treatments."

Jasper's dearest friend is his nephew, Edwin "Ned" Drood (David Manners), but the older man also is half-crazed with jealousy because he secretly loves Edwin's fiancée, Rosa Bud (Heather Angel). Edwin and Rosa, the lovers of Jasper's opium nightmares, were betrothed in infancy but are not really in love. Jasper confides to Edwin his hatred of the gloomy cathedral: "No monk... could have been more tired of it... He could take to carving demons for relief... Must I take to carving them out of my heart?"

Demons of the heart and the mind are the essence of this second of Universal's robust adaptations of Charles Dickens' most foreboding novels. Early in 1934, Stuart Walker had directed a commendable *Great Expectations*, with Henry Hull as the mysterious fugitive Magwitch, a role that Universal had first planned for Karloff. (Many viewers of the film today mistake Hull for Karloff.) Even though *Great Expectations* fared poorly at the box office—insiders joked that the elder Carl Laemmle had decided not to pick up Dickens' option—Walker was given a substantial budget to film *Mystery of Edwin Drood*. A script by Leopold Atlas and Bradley King was completed in August of 1934 but then recalled for revision by John L. Balderston and later supplemented by Walker's stage collaborator, Gladys Unger.

Because the novel—patently a foreshadowing of Mr. Stevenson's *Jekyll & Hyde*—was left uncompleted upon Dickens' death in 1870, it was necessary to devise an ending. More than 120 authors had weighed in as to how Dickens might have resolved the tale. (The strangest of these attempts was that of Thomas P. James, an itinerant printer in Vermont, who in 1872 announced that he had established contact with the spirit of Charles Dickens and found himself appointed to complete *Drood*. Which he did: The following year's published result earned such raves as a Boston newspaper's assertion that "James could not have written this book without help from Dickens—be it spiritual or otherwise, we do not know." Sir Arthur Conan Doyle, creator of Sherlock Holmes and a devotee of spiritualism, concluded later that James had shown no literary talent before or after the manuscript. "If [the conclusion] be indeed a parody," declared Doyle, "it has the rare merit... of never accentuating or exaggerating the peculiarities of the original.")

For the Universal production of 1935, Karloff had been slated to portray the opium fiend. Another English actor, Frank Lawton, was supposed to follow his role in James Whale's *One More River* with that of Jasper's intended fall guy, Neville Landless. Script problems caused postponements, necessitating cast changes between early September, when production was scheduled to commence, and November 14, when shooting actually started. By then, background scenes had been filmed in Rochester, England, by a second unit organized by David Bader, of Universal's London office. Art director Albert S. D'Agostino had reshaped Universal's permanent European village set to resemble Dickens' Cloisterham; designed impressive sets, utilizing elements of the cathedral built for 1923's *The Hunchback of Notre Dame*; and assembled an underground crypt, incorporating details built for *The Phantom of the Opera* (1925) and *Dracula* (1931).

Claude Rains, upon completing *The Man Who Reclaimed His Head*, was scheduled to portray Dr. Pretorius in *The Return of Frankenstein* (which became *Bride of Frankenstein*). Additional juggling put Rains in the role of Jasper. Douglass Montgomery replaced Lawton, who had gone to MGM to take the title role in another adaptation from Dickens, *David Copperfield*. There were additional delays as dozens of children were tested for the role of a

Douglass Montgomery and Heather Angel

tattered youngster who aids in solving the mystery. Georgie Ernest, later to become a perennial member of 20th Century-Fox's *Jones Family* series, became the worthy choice.

Mme. Hilda Grenier, an authority on Victorian England and a confidante of the Royal Family, was engaged to ensure authenticity. The strictness of Victorian manners is scrupulously observed throughout. It is particularly consistent with the Victorian code, for example, that David Manners' Edwin Drood suspects nothing of his uncle's drug dependency or lust for Rosa, and that Rains' John Jasper can pursue a forbidden secret life with impunity, so long as he keeps up the proper appearances.

The complications are intensified with the arrival from Ceylon of Neville Landless (Montgomery) and his sister, Helena (Valerie Hobson). Edwin is attracted to Helena, and Neville falls in love with Rosa. Neville discloses that he has been banished to England because he had threatened his stepfather while protecting Helena. Neville's resentment of Edwin leads to an argument, which Jasper quells. Rosa confides that Jasper "haunts my thoughts like a ghost... seems to lapse into some frightful dream and takes me with him."

Edwin angrily tells Neville: "We English don't encourage fellows with dark skins to admire our girls." Neville takes up a knife, puts it down, and leaves. Neville decides to make amends with Edwin. Jasper bruits it about that Neville threatened Edwin's life.

Grewgious (Walter Kings-ford), Rosa's guardian, gives Edwin a ring that had belonged to Rosa's mother, who asked that the trinket be "given from the grave" at Rosa's wedding. Edwin tells Rosa he will step aside because of her love for Neville. Jasper visits an ancient Norman crypt beneath the cathedral and notices a quantity of quicklime.

A crone (Zeffie Tilbury) travels from London to report that one Mr. Horridge, a customer at her opium den, has raved of his desire to strangle someone named Ned. Edwin has gone missing. Neville, accused of doing away with Edwin, volunteers to lead a search. Jasper collapses when he learns that Edwin and Rosa had decided not to marry. Neville decides he must go away until he can clear his name. A bearded old man called Datchery comes to the village. Only Grewgious knows that Datchery is a disguised Neville. Grewgious has learned that Jasper is an addict and that he has made a key to the crypt.

"Over and over again, always in the same way, hundreds of thousands of times, I've done it," Jasper cries as he dreams of killing and the hag listens. "It was pleasant to do. When it was finally done, it seemed not worth the doing—it was done so soon... *Rosa*!" He grasps the crone's throat and almost strangles her before he wakes. The hag returns to Cloisterham and, sighting Jasper, identifies him to Datchery as the murderous Mr. Horridge. Datchery hurries to fetch Sapsea (E.E. Clive), the mayor. They return to find the woman slain.

Datchery enlists Deputy (Georgie Ernest), a ragamuffin who works at the churchyard, to take him to the sexton, Durdles (Forrester Harvey). They find the quicklime depleted and a sarcophagus opened and resealed. The sarcophagus is opened to reveal the outlines of a body and a few bones in a bed of quicklime. The wedding ring carried by Edwin lies encrusted among the remains.

A consoling interlude in ...*Drood*

"*Ned*! What have I done?" Jasper shouts as he flees to the church tower. The great bells toll. Shattered by remorse, Jasper cries out: "Rosa, the journey is made!" and leaps to his death. Later, the bells ring again—for the marriage of Rosa and Neville.

Extra personnel were hired to provide mid-Victorian wardrobes and character makeups for 488 cast members. Jack Pierce claimed that he and his staff used 2,200 pounds of crepe hair and greasepaint during the course of production. In making up Montgomery as the aged Datchery, Pierce fashioned a white wig and beard of natural hair and transformed the actor's nose into an aquiline beak of bone and collodion. For Rains, he devised a subtle makeup to differentiate between the good and evil aspects of Jasper's personality. For the dark side, he made barely perceptible changes in the eyes, ears, nose and mouth. Sideburns were tapered, and false wisps were added to the hair over the ears. This, plus some of the Frankenstein Monster's gray-green greasepaint, made the ears seem thinner and pointed. The eyebrows were brought closer together with a mascara pencil, and the lips were painted down to make the mouth into a slit.

Rains gives a superb accounting of the conscience-stricken murderer, a vulnerably human but nonetheless frightening monster. He is properly evil when skulking among the shadows or raving about his crime while in an opium stupor, yet entirely pitiable during his less murderous moments. Montgomery's passionate young man and his stooped geezer are well-conceived characters, the latter being unrecognizable as Montgomery. David Manners makes a bright and sympathetic Ned, Heather Angel a primly attractive Rosa and Valerie Hobson an enchanting Helena.

The lesser characters are true to Dickens in every respect, particularly Francis L. Sullivan (who can be seen in many movie versions of Dickens' novels) as the lovable Septimus Crisparkle; Walter Kingsford as the gruff but kindly Grewgious; Forrester Harvey as a happily intoxicated Durdles; Georgie Ernest as the sharp and cheeky Deputy; E.E. Clive as the pompous mayor; and Zeffie Tilbury (a most remarkable character woman, herself possessed of a Dickensian name) as the opium pusher who develops a self-sacrificing sense of justice.

One never is conscious of the confines of the studio. There are many clever transitions, typified by the cathedral spire of Rains' caricature-of-Freud dream fading into a bedpost in the opium den. The fateful gathering on the night of the murder is shown from outside the house, involving the audience more in voyeurism than in any illusion of participation. The storm is a marvelous piece of special-effects work. There is atmosphere of a superior kind in the gloomy hunt for the missing Ned, with torches flickering in the rain and vapors of breath puffing from the searchers.

An enhancement throughout is an imposing score by Edward Ward (who had also done *Great Expectations*), consisting of no fewer than 89 cues. It is highly effective during the storm sequence and in the climactic moments in the cathedral. The score also utilizes selections from Handel, Haydn and Bossetti.

Stuart Walker was 48 at the time—a scholarly man who had long since earned fame for contributions to the legitimate theater. Kentucky-born, Walker had left his job with a creosoting company to attend the American Academy of Dramatic Arts in New York City. He soon found employment with David Belasco as an actor, reader, stage manager and director. In 1915, Walker set out on his own as a playwright, actor and producer, designing and patenting a portable stage, complete with lighting equipment, that could be set up in an hour. His company, Stuart Walker's Portmanteau Theatre, played in some 70 cities, performing scenarios written by Walker. One of these, *Six Who Pass While the Lentils Boil*, ranked for generations as one of the most-often-performed American one-act plays.

Walker's patented x-ray system of stage lighting, utilizing mirrors and a primary-color process, was particularly influential. In 1918, he introduced the spotlight system, which became the most popular method of stage lighting. He operated repertory companies in Indianapolis and Cincinnati. Walker's dramatizations toured North America for many years, and he gained widespread recognition for his stagings of Lord Dunsany's satirical fantasies.

In 1930, Walker wrote several scripts for Columbia and then joined Paramount Publix Corp. as a producer-director. During the next three years, he made several pictures, among them the war drama, *The Eagle and the Hawk*, with Fredric March, Cary Grant and Carole Lombard. He joined Universal in 1934 to direct the two Dickens films, which were followed by *Werewolf of London* (1935). He quit directing after the mid-1930s, but carried on as a producer and occasional screenwriter until his death in 1941.

A World Film Corp. adaptation of *The Mystery of Edwin Drood*, from 1914, allows Edwin Drood (as played by Rodney Hickok) to survive the treacheries of his uncle (Tom Terriss, who also served as screenwriter), the better to exonerate Neville Landless (Paul Sterling). This version finds Helena Landless (Margaret Prussing) impersonating the mysterious Mr. Datchery. A Broadway musical version of *Drood* opened in 1985.

CREDITS: An Edmund Grainger Production, Produced by: Carl Laemmle, Jr.; Director: Stuart Walker; Based upon: Charles Dickens' Novel, *The Mystery of Edwin Drood*; Screenplay: John L. Balderston and Gladys Unger; Adaptation: Leopold Atlas and Bradley King; Art Director: Albert S. D'Agostino; Photographed by: George Robinson; Music: Edward Ward; Piano Music: James Dietrich; Technical Advisor: Mme. Hilda Grenier; Special Effects: John P. Fulton; Editor: Edward Curtiss; Makeup: Jack P. Pierce; Second Unit Director: David Bader; Matte Effects: Jack Cosgrove and Russell A. Lawson; Effects Cameraman: David S. Horsley; Set Décor: R.A.

Gausman; Western Electric Sound by: Lawrence Aicholtz; Assistant Directors, Phil Karlstein and Harry Mancke; Running Time: 86 minutes; Released: February 4, 1935

CAST: Claude Rains (John Jasper); Douglass Montgomery (Neville Landless); Heather Angel (Rosa Bud); David Manners (Edwin Drood); Valerie Hobson (Helena Landless); Francis L. Sullivan (Mr. Crisparkle); Walter Kingsford (Hiram Grewgious); E.E. Clive (Thomas Sapsea); Forrester Harvey (Durdles); Louise Carter (Mrs. Crisparkle); Ethel Griffies (Miss Twinkleton); Zeffie Tilbury (Opium Den Hag); Vera Buckland (Mrs. Tope); Elsa Buchanan (Tisher); Georgie Ernest (Deputy); J.M. Kerrigan (Chief Verger Tope); Adele St. Maur (Cook); Anne O'Neal (Maid); Walter Brennan (Talkative Villager); Will Geer (Lamplighter); John Rogers, D'Arcy Corrigan and Harry Cording (Opium Smokers)

MARK OF THE VAMPIRE
(Metro-Goldwyn-Mayer Corp./Loew's, Inc.; 1935)

Fear grips the Czech village of Visoka; the long-dead Count Mora (Bela Lugosi) and his equally defunct daughter, Luna (Carol Borland), are said to have risen. The beloved Sir Karell Borotyn (Holmes Herbert) is found slain—throat punctured, blood drained. Dr. Doskil (Donald Meek), the local physician, blames vampires. Inspector Neumann (Lionel Atwill) suspects some human fiend.

Sir Karell's daughter, Irena (Elizabeth Allan), becomes a house guest of Baron Otto (Jean Hersholt). Her fiancé, Fédor (Henry Wadsworth), survives an attack. Irena finds wounds about her throat. Apparitions of Mora and Luna are seen. When Irena is attacked, Professor Zelen (Lionel Barrymore) is summoned; he declares that Sir Karell has joined the undead; the body has disappeared.

Zelen leads a search, proposing to behead the vampires before nightfall. Otto finds what he believes to be the body of Sir Karell and starts to sever the head when Zelen stops him.

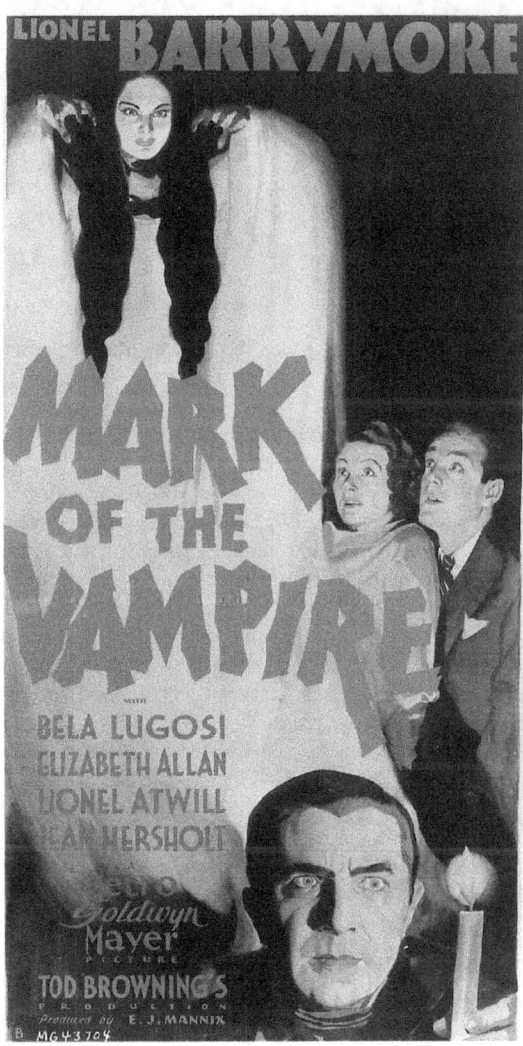

Irena seems to have succumbed to the vampires' will. Zelen hypnotizes Otto into re-enacting the events of the night Sir Karell died. In the study, Irena sobs that she cannot carry on; the man whom Otto had nearly beheaded, she says, resembles her father too closely. She rallies at the insistence of Neumann and Zelen.

In his hypnotized replay, Otto steals back in, ready to drain his host's blood. Neumann and company seize Otto, and Zelen breaks the hypnotic spell.

Count Mora, now revealed as an actor hired by the investigators, and his colleagues are seen removing their makeups and packing to leave. The Count waxes eloquent: "This vampire business—it has given me a great *idea*... I will be greater than any *real* vampire!" His partners advise him to get busy with the loading.

A delightful sham, is Tod Browning's *Mark of the Vampire*. The picture showcases such genius at production and such a concentration of Grand Manner acting as to compensate generously for the viewer's likely outrage at being cheated of any supernatural payoff. (The picture is, of course, a remake-with-embellishments of Browning's *London after Midnight* [1927], a Lon Chaney-starrer whose archival elements were presumably destroyed

A vampiric—or is it?—household

in an MGM vault fire during the 1960s — the most famously lost of all American films. Many hoaxes, including a counterfeit digital-video disk package, have surfaced to suggest *London*'s survival intact. In 2002, a truer representation came about: The restorationist Rick Schmedlin assembled an impressive featurette-facsimile from some 200 production stills, on behalf of the Turner Classic Movies television network.)

Its shaggy-dog plot twist notwithstanding, *Mark of the Vampire* still delivers a proper (if caricatured) abundance of fearful atmosphere, particularly in a sequence where a village hag snags her clothing while fleeing from a bat in a graveyard, and in another where an ersatz vampire soars through the castle. Bela Lugosi's scowling countenance (seen here much as in 1931's *Dracula*, with a bullet wound added); views of the cavernous castle interiors; and a precipitous low-angle shot of a rushing carriage are genuinely unnerving. In the inevitable comparisons with Tod Browning's *Dracula*, Browning's return to the turf in *Mark of the Vampire* fares well. Where the earlier film veers drastically from its opening aura of timeless evil, *Mark* holds throughout to a crushing sense of Old World rural superstition.

The killer's *modus operandi* requires the greatest suspension of disbelief. The question of what Jean Hersholt did with all that blood catches one as much off-guard as the abrupt realization that "the play's the thing"—that Lionels Atwill and Barrymore have resorted to such an elaborate masquerade. The screenplay stems from a scenario by director Browning called "The Vampires of Prague." This, in turn, is a reworking of the scenario for *London after Midnight* (1927), which derived from Browning's story, "The Hypnotist"—an early example of the plot-to-unveil-a-plot theme popularized many years later in the French-made *Les Diaboliques* (1955). (Co-screenwriter Guy Endore, the author of *The Werewolf of Paris* and *Babouk*, was a *bona fide* eccentric who startled the studio folk by going about even on the coldest days in sandals.)

Browning, who had been dubbed "the Edgar Allan Poe of the screen" by the studio's publicists in view of his offbeat silent pictures with Chaney, declared to the press that he relied upon vast settings to provide an unsettling framework: "Dialogue and description could not produce such an effect. Attempts to describe the gnawing fear of a vampire cult would only weaken the idea"—and indeed, Barrymore has only one speech in this direction—"but a weird, desolate sky, fantastic cloud-images and the right lighting impress the effect on the brain through the eye. The sky was used with different effects throughout the picture. We built our sets before it, tore them down and built more, so that the weird sky was always the shadow behind the action."

Such a commitment to the visual imperative had worked to Browning's advantage on *Dracula*, and it proved still more effective on *Mark of the Vampire*, which, with the remarkable James Wong Howe in charge of cameras, is above all a treat to the eye. Years later, Howe related to us his fascination with what he called "big skies," achieved in indoor settings through the projection of forms. When he shot *Hud* in Northwest Texas during the early 1960s, Howe was delighted to find his "big skies" a natural part of the scenery.

The planetarium-styled sky of *Mark* was a huge cyclorama, built to traverse the length of a sound stage and given its effects by projected clouds. Howe said that Browning was "very old-fashioned" in his strict handling of actors and staging but permitted great freedom in innovative cinematography—a godsend to Howe, whose devotion to photographing a setting "just as the eye would see it" is shown here to good advantage.

Great pains were taken to advance and embellish the legendry of vampirism. A byword in the dialogue is *bat-thorn*, as opposed to the more conventional garlic and wolf's-bane. Creatures presented to flavor the eerie doings include assorted dogs, two timber wolves (borrowed from a Los Angeles zoo), a rat and a great horned owl. The properties department provided mechanical bats and spiders. *Mark of the Vampire* was the proving ground for a fog-producing machine that used a mist slightly denser than air. Compressed into forms and then released, the mist theoretically would expand, retaining a semblance of the original shape—but only on days of low atmospheric pressure. The crew was obliged to watch a barometer to know when the effect could be employed. Mechanical problems plagued the staging of the part where the vampire girl drifts aloft. "It took us days to get that one scene," Howe told us.

MGM touted a "modern psychological orchestration," and the picture *does* have a uniquely maudlin score—but not of the type first commissioned. A leading composer-conductor at the studio, Herbert Stothart, delivered music that would represent the lead

A symbolic publicity shot for *Mark of the Vampire*

A shot is readied on the *Mark of the Vampire* set.

players with individual instruments (droll bassoon for Lionel Barrymore's grouchy hypnotist, muted trumpet to echo Lionel Atwill's clipped voice, dour French horn for Lugosi and so forth). Stothart's work was publicized in connection with the film but is not heard in the released version, having been set aside for a more understated score that is dominated by low-register and often dissonant groanings from a pipe-organ.

The domineering Atwill and Barrymore contrast nicely with the befuddled Hersholt, who is more suave a villain than usual. The scene where Hersholt almost beheads a mock vampire triggers one of Barrymore's best-ever outbursts of pompous bluster: "Why, their fury would follow us to the ends of the *earth*!" Teen-aged Carol Borland is chilling in her silence, broken once by a reptilian hiss. Howe said Rita Cansino (later, Hayworth) came close to landing the part; Miss Borland was selected for her unusual eyes, which lent themselves to good photographic effects, and by virtue of her stage experience with—and a recommendation from—Lugosi. As a Czech Dracula, Lugosi conveys menace without a line of dialogue, then steps out of character to end the show on a comical note. Lugosi, Howe recalled, "was a very funny guy—seemed to think he really *was* a vampire." The appropriately surnamed Donald Meek has some amusing moments as a scared-silly doctor intimidated by the pragmatic Atwill. The other players of consequence are innocuously competent.

The rapid-fire action of *Mark of the Vampire* is not so much the result of strategy as of last-minute scissoring. MGM whacked 20 minutes between preview and release.

CREDITS: Producer: Edward J. Mannix; Director and Original Scenarist: Tod Browning; Screenplay: Guy Endore and Bernard Schubert; Reworked from: Browning's 1927 Film *London after Midnight*, His Scenario "The Vampires of Prague" and His Story, "The Hypnotist";

Recording Director: Douglas Shearer; Art Director: Cedric Gibbons; Associates: Harry Oliver and Edwin B. Willis; Gowns: Adrian; Photographed by: James Wong Howe; Editor: Ben Lewis; Music: Edward Ward, Domenico Savino and Dr. William Axt; Organ Music Composed and Performed by: Price Dunlavy; Gypsy Songs Arranged by: Frank J. Virgil; Assistant Director: Harry Sharrock; Second Cameraman: Charles Salerno, Jr.; Photographic Effects: Warren Newcombe; Western Electric Sound: G.A. Burns, S.J. Lambert, Ralph Pender, R.L. Stirling, Don Whitmer, James Graham, T.B. Hoffman, Mike Steinore and M.J. McLaughlin; Running Time: 80 Minutes at Preview, 60 Minutes in Release; Released: April 26, 1935

Lugosi and Borland

CAST: Lionel Barrymore (Zelen); Elizabeth Allan (Irena); Bela Lugosi (Count Mora); Lionel Atwill (Newmann); Jean Hersholt (Otto); Henry Wadsworth (Fédor); Donald Meek (Dr. Doskil); Jessie Ralph (Midwife); Ivan Simpson (Jan); Franklyn Ardell (Chauffeur); Leila Bennett (Maria); June Gittleson (Annie); Carol Borland (Luna); Holmes Herbert (Karell); Michael Visaroff (Innkeeper); James Bradbury, Jr. (Vampire); Egon Brecher (Coroner); Rosemary Goltz (Village Woman)

LET 'EM HAVE IT
(Reliance Pictures, Inc./United Artists Corp./Astor Pictures Corp.; 1935)

Let 'Em Have It is a purebred ancestor of the cycle of highly realistic crime dramas of more than a decade later. Its subject matter alone would put the film well ahead of its time, although its impact was blunted in 1935 by the release just two weeks earlier of Warners' *G-Men*, a similarly progressive film that created a sensation by taking the vantage of the authorities rather than the outlaws.

Edward Small did likewise with *Let 'Em Have It*, which was filmed almost simultaneously, but Warners reached the box office first. *Let 'Em Have It* is the more realistic film. Where both employ a semidocumentary approach, the Warners picture was tailored as a showcase for James Cagney. Small went with a strong ensemble cast, with reduced emphasis on star appeal. Director Sam Wood holds to low-key portrayals. The Grand Guignol touches—a show-stopping mutilation of the villain and a grotesque finale—are all the more effective for the contrast they strike with the overall tone. But we're getting ahead of the game once again, and the game goes like this:

The F.B.I. accepts three recruits: attorney Mal Stevens (Richard Arlen), sportsman Van Rensseler (Harvey Stephens) and cowboy Tex Logan (Gordon Jones). The new friends foil the kidnapping of Eleanor Spencer (Virginia Bruce), a debutante. Her chauffeur, Joe Keefer (Bruce Cabot), suspected of engineering the plot, draws a three-year sentence for illegally packing a gun. Eleanor considers Keefer innocent and helps secure his parole. Keefer's release triggers a new rampage.

Eleanor's kid brother, Buddy (Eric Linden), so admires the three agents that he gains a Justice Department appointment. Working undercover for Stevens, Buddy locates the Keefer

gang's hideout. Keefer recognizes Buddy and kills him. Eleanor blames Stevens, who has fallen in love with her.

Keefer, now promoted to Public Enemy No. 1, forces a plastic surgeon (George Pauncefort) to alter his features and then kills the doctor. Later, at a backwoods refuge, he removes the bandages in the presence of his henchmen. To everyone's horror, Keefer's features have been mutilated—and his initials carved into his face.

Stevens falls into the hands of the gang. Stevens and Keefer fight atop a staircase. Keefer falls through a balustrade and lands impaled on the railing. Stevens and Eleanor are reunited.

Bruce Cabot plays the gang boss here to such near-perfection as to steal the show. Late in the film, he sports an elaborate horror makeup that would have suited even Boris Karloff. "That makeup was very painful," Cabot told us in 1967. "I had to check in before daylight every morning, and it took three men about six hours to make me up. Then, I couldn't take it off until after work each night. This happened every day for 10 days."

Richard Arlen, Harvey Stephens and Gordon Jones are splendid as the G-Man Musketeers, with Eric Linden as their tragic D'Artagnan, and Virginia Bruce makes a charming heroine. Barbara Pepper does well as a gang moll, and Harry Woods, Donald Kirke, Mathew Betz and Paul Fix stand out among a fine group of heavies.

Forensic operations are depicted in fascinating detail. It is shown, for example, how one's features can be reconstructed from the bite-marks in an apple, and how a strand of hair and a footprint can yield a description.

Direction and script place more emphasis on characterization and significant detail than on momentum. The photography follows suit with a minimum of glamour effects, achieving the naturalistic urgency of a newsreel. This sense of authenticity is advanced by a sparseness of background music—opening and closing patriotic strains, action passages for a war-on-crime montage and incidental popular tunes. The picture was filmed at the RKO-Pathé studio.

CREDITS: Presented by: Harry M. Goetz and Edward Small; Producer: Edward Small; Director: Sam Wood; Screenplay: Joseph Moncure March and Elmer Harris; Photographed by: J. Peverell Marley and Robert Planck; Music: Hugo Riesenfeld; Additional Music: Edward Powell, Alfred Newman, Charles Rosoff and Constantin Bakaleinikoff; Songs: "My Sweet Jeanette," by Wayne Allen, "Moon of Monte Cristo," by Richard Whiting & Sidney Clare and "Song of Surrender," by Harry Warren & Al Dubin; Art Director: John Ducasse Schulze; Technical Direction: Capt. Don Wilkie; Editor: Grant Whytock; Montage Effects: Slavko Vorkapich; Assistant Director: Nate Watt; Photographic Effects: Paul Eagler; Matte Paintings: Jack Robeson; Cameramen: Harry David and William Snyder; Sound: Frank Maher, Roger Heman and Vinton Vernon; Stunt Supervisor, Cliff Bergére; Running Time: 92 minutes; Released: May 17, 1935

CAST: Richard Arlen (Mal Stevens); Virginia Bruce (Eleanor Spencer); Alice Brady (Aunt Ethel); Bruce Cabot (Joe Keefer); Harvey Stephens (Van Rensseler); Eric Linden (Buddy Spencer); Joyce Compton (Barbara); Gordon Jones (Tex); J. Farrell MacDonald (Mr. Keefer); Bodil Rosing (Mrs. Keefer); Paul Stanton (Department Chief); Robert Emmett O'Connor (Police Captain); Jonathan Hale (Scientist); Hale Hamilton (Ex-Senator Reilly); Dorothy Appleby (Lola); Barbara Pepper (Milly); Mathew Betz (Thompson); Harry L. Woods (Big Bill); Clyde Dilson (Pete); Matty Fain (Brooklyn); Paul Fix (Sam); Donald Kirke (Curley); Eugene Strong (Dude); Christian Rub (Henkel); Eleanor Wesselhoeft (Mrs. Henkel); Wesley Barry (Walton); Ian MacLaren (Reconstructionist); George Pauncefort (Dr. Hoffman); Joseph King (Instructor); Clarence Wilson (Reynolds); Katherine Clare Ward (Ma Harrison); Landers Stevens (Parole Chairman); Sidney Bracy (Butler); Dave O'Brien (Agent); Tom London (Guard)

THE BLACK ROOM
(Columbia Pictures Corp.; 1935)

Boris Karloff "splits the very atom of his soul" in *The Black Room.*

Boris Karloff splits the very atom of his soul in Roy William Neill's *The Black Room*, a profoundly stylish period melodrama that seems to belong more to the Universal manner—particularly, *Bride of Frankenstein* and *Tower of London*—than to anything else that Columbia ever delivered, before or after. Karloff serves *The Black Room* as both kind-hearted aristocrat and perverted tyrant, twins who have long been separated for purely superstitious reasons. The element of superstition seems mere window-dressing for a story that has more to do with madness and murder, until the notion of an ancestral curse reasserts itself for a respectably ironic finale.

Whenever twins are born to the lordly de Berghman family, legend holds that the later arrival is fated to kill the elder. In this outcropping of twins, Anton, the younger, is sent away as a precaution. Years later, Gregor (Karloff) has so alienated his feudal subjects that he calls for the return of his brother—the better to keep hidden his murderous secret life. Anton (Karloff) suspects treachery, but he accepts shared responsibility for governing the village.

The antagonisms commence early on, when Anton falls for Thea Hassel (Marian Marsh), daughter of a military official, and never mind that Gregor has designs on Thea despite her greater fondness for Lt. Albert Lussan (Robert Allen). Gregor claims Mashka (Katherine De Mille), a servant, as his latest victim when she threatens to reveal their affair. Gregor calms an angry mob by renouncing his title.

Gregor ushers Anton to the castle's fabled Black Room, which had served as a torture chamber in times past. Anton, upon seeing the remains of Mashka, realizes that Gregor means to kill him. Which Gregor does. Gregor then commences to impersonate Anton, down to the finest detail of a paralyzed arm, and manages to fool everyone but Anton's dog, Thor (played by a splendidly trained Mastiff named Von), and Thea's father, Col. Hassel (Thurston Hall). Hassel is slain, and Gregor sets up Lussan to take the rap. En route to marry Thea, Gregor is attacked by Thor. The dog forces Gregor into a pit in the Black Room, where the villain is impaled upon a knife clutched by Anton's corpse. Thus is the family curse fulfilled—assuming that one believes in family curses.

No one is likely to confuse Roy William Neill with James Whale, for the directors were leagues apart in style and sensibilities, to say nothing of Neill's greater span of experience. Neill is most vividly remembered as a master of headlong pace, which served him well on most of the Universal *Sherlock Holmes* pictures, on 1943's *Frankenstein Meets the Wolf Man*, and on actioners, romancers and comedies dating from 1920. But a Whale-like attitude and technique surface all through *The Black Room*, which boasts atmosphere, sardonic wit, a painterly anti-realism (in the lowering cloudscapes and angular exterior sets) and an immersion-in-place-and-period to compare with Whale's 1935 gem, *Bride of Frankenstein*. The mannered and measured performances match the setting ideally, especially those of the good Karloff, of the virginal Marian Marsh, and of Thurston Hall as the upstanding Col. Hassel and Robert Allen as the framed-for-murder romantic lead. Katherine De Mille and the wicked Karloff impose a pleasingly lustful coarseness in counterpoint to the uppercrust Tyrolean milieu. The Canadian-born adopted daughter of Cecil B. De Mille is first-rate as a defiant servant whose forbidden affair with the overlord can only end in tragedy.

Karloff is doubly fine here, and the Karloff-with-Karloff pairing is a marvel of refined opticals, editing and doubling. It comes as a small astonishment that the TV-commercial image pirates of recent times have neglected to corrupt one of *The Black Room*'s Karloff-times-two scenes into some prime-time pitch for Doublemint Gum, which would be, really, no greater an affront to the cinematic heritage than Fred Astaire and his vacuum-cleaner dancing partner. Anton is no particular stretch for Karloff's natural-born benevolence. The actor applies a more robust zeal to Gregor, establishing the evil twin as one who has long since found murder and eroticism to be kindred interests. Especially rich, in its cringe-inducing way, is a scene where the juice of a ripe pear inspires Gregor to rethink the Old Testament: "Adam should've chosen a *pear!*"

CREDITS: Producer: Robert North; Director: Roy William Neill; Screenplay: Arthur Strawn (from His Story) and Henry Myers; Photographed by: Allen G. Siegler; Art Director: Stephen Goosson; Assistant Director: C.C. Coleman; Editor: Richard Cahoon; Costumer: Murray Mayer; Music: Louis Silvers; Sound: Edward Bernds; Running Time: 75 Minutes; Released: July 25, 1935

CAST: Boris Karloff (Anton and Gregor); Marian Marsh (Thea Hassel); Robert Allen (Lt. Albert Lussan); Thurston Hall (Col. Hassel); Katherine De Mille (Mashka); John Buckler (Beran); Henry Kolker (Baron de Berghman); Colin Tapley (Lt. Hassel); Torben Meyer (Peter); Egon Brecher (Karl); John M. Bleifer (Franz); Fredrik Vogeding (Josef); Edward Van Sloan (Doctor); Lois Lindsey and Phyllis Fraser (Bridesmaids); George Burr MacAnnan (Majordomo); John Maurice Sullivan (Archbishop); Reginald Pasch (Tailor); Robert Middlemass (Prosecutor); Marion Lessing (Marie); George MacQuarrie (Chief Justice); Edith Kingdon, Carrie Daumery, Grace Goodall, Eric Mayne, Edwards Davis, Count Rudolf von Stefinelli and Wilfrid North (Members of Court); Von (Thor); Sidney Bracy (Hairdresser); Helena Grant (Housekeeper); Joseph Singer (Raoul); Victor DeLinsky (Michael); Paul Weigel, Bert Sprotte and Michael Mark (Peasants); James Gordon, Richard Lancaster and Bert Howard (Gentlemen); Hans von Morhart (Servant); Ivan Linow and Abe Dinovitch (Gatemen); the Bleifer Twins (Anton and Gregor as Boys); John Beck (Court Clerk); Alexander Melesh and Enrique Acosta (Judges)

THE EAGLE'S BROOD
(Harry Sherman Productions, Inc./Paramount Productions, Inc.; 1935)

> My home ain't here—it's 'way out in the West,
> 'Way up high in those mean old mountains,
> Where the eagle builds his nest.
> —Texas Yodeler Luther Joe Pybus, "Mean Old Mountains Blues" (1934)

The novelist Clarence E. Mulford gave the culture an iconic hero in a 1912 book called *Hopalong Cassidy*—a hard-charging adventure centered on a character as rugged and as ornery as the Western frontier itself. The continuing published adventures of Cassidy caused a popular sensation over the long haul. In the summer of 1935, the franchise became the best thing that ever happened to the snappy tough-guy actor William Boyd, whose fortunes had lapsed right along with the U.S. economy of the Great Depression.

Boyd (1898-1972) had been a reigning star of the silent screen and a favored player of Cecil B. DeMille, D.W. Griffith and Lewis Milestone, with assignments dating from the early '20s. Boyd made the transition to talking pictures gracefully enough, but he found a troublesome doppelganger with whom to reckon: The other William Boyd was a similarly tough, somewhat older personality who was primarily associated with the legitimate theater but also tackled movie roles, including the no-guff lawman in 1931's *Murder by the Clock*. Each had a taste for carousing—although the other Boyd veered nearer criminal activity, with ties to the rum-running and prostitution rackets—and each was continually blamed for the other's escapades. A 1931 booze-and-gambling scandal involving the more deliberately scandalous William Boyd was the last straw, with some newspapers running the wrong actor's photograph in connection with the lurid stories that resulted.

But the actors found a surprisingly amicable solution: William Boyd, the Hopalong Cassidy-

to-be, became Bill Boyd while his namesake became William "Stage" Boyd. Upon the death of "Stage" in 1935, Bill retrieved his right name and proceeded to parlay the Hopalong portrayal into a lasting, however narrow, stardom. (Yet another Bill Boyd, a Texas-bred bandleader who billed himself as "the Cowboy Rambler" and starred in a handful of small-time Westerns as a sideline, was less the annoyance, being primarily a recording artist.)

Most people who remember Cassidy nowadays are of the post-WWII generation, and their impression of the character derives from his more lighthearted United Artists pictures of 1942 and onward. These led to an original-for-TV series. Although no one but Boyd ever played the character, there are two distinct periods of the *Hopalong Cassidy* movies. The Paramount *Cassidy*s of 1935-41 are an altogether grimmer lot, in which Boyd's approach is as uncompromising as the bedevilments that dog Cassidy's tracks. When this Cassidy laughs or even cracks a smile, he's usually amused by the destruction he has brought down on the bad guys, who deserve the worst he can dish out.

The Eagle's Brood is the grimmest, and the most nearly perfect, of the lot. The yarn hangs on a rumor that a notorious Mexican bandit known as El Toro is returning to the States. Which El Toro means to do, but only because his son and daughter-and-law have been murdered while en route homeward. His grandson, Pablo (George Mari), is in hiding from the killers. Joining the manhunt are enforcer Cassidy and his pal, Johnny Nelson (Jimmy Ellison). Cassidy lands in a quicksand sinkhole but is rescued by El Toro (William Farnum). El Toro begs Cassidy to let him proceed. Cassidy promises to rescue Pablo—on condition that El Toro return to Mexico.

Cassidy follows a slim lead to a cantina, where a dancer named Dolores (Joan Woodbury) has been sheltering Pablo from mob boss Big Henry (Addison Richards). Dolores is slain and declared a suicide. Johnny, however, has witnessed her murder from hiding. Cassidy advises Johnny to keep mum—for Cassidy intends to infiltrate the gang. Johnny takes the child to a mountainside stronghold. Cassidy plots to dismantle the gang, which has grown to doubt his loyalty. Finally, Big Henry wounds Johnny and is preparing to kill Pablo when Cassidy, outwitting his own captors, attacks and maneuvers Henry into a fatal fall.

Brisk and often hair-raising, *The Eagle's Brood* found itself banned outright in Norway because of its high violence quotient. The censors in Denmark scissored the film heavily. Mayhem is less the point, however, than the seething mob-boss portrayal from tall and stately Addison Richards—seen oftener as a man of official authority in many bigger pictures—and Boyd's driven impersonation of an almost-outlaw on an errand of mercy and incidental vengeance. The slaying of Joan Woodbury's sympathetic gang-moll character is a harrowing touch, and the child player, Mexican-born George Mari, seems convincingly in danger throughout. Miss Woodbury accepted the début role under her actual name, Nana Martinez, but rechristened herself soon thereafter; the publicity materials, as late as a Goodwill Pictures reissue of the 1940s, cite Nana Martinez, but published reviews mention Joan Woodbury.

Jimmy Elison is, as usual, a winning sidekick who accounts for plenty of the heroism. George "Gabby" Hayes, who was in 1935 just gaining momentum in a crucial transition from villainous roles to comical-sidekick parts, takes a middle ground here as a talkative bartender in cahoots with the owl hoots. William Farnum manages some touching moments as the bereaved bandit chief, although the Boston-born veteran character man never quite appears authentically Mexican.

The Eagle's Brood was shot during early-middle October of 1935 on location in the Mother Lode region of California's High Sierras, where it proved necessary to set up a short-wave rig to maintain contact with the civilized world. A brush fire broke out early on, delaying Boyd's arrival at his own starring project. Boyd recalled years later that, while motoring to the *Brood* site, he encountered a backwoodsman who informed him: "Yew cain't go up thar. They's a *fahr* up yonder." Boyd told us: "It took me a few beats to realize what I thought he was saying. So I said, 'Aw, heck, it's not so *far*.' And he said, 'Naw! I mean, they's a *fahr*!' Finally, I spotted some

smoke—it wasn't much of a fire—and caught on. I told him, 'Oh, yeah. A *fahr*.' He said, 'Thet's whut ah *said*. Yew *deef* or sump'n?'"

Early though *Brood* fell within the *Cassidy* mythology, Boyd already had begun accumulating a loyal base of fans. One admirer visited the shooting location to present Boyd with a gift of several antique firearms. "He said he wanted to see 'Hoppy' Boyd," the star told us. "So I introduced myself to him. 'I'm your man,' I says. He says, 'You ain't Boyd—don't look nothin' like him at all.' I says, 'Well, I sure as heck *am* William Boyd.' I was beginning to think that old William Boyd-vs.-William Boyd business was starting up all over again. Finally, he says, 'Well, if you're Hopalong Cassidy Boyd, then where's your makeup?' I told him I never much went in for makeup, and finally it dawned on him he was talkin' to the guy he'd come out to meet."

The series-launcher, *Hop-Along Cassidy* (complete with peculiar hyphenated spelling), had arrived in August of 1935. Over the next five years, the Paramount series would grow to 13 in number—plus a reissue of *Hop-Along Cassidy*, rechristened *Hopalong Cassidy Enters*. Each provided a welcome hard-charging alternative to the relentlessly emerging cowboy-crooner style. Paramount sold the *Cassidy* rights in 1942 to United Artists, which found a new audience with a more generally upbeat approach. (A late entry, 1948's *The Dead Don't Dream*, is a welcome throwback, what with its tale of nocturnal smotherings in a shunned roadside lodge.) Boyd, a savvy investor, bought the television rights and aired abbreviated versions via NBC during 1949-51, then launched the broadcast-specific series of 52 episodes. By the early '50s, Boyd-as-Cassidy was an industry in his own right, his face and signature adorning toy-store merchandise from cap pistols to schoolkids' lunchboxes. Which wouldn't have meant a great deal to the leaner, meaner Hopalong Cassidy of the 1930s.

The *Variety* review mis-stated the title as *The Eagle's Blood*; that same typographical glitch occurs in the film's copyright registration.

CREDITS: Associate Producer: George Green; Director: Howard Bretherton; Assistant Director: Ray Flynn; Screenplay: Doris Schroeder and Harrison Jacobs; Based upon: the Character Created by Clarence E. Mulford; Photographed by: Archie Stout; Incidental Music: Sam H. Stept and Sidney Mitchell; Editor: Edward Schroeder; Sound: Earl Sitar; Running Time: 61 Minutes; Released: October 25, 1935

CAST: William Boyd (Hopalong Cassidy); George "Gabby" Hayes (Spike); Jimmy Ellison (Johnny Nelson); William Farnum (El Toro); Addison Richards (Big Henry); Nana Martinez [Joan Woodbury] (Dolores); Frank Shannon (Mike); Dorothy Revier (Dolly); Paul Fix (Steve); Al Lydell (Pop); John Merton (Ed); George Mari (Pablo); Juan Toreña (Esteban); Henry Sylvester (Sheriff); and Frank McGlynn, Jr., Ethel Wales, Thomas Pogue

SHOW THEM NO MERCY!
(20th Century Pictures, Inc./20th Century-Fox Film Corp.; 1935)

The criminal underworld is the setting of the first *all*-talking feature, *The Lights of New York* (1928). The film is not particularly well made, but it proved to the fledgling talkie industry that gangland jargon, muttered if not uttered, and the sounds of savage misbehavior added a great deal of charm to such a story. The next dozen years saw a large number of gangster thrillers, much to the horror of the censors and many of the critics. Despite efforts ever since to stem the mayhem, the genre continues to flourish. Among the many actors who achieved renown in these films were Edward G. Robinson of *Little Caesar* (1931), James Cagney of *The Public Enemy* (1931), Paul Muni and George Raft of *Scarface* (1932), Humphrey Bogart of *The Petrified Forest* (1936) and Richard Widmark of *Kiss of Death* (1948). From the gangster films came innovations in styles of acting, writing and footage-cutting—fundamental developments in the evolving art of the talking picture.

The guiding intelligence of the genre was Darryl F. Zanuck, who as chief of production at Warner Bros.-First National launched such pacesetters as *Little Caesar* and *The Public Enemy*. Zanuck left Warners in 1933 to establish 20th Century Pictures, an aggressive, well-heeled independent company allied with United Artists. So successful was the venture that a merger with an ailing old-line major studio, Fox Film Corp., took place in 1935, with Zanuck elected vice president for production. The first group of 20th Century-Fox releases included *Snatched!*—one of Zanuck's independent productions and his first gangster film since his days at Warners. Written by Kubec Glasmon, co-author of *The Public Enemy*, the film took its cue from the Weyerhauser kidnap case, lately cracked by the F.B.I.

The Production Code Administration refused to sanction a film that would convey the details of an abduction. A canny rewrite had the story begin *after* the crooks have collected a ransom. The man and wife and baby held by the kidnappers became a family that blunders into the gang's hideout.

Joe and Loretta Martin (Edward Norris and Rochelle Hudson), driving to California with their baby son and a pet terrier, are caught in a Midwestern rainstorm. They seek shelter in a desolate farmhouse. The place proves occupied. The inhabitants—Tobey (César Romero), Pitch (Bruce Cabot), Buzz (Edward Brophy) and Gimp (Warren Hymer)—are in hiding with a satchel of payoff loot. Pitch wants to kill the interlopers, but Tobey, the gangleader, orders them locked away.

The Justice Department has organized a manhunt. The criminals have made a clean getaway, but the serial numbers of the ransom bills are known. The kidnappers grow edgy. Pitch, drinking heavily, becomes surly except when exercising his macabre sense of humor on Buzz. Pitch continues to threaten Joe and his family, alienating Tobey. Tobey orders Joe to visit a nearby town and pass off some of the loot. Loretta and the child are held hostage. The money draws the authorities. Buzz and Gimp decide to leave, taking part of the money. Cornered by federal agents, Buzz is killed. Gimp becomes a churchgoer, placing large bills in the collection plates and

An unholy alliance

Tensions develop among the kidnap gang

taking change. He, too, is killed by government agents.

Pitch leaves after a disagreement, but he returns and convinces Tobey they should remain partners. As soon as Tobey turns his back, Pitch guns him down, then goes after the escaping Martins. Pitch takes aim on Joe. Before he can squeeze the trigger, Pitch is riddled with bullets from his own machine gun, wielded by Loretta.

The working title, *Snatched!*, required changing before the Production Code Administration—as nasty-minded as ever, and perpetually on the lookout for *double-entendres*—would grant a Purity Seal. (And yes, the Code used the term *Purity Seal* with all due seriousness.) Hence the clumsy rechristening as *Show Them No Mercy!* After some finagling, Zanuck was permitted to retain a startling special-effects scene in which a machine-gun salvo stitches a gash across the bared chest of Bruce Cabot; some regional censors chopped the scene. Wailing also was heard from the religious sector because one of the gangsters is shown using church services to pass ill-gotten currency.

By 1935, the industry had so knuckled under to censorship that, generally, the emphasis had shifted from criminals to law enforcement, as in *G-Men*, *Let 'Em Have It* and *Public Hero Number One*. This switch at first created a shock-of-the-new sensation but soon became the stodgy rule—to which *Show Them No Mercy!* is a refreshing exception. It shows the federal men in a heroic light but keeps them very much in the background; the main narrative concerns itself with the horrifying plight of the trapped family and the mental deterioration of the fugitives as they crack under the very pressures they have created.

Director George Marshall, who had started out in 1914 with Universal, would gain his greatest renown as a master of comedy (1939's *You Can't Cheat an Honest Man*, 1940's *The Ghost Breakers*) and large-scale frontier pieces (1939's *Destry Rides Again*, 1948's *Tap Roots*). With the fast-moving and hard-bitten *Show Them No Mercy!*, Marshall forcefully invaded the turf of William Wellman and Archie Mayo and Howard Hawks. The cold and snappy photography suits to perfection the compact relentlessness of the yarn.

Rochelle Hudson and Edward Norris are fine as the menaced couple, representing well the courageous young adults of America's Depression Era. The kidnappers are superbly played, each actor contributing a distinctive portrayal. César Romero, in what he told us was his favorite role, creates a character he called "cruel, ruthless, cowardly,... [with] slim slits in his shell which allowed a little kindness to show through [and] simply made his general character darker by contrast." Romero's flashy gangleader is ironically sympathetic at times, as when he sings the popular tune "Oh, You Nasty Man" while contemplating a pile of money, or when he refuses (albeit for selfish reasons) to permit the slaughter of the prisoners. Warren Hymer, the movies' perennial dumb lug, adds dimension to his usual characterization by revealing glimpses of the brute behind the simple-minded façade. Small, squeaky-voiced and balding Eddie Brophy provides a remarkable study of a semi-comical social parasite driven to near-dementia.

Bruce Cabot's terrifying performance bests even his psychopathic hoodlum of *Let 'Em Have It*. Initially perceived as merely a primitive sort on good terms with his accomplices, Cabot gradually is revealed as a sadist whose idea of a joke is to torch a newspaper under which Brophy is sleeping. Under the influence of alcohol, he becomes increasingly vicious, degenerating at length into savagery. Cabot told us: "I based my interpretation in part upon the personality of [Vincent] 'Mad Dog' Coll"—a New York racketeer whose demise was welcomed even by his confederates. (A similarly striking interpretation of Coll is that of Nicolas Cage in his uncle Francis Ford Coppola's 1984 picture, *The Cotton Club*.)

Too bad that *Show Them No Mercy!* has not the reputation enjoyed by some of the earlier gang melodramas, for it is the equal of the best in the field. The plot of *Show Them No Mercy!* was recycled by 20th Century-Fox as a Western—and a very good one, at that—called *Rawhide* (1951), with Tyrone Power and Susan Hayward.

CREDITS: A Darryl F. Zanuck Production; Presented by: Joseph N. Schenck; Associate Producer: Raymond L. Griffith; Director: George Marshall; Story by: Kubec Glasmon; Screenplay: Henry Lehrman; Photographed by: Bert Glennon; Art Director: Jack Otterson; Editor: Jack Murray; Western Electric Sound: W.D. Flick and Roger Heman; Music: David Buttolph; Special Effects, Fred Sersen, Louis J. Witte and J.O. Taylor; Second Cameraman: Irving Rosenberg; Music Recording, Vinton Vernon; Produced at: Metropolitan Studio; Running Time: 75 minutes; Released: December 6, 1935

CAST: Rochelle Hudson (Loretta Martin); César Romero (Tobey); Bruce Cabot (Pitch); Edward Norris (Joe Martin); Edward Brophy (Buzz); Warren Hymer (Gimp); Herbert Rawlinson (Kurt Hansen); Robert Gleckler (Gus Hansen); Charles C. Wilson (Clifford); William B. Davidson (Chief Haggerty); Frank Conroy (Reed); Edythe Elliott (Mrs. Hansen); William Benedict (Willie); Orrin Burke (Judge Fry); Boothe Howard (Lester Mills); Paul McVey (Dr. Peterson); and Edward LeSaint

UNCIVILIZED
a.k.a.: PITURI
a.k.a.: PITURI (IT MAKES THEM UNCIVILIZED)
(Expeditionary Films, Ltd.; 1936)

Here we have a little-known film without which Paul Hogan's extraordinarily popular *"Crocodile" Dundee* adventure-comedies of times more recent might not exist. Hogan, a born-and-bred Australian whose brief but crowd-pleasing big-screen career hangs on the portrayal of a rugged outback adventurer named Mick "Crocodile" Dundee, volunteered as much in 1986 when we brought up the name of Charles Chauvel during the U.S. press tour for that first *Dundee* picture.

"Chauvel!" Hogan replied. "The Aussie Griffith! Did you ever hear of a picture of his called *Uncivilized*? You *must*'ve, or you'd not've mentioned him.

"You might say this first *Crocodile* picture is my way of paying notice to Chauvel, to *Uncivilized*, which I've loved ever since I saw it as a lad. Of course, there's a little of *Tarzan's New York Adventure* in *Crocodile*, as well, and a little of a forgotten picture called *Wallaby Jim of the Islands*—but yes, my big influence here is *Uncivilized* and its white-savage hero."

Australian novelist Beatrice Lynn (Margot Rhys) learns from her publisher that the public has tired of her drawing-room stories—she should write something hot-blooded. She undertakes to search for the fabled Mara, half-wild white king of a remote tribe. Beatrice is captured by Akbar Jahn (Ashton Jarry), an Afghan camel-trader, who sells her to Mara (Dennis Hoey) in exchange for permission to traffic in pituri, a narcotic made from a wild shrub. Mara seems as savage as his subjects.

Mara wants Beatrice as his mate, but so does the tribal witch doctor, Vitchi (E. Gilbert Howell), who uses pituri to enslave the tribesmen. Trask (Kenneth Brampton), a smuggler, haunts the area, planning to steal the tribe's treasure. Sondra (Marcelle Marnay), a beautiful half-caste who loves Mara, tries to poison Beatrice with an overdose of pituri. Beatrice is saved by Mara's medicine, but the effects of the drug fill her with desire. Angered that the woman who has spurned him should want him only when under the influence, Mara bans the use of pituri.

Tiki causes an uprising, only to be slain when government agents intervene. Trask is taken into custody by Inspector Peter Radcliffe—the supposed Afghan. Beatrice decides to remain with Mara.

Geographic isolation has long kept Australia from competing fully in the world film trade. There has been an active movie industry in Australia from the earliest days, however. For several decades, its most aggressive and productive practitioner was Charles Chauvel, president

Dennis Hoey at large in the wilderness.

of Expeditionary Films, Ltd., with headquarters in Sydney. Adventure was Chauvel's specialty, and his approach was very like that which characterized the making of Robert Flaherty's *Nanook of the North* (1921) and the Cooper-Schoedsack *Grass* (1925) and *Chang* (1927). For his on-location films, Chauvel shipped over much of the South Pacific, worked under great difficulty in the jungles of Cape York, and staged an Anzac Army spectacle in the Great Australian Desert.

Most of *Uncivilized* was filmed in the Northern and Northeastern jungles, in the Kimberly Mountains and in the central desert, with night scenes and interiors completed in Sydney. The company found itself plagued by mosquitoes and an astonishing variety of deadly snakes. One of the crew was snakebitten and, far removed from the nearest white doctor, was treated by natives who lanced the wound, sucked the venom, and applied a poultice of clay. (The victim survived.)

In December 1935, Chauvel returned to Sydney with tribesmen from Palm Island, along with a number of gigantic pythons, which he had purchased from them for eight shillings per foot. (And yes, they *do* have pythons in Australia.) A celebration at the new Pagewood Studio came complete with tribal rituals.

Uncivilized is an elemental melodrama rather along the lines of *Trader Horn* (1930). There are magnificent backgrounds, especially in a river trip through mangroves and jungles into the mist-shrouded mountains. There are numerous scenes depicting the folkways of tribes then untouched by civilization (it's a different story today). Most memorable is a *corroboree*—a spectacular nighttime celebration—which is photographed with a documentarian's attention to detail.

The story, for all its basic simplicity, develops twists and turns that are at times difficult to follow. In some ways, the picture differs little from suchlike American-made films; there's even a renegade named Trask, without whose kind no jungle adventure is truly complete. There are occasional lapses into crude production methods and ragged editing, but for the most part the film is well done, with imaginative photography by the top-ranked Tasman Higgins and a fresh musical score worthy of the concert hall. The spidery witch doctor is worthy of any Who's Who of movie fiends.

Because of scenes involving narcotics, liberal use of swear words, some heated romantic business and a tasteful in-the-buff swimming scene for Margot Rhys, *Uncivilized* was denied the U.S. film industry's Production Code Purity Seal. It was seen chiefly in burlesque theaters. Later, the title was changed to *Pituri*, occasionally with the subtitle *It Makes Them Uncivilized*. Such was the fate in America of one of Australia's best-respected films.

The rugged Mara is Dennis Hoey, an operatic baritone who later came to Hollywood—and is most vividly remembered as the bumbling but thoroughly well-civilized Inspector Lestrade in the Basil Rathbone–Nigel Bruce *Sherlock Holmes* pictures of the 1940s. Hoey is very much the Victor McLaglen type here, hardly handsome in a matinee-idol sense but very much a man of strength, initially menacing but at length sympathetic. Miss Rhys is a beautiful and accomplished leading lady, and Ashton Jarry is effective as a Secret Service agent in disguise. It is the aborigines to whom the show rightfully belongs, however, in a fascinating study of a primitive culture.

CREDITS: Producer and Director: Charles Chauvel, from His Scenario; Original Story: E.V. Timms; Photographed by: Tasman Higgins; Music Composed and Conducted by: Lindley Evans; Dance Director: Richard White; Special Effects: George D. Malcolm; Running time (in U.S.), 77 minutes: Australian Release: During Early 1936; U.S. Release: 1936-40

CAST: Dennis Hoey (Mara); Margot Rhys (Beatrice Lynn); Ashton Jarry (Akbar Jahn); Marcelle Marnay (Sondra); Kenneth Brampton (Trask); Victor Fitzherbert (Hemmingway); E. Gilbert Howell (Vitchi); Edward Silveni (Salter); P. Dwyer (Blum); Rita Aslim (Nardin); John Fernside (Captain); Jessica Malone (Secretary); Richard Mazar (Tong); Z. Gee (Tiki); D. McNiven, P. Rutledge and C. Francis (Troopers); and a Cast of Aboriginal Tribespeople

Tod Slaughter lives admirably up to his surname.

SWEENEY TODD, THE DEMON BARBER OF FLEET STREET
(George King Productions/MGM-British; 1936)

Tod Slaughter is, put mildly, an acquired taste. In some free-for-all of extravagant acting he could have—even if bound and gagged—out-hammed Charles Laughton, Robert Newton, Sir Cedric Hardwicke, Vincent Price and Bela Lugosi combined. As a lecherous scoundrel (his customary role), Slaughter makes W.C. Fields look as bland as Freddie Bartholomew. When offered a motive and the opportunity to commit murder, Slaughter does so with a chuckle and often a witticism. Those of us who treasure his work seldom win any converts, however.

N. Carter "Tod" Slaughter (1885-1956) was a lifelong producer-actor in the provincial theaters of England. His specialty lay in staging Victorian scenarios (which he termed "new-old melodramas") in an authentic style. The results were both comical and horripilating, the humor arising from the knowingly florid acting and dialogue rather than any attempt at parody. Far from the forerunner of "camp" (whatever that nebulous anti-distinction is supposed to mean) that some wrongheaded souls have called him, Slaughter actually was a master at re-creating a bygone school of theater in a straightforward manner. The closest anyone else has come to this approach is Kenneth Branagh, whose 1994 filming of *Mary Shelley's Frankenstein* descends straightaway from Slaughter. Which, of course, is why most of the critics skewered the Branagh *Frankenstein* as overripe corn: The shallow-minded trendies had no idea of where the approach was coming from and could scarcely be bothered to inquire.

Portly but lean-legged, Slaughter cut an undeniably frog-like figure. His large, heavy-lidded eyes, a generous wedge of a nose, a crocodilian smile and an oily voice—all these, he would combine with his over-exaggerations of the naturally exaggerated Grand Manner to convey an impression of unbridled lust and self-congratulatory evil.

George King was a producer-director who delivered both Quota Quickies (under a British government-mandated, mostly hackwork system to keep American films from overrunning U.K. screens) and more prestigious pictures, when allowed the resources. King decided in 1935 to produce one of Slaughter's more popular touring shows, *Maria Marten, or the Murder in the Red Barn*. The film proved almost a literal replay of the stage version, enacted on substantial studio sets and in highly scenic countryside locations. Sold to MGM-British for its Quota program, *Red Barn* enjoyed a certain success within the Empire and eventually received scattered bookings in America. Slaughter would grace more than a dozen films; most were based upon his stage shows and produced by King.

Johnny Singer and Tod Slaughter

The second King-Slaughter picture, *Sweeney Todd, the Demon Barber of Fleet Street*, is their most famous, partly because of the enduring legend thus invoked. The original play, *The String of Pearls*, was written in 1847 by George Dibdin-Pitt; Slaughter had performed it often. The film version was made at the new Sound City at Shepperton, an elegant seven-stage studio on a 60-acre country estate, complete with a manor house. Without spending an unusual amount of money, King managed to pull together some fairly impressive sets of Fleet Street as seen during the early 1800s. These, he peopled with a fine lot of extras in Dickensian costumes. The cellar that figures in the Demon Barber's machinations is an appropriately grim, rat-infested place. There are good period interiors, a trading ship with back-projected seas and a jungle stage.

In London, in 1936, a grouchy customer at a barbershop inquires about a framed cartoon labeled "Sweeney Todd Ready To Give a General Polishing-Up." The barber replies that his ancestor, Sweeney Todd, was history's greatest exponent of the razor. He tells the story:

At the waterfront of a century ago, Sweeney Todd (Tod Slaughter) watches the good ship *Golden Hope* unload its cargo. The first mate, Mark (Bruce Seton), and seaman Pearly (Jerry Verno) receive a fond welcome from their sweethearts, Johanna Oakley (Eve Lister) and her maid, Nan (Davina Craig). Johanna's father (D.J. Williams), owner of the ship, doesn't approve, nor does his silent partner, Todd, who has designs on Johanna. Todd gives Oakley a large amount of money: "The fruits of my razor—so many, I've polished off."

One Mr. Findley (Herman Pierce), carrying a bag of jewels, is invited by Todd to receive "a general polish-up." Todd pulls a lever that causes Findley to go tumbling into the basement, then hastens downstairs to dispose of the victim. The remains are taken in charge by Mrs. Lovatt (Stella Rho), a next-door baker whose meat pies are famed for their distinctive flavor.

Mark survives a native uprising during an African expedition and returns a wealthy man. He is invited to Todd's shop and lands in the basement. Mark is saved, however, by Mrs. Lovatt, who resents Todd's attentions to Johanna. Mr. Parsons (Billy Holland), who fences Todd's stolen finery, pulls a blackmail scam and winds up in the basement. Mark visits, in disguise. Todd murders Mrs. Lovatt and plots arson to destroy the evidence. Finding Johanna snooping about, Todd knocks her unconscious, then sets the fire and scrams, only to return when he spots an opportunity to attack Mark. Todd falls into the deadly chair and is plunged into the conflagration.

So ends the modern-day barber's story. The customer senses an aroma from the meat-pie shop next door. The barber strops his razor—and looks up to see his customer running away.

The chewy dialogue, delivered with chops-licking sincerity by Slaughter, is delightful. Looking over a mass of humankind, he remarks: "A lovely lot of throats, the lot of them... Rich, and mellow to the razor." A customer, seeing Todd give an orphan-boy assistant (Johnny Singer) a penny for a pie, observes that Todd has a kind heart. "Tender as a chicken, sir. My one weakness," Todd responds just before he sends his customer hurtling into the cellar. Another patron is informed: "When I've finished with you, you won't know yourself... a *beautiful* throat for the razor, sir."

Lechery and vanity are crucial to any Slaughter portrayal. "Pearls for your teeth, rubies for your lips and sapphires for your eyes," he tells the young woman of his choice as he presents her with ill-gotten jewelry. We see him applying dye to his hair before he goes calling on the lovely Johanna, who is set forth with proper innocence by Eve Lister. Bruce (later, *Sir* Bruce) Seton is the stalwart hero.

More conventional comedy is supplied by Jerry Verno, as Seton's shipmate, and by Davina Craig as a dotty maidservant. At one point, the action slows just long enough to reveal Verno in the basement, enjoying one of the notorious meat pies.

The later Slaughter melodramas are slicker and more cinematically coherent, especially *The Face at the Window* and *Crimes at the Dark House* (both from 1939). But the quintessential Tod Slaughter—and the ultimate rendering of *Sweeney Todd*, despite many stage-and-screen interpretations since—is the image of the batrachian tonsorial artist, chuckling in anticipation as he creeps down the cellar stairs, open razor at the ready.

CREDITS: Producer and Director: George King; Screenplay: Frederick Hayward; Based upon: George Dibdin-Pitt's 1847 Play, *A String of Pearls*; Dialogue: H.F. Maltby; Assistant Director: Ronnie Kinnoch; Production Manager: Billy Phelps; Photographed by: Jack Parker; Art Director: Percy Bell; Editor: John Seabourne; Visatone System Sound by: J. Byers; Continuity: Olga Brook; Cameraman, Ronald Neame; Running Time, 68 minutes; U.K. Release: March of 1936, Reissued 1940; U.S. Release: 1936-38

CAST: Tod Slaughter (Sweeney Todd); Stella Rho (Mrs. Lovatt); Johnny Singer (Tobias); Eve Lister (Johanna); Bruce Seton (Mark); D. J. Williams (Stephen Oakley); Davina Craig (Nan); Jerry Verno (Pearly); Ben Souten (Beadle); Billy Holland (Mr. Parsons); Herman Pierce (Mr. Findley), Aubrey Mallallieu (Trader Peterson)

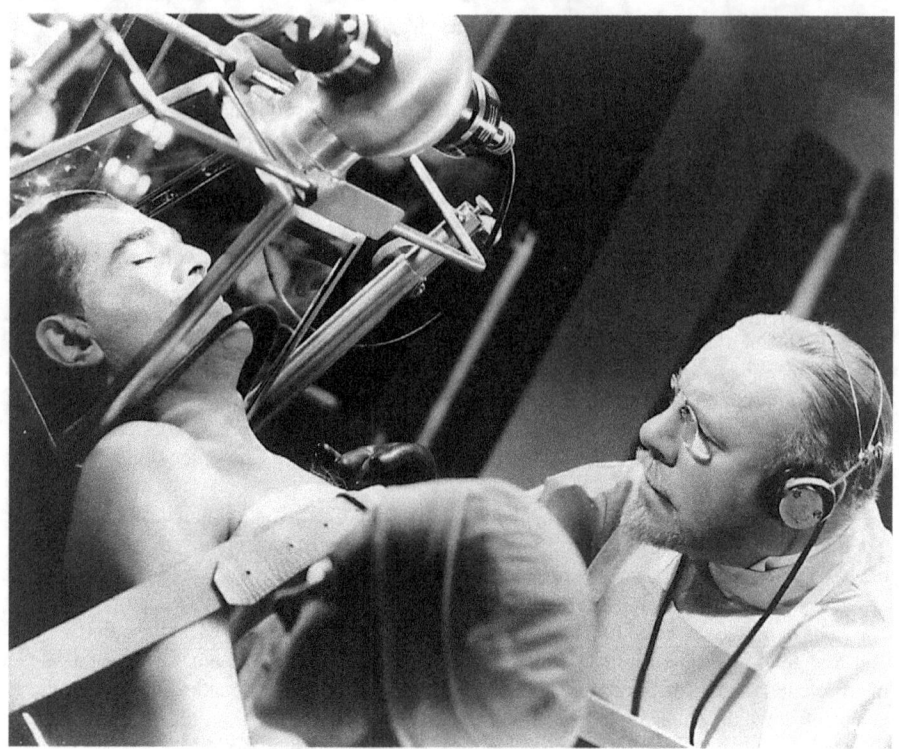
Edmund Gwenn readies Karloff for a resurrection.

THE WALKING DEAD
(Warner Bros. Pictures, Inc.; 1936)

Each studio that produced horror movies had its distinctive approach. Warners' efforts during the silent and early sound periods are generally heavy on Gothic atmosphere and broad comedy. Two pictures from 1931 starring John Barrymore, *Svengali* and *The Mad Genius*, break that mold decisively as pure Gothics, beautifully produced and performed but hardly runaway crowd-pleasers. Then, *Dr. X* and *The Mystery of the Wax Museum*, Warners' Technicolor chillers of 1932-33 (and both directed by Michael Curtiz), set the unique Warners style for the long term. In these, the Gothicism combines with elements of the gangster features for which Warners was famous, and a considerable leavening of comedy often rises. Traditional horror motifs and characters are intermingled with bootleggers, dope peddlers and addicts, smart-alecks from the newspaper racket, hard-boiled cops and slumming socialites. Here, too, figures the fast-editing technique (aptly called "visual shorthand") that is integral to the studio's mobster yarns—a drastic break from the statelier pacing of most horror films. This approach holds fast with *The Walking Dead*, as well as such later efforts as *The Return of Dr. X* (1939) and *The Smiling Ghost* (1941). (But *Sh! The Octopus*, from 1937, is across-the-board comical, except for an oppressive atmosphere and one bracing moment of cathartic horror. Go figure, as the wise old Oriental saying advises.)

The Walking Dead, first of Boris Karloff's handful of star vehicles for Warner Bros., is handsomely produced and generously peopled with top-notch backup talents. Michael Curtiz was in the upper echelon of Warners' contract directors. Certainly, *The Walking Dead* is among

Karloff's better pictures, one that has aged most impressively. In large measure, this quality can be credited to the intelligent script, whose contributing writers were more keenly interested in developing a believable and provocative yarn than in trying to scare the bejeezus out of the customers.

Then, too, there is the surehanded direction of Curtiz, that much-maligned tyrant of the Warners lot, who had the know-how to make *any* type of picture better than it could have been done by almost anyone else. Amazingly versatile, Curtiz is best remembered for his large-scale historical epics—*Moon of Israel* (1924), *Noah's Ark* (1928), *Captain Blood* (1935), *The Charge of the Light Brigade* (1936), *The Adventures of Robin Hood* (1938), *The Private Lives of Elizabeth and Essex* (1939), *The Sea Hawk* (1940), etc., etc., etc. and so forth, not to mention the divergent likes of *Casablanca* (1943) and *White Christmas* (1954). It is difficult to imagine the volatile, Budapest-born director teamed with the gentle Englishman Karloff, but the results are splendid.

Execution—and worse—await Boris Karloff.

Stephen Martin (Kenneth Harlan), a crooked politician, is on trial before Judge Shaw (Joseph King). His defender is Nelson (Ricardo Cortez), a slick society lawyer who is the secret leader of Martin's political machine. Other members are Loder (Barton MacLane), Merritt (Robert Strange) and Blackstone (Paul Harvey). Martin lands a stretch in prison, and a contract is put out on the judge.

John Elman (Karloff), a former concert pianist who once was sentenced in Shaw's court for killing his wife's lover, is selected as the fall guy. The escaping killers are seen by Nancy and Jim (Marguerite Churchill and Warren Hull), sweethearts who are warned to keep mum.

Nelson volunteers to defend Elman. Comes the day of execution, and Jimmy and Nancy confide in their employer, Dr. Beaumont (Edmund Gwenn), a research scientist. Beaumont phones Nelson, who delays getting word to the authorities until too late. Beaumont, who has long sought to revive the dead, arranges to have the body rushed to his laboratory.

So Elman lives again—a crippled shell with no apparent memory. Nancy, conscience-stricken, cares for him tenderly. One day, she plays a selection on the piano that proves to be a trigger. (It is the cloister music from Rubenstein's *Kamenoi Oistrow*.) Elman approaches the piano and plays. Nelson and District Attorney Werner (Henry O'Neill) enter. Elman glares at Nelson and orders him to leave.

Werner suspects Nelson framed Elman. Werner and Beaumont arrange a recital for Elman, making certain that Nelson, Loder, Blackstone and Merritt attend. So unnerved are the suspects that Werner is convinced of their guilt. Elman begins a campaign to confront and question his betrayers, who die in rapid order. Elman takes solace in visits to a cemetery. Finally, Nelson and Loder stalk Elman, and Loder opens fire on the living dead man.

Beaumont questions Elman desperately. Elman warns him, "Leave the dead to their maker." Nelson and Loder are electrocuted when their car swerves into a power station. Elman rallies. "Now, I think I can remember," he murmurs. "After the first shock there was a great feeling of peace. And then—" Death halts his statement. Beaumont, ever the unfeeling scientist, remarks

Karloff, revived

disappointedly: "It will never be known."

The photography meshes well with Curtiz' liking for angular compositions and significant shadow patterns. A daringly Expressionistic device occurs during the recital. The lighting of each close-up, of both accuser and accused, changes on camera. Hugh Reticker's settings are realistic yet mesh well with the calculated eccentricities of the photography.

The resurrection scenes are surprisingly convincing, being based on actual experiments of the day. Shown in operation is a replica of the Lindbergh Heart, or Perfusion Pump, which was developed by famed pilot Charles A. Lindbergh under the supervision of the Nobel medalist Dr. Alexis Carrel, of the Rockefeller Institute. During the operation, Karloff lies on a replica of a tilting device used by Dr. Robert Cornish, a Berkeley scientist who claimed to have revivified a dog, and who portrayed himself, more or less, in an orphaned Universal picture called *Life Returns* (1934-38). This superbly edited montage of wild angles and swiftly changing vantages is accompanied by pulsating music.

Karloff creates in John Elman a creature of surpassing otherworldliness, who is not only viewed with sympathy but also is the *only* wholly sympathetic character. This, despite a forbidding makeup created by Perc Westmore. Karloff was built up four inches taller than he had stood before going to the chair. The left side of his body seems shrunken and partially paralyzed, and his face is shaded and highlighted accordingly. The eye-sockets appear sunken through strategic darkening, and the left eye is smaller than normal, an effect achieved with false eyelids. The other eye is distended by hidden clips. A streak of white hair distinguishes Karloff's Death Row haircut.

Villains of the darkest hue are arrayed against Karloff: The broodingly handsome Ricardo Cortez, the movies' first Sam Spade (in 1931's *The Maltese Falcon*), exudes a crafty menace as the crooked lawyer and gangleader. Robert Strange and Paul Harvey are realistic political schemers. Barton MacLane, the loudest and meanest of the Warner Bros. gangsters, sets forth with chilling conviction a figure of brute instincts. Joseph Sauers (later known as Joe Sawyer) gives an unusual portrayal of a coldly efficient killer, taking thorough charge of one scene in which he coolly defeats his employers at billiards while boasting of his plans for the doomed judge.

Even the good guys let Karloff's Elman down, although most of them try to make amends. The romantic leads withhold crucial information. The state's attorney rightly suspects a frame-up, but he will not let such misgivings stand in the way of a voter-pleasing conviction. The scientist, perceived initially as a kindly sort (and who could be more lovable than Edmund Gwenn?), proves a cold-hearted zealot.

Eventually Beaumont tells Werner that he wants to try to "unlock" Elman's mind with a likely fatal brain operation: "But it's worth that chance!... Things that no man has ever dreamt of will be in *my* reach—*think* of it!" The D.A. *does* think of it—and of the crooks he'll be able to prosecute—and nods. And when Elman dies again, Beaumont registers only frustration.

CREDITS: Director: Michael Curtiz; Screenplay: Ewart Adamson (from a Story by Adamson and Joseph Fields), with Peter Milne, Robert Andrews and Lillie Hayward; Photographed by: Hal Mohr; Editor: Thomas Pratt; Dialogue Director: Irving Rapper; Art Director: Hugh Reticker; Gowns: Orry-Kelly; Musical Director: Leo F. Forbstein; Music: Bernhard Kaun; Special Effects: Fred Jackman, Edwin A. DuPar, Paul Detlefsen and James Gibbons; Sound: Stanley L. Jones, Gerald Alexander and Harold Shaw; Makeup: Perc Westmore; Operative Cameraman, Robert Surtees; Stills: Mac Julian; Running Time: 66 minutes; Released: March 14, 1936

CAST: Boris Karloff (John Elman); Ricardo Cortez (Nelson); Edmund Gwenn (Dr. Beaumont); Margurite Churchill (Nancy); Warren Hull (Jimmy); Barton MacLane (Loder); Henry O'Neill (Werner); Joseph King (Judge Shaw); Addison Richards (Warden); Paul Harvey (Blackstone); Robert Strange (Merritt); Joseph Sauers (Trigger); Eddie Acuff (Betcha); Kenneth Harlan (Stephen Martin); Miki Morita (Sako); Ruth Robinson (Mrs. Shaw); James Burtis and John Kelly (Bodyguards); Adrian Rosley (Florist); Frank Darien (Caretaker); Wade Boteler and Edward Gargan (Guards); Gordon Elliott (American Announcer); Crauford Kent (English Announcer); Earl Hodgins, Eddie Shubert, Larry Kent, Milt Kibbee, Charles Marsh, Isabelle LaMal, Lucille Collins, Charles Sherlock and Paul Panzer (Reporters); James Pierce (Gunman); Lee Phelps, Tom Brower, Harry Hollingsworth and Lee Prather (Bailiffs); George André Beranger (Servant); Nick Moro (Cellist Convict); William Wayne (Trusty); Edgar Sherrod (Priest); Chris Corporal, Tom Schamp, Ed Carli and Jim Pierce (Prisoners); Boyd Irwin (British Doctor); Jean Perry (French Doctor); Nicholas Kobliansky (Russian Doctor); Paul Irving, Malcolm Beach and Malcolm Graham (Guests); Sarah Edwards (Physician); Harrington Reynolds (Doctor); Edward Peil Sr. (Train Engineer); Alphonse Martel (Florist); Michael Curtiz (Intern)

One of Paul Minine's elaborate settings for *Broken Blossoms*

BROKEN BLOSSOMS
(Twickenham Film Corp./Imperial Pictures Corp.; 1936)

D.W. Griffith's *Broken Blossoms* (1919) is one of the more exquisite productions of the silent screen. Drawn from a lurid short story in Thomas Burke's *Limehouse Nights*, the film is a directorial *tour-de-force* that utilizes harsh naturalism to convey spiritual beauty through shabbiness and violent bigotries. Its casting is superb: Richard Barthelmess as a tender-hearted Buddhist, Lillian Gish as a tragic waif and Donald Crisp as a sadist. Elaborate tinting and toning lend a delicacy to the cruelly grim picture.

In July 1935, Griffith found himself in London, where he signed with Julius Hagen, head of the tiny but very busy Twickenham studio, to remake *Broken Blossoms* as a talkie. Inactive in pictures since the failure of his redemption drama *The Struggle* (1931), Griffith went to work with enthusiasm but soon became quarrelsome over the script. When filming began in September, further disagreements erupted over the casting of the female lead. Griffith withdrew in exchange for what he called "a gratifying sum." He was replaced by the studio's production supervisor, the German director Hans Brahm, who as John Brahm would achieve distinction in America with such films as *The Lodger* (1944), *Hangover Square* (1944), *Guest in the House* (1944) and *The Locket* (1946).

The screenplay is the work of Emlyn Williams, author of such successful plays as *Night Must Fall* and *The Corn Is Green*. Williams also plays the Barthelmess role. Curt Courant, one of the best of the Continental cinematographers, came aboard at Brahm's behest.

Chen (Williams), a Buddhist missionary broken by the harshness of Western society, opens an antiques shop in London's Limehouse district. He meets Lucy Burrows (Dolly Haas), a fragile beauty in her teens. Lucy's father is Battling Burrows (Arthur Margetson), an East End prizefighter. It is Burrows' custom to beat Lucy, for she resembles her dead mother, whom Burrows hated.

One night, Chen finds Lucy, collapsed in the snow, and carries her to his house. As he nurses her back to health, Chen falls in love. Robing her in silk and lodging her in a shrine of a room, he worships the girl as he would a princess of Ancient Cathay.

Burrows is enraged to learn of Lucy's new situation. The brute proceeds to Chen's house and catches the girl unprotected, beating her unmercifully. Chen finds the battered corpse of Lucy. His vows to Buddha cast aside, Chen kills Burrows and carries Lucy to her shrine, where he takes his own life.

Several critics railed at Twickenham for making a "gruesome" and "horrifying" version of a classic film that they remembered as "spiritual" and "poetic." Actually, the remake is almost a literal translation of the original, and the horrors descend from Burke and Griffith—although certainly the addition of sound renders things all the more harrowing. The direction is firm, the photography is delicate, and the work of Brahm's wife, the Austrian Dolly Haas, is first-rate, as astonishing as the Gish original. In these particulars, the picture is fully the equal of its 1919 model. However, Emlyn Williams—his own excellence as an actor notwithstanding—is far less affecting than Barthelmess, and Arthur Margetson runs a poor second to Crisp.

Much of the picture was filmed in Limehouse in the actual places described by Thomas Burke, and the baleful atmosphere of the West India Docks is palpable. This realism stands in contrast to a dreamlike depiction of Chen's monastery in China, a deliberate rendering of the unreality of the priest's cloistered youth. These settings are the work of a well-known artist, Paul Minine.

CREDITS: Producer: Julius Hagen; Director: Hans (John) Brahm; Screenplay: Emlyn Williams; Based upon: Thomas Burke's Story, "The Chink and the Child," and D.W. Griffith's Motion Picture of 1919; Lighting Cameraman: Curt Courant; Operative Cameraman: Hal Young; Editors: Jack Harris and Ralph Kemplen; Production Supervisor: Bernard Vorhaus; Art Director: James Carter; Special Settings: Paul Minine; Visatone Sound: Baynham Honri and Carlisle Mounteney; Musical Director: W.L. Trytel; Music: Karol Rathaus; Running Time: 87 minutes; U.K. Release: During May of 1936 via Imperial Pictures Corp.

CAST: Dolly Haas (Lucy Burrows); Emlyn Williams (Chen); Arthur Margetson (Burrows); Ernest Sefton (Manager); C.V. France (High Priest); Basil Radford (Mr. Reed); Edith Sharpe (Mrs. Reed), Ernest Jay (Alf); Bertha Delmore (Daisy); Gibb McLaughlin (Evil Eye); Donald Calthrop (Old Chinaman); Kathleen Harrison (Mrs. Lossy); Kenneth Villiers (Missionary); Jerry Verno (Bert); and Dorothy Minto, Sam Wilkinson

TROUBLE FOR TWO
(Metro-Goldwyn-Mayer Corp./Loew's, Inc.; 1936)

A toast to death...

The filmgoer who insists upon categorizing pictures according to genre might go nuts trying to pigeonhole *Trouble for Two*, MGM's adaptation of Robert Louis Stevenson's "The Suicide Club," from *The New Arabian Nights*. A Ruritanian romance, a comedy, a swashbuckler and a mystery-horror thriller all in one, this handsomely staged entertainment met an end typical of what became of most such costume melodramas during the middle 1930s: failure at the box office.

The tale probably would have fared better four years earlier, when Universal came within days of putting it into production as a Karloff vehicle scripted by John L. Balderston, scenarist of several of the studio's most effective chillers. At MGM, the most star-conscious of studios during the heyday of the star system, the story proved primarily a showcase for two glamorous and sophisticated personalities, with fewer terrors than Stevenson, or Balderston, would have wished. Robert Montgomery and Rosalind Russell are at their sparkling best, well served by witty dialogue, elaborate costuming, impeccable makeup, glistening photography and a top-drawer supporting cast.

In 1880, the Royal Family of Karovia presses for an arranged marriage between Karovian Crown Prince Florizel (Montgomery) and Princess Brenda of Irania. Florizel, who remembers Brenda as an unappealing brat, is allowed one last adventure before he must settle down. He ships out for England with his guardian, Col. Gerry Geraldine (Frank Morgan).

Florizel meets an alluring adventuress (Miss Russell), who sends him on a fool's errand. Later, a young wastrel named Northmore (Louis Hayward) leads Florizel and Gerry to a place called the Suicide Club. The strange woman watches from hiding.

The club's glowering president (Reginald Owen) displays a ritual in which he deals cards to the members. The Ace of Spades is the card of death, and its recipient is the next to die. The recipient of the Ace of Clubs becomes the executioner. The mysterious beauty enters. She receives the Ace of Clubs and Northmore the Ace of Spades. Northmore's obituary notice appears in the next day's newspapers. At another meeting, the lady again receives the Ace of Clubs. The lethal Spade falls to Florizel. The woman breaks down and says she cannot continue. She explains that she had sent Northmore away and planted a false report of his death.

Florizel and the woman find themselves under attack by the club's president. She explains that she is a princess of Irania, and that she ran away rather than marry someone she had despised as a child. Recognizing Florizel on the ship, she had decided to learn more about him from a strategic distance. They decide to return to Karovia—but Florizel and Gerry are lured into a trap. The president is revealed to be one Dr. Noel, a Karovian exile. Florizel escapes, but Gerry is taken hostage.

Florizel now must rescue Gerry and dismantle the Suicide Club as a matter of Karovian diplomacy. Florizel is led to a deserted house, anticipating a duel. Two men are digging a grave. Florizel stalls until help arrives—a military contingent recruited by the princess. Florizel insists upon a duel, which proceeds to the edge of the open grave. Run through, the dying Noel falls into the pit. The royal wedding takes place as planned.

It is gratifying that J. Walter Ruben, one of the more versatile directors of Old Hollywood in that emerging talkie era, chose to lavish such care upon the yarn's weird and eccentric aspects, which might otherwise have been lost among the script's prevailing elements of glamour and romance. Reginald Owen—whose own versatility may be gauged by the fact that in different films he had portrayed both Sherlock Holmes *and* Dr. Watson, as well as a splendid Ebenezer Scrooge—makes a wonderful menace. Looming from the darkness, his aquiline features accented by a sinister makeup with a domed forehead and shaggy eyebrows, Owen suggests Conan Doyle's written descriptions of Holmes' archenemy, Prof. Moriarty. A haunting musical theme by Franz Waxman adds a chilling emphasis to Owen's presence. Backup villainy is capably provided by the sculptor and actor Ivan Simpson (in a role reminiscent of his sniveling manservant in multiple stage-and-screen versions of *The Green Goddess*), and by an assortment of skulking ruffians.

The beloved Frank Morgan is capital as the courageous but comically flustered bodyguard. Effectively offbeat touches are added by Louis Hayward and by Walter Kingsford as, respectively, the youngest and eldest of the alienated flakes who have joined the Suicide Club. (Hayward was destined soon to achieve stardom, and eventually to star in another takeoff on R.L. Stevenson, 1951's *The Son of Dr. Jekyll*.) E.E. Clive is a delight as a kindly king.

The dialogue has a nice sense of period about it. "Well, sir, here we are," Florizel tells Dr. Noel as he forces him to the edge of a yawning grave. "I must not detain you." Charles Clarke's photography could not be bettered; it captures the elegant, the humorous and the bizarre aspects of the adventure with equal radiance on all fronts.

CREDITS: Producer: Louis D. Lighton; Director: J. Walter Ruben; Screenplay: Manuel Seff and Edward E. Paramore Jr.; Contributing Authors: A.E. Thomas, A. W. Hannemann, Keene Thompson, Jack Murray, Allen Boretz and Vincent Lawrence; Based upon: Robert Louis Stevenson's 1895 Story, "The Suicide Club"; Music: Franz Waxman; Art Director: Cedric Gibbons; Associates: Joseph C. Wright and Edwin B. Willis; Photographed by: Charles G. Clarke; Editor: Robert J. Kern; Sound: Douglas Shearer; Special Effects: A. Arnold Gillespie, Warren Newcombe and Tom Tutwiler; Costumes: Dolly Tree; Assistant Director: Dolph Zimmer; Makeup: Jack Dawn; Sound System: Western Electric; Running Time: 83 minutes; Released: May 22, 1936

CAST: Robert Montgomery (Prince Florizel); Rosalind Russell (Miss Vandeleur); Frank Morgan (Col. Geraldine); Reginald Owen (President); Louis Hayward (Northmore); E.E. Clive (King); Walter Kingsford (Malthus); Ivan Simpson (Collins); Tom Moore (Maj. O'Rook); Robert Greig (Fat Man); Guy Bates Post (Ambassador); Pedro de Cordoba (Sergei); Leyland Hodgson (Capt. Rich); Pat O'Malley (Ship's Captain); Dorothy Arville (Singer); Carola Alena (Gypsy Dancer); and Forrester Harvey, Edgar Norton, Sidney Bracy, Paul Porcasi, Philo McCullough, Léonard Carey

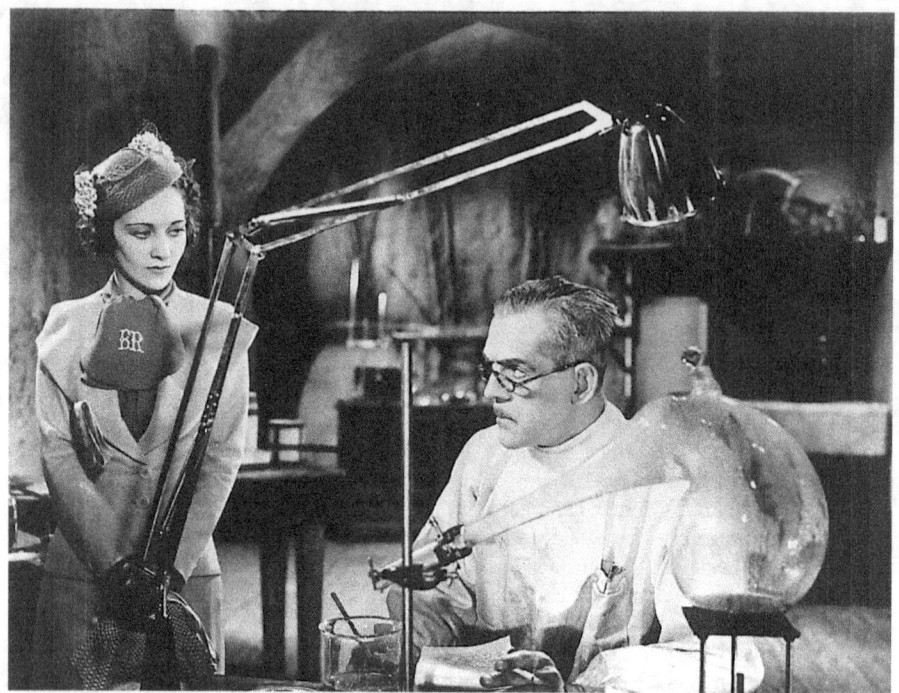

Karloff's emphatic and spirited acting is at odds with the stodgy pacing of *Juggernaut*.

JUGGERNAUT
a.k.a.: THE DEMON DOCTOR
(Twickenham Film Corp.; 1936)

Boris Karloff's mad-doctor persona must date technically as far back as James Young's *The Bells* (1926), in which the actor holds forth as a Caligari-like mesmerist, pre-dating his larger indelible typecasting as a creation, more so than a practitioner, of renegade science. The operative distinction in Karloff's 1932 star turn as Sax Rohmer's Dr. Fu Manchu is the rank of *Doctor*. Karloff's enactments in *The Mummy* (1932) and *The Ghoul* (England; 1933) are handily as much scientist/sorcerers as supernaturally motivated stalkers. His Im-Ho-Tep in *The Mummy* is nothing so much as a Romeo of the occult—a primitive savant of Ancient Thebes who, damned by intolerant contemporaries for a forbidden love, returns to life in the 20th Century to get cracking on some unfinished business. And of course Karloff's combustible Midas in *The Invisible Ray* (1936) bears mentioning here, even though the role proves as monstrous as it is a case of maddened genius.

It took the back-to-back British productions of *Juggernaut* and *The Man Who Changed His Mind*, however, to cinch the mad-doctor image that would define Karloff's work well along into the WWII years: an utterly human sophisticate, perhaps more sinned-against than outright sinner, and driven more by the maverick healing urge than by any mechanically fantastic plot devices. (Karloff's heroic *Mr. Wong* pictures at Monogram are a self-contained packet, more a holding pattern than a process of development or variations upon a theme.)

It was at Columbia Pictures, with sidetracks to *The Ape* at Monogram and to *Night Key* and *Black Friday* at Universal, that Karloff perfected this style, risking repetitive monotony—"a string of kindly old doctors or scientists whose experiments go horribly wrong," as the historian Phil Hardy has put it—to compile an insular *oeuvre*-in-miniature. Returning to Universal for

House of Frankenstein in 1944, Karloff would come full-circle to the immersion in gleefully thoroughgoing wickedness with which he had distinguished *The Mask of Fu Manchu* at MGM.

The British-made forebears of this approach are of especial interest on a variety of counts: Karloff is fascinating to watch at work in the mannered drawing-room (melo)dramatic context of his native society; the pictures place the scientific extravagances at the service of emotional intensities; and each grants Karloff a more imaginatively fulfilled death scene than the Columbias generally would allow him.

Juggernaut finds one Dr. Sartorius (Karloff) financially frustrated in a quest to find a cure for polio. He is called upon by Lady Yvonne (Mona Goya), the glamorous wife of Sir Charles Clifford (Morton Selden). The conniving Yvonne has encountered increasing difficulty in obtaining money to supply the wants of her opportunistic lover, Capt. Arthur Halliday (Anthony Ireland). Yvonne arranges for Sartorius and his nurse, Eve Rowe (Joan Wyndham), to settle in at the Clifford mansion to care for the ailing Sir Charles. If Sartorius will help Yvonne gain control of the Clifford fortune, he will be given the £20,000 he needs to conclude his experiments.

Lord Clifford grows noticeably weaker. Suspecting his wife's infidelity and knowing well her free-spending ways, he assigns power-of-attorney authority to his son, Roger (Arthur Margetson). Roger catches Halliday and Yvonne in a clinch and angrily informs her of the new situation. Yvonne confronts Lord Clifford, who collapses. Sartorius arrives to administer an injection. As Roger drags Yvonne from the room, she sinks her teeth into his hand. Lord Clifford dies.

Eve takes the syringe to a chemist for analysis. Sartorius and Yvonne conspire to poison Roger. Sartorius intercepts the chemist's report. Roger has begun to feel the effects of the gradual poisoning, and Sartorius insists upon treating him for tetanus. Eve bursts in, just in time to halt another lethal injection. The butler, who had seen Yvonne poisoning Roger's drinking-water, has already summoned the law. Sartorious plunges the needle into his own arm and falls dead.

The stiff-as-starch unfolding of the soap-operatics must struggle for dominance throughout with Karloff's forceful portrayal; he prevails, despite some tedious stretches. The villainy is more or less equally shared by the coldly beautiful Mona Goya, as a proto-trophy wife whose treacheries have not so noble a motivation as the dirty deeds of Karloff's Dr. Sartorius.

CREDITS: Producer: Julius Hagen; Director: Henry Edwards; Story: Alice Campbell; Screenplay: Cyril Campion and H. Fowler Mear; Additional Dialogue and Adaptation: Heinrich Frankel; Photographed by: Sidney Blythe and William Luff; Editor: Michael Chorlton; Art Director: James Carter; Musical Director: W.L. Trytel; Running Time: 73 Minutes; U.K. Release: September 8, 1936; U.S. Distribution: Grand National Pictures, Inc.

CAST: Boris Karloff (Dr. Sartorius); Joan Wyndham (Eve Rowe); Arthur Margetson (Roger Clifford); Mona Goya (Lady Yvonne Clifford); Anthony Ireland (Capt. Arthur Halliday); Morton Selden (Sir Charles Clifford); Nina Bouciault (Mary Clifford); Gibb McLaughlin (Jacques); J.S. Roberts (Chalmers); V. Rietti (Dr. Bosquet)

Karloff reserves the right to change his mind.

THE MAN WHO CHANGED HIS MIND
a.k.a.: THE MAN WHO LIVED AGAIN
a.k.a.: DR. MANIAC
a.k.a.: THE BRAIN SNATCHER
(Gaumont-British Picture Corp./Gainsborough Pictures, Ltd./
Gaumont-British Picture Corp. of America; 1936)

Unique among Boris Karloff's trio, not to say trilogy, of U.K.-made Depression-Era chillers, *The Man Who Changed His Mind* defies convention in ways beyond the grasp of *The Ghoul* (which is, essentially, an emulation of the Universal style) and moves like a bandit by contrast with the ever-so-British plodding of *Juggernaut*. Robert Stevenson's *The Man Who Lived Again* benefits especially from the screenwriter teaming of the master-of-horrors John L. Balderston and the extraordinarily droll Sidney Gilliat, better known as a writer for Alfred Hitchcock. Even the (authentic) title is brilliantly written—a splendid pun, bridging the literal and figurative realms in a few gemlike words. The film's Americanized proxy titles take a line of lurid lesser resistance.

Karloff's quest here is eternal life, achieved by means more complex than just good clean living, with selfish side-interests: "I understand—I'm *old*," he tells the lovely Anna Lee after she has rejected him in favor of John Loder. "But... with this new power, I needn't *remain* old. I can take a new body, a *young* body, and keep my own brain. And you, *too*—you won't always be young. When you grow old, I can give *you* a new body. *Think* of it: I offer you eternal youth, eternal *loveliness*!"

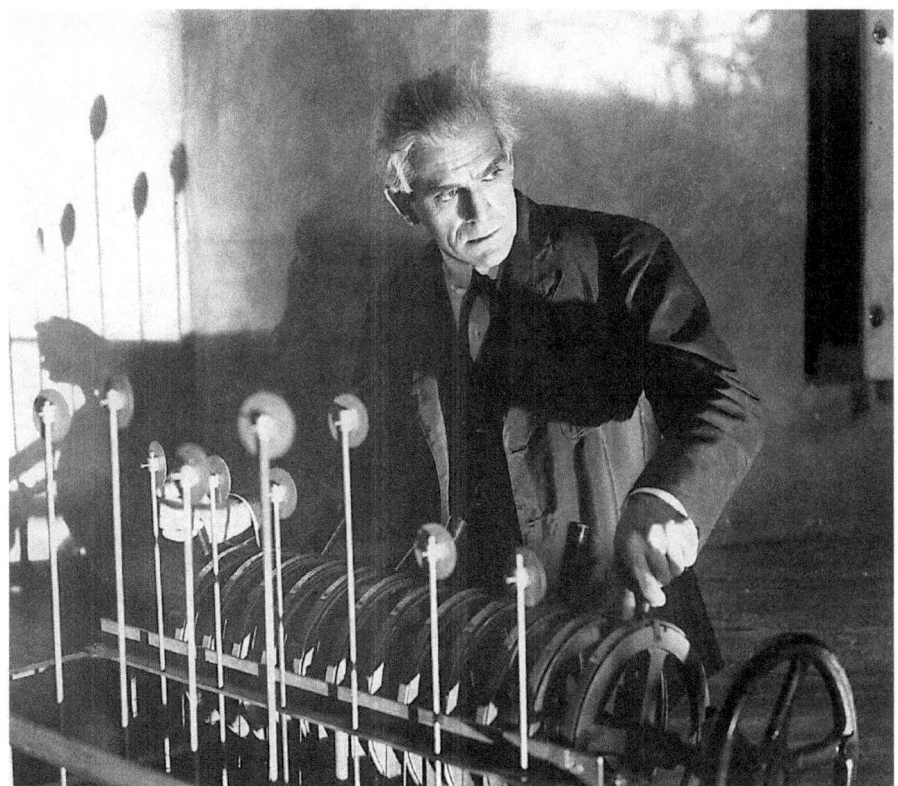

Karloff, in his element

His unorthodoxy has estranged the eminent Dr. Laurience (Karloff) from his colleagues. Working in solitude, his only companion a malicious invalid named Clayton (Donald Calthrop), Laurience realizes he is nearing success and summons Dr. Clare Wyatt (Miss Lee), a brain surgeon. Laurience achieves unimpeachable results in an exchange of minds between apes.

Lord Haslewood (Frank Cellier), a publisher, bankrolls Laurience's project. Claire becomes romantically involved with Haslewood's son, Dick (Loder). But when the British Medical Society rebuffs Laurience and Lord Haslewood begins to doubt the radical experiments, Laurience decides to use his discoveries for crueler purposes.

Clayton's vile spirit is transferred into Lord Haslewood's body, ensuring continued support—until the tycoon proves to have an inoperable heart condition. Clayton/Haslewood now demands the body of Dick Haslewood.

Laurience, however, intends to transmit his own intellect into the youth's body. Clare realizes that the unthinkable has occurred when Dick suddenly takes up Laurience's habit of chain-smoking. After a wild pursuit, an onslaught of poison gas, a fatal fall and a re-transmigration of minds, Dick Haslewood is restored. Laurience, dying, is forgiven by Clare, who promises to destroy the doctor's invention.

Frank Cellier is especially good as the big shot who proves both friend and foe to Karloff, lapsing convincingly from pomposity to malice when the mind-swap proves a success. Anna Lee is almost a gutsier, more defiant Renfield to Karloff's vampire-of-the-mind, who lives in Dracula-style isolation and whose distant laboratory is regarded with a superstitious awe by the locals. John Loder is a hapless and helpless romantic lead, but he does well at mimicking the Karloff mannerisms.

Karloff relishes the ripe dialogue of *The Man Who Changed His Mind*.

Karloff relishes the ripe dialogue. After a rebuke by his fellow scientists, his eyes narrowed to slits, he hisses: "All right! I'll keep it to myself, I'll *use* it for myself—and I'll use it for my own *ends*!" While strangling the transformed Cellier, Karloff taunts his victim: "There's no further need for *you*. Thanks to you, the boy's on his way to the Institute, where I'll take his body and he'll take *mine*—the body that'll be hanged for *murder*!"

Kent, England-born Anna Lee, whose acting career continued apace into the middle 1990s, spoke with us during the 1980s of Karloff's enthusiasm for *The Man Who Changed His Mind*: "That was the first picture I made with Boris, along with John Loder and a pair of chimpanzees. What a jolly company! Years and years later [in 1946], Boris and I would make *Bedlam*, in Hollywood, with Val Lewton, and the renewed friendship clicked immediately, as though not a tick had passed since our English film.

"And what a dear, gentle, loving man Boris was! Cherished the badman roles, he did—and I think that was because he could bring so much passion to them. He loved the opportunity to bring a poetic interpretation to a ferocious speech. Boris never did just a line reading; he *interpreted* everything he was given to speak. You listen to his rants today, in the motion pictures, and it's as though he were reciting poetry.

"That was a common ground for us, for that matter," Miss Lee continued. "Boris loved poetry, and so did I. I kept trying to surprise him with some favorite verse of mine—but, you know, I could *never* find a poem that Boris didn't know!"

Robert Stevenson had weighed in as a director in 1932 and resettled in Hollywood in 1940, keeping busy well into the '70s. *The Man Who Lived Again* proved to be his only out-and-out horror picture, although the bombastic 1944 version of *Jane Eyre* is hardly without its eerie qualities. As a favored director for the Disney machine, Stevenson would deliver such fantastic oddities as *Darby O'Gill and the Little People* (1959) and *The Absent-Minded Professor* (1961).

CREDITS: Director: Robert Stevenson; Screenplay: Sidney Gilliatt, L. DuGarde Peach and John L. Balderston; Photographed by: Jack Cox; Music: Louis Levy; Art Director: Vetchinsky; Gowns: Molyneaux; Sound: W. Salter; Editor: R.F. Dearing; Cutter: Alfred Roome; Makeup: W.T. Partleton; Animal Supervision: Momo; Running Time: 66 Minutes; U.K. Release: September 11, 1936; Reissued as *Dr. Maniac* by: Favorite Films, Inc.; and as *The Brain Snatcher* by: Vogue Pictures

CAST: Boris Karloff (Dr. Laurience); Anna Lee (Dr. Clare Wyatt); John Loder (Dick Haslewood); Frank Cellier (Lord Haslewood); Donald Calthrop (Clayton); Cecil Parker (Dr. Gratton); Prof. Holloway (Lyn Harding); D.J. Williams (Innkeeper); Sam and Gonette (Chimpanzees)

NIGHT KEY
(Universal Pictures Corp.; 1937)

An ensemble still from the *Night Key* shoot

Even his one wholly benevolent, non-horrorific star turn at Universal finds Boris Karloff in a tense and unseemly situation: He is a betrayed and justifiably dodgy genius of an inventor in *Night Key*. The role dovetails with the greater body of Karloff's mad-doctor pictures—with less a stretch than one might expect.

Dave Mallory (Karloff) has been nosed out of the rights to a sophisticated burglar-alarm system by a former partner, Steven Ranger (Samuel S. Hinds). Mallory, working in haste against failing eyesight, contrives a device that renders the earlier invention obsolete; he demonstrates the new gizmo to Ranger, who agrees to utilize it on a royalty basis. Mallory believes he has assured his daughter, Joan (Jean Rogers), of security—until he learns that Mallory has bought into the new alarm only to keep it off the market. Enraged, Mallory informs Ranger: "What I create, I can destroy." (The situation is very like that which would drive Bela Lugosi to a fugue of murderous invention in 1940's *The Devil Bat*.)

Mallory contrives to neutralize the Ranger system. He and a small-time burglar called Petty Louie (Hobart Cavanaugh) enter Ranger-protected establishments, stealing nothing but leaving humiliating evidence. Ranger assigns a security guard, Jim Travers (J. Warren Hull), to find Mallory. Travers meets Joan and falls in love with her. John "the Kid" Baron (Alan Baxter), a gang leader, abducts Joan and forces Mallory to help burglarize the Ranger-protected shops. Mallory defies the mob with an electrical blaster. He and Petty Louie nearly escape, but Louie is slain.

Travers breaks from Ranger to help Joan and her father. Baron and his mob flee with Mallory and Joan, but Mallory causes the car to crash, enabling the police to dismantle the gang. Ranger, in a generous turnabout, declines to press charges against Mallory, welcomes him into a lucrative new partnership, and helps to find a cure for Mallory's failing vision.

If Karloff had longed for a change of pace, he certainly found it in *Night Key*, which exploits his grandfatherly presence—at only age 50—in ways that prefigure his work of much later years as a player on the televised *Shirley Temple's Storybook Theatre* and as a narrator of fairytale recordings for children. *Night Key* is, even so, hardly a kiddie picture: Karloff's furious indignation is as intense as ever, and his displays of malicious mischief suggest such a subversive guerrilla intellect that it's a wonder the Production Code's Status Quo enforcers did not object. His sentimental streak shows impressively, too—but of course that innate tender-heartedness figured, as well, in many of his more monstrous portrayals. *Night Key* was a contract-honoring throwaway in the larger scheme of Karloff's career, but its timing was strategic: In the midst of an international embargo on horror films, the picture demonstrated Karloff's versatility to an industry that might otherwise have let him fade out with the endangered genre.

The supporting ranks are ably filled, especially by *Flash Gordon* heroine Jean Rogers and cliffhanger champ-in-waiting Warren Hull. Hobart Cavanaugh is effective as a comic-relief

Karloff registers a saddening sense of betrayal in *Night Key*.

player turned tragic, and Samuel S. Hinds fares well as a socially upstanding patent thief who finally sees the error of his ways. Lloyd Corrigan was nearing the end of his directing career when he helmed *Night Key*. The rotund Corrigan turned wholeheartedly to acting by the end of the '30s, specializing in chipper and/or henpecked character parts.

CREDITS: Associate Producer: Robert Presnell; Director: Lloyd Corrigan; Screenplay: Tristram Tupper and John C. Moffitt; Story: William Pierce; Photographed by: George R. Robinson; Art Directors: Jack Otterson and Loren Richards; Film Editor: Otis Garrett; Special Effects: John P. Fulton; Music: Leo Forbes; Sound: Bernard B. Brown; Technician: Jesse Bastian; Gowns: Vera West; Makeup: Jack Pierce; Electrical Effects: Kenneth Strickfaden; Running Time: 67 Minutes; Released: May 2, 1937

CAST: Boris Karloff (Dave Mallory); Jean Rogers (Joan Mallory); J. Warren Hull (Jim Travers); Hobart Cavanaugh (Petty Louie); Samuel S. Hinds (Steven Ranger); Alan Baxter (John "the Kid" Baron); Dave Oliver (Mike); Edwin Maxwell (Kruger); Ward Bond (Finger Man); Frank Reicher (Karl); George Humbert (Spinelli); George Cleveland (Adams); Charles Wilson (Capt. Wallace); Ethan Laidlaw (Gangster); Frank Hagney (Hoodlum); Jim Hanlon (Announcer); Charles Sullivan (Cab Driver); Ralph Dunn (Shipping Agent)

THE ATTIC OF TERROR *et Seq.*
(Warner Bros., Inc./The Vitaphone Corp.; 1937-39)

Seekers after mystery haunt strange places: They look for inspiration to Ancient Egypt, to ruined Anghkor, to Loch Ness, to the Devil Horse Jungles of forgotten Siam, to the inbred and hostile moonshine country of the American Southland or to what few unexplored regions this shrunken planet has managed to hold in secret. The results of their searching can be as enriching to the culture as the unearthed treasures of the Pharaohs or the heights of artistry to which the likes of Rudyard Kipling and O. Henry and Ambrose Bierce and Irvin S. Cobb were moved by their own restless explorations.

The invention of moving pictures, toward the end of the 19th Century, brought such seekers ever nearer the objective of sharing their adventures with a massed audience. Explorers including Theodore Roosevelt, Martin and Osa Johnson, Merian C. Cooper and Ernest B. Schoedsack, Frank "Bring 'Em Back Alive" Buck and even that globetrotting champion cowboy Ken Maynard seized upon the potential of portable moviemaking as a means of capturing their exploits on the spot—the better to capture, in turn, the popular fancy with the power of the projected image. Inevitably, the filmmaking urge would lead homeward: Once some Great Adventure had been documented, only within the sheltering confines of civilization could the raw footage be refined to a commercially viable essence. Cooper and Schoedsack, the most remarkable of those expeditionary moviemakers, brought so great an influence to bear upon the Hollywood establishment that their 1932-33 production of *King Kong*—purely a studio concoction, though based upon the partners' ventures as jungle-prowling cameramen—has become more famous today than it was in first release.

Many are called, but few are chosen. For every rousing adventure movie that will be remembered beyond its makers' lifetimes, any number of others must lie forgotten within their own strata of history. Likewise for the makers of those disremembered pictures, many of whom led lives as harrowing and as adventurous as anything they ever committed to the page or the screen. Such has been the fate of Warner Bros.' "The Attic of Terror" and the long-running series

that it launched—and of Floyd Gibbons (1887-1939), the veteran war correspondent-turned-radio personality who created that series.

Gibbons' days of hair's-breadth desperate adventure were for the most part behind him when he approached Warners during 1936 with a pitch for a series of true-to-life hair-raisers for the picture-show market. Gibbons was not looking here to his own exploits for inspiration, but rather to that vast audience that had since 1929 made him a phenomenally popular radio journalist, starting out with fellow commentator Lowell Thomas on the NBC network. Putting together a loose-knit organization he called the Adventurers' Club, via the influence of his Thursday-night *Headline Hunters* broadcasts over the CBS network, Gibbons convinced Warners to ante up thousands of prize dollars for "the best true-adventure stories" submitted from September 1, 1937, to May 15, 1938. The yarn considered the most sensational would snag $1,000; all those selected for filming would earn $250 each, with another $25-a-pop going to the runners-up chosen for use on Gibbons' radio program. Their telling on radio would be distinctive, related in the not-quite-frenzied manner that had become Gibbons' trademark. He often said he learned to speak rapidly, and with precise diction, because "there always seems more to say than there is time to say it, and I dislike leaving out the interesting details."

"Everybody has had at least one adventure, and there's movie material in everyone's life," declared Gibbons. "No one knows that better than I do."

By the time Warner Bros. and its affiliated Vitaphone Corp. announced the formal contest, Gibbons had already selected a lead-off story and commissioned its adaptation to the screen, collaborating with scriptwriter Ira Genet and veteran silents-into-talkies director Joseph E. Henabery. The contest was barely a month under way when Warners released the 20-minute featurette "The Attic of Terror," a backwoods Southern Gothic based upon a close shave recollected by one Edward Capps, a canned-tamale tycoon from Detroit.

Short subjects were all over the moviemaking map in those days. They ranged from cartoons and slapstick comedies, to newsreels and sports revues, to documentary-like pieces and quick-sketch romances and thrillers, and they varied in length from one reel (five to 10 minutes) to three reels (half an hour, more or less). The shorts played the same uptown and neighborhood theatres as the feature-length attractions, serving as warm-up acts that gave the customers a greater sense of getting their money's worth.

Warner Bros. had an especial liking for weird-mystery shorts. Director Henabery spent the 1930s as Warners' most dependable short-subject helmer, headquartering at the Vitaphone Studio in Brooklyn. Warners' Eastern satellite seldom made anything more out-of-the-ordinary than the *Your True Adventures* series, which became a favorite diversion of Alfred Hitchcock and seems likely to have influenced RKO-Radio producer Val Lewton's insistence upon showing "those extraordinary things that happen to ordinary people." Though announced to run for 13 installments, *Your True Adventures* proved so popular that its span was extended to 17 during nearly two years. Ticket-selling appeal was so strong that the yarns probably would have continued if not for the death of Gibbons, the series' combustible intellect, in 1939. The greater fascination was that the tales were arguably factual—though helped along by dramatic license—and that anyone with a tale to tell could play.

"The Attic of Terror," whose work-in-progress title had been "Mr. Capps and the Corpse," derives from Edward Capps' memoir of his early years as a traveling salesman for a tobacco company. Capps is played at age 22 by Chester Stratton, who never caught on as a feature-film player despite impressive work on stage and in the short-subject realm.

The film catches up with Capps as he comes charging on horseback into a customer-rich region of Kentucky's Cumberland Mountains, hoping to overtake a rival salesman named Gus Lobe. Sidetracked by a terrific storm, Capps seeks shelter at the cabin of an elderly couple known as Clayt and Maw (William Morrow and Jane Fawcett). Reassured by their welcome, Capps enjoys a meal in expectation of riding on after the rain has stopped.

"Gosh!" Capps says. "Looks like it's never going to let up!" He asks whether his hosts might grant him lodging for the night.

"You ain't aimin' to leave afore we're up?" asks Clayt.

Capps, taking the hint, says, "I guess I'd better pay you now, huh?"

"Aw, that's all right," Clayt replies, and shows Capps to the attic.

Upstairs, Capps notices two beds—one of them, occupied. Clayt nonchalantly explains that the blanketed figure is "a daid man. Jus' went to sleep an' didn't wake up. Been waitin' for it to stop rainin' so's we could take him out." Capps balks at bunking up in close quarters with a stiff, but he decides to stay after Clayt reminds him, "It's mighty damp outside."

Capps falls into an uneasy slumber but is awakened suddenly by voices that he at first dismisses as a dream. It is still night, and the storm continues. Capps sees a light through a crack in the floor. Peering through a knothole, he sees Clayt, Maw and a massively built man (Al Ochs) emptying the saddlebags from Capps' horse.

"Thar ain't no money hyar," Clayt complains, to which Maw adds: "He mus' hev it on him." The big man asks what their next step should be. Clayt asks, "Well, d'ye want the money?"

The hillbillies attack

Wide awake now and fearing for his life, Capps rushes to the other bed, draws back the blanket and sees the face of Gus Lobe, his competitor. Lobe's skull has been shattered. Certain that his hosts will be coming upstairs any moment now, Capps changes places with the corpse.

The two men climb into the attic and approach Capps' bed. The tall man raises a club to strike, but he is interrupted by a knock from downstairs. Maw admits two neighbors. Clayt and the tall man return downstairs.

Capps, certain he will be killed sooner or later, seizes a water pitcher and rushes downstairs on a rickety ladder, hurling the pitcher into the midst of his surprised hosts and then rushing outdoors. Before the murderous hillbillies can react, Capps has reached his horse and made a dash for safety. He returns the next day with a posse, assuring prompt justice for the killers. "The Attic of Terror" ends with Floyd Gibbons' introduction of the real Edward Capps, who accepts payment for the use of his story. Capps seems every bit the level-headed work-ethic American squire, the type who could relate such an experience with a straight face and a clear conscience.

Typical of the Warners shorts, "The Attic of Terror" cracks along with the pace of a fever-dream, allowing for efficient character introductions and getting right to the point of the title. Though the telling is unremittingly grim, the film seems almost a rough-sketch template for Paramount's famous Fred MacMurray starrer *Murder, He Says* (1945), a gallows comedy of the old-dark-house school, set among a clan of degenerate hill folks. The acting in "Attic" is uniformly good—and surprisingly cinematic, given the players' stagebound origins—and the menacing characters seem authentically rustic, with an especially strong command of dialect. Future television star Phil Silvers puts in a small appearance in the framing segment.

Joseph Henabery (1888-1976) had come to the movies in 1913 as an actor, signing on additionally as an assistant to D.W. Griffith for *The Birth of a Nation* and *Intolerance* (1915-16). Henabery soon weighed in as a director under Griffith's supervision and matured rapidly as a favored artist with Douglas Fairbanks' production company, then with Paramount and First National, among other old-line major studios. Henabery's Hollywood years were spent on pictures starring such name-brand players as Roscoe "Fatty" Arbuckle, Betty Compson and Rudolph Valentino. Upon the decisive arrival of talking pictures during 1929-30, Henabery resettled back East with Vitaphone. He stuck with the short subjects until 1943, when he returned to featuremaking with *The Leather Burners*. This was his last feature-lengther until 1948, when he delivered a mental-hygiene feature called *Shades of Grey* for the U.S. military, and then retired.

Floyd Gibbons was perpetually on the lookout for what he called "that certain story" that would scoop the competition, and he seems to have found it time and again—not only in this Warners series, but also in a larger career that had landed him in the major leagues of journalism and battlefront heroism during World War I.

Gibbons told an interviewer in 1937: "Plunk me down in any town… without a dime or any more clothes than I have on my back, and under a different name, so that nobody knows me—and I'll bet that within a day I'll have… a story that no other reporter in town has. And on the strength of it, I'll get a job."

That commanding aggressiveness was no pose. The Warners Bros. publicity department scarcely needed to justify calling Gibbons "a thrill dispenser" because it could refer simply to the newsman's track record of having "literally courted danger."

By 1918, Gibbons had become a ground-zero correspondent in France for the Chicago *Tribune*. On June 6, he went over the top with the first assault in the historic Battle of Belleau Wood. Gibbons was accompanying Army Maj. John Berry, who fell wounded while leading the charge. Rushing to assist Berry, Gibbons was struck in the left shoulder by a burst of German machine-gun fire. A bullet hit one arm, but Gibbons persisted, only to be halted by a third bullet that tore out his left eye and shattered his skull. He lay as if dead for hours, finally crawling to safety under cover of night. His show of gallantry under fire earned Gibbons two citations from the French government.

His success as a radio announcer notwithstanding, Gibbons long continued to take to the high country in search of adventure and "that certain story." As late as 1936, even as his CBS segments chronicling other people's wilder experiences were pointing toward the Warners series, Gibbons spent a stretch covering the Spanish Civil War. Radio and the movies, however, held the greater charm for him at this stage of a distinguished and flamboyant career.

It was, indeed, the true-to-life adventures—his own—that had landed Gibbons a berth in the radio-personality racket.

"I was finishing the manuscript of my novel, *The Red Napoleon*," Gibbons wrote in press notes for Vitaphone, "and it was necessary for me to have some technical data on radio operation." In the course of a research meeting with NBC's brass, someone suggested that Gibbons' wartime experiences might make good broadcast fodder.

"For several years," a Warners publicist wrote in 1937, "[Gibbons] has been broadcasting thrill stories sent him by fans—and now his air-adventuring has taken a new turn."

That turning point yielded, over a respectably long haul, one of the most brightly sustained series in the history of the short-form melodrama. *Your True Adventures* bears mentioning in the same breath with the *Pete Smith Specialties*, Robert Benchley's droll one-reelers, cartoons from the houses of Fleischer and Warner, and Hal Roach's *Our Gang* adventures—to name a handful of those series that would elevate the short subject beyond the program-filler level.

Beyond "The Attic of Terror," the balance of the series (all directed by Joe Henabery) would be: "Night Intruder" (Screenplay: Ira Genet; two reels; issued July 23, 1938); "Trapped Underground" (Genet; two reels; August 20, 1938); "Toils of the Law" (Genet; 11 minutes; October 15, 1938); "Defying Death" (Genet; 12 minutes; November 28, 1938); "Fighting Judge" (Cyrus D. Wood; one reel; November 29, 1938); "Identified" (Wood; two reels; December 15, 1938); "Human Bomb" (Burnet Hershey; one reel; December 16, 1938); "Treacherous Waters" (Genet; 10 minutes; December 23, 1938); "High Peril" (Hershey; 12 minutes; February 20, 1939); "A Minute from Death" (Hershey; one reel; March 4, 1939); "Chained" (Hershey; 12 minutes; April 1, 1939); "Voodoo Fires" (Hershey; one reel; May 6, 1939); "Haunted House" (Hershey; 12 minutes; June 3, 1939); "Lives in Peril" (Hershey; 11 minutes; July 1, 1939); "Three Minute Fuse" (Hershey; 11 minutes; July 29, 1939); and "Verge of Disaster" (Hershey; 11 minutes; August 26, 1939).

CREDITS: Director: Joseph Henabery; Screenplay: Ira Genet; Based upon: An Autobiographical Account by Edward Capps; Photographed by: Ray Foster; Running Time: Approx. 20 Minutes; Released: October 18, 1937

CAST: Floyd Gibbons (Himself); Jane Fawcett (Maw); William Morrow (Clayt); Chester Stratton (Edward Capps); Al Ochs (Ike); Cliff Heckinger and Howard Negley (Mountaineers); Alexander Campbell (Johnson); June Nash (Secretary); Ralph Riggs (Reporter); Phil Silvers (Photographer); Edward Capps (Himself)

THE SPIDER'S WEB
(Columbia Pictures Corp.; 1938)

The first two episodes reveal... more thugs being killed in five reels than in most other complete serials.
—From the *Motion Picture Exhibitor* Review

"Got a couple of prisoners... if they're still alive."—Warren Hull, as the Spider

Some four generations before the Disney machine made *Arachnophobia* something of a household word in 1990—and longer than that before a picture shot under the dumbed-down title of *Arac Attack* would dumb down itself even further to the hyphen-deficient *Eight Legged Freaks* for a 2002 release—the motion-picture industry had begun exploiting a fascinated abhorrence of spiders among its massed audience.

This squeamish popular appeal ranges well beyond such overliteral representations as Universal-International Pictures' *Tarantula* (1955) and American International Pictures' *Earth vs. the Spider* (1958)—that is, films whose menaces can be taken at a bigger-than-real face value. There remains a broader and more imaginative variety of movies that make much of suggesting the spider-like traits of entrapment, toxicity and aggression in human characters.

Paramount Pictures' production of *The Spider* and Fox Film Corp.'s *The Spider and the Fly* (both from 1916) represent early applications of the tactic. Robert G. Vignola's *The Spider* is a culture-clash drama set among the decadent French upper class, with Pauline Frederick as a scheming woman whose web of intrigues becomes her undoing. J. Gordon Edwards' *The Spider and the Fly*, also set in France, allows its spidery vamp (Genevieve Hamper) to get religion and settle into missionary work—but not before her venomous ways have wrecked a handful of lives.

Two of the Fleischer Bros. studios' more striking animated shorts, *Mother Goose Land* (1933) and *The Cobweb Hotel* (1936), vary the theme to unnerving effect by mingling behaviors of human and spider in cartoon villains who are as scary as they are comical. And the David O. Selznick production of *Gone with the Wind* (1939) takes especial pains to liken the man-trapper instincts of Vivien Leigh's Scarlett O'Hara to those of a spider. To say nothing of Fox's 1931 production of *The Spider*, which gets talked to death elsewhere in this volume.

Any number of the screen's predatory miscreants have raised the ante on menace via suggested spidery traits: One finds the human-sacrificing tribe of Spider Men in 1935's *The Lost City*; the Spider Gang in 1937's *Dick Tracy*; Jill Banner's queasy title portrayal in 1964's *Spider Baby*; and especially Gale Sondergaard's invitation to typecasting in *Sherlock Holmes and the Spider Woman* (1944) and a Holmes-less spin-off, *The Spider Woman Strikes Back* (1946).

Handily the most ruthless and unrelenting of the movies' figurative arachnids—though as much a hero as a menace—is Warren Hull's star turn in two serials from Columbia Pictures, *The Spider's Web* (1938) and *The Spider Returns* (1941). The merciless protagonist and his entourage derive from characters developed in 1933 by the author Reginald Maitland Thomas Scott for *The Spider, Master of Men*, from an idea conceived by publisher Henry "Harry" Steeger, president of Popular Publications.

R.T.M. Scott committed something akin to self-plagiarism in patterning the Spider and his entourage after characters from Scott's 1927 novel, *Aurelius Smith, Detective*. The Spider's civilian career derived from Steeger's interest in the corporate sector. Steeger also cited the high-adventure films of Douglas Fairbanks as an inspiration. Scott defined the Spider along traditional masked-avenger lines—a well-to-do sort pursuing a secretive crimebusting life, with a sweetheart/assistant and a servant/sidekick of exotic origins—but raised the stakes by heightening the character's appetite for violence. This Spider would be as well feared and despised by the law, as by the criminal element.

The pulp-magazine Spider's nearest kindred souls were the better-mannered characters known as Doc Savage and the Phantom Detective, both of whom also surfaced in 1933, and of course the Shadow, whose adventures had commenced publication in 1931. Steeger acknowledged that his launching of *The Spider* was predicated upon Street & Smith's success with the Shadow. These characters, to a man, descended from such key figures of mythology and popular fiction as the Teutonic culture's Siegfried (portrayed on film in 1924), a Parisian newspaper's Fantomas (first brought to the screen in 1913) and Broadway's the Bat (adapted to the screen in 1926 and 1930). The pulp heroes, in turn, would herald the arrival of any number of comic-book vigilantes, beginning during the 1930s.

For all his traditionalism, however, the Spider remains a breed apart. In a prolific pulp-fiction industry—whose low-rent publishers presented tens of millions of words every month in hundreds of magazines that thrived on sensationalized one-upsmanship—the Spider carried on for just over 10 years as the pulps' most reliably brutal heroic presence, committing one act of mayhem after another in the name of justice and fair play. His 118 short-novel adventures live admirably up to the promise of their titles (the likes of *The Devil's Death-Dwarves*, *Overlord of the Damned* and *The Pain Emperor*) with an unforgiving deterrent. In their view of Due Process and rehabilitation as unattainable ideals, the tales also argue that Richard "the Spider" Wentworth has more in common with such classier practitioners of heroic vengeance as Seabury Quinn's Jules de Grandin, Leslie Charteris' the Saint, John P. Marquand's Mr. Moto and Ian Fleming's James Bond than with any other masked-vigilante type.

Similarly, the Columbia production of *The Spider's Web* (not to be confused with like-titled films from 1912, 1916 and 1927) has as much in common with the brooding film noir style as it does with its own adventurous chapter-play tradition. It is the first serial to be based upon a pulp-magazine character. (The Shadow had been featured in six two-reel shorts at Universal during the early '30s and two inadequate features from Grand National during 1937-38.) And of course, the stories that gave the noir idiom its foundation—the works of Cornell Woolrich, Dashiell Hammett, Raymond Chandler *et al.*—had originated in the pulps.

An exaggerated sense of urgency is a foregone conclusion in the serials, from cliffhangers of the silent screen through the medium's dying gasps of the middle 1950s. *The Spider's Web* compounds this thrill-quotient value with an unusually noir-mannered morbid desperation. The serial strives, as well, to have its hero fall short of likeability, however just his cause. (*The Spider Returns*, produced only three years later but under markedly different circumstances, is quite another matter—about which, more later.)

By the autumn of 1938, when *The Spider's Web* arrived as a week-to-week attraction, a former newspaperman named Norvell Page had long since taken over the writing of the character's magazine exploits. Working under the pseudonym of Grant Stockbridge, Page nurtured in the character a viciousness that would place *The Spider* magazine on a par with the horror-anthology pulps of its day.

It could hardly be taken for granted that Hollywood would represent the pulps' sensibilities with accuracy in a *Spider* film. The industry's system of institutionalized censorship had reasserted itself powerfully only four years earlier, claiming Edgar G. Ulmer's *The Black Cat* (1934) as a major sacrifice and sending up signals that, coupled with an English/European ban on horror films, brought on the genre's near-extinction in cinema during the latter 1930s.

But during those feeble few years for horror movies, serial filmmaking remained a reliable outlet, less readily targeted by the censors. Grotesque extravagances of villainy flourished in the serials where the same values had withered in the feature-film sector. Columbia's inexperienced chapter-play subsidiary had farmed out earlier such efforts to the Weiss Bros.' independent company. With its in-house production of *The Spider's Web*, Columbia delivered a serial that not only does justice to the idiom but also apologizes most persuasively for the studio's inept first stab at serial filmmaking, the out-sourced production of *Jungle Menace* (1937; later seen in a feature-length condensation as *Jungle Terror*). *Web* is among the few Columbia serials that bear mentioning in the same breath with the more consistently worthy serial output of Republic and Universal; it approaches the dark ferocity of *Drums of Fu Manchu* (Republic; 1940) and *The Phantom Creeps* (Universal; 1939).

The Spider's Web, directed by Ray Taylor and James W. Horne, opens ominously with the arrival of a white-hooded troublemaker known as the Octopus. (It bears noting that by having a black-clad hero and a villain dressed in white, Columbia pulled an unusual inversion of a tradition. Of course, so had the Ku Klux Klan.) The Octopus, who walks as though crippled and sports a prosthetic arm, presides over a mob that seeks to wreck transportation systems as a means of controlling U.S. commerce. The Octopus guns down a captive industrialist with a hidden weapon—the false limb is a decoy—and announces that his next victim will be Richard Wentworth. (*The Octopus* became a short-lived companion magazine to *The Spider* at Popular Publications. The single issue of *The Octopus* magazine bore a date of February 1939 and featured the novelette *The City Condemned to Hell*, bylined as the work of one Randolph Craig—a house name; the author was in fact Norvell Page. Sluggish sales prompted Henry Steeger to rechristen the second issue *The Scorpion*.)

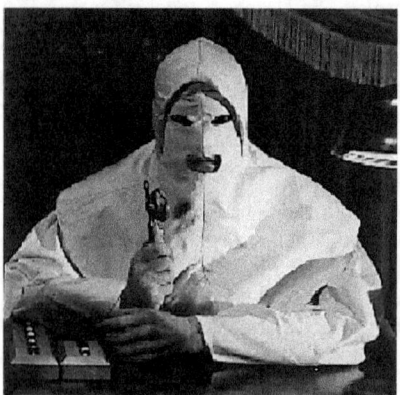

The Octopus is the ominous villain of *The Spider's Web*.

Now, Wentworth (played by Warren Hull) is a socialite and respected amateur detective. Only a few intimates know that Wentworth also is the masked vigilante known as the Spider, whose methods have not only terrorized the underworld but also provoked the law to put a price on his head.

Wentworth claims to have retired his Spider routine, and he and his spirited confidante and impatient fiancée, Nita Van Sloan (Iris Meredith) are planning an overdue wedding. Wentworth and his cohorts Ram Singh (Kenneth "Kenne" Duncan) and Jackson (Richard Fiske) understand, however, that the Octopus' racket requires a fierce response. So the Spider's retirement proves to have been a mere sabbatical. Wentworth also masquerades now and again as a gruff, one-eyed safecracker named Blinky McQuade, who can move freely among the criminals who might lead the Spider to the gang boss.

The Spider's Web sustains a breathtaking pace throughout 15 chapters, thanks in great measure to the efficiency of the serial sector's standard two-director system; to Allen G. Siegler's straightforward but moodily lighted photography; and to the generous deployment of Morris Stoloff's stirring orchestral passages. Siegler was one of Columbia's dependables, a veteran cinematographer whose career had begun with the Edison studios early in the century and includes the respected Karloff vehicle *The Black Room* (1935). Stoloff was head of Columbia's music department and, with *Web* as his lone exception, left the serial-scoring chores to others.

Web's screenplay—a barrage of angry energy from Robert E. Kent, Basil Dickey, George Plympton and Martie Ramson—accommodates an alarmingly high body count. In a cast of only seven principals but approximately 130 bit players, some poor fool falls victim every several minutes to either the Spider or the Octopus. The expendables include the notable likes of Nestor Paiva (popular villain in the long-running play *The Drunkard*), Ernie Adams, Harry Semels and

Bert Young. Dominant among the heavies is the excellent Marc Lawrence, whose portrayals of gangsters for more than 50 years add up to a body of real artistry. The players include former matinee idols (Edward Earle and Edward Hearn); lapsed comedy stars (Harry Myers, Kit Guard and Eddie Featherston); Western-movie veterans (Lane Chandler, Bill Patton, Eddie Cobb and Tom London); and bygone sports stars (Oscar "Dutch" Hendrian and Frank Hagney). There are even roles for Joan Blondell's kid sister, Gloria Blondell, and the lovely Ann Doran.

The mortality rate may be gauged by *Web*'s first chapter, "Night of Terror." An opening montage establishes 100 fatalities in a train wreck; a car full of people being forced over a precipice; an airport in flames; and the explosion of a building. The Octopus dispatches two victims. Wentworth kills two men outright and lands a third in a hospital, where the injured party is slain by a cohort to prevent blabbing. Ram Singh racks up numerous casualties on his own.

If the two-director system can be considered integral to the success of *The Spider's Web*, then its abandonment for *The Spider Returns* might account for the failings of the sequel. The partner-director approach was a discovery of a tiny nothing-but-serials studio, Mascot Pictures, which in 1932 had brought in B. Reeves Eason to relieve a temporarily ailing Ford Beebe on *The Shadow of the Eagle*. The pinch-hitter assignment proved such a relief to the labor-intensive chore of filming a chapter-play—permitting one director to set up the next day's shoot while the other was busy on the set—that it became a standard approach.

The Spider Returns, from a screenplay by George Plympton and Jesse A. Duffy and directed solo by James Horne, offers scarcely more than a wartime replay of *Web*'s story. Here, a hooded villain called the Gargoyle commands a mob bent upon crippling the American defense system. Kenne Duncan returns as Ram Singh. Newcomer Mary Ainslee, an energetic and appropriately vulnerable beauty but an unpersuasive screamer, picks up the Nita Van Sloan character—who in this instance has been reduced to a more conventional ingénue-type. Championship stunt artist Dave O'Brien takes over the Jackson role with pleasing results, while repeating his more strenuous chores as Hull's action double.

Warren Hull's consistently tough portrayal is a saving grace of the No. 2 serial. Hull plainly relishes the assignment, especially when his surly hoodlum character, McQuade, must resort to violence or the Spider must take the offensive. Lee Zahler's musical score has a robust timbre—heavy on the low brass and alto-range strings and woodwinds—at odds with the shallowness of the retreaded story. Zahler's old-fashioned melodic sense (and his cues had sounded old-fashioned even during the 1930s) is quite a departure from Stoloff's progressive score for *The Spider's Web*. The screenplay substitutes tough-guy posturings, all threats and insults, for narrative substance, and thrilling action is in short supply by comparison with *Web*. A fantastic invention that figures prominently in *Returns* is a laughable contraption. The photography, by James S. Brown, Jr., is unremarkably competent. (Brown was another credentialed pioneer, having started out with Edison in 1912 and distinguished himself as a combat photographer during World War I. Brown's career was damaged by a pugnacious nature and chronic ill health; he killed himself in 1949 at age 57.)

If only one of *Web*'s directors could have returned to helm *The Spider Returns*, it should have been Ray Taylor instead of James Horne. Horne was no slouch—at least, not at slapstick comedy—and had amassed serial credentials dating from the 1910s. Best known as a director of such beloved Laurel & Hardy entries as "Our Wife" and *Way Out West,* Horne returned to serials in his later years. His solo assignments for Columbia (also including *The Iron Claw* and *The Green Archer*) are marked by a tedious sense of pacing and bits of inappropriate knockabout comedy. Horne died at 62 in 1942.

By contrast, Ray Taylor was a master of virile action, having apprenticed under the brilliant taskmaster John Ford following World War I before securing a run of short-subject assignments all his own and gaining ground as a serial director on *Fighting with Buffalo Bill* (1926). Taylor's generally splendid talking-picture serials include *The Return of Chandu* (1936), *Dick Tracy* (1937, with co-director Alan James), and *Flash Gordon Conquers the Universe* and *The Green Hornet*

Warren Hull as The Spider

(both from 1940, and both co-directed with Ford Beebe). Serial favorite Buster Crabbe once told us he considered Taylor the finest of all the cliffhanger directors. Taylor remained prolific in serials and occasional features—most notably, Universal's *The Michigan Kid* (1946)—until 1949. He died at 64 in 1952.

The Spider himself, Warren Hull, was born in 1903 in Gasport, New York. He entered show business as a radio announcer and light-operatic baritone and came to Hollywood during the middle 1930s, quickly catching on as a dapper and confident second-string leading man in such pictures as *The Walking Dead* and *Love Begins at 20* (both from 1936) and *Night Key* (1937). Hull registered more dynamically as the Spider, an enactment that led him to title portrayals in the serials *Mandrake the Magician* (1939) and *The Green Hornet Strikes Again* (1941) in addition to a continuing run of feature assignments. Hull came full-circle with *The Spider Returns*, then left the movies after *Bowery Blitzkreig* (1941) to concentrate on broadcasting.

Hull found a more grotesque prominence in 1948, when he became host of a bizarre quiz program called *Strike It Rich*. Originating on radio but emerging in 1951 as a television hit, the show featured genuinely pitiable contestants whose correct answers to simple questions would win such prizes as hearing aids, artificial limbs and teeth and all manner of medical treatments. Hull frequently became tearful during these contests, which at length provoked an investigation by New York's welfare bureaucracy. *Strike It Rich* weathered the controversy, and Hull remained its emcee until the program's cancellation at the start of 1958. Warren Hull died in 1974.

The scrappy leading lady of *The Spider's Web*, Iris Meredith, was a favorite of the matinee-Western crowd because of her many appearances opposite Charles Starrett and Wild Bill Elliott. She also was the most memorable leading lady of the Columbia serials, appearing as well in *Overland with Kit Carson* and *The Green Archer*.

Stunt ace Dave O'Brien was a burly West Texan who had come to Hollywood from a song-and-dance career, scoring as a bit player and action specialist until such scruffy assignments as *Reefer Madness* (1936) and *Devil Bat* (1940) allowed him to display an unusual scene-stealing ability. O'Brien starred in Columbia's *Captain Midnight* serial in 1942 and remained busy in feature films well into the 1950s, but he left his strongest popular impression as the put-upon, pratfalling Everyman in the *Pete Smith Specialties* comedy shorts for MGM. O'Brien later became a gagwriter for Red Skelton and a director in the realm of television. He died in 1969.

And yes, the Kenneth Duncan who plays Ram Singh is the Kenne Duncan who later became part of the entourage of the earnestly inept filmmaker Edward D. Wood, Jr. Duncan's serene-but-deadly portrayal in the *Spider* serials is a real detour for an actor who had long specialized in snarling Western heavies.

The wild world of the pulp magazines was often evoked in weird-mystery features and Westerns based on pulp yarns, and several Columbia serials of pulp origin followed *The Spider's Web*, including *The Shadow* (1940) and *Chick Carter, Detective* (1946). *Web*, driving full-force with a wealth of ruthless ferocity, remains the standard by which the pulp-origin serials must be measured.

CREDITS: Executive Producer: Irving Briskin; Producer: Jack Fier; Directors: Ray Taylor and James W. Horne; Screenplay: Robert E. Kent, Basil Dickey, George Plympton and Martie Ramson; Based upon: Stories and Characters Developed by Henry Steeger, Reginald Maitland, Thomas Scott and Norvell Page for *The Spider, Master of Men* Magazine; Photographed by: Allen G. Siegler; Musical Score by: Morros Stoloff; Additional Compositions by Mischa Bakaleinikoff, Sidney Cutner and Ben Oakland; Editor: Richard Fantl; Running Time: 15 Weekly Episodes; Released: Following Hollywood and New York Previews during August-September 1938

CAST: Warren Hull (Richard Wentworth/The Spider); Iris Meredith (Nita Van Sloan); Richard Fiske (Jackson); Kenneth Duncan (Ram Singh); Dave O'Brien (Stunt Double for Warren Hull); Forbes Murray (Commissioner Stanley Kirk); Marc Lawrence (Steve Harmon); Charles Wilson (Chase); Beauregard Bonifacio (Corner Man); Donald Douglas (Jenkins); Lester Dorr (Frank Martin); Edward Earle (J.R. Adams); Eugene Anderson, Jr. (Johnnie Sands); Ernie Adams (Merkel); Ernie Alexander (Reporter); Sam Ash (Dover); Harry A. Bailey (Dr. Gaylord); Jimmie Baker, Ed Randolph and Harry Tenbrook (Powerhouse Workers); Brooks Benedict (Chauffeur); Harry Bernard (Watchman); Beatrice Blinn (Steno); Gloria Blondell, Ann Doran and Larry Wheat (Secretaries); Roy Brent (Railroad Worker); Ralph Brooks (Chambers); Frank Bruno (Monk); Buel Bryant, Earle D. Bunn, Steve Clark, Steve Clark, Jerry Frank, Roger Gray [as Grey], Kit Guard, Charles "Jockey" Haefeli, Frank Hagney, Charles "Chuck" Hamilton, Oscar "Dutch" Hendrian, George Hoey, Reed Howes, Dick Jensen, Ray Johnson, Jack Lowe, Sam Lufkin, Ed McCabe, Frank Mills, Joe Palma, Bill Patton, Charles Phillips, Al Rhein, Harry Semels, Dick Stanley, Walter Stiritz [as Stirritz], Harry Strang, Joe Sully, Dirk Thane, George Turner and Bert Young (Henchmen); George De Normand, Bud Geary and Duke York (Henchmen/Stunt Doubles); Lew Caits (Blade); James Carlisle (Fire Captain); Lane Chandler (Trigger); Edmund Cobb (Police Dispatcher); Harry Cornell [as Cornella] (Brownie); Kernan Cripps (Officer Mulvaney); Beatrice Curtis (Kate Sands); Dick Curtis (Malloy); Sidney D'Albrook (Spike); Lou Davis (Harry Stone); Harry Depp (Oswald); Dick Dickinson (Customer at Bus Depot); Jessie Perry, Rose Plummer and Anne Schaefer (Women at Bus Depot); Charles Dorety (Mort); Curley Dresden (Henchman and Driver); Art Dupuis (Radio Man); Dick Durrell (Charlie Dennis); Carl Faulkner, Charles McMurphy, Frank O'Connor, Jack Richardson, Ed Schaefer and William Witney (Policemen); Al Ferguson (Bus Mechanic); Eddie Fetherston (Tom); Bess Flowers (Carlotta Cobb and Myrtle); Eddie Foster (Lefty); Byron Foulger (Allen Roberts); Jack Gardner (Reporter); Bill Gavier (Louis); Gordon Hart (J. Mason); Jack Harvey (Marvin); Edward Hearn (Desk Sergeant); Jack Hennessy (Second Chauffeur); Al Herman (Spike McLean); Russell Heustis (James); Bentley "Ben" Hewlett (Joseph Crane); Harry Hollingsworth (Police Inspector); Al Klein (Saber); Bob Kortman (Joe); Edward Le Saint (Doctor); Tom London (Bank Guard); Chet Lynn (Jim); Stanley Mack (Nick); Bud Marshall (Police Dispatcher); Ralph McCullough (Reuben); Malcolm "Bud" McTaggart (Elevator Attendant); Lew Meehan (Burke); Tony Merlo (Chauffeur); Bruce Mitchell (Policeman and Henchman); King Mojave (Mike); Harry C. Myers (Detective); Wedgwood Nowell (Allen); Nestor Paiva (Red); Claude [as Claud] Payton (Radarez); Edward Peil, Sr. (Officer Jones); Jack Perrin (Interne); Bob Perry (Tim Spencer); Lee Prather (Editor Morris); Gus Reed (Frank); Cyril Ring (Henry Blake); John Roy (Police Scientist); Cy Schindell (Cadman); Dick Scott (Joe); Cap Severn (Farm Wife); Charles Sherlock (Detective); Ernest "Ernie" Shields [as Shield] (Man); Lee Shumway (Police Sergeant); Reginald Simpson (Gordon); Johnny Sinclair (Writer); Tom Steele (Gunman and Stunt Double); Gene Stone (Cashman); George Taylor (Whitey); Henry Taylor (Wilson); Victor Travers (Brand); John Tyrrell (Grafton); Francis Walker (Farmer and Stunt Double); Paul Whitney (Gray); Roger Williams (Driver); Dan Wolheim (Bartender); William Worthington (Cantlon); and Herman Marks, Jerry Jerome

Karloff tests a death-defying apparatus.

THE MAN THEY COULD NOT HANG
(Columbia Pictures Corp.; 1939)

Although most of us might regard a day in court with dread, many actors look forward to facing a judge and jury—on stage or on camera, anyhow, where even one's fate is at the disposal of dramatic license. George Arliss, Gregory Peck, Paul Muni, Claude Rains, Lionel Barrymore, James Stewart and Lee J. Cobb are among that inspired lot who have given some of their finest performances while arguing cases with life and/or human dignity at stake.

Scenarists are equally enthusiastic about writing eloquent dialogue for sound-stage courtrooms. Karl Brown, a great cinematographer-turned-screenwriter, was no exception. Brown's favorite courthouse oratory was tailored for his friend Boris Karloff, in *The Man They Could Not Hang*. Director Nick Grinde and cinematographer Benjamin Kline placed Karloff in slatted light from a large window. Decked out to dashing effect in a styled wig (his head had been shaved for Universal's *Tower of London*), Karloff brought Brown's words to life with British élan.

Portraying Dr. Henryk Savaard, whose experiment in putting a volunteer to death in expectation of bringing him back to life was ruined by police interference, Karloff calmly states his case before a stern judge (Charles Trowbridge), a jury (with Dick Curtis, a favorite villain of the Western movies, as the foreman) and a houseful of extras. Karloff likens surgery as it is known to "trying to repair a motor that's still running," adding that his method would make it possible to "replace vital organs that have been worn out." He wants to "make death our servant instead of our master."

There is a ferocity underlying Karloff's mannered civility, however, and an imperious indignation that establish this Dr. Savaard as more a doer of deeds than an arguer of lost causes.

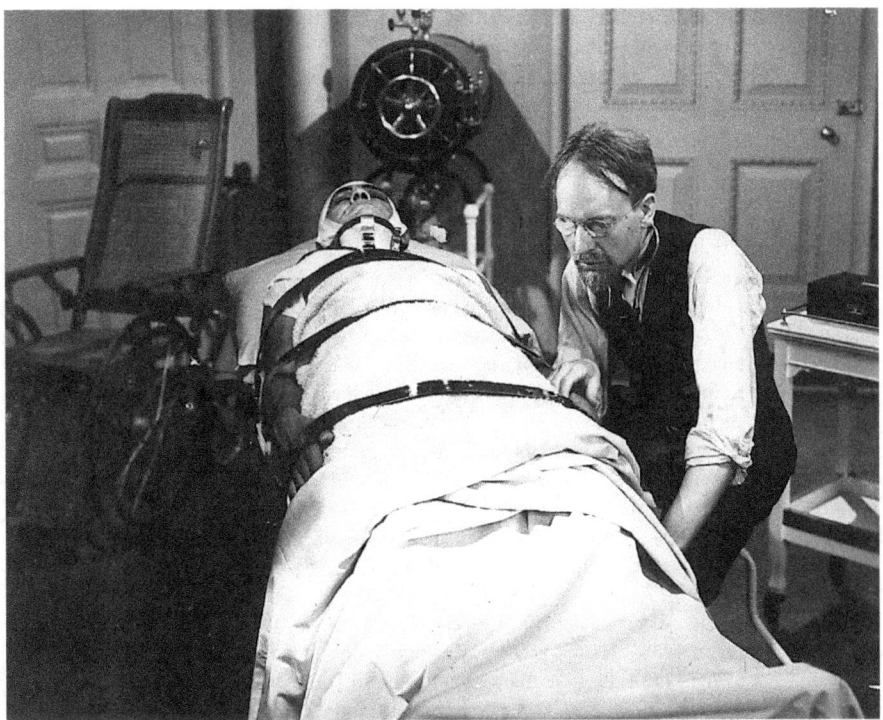

Byron Foulger, in *The Man They Could Not Hang*.

And Savaard's cause seems lost, indeed. The district attorney (Roger Pryor) shreds the thesis, commanding a verdict of guilty and a sentence to hang. Savaard asks "the privilege of addressing this court for two minutes," then:

"You who have condemned me—I *know* your kind. Your forebears poisoned Socrates, burned Joan of Arc, hanged, tortured all those whose only offense was to bring light into darkness..." To the prosecutor: "...When your last moment comes, remember that you killed the one man who could have made your life secure." And to the judge: "... [Y]ou will be overtaken by a punishment far more terrible than anything you can do to me." (On that same sound stage a year later, again with director Grinde and camera chief Benjamin Kline and enacting another Karl Brown yarn called *Before I Hang*, mercy killer Karloff again would get the noose from Trowbridge, one of Old Hollywood's perennial jurists. Half a century down the line, Dr. Kevorkian was getting away with just such shenanigans right and left.)

But we were talking about *The Man They Could Not Hang*: Savaard's disciples and devices bring him back from the dead. The healer begins a methodical campaign of revenge, which has escalated to half the jury before a newspaper reporter (Robert Wilcox) senses a pattern here and finds Savaard's surviving persecutors in urgent danger. Savaard is up to a ninth kill when his daughter (Lorna Gray) causes an interruption. She is slain in the resulting mêlée. Savaard, mortally wounded, musters the strength to bring her back to life. He demolishes his revolutionary gizmo before death can claim him.

The beauty of *The Man They Could Not Hang* lies less in the desultory and-then-there-were-none plotting than in the richly defined person of Henryk Savaard. If only one can let it slide that its own studio regarded the picture as assembly-line fare, that nobody in charge was particularly trying to Make Art, then Karloff's interpretation of Brown's vivid narrative voice emerges as art of a high order. If Dr. Savaard has a bad attitude here, that can only be because somebody imposed it upon him, and what he does with that bad attitude is to give it back in spades. The tragedy is not that a handful of holier-than-thou bourgeois bottom-feeders get done away with, but rather that society has denied itself a crack at a medical miracle by entrusting justice to the assembled jerks of this narrow-minded courtroom. The trouble with democracy is that it's too blasted democratic.

Karloff's show of rage is so nearly Shakespearean in its savagery that it sits quite unsteadily upon the hack-plotting pulp-fiction framework. Brown was handier at matching the right words with the right deeds than at contriving the situations. It is a singular letdown that Dr. Savaard's undoing comes in the form of a common journalistic snoop and a demise better suited to some punk hoodlum. It is a major compensation that Savaard at last proves the validity of his breakthrough—and then takes the secret to the grave.

And so what was Karl Brown—a protégé of D.W. Griffith and the celebrated photographer of *The Covered Wagon*—doing writing B-movie screenplays, anyhow? This circumstance has its origins in the year 1926, when Brown journeyed to the Great Smoky Mountains to produce, write and direct the Neorealist epic, *Stark Love*. The time away cost Brown considerable momentum with the short-memoried Hollywood establishment, and upon his return he found it difficult to land new assignments as a cinematographer. So he began directing, a task that he disliked, and then parlayed an abiding interest in writing into a successful new career. Brown's first published writings had occurred during the 1920s in *The American Cinematographer* magazine, which he also served as associate editor. Brown was 93 and again writing for the journal of the American Society of Cinematographers when he died in 1990.

CREDITS: In Charge of Production: Irving Briskin; Producer: Wallace MacDonald; Director: Nick Grinde; Screenplay: Karl Brown; Story: Leslie T. White and George L. Sayre; Photographed by: Benjamin Kline; Film Editor: William Lyon; Musical Director: M.W. Stoloff; Art Director: Lionel Banks; Sound Engineer: George Cooper; Musical Score by: Joseph Nussbaum, Ben Oakland, Gregory Stone, George Parrish, Nico Grigor, William Grant Still, Dr. Karol Rathaus and Rex H. Bassett; Running Time: 65 Minutes; Released: August 17, 1939

CAST: Boris Karloff (Dr. Henryk Savaard); Lorna Gray [a.k.a. Adrian Booth] (Janet Savaard); Robert Wilcox ("Scoop" Foley); Roger Pryor (District Attorney Drake); Don Beddoe (Lt. Shayne); Ann Doran (Betty Crawford); Joseph De Stefani (Dr. Stoddard); Charles Trowbridge (Judge Bowman); Byron Foulger (Lang); Dick Curtis (Kearney); James Craig (Watkins); John Tyrrell (Sutton); Ian MacLaren (Priest); Harlan Briggs (Parker); George Anderson (Warden); Stanley Brown (Roberts); Flo Campbell (Housewife); John Dilson (King); Robert Sterling, Franklin Parker and Walter Sande (Newspapermen); Frank Jaquet (Fat Man); Charles Miller (Dr. Avery); Cyril Thornton (Butler); Sam Ash (Druggist); Larry Lund (Court Clerk); Bill Lally (Bailiff); Stanley Blystone (Guard); Charles McAvoy (Prison Official)

Lugosi and Greta Gynt

DARK EYES OF LONDON
a.k.a.: THE HUMAN MONSTER
(Argyle British Productions, Ltd.; 1939)

Bela Lugosi, an abler talent than his industry or even Lugosi himself came prepared to acknowledge, had become in 1931 the first actor for whom horror films would both define and frustrate a career. Within months of that year's release of *Dracula*, the watershed starring vehicle for Lugosi, Boris Karloff had followed suit with his career-cinching portrayal of the Monster in *Frankenstein*. But where Karloff's greater studio-politicking skills—not to mention a more thorough Americanization, what with both artists being immigrants—helped him to deal constructively with the perils of casting-to-type, Lugosi found himself virtually enslaved to his bogeyman celebrity.

The crunch came during 1936-37: The embargo on such pictures from Hollywood's lucrative U.K. and European markets caused almost two years' official abandonment of the genre, with subversive exceptions (see our book *Forgotten Horrors 2: Beyond the Horror Ban*). Karloff retrenched into more generalized character assignments, a holding pattern that demonstrated his versatility and kept his name prominent pending a reassertion of the popular appetite for unabashed chillers. Lugosi lapsed into impoverished obscurity—gracing only one high-adventure shocker, the 1937 serial *S O S Coast Guard*, and losing title to his imposing residence in the Hollywood Hills. He had leased a house, plainer by far, only a short distance from Universal Studios—the scene of his greater stardom—when 1939 saw a renewed demand for his distinctive gifts.

A showman named Emil Umann had launched the revival almost unwittingly in 1938, tapping a pent-up popular demand by booking a lineup that included *Dracula* and *Frankenstein* into the Regina Theatre in Beverly Hills. This provocation of a comeback for the genre translated into a triumphant reversal-of-fortune for Lugosi, who at age 57 soon found himself toplining Universal's horror serial *The Phantom Creeps*; rejoining Karloff at Universal for *Son of Frankenstein*, their first teaming since 1936's *The Invisible Ray* and their only shared venture to allow Lugosi the meatier role; taking a high-comedy supporting turn at MGM in *Ninotchka*; and journeying to England to star in *Dark Eyes of London*.

Scotland Yard is on the spot to find a pattern in the drownings of five generously insured citizens. "An extraordinary coincidence," declares Dr. Feodor Orloff (Lugosi), a small-time lender and insurance broker, when Inspector Larry Holt (Hugh Williams) notices that Orloff's agency has paid off to absentee beneficiaries in the deaths.

Orloff's latest customer is struggling inventor Henry Stuart (Gerald Pring), whom Orloff counsels to support a haven known as Dearborn's Home for the Destitute Blind. Proprietor Dearborn is a saintly, sightless oldster who dispenses meals and sermons with a missionary zeal. Orloff, who admits to being a banished physician, frequents the shelter—whose clinic contains such ominous furnishings as a cast-iron tank and an array of electronic equipment. Dearborn's helper, a blind and disfigured hulk called Jake (Wilfrid Walter), accepts encoded messages from Orloff via Lew (Arthur E. Owen), a blind-and-mute street musician. Complicating Holt's progress is the arrival of Fred Grogan (Alexander Field), a forger extradited from America. Grogan's escort, Chicago Police Lt. O'Reilly (Edmon Ryan), extends his stay to study Scotland Yard's procedures. Also newly arrived is Diana Stuart (Greta Gynt), Henry's daughter.

Stuart turns up as the latest victim in the Thames' mud flats. Grogan, freed on bail, is coerced by Orloff to imitate Stuart's signature. Holt and O'Reilly decide to confront Grogan— but too late: Jake has drowned the forger in his bathtub. "Don't they ever *shoot* anybody in this country?" O'Reilly asks Holt.

Orloff gains Diana's confidence and secures for her a job with "a very dear friend, who runs a home for the blind." Holt intercepts Diana and, taking advantage of her eagerness to expose the killer, enlists her help. Lew is placed in restraints in the Dearborn clinic. "You're blind, and you can't speak. But you can *hear*," Orloff snarls accusingly—then deafens the man with an electrical jolt.

Diana uncovers evidence of her father's visit to the shelter. While telephoning Holt, she is attacked in her rooms by Jake, whom she disables with a lamp. Jake escapes through a window just as Holt and O'Reilly arrive. Returning to the shelter, Diana finds a piece of jewelry bearing her father's initials. Confronted with the item, Dearborn unthinkingly *looks* at it and reveals himself to be Orloff. Diana manipulates Jake into turning on Orloff. By the time the law arrives, Jake, mortally wounded, has hurled Orloff to his death.

Challenged to deliver two pivotal impersonations well removed from his own age range (the wicked Dr. Orloff is said to be 48; the mild Mr. Dearborn appears a good generation older), Lugosi undertakes a thoroughgoing immersion in character that gives the climactic unmasking a keen edge of surprise. He is helped along, of course, in the Dearborn part by the dubbed voice of an uncredited Oliver B. Clarence, a busy English character man who is best remembered today as the Aged Parent in David Lean's *Great Expectations* (1946). No amount of vocal coaching could have subdued Lugosi's rich Hungarian accent. But Dearborn's physical presence is vastly more than a white wig and mustache and smoked eyeglasses: Lugosi's oily arrogance vanishes during the masquerade as the kindly missionary—his enactment benefited from technical advice supplied by England's National Institute of the Blind—and his hesitant motions bespeak a superb sense of timing. Lugosi cautiously lets slip clues that the do-gooder might know more than he lets on, and in one delicious moment when the plucky leading lady, Greta Gynt, remarks admiringly on the ease with which he moves about, Lugosi hesitates guiltily before managing a disarming reply about how "every sorrow... has its compensation."

Lugosi uses the Orloff role to embody all his admirers had expected of him since *Dracula*. Orloff's history as a disgraced healer is never adequately explained, but tantalizing hints

Lugosi unleashes a tragic beast.

validate the queasy mad-doctor sequences and allow for a classic-manner Lugosi speech: "I wanted to devote my life to the healing of mankind... ," Orloff snarls. "But they got together—these narrow-minded, prejudiced medical men—to see how they could ruin me. 'Brilliant but unbalanced'—*that* was the verdict." Then, relaxing, he adds: "And so, I serve the blind."

The screenplay retains source-author Edgar Wallace's not-quite-whodunit structure and attention to procedural detective work but concentrates throughout on the atrocities. The British Board of Film Censors formally inaugurated its H Certificate ("horrific; persons under 16 not admitted") on *Dark Eyes of London*, and with abundant reason: The portrayal of handicapped paupers as pawns of a murderer is disturbing enough, but specific moments—a body afloat in the muddy Thames; the hulking Wilfrid Walter's *Old Dark House*-like rampage; the drowning of a likable felon; the torture of a helpless blind man; and Lugosi's agonized drowning—convey a terror that transcends shock value. The asylum is a claustrophobic wonder, its nightmarish qualities compounded by precipitous camera placements and light-and-shadow effects. Most of the settings, both real and of the studio, seem calculated to create an ugly and oppressive atmosphere.

As the chief detective, Hugh Williams offsets his boyish appearance with a relentlessness that borders on cruelty. The American cop is played by Edmon Ryan with an extroverted boorishness that belies an efficient determination, and his wisecracks supply a helpful leavening. As the heroic young woman who plays along with Williams' game of entrapment, Greta Gynt supplies so much more than a decorative presence that her romantic attraction to Williams at the fade-out feels artificial. Shakespearean stage player Walter's turn as the hideous blind killer is surprisingly understated, and his relationship with the Lugosi character(s) suggests that director/co-author Walter Summers had studied the teamings of a monstrous Boris Karloff with a manipulative Lugosi in *The Raven* (1935) and *Son of Frankenstein*, which had been issued earlier in 1939. *Dark Eyes of London* proved influential in its own right and in short order, defining the resentful Lugosi characters of *The Devil Bat* (1940) and *Black Dragons* (1942) and serving virtually as a template for another Lugosi vehicle, *Bowery at Midnight* (1942).

A noted realist among British directors, Walter Summers had entered the film industry from a childhood stage career while still in his teens, landing his first directing assignment at age 27 in 1923. *Dark Eyes of London* was his next-to-last picture. His son, Jeremy Summers, became a director in England some 20 years later, specializing in modestly budgeted thrillers.

CREDITS: Producer: John Argyle; Director: Walter Summers; Screenplay: Patrick Kirwan, Walter Summers and J.F. Argyle; Additional Dialogue: Jay Van Lusil; Based upon: Edgar Wallace's Novel; Photographed by: Bryan Langley; Music Composed and Arranged by: Guy Jones; Organ Music: C. King Palmer; Production Manager: H.G. Inglis; Production Assistant: George Collins; Recording Supervisor: H. Benson; Sound Recording: A.E. Rudolph; Film Editor: E.G. Richards; Art Director: Duncan Sutherland; Assistant Director: Jack Martin; Camera: Ronald Anscombe; Grateful Acknowledgment to: National Institute of the Blind; World Distribution: by Pathé Pictures, Ltd.; U.S. Distribution: Monogram Pictures Corp.; Produced at: Welwyn Studios, Garden City, Herts; Running Time: 76 minutes (U.S., 73 minutes); U.K. Release: During October of 1939, Reissued: 1945 and 1950

CAST: Bela Lugosi (Dr. Orloff); Bela Lugosi (Mr. Dearborn, voiced by Oliver B. Clarence); Hugh Williams (Inspector Holt); Greta Gynt (Diana Stuart); Wilfrid Walter (Jake); Edmon Ryan (Lt. O'Reilly); Julie Suedo (Secretary); Alexander Field (Grogan); Arthur E. Owen (Lew); Gerald Pring (Henry Stuart); Bryan Herbert (Walsh); May Halliatt (Policewoman); Charles Penrose (Drunkard)

Treachery is afoot in the realm.

TOWER OF LONDON
(Universal Pictures Corp.; 1939)

No age is without its ruthless men... A web of intrigue veils the lives of all who know only too well that today's friends might be tomorrow's enemies.—From the Prologue

The most ruthless of Real World villains, according to the persuasive arguments of Rowland V. Lee's 1939 production of *Tower of London* (and to Shakespeare, and to history's saner voices), was Richard, Duke of Gloucester, destined to become King Richard III. Here we have the story of how *Tower of London* came to be—and of how it has come to transcend Universal Pictures' so-called horror-movie cycle of which circumstance, and publicity-department strategy, made it a part. Yes, and *Great Expectations* and *The Love Captive* and *East of Java* and even Ken Maynard's *Smoking Guns* would be remembered today as Depression-Era Universal shockers, had the advertising machinery seized upon those pictures' weirder qualities.

Much of Richard's infamy is found crystallized in Shakespeare's plays, *King Henry VI* and *The Life and Death of King Richard III*, in which the conniving hunchback ("an envious mountain 'pon my back... legs of an unequal size...") murders his way to the throne. History's crockheaded revisionist sector maintains, however, that Richard was a just ruler who became a victim of posthumous defamation by his assassins, the Tudors. (See Vincent Price's comments in our Afterword.) Even after workmen repairing a stairwell found the skeletons of two boy bluebloods who were among Richard's victims, it was suggested that the children were slain by the Tudors. As to deformity, the official portrait reveals a pleasant-looking man—although the

The Definitive Edition

right shoulder rides higher than the left. And was there ever a royal portraitist with the gall or the gumption to paint an unflattering portrait of his king?

Tower of London was shepherded by producer and director Rowland V. Lee and his screenwriter brother, Robert N. Lee. The Lees had worked together since scripting 1922's *Shirley of the Circus* at Fox. Their collaborations were antagonistically productive: "We write it out and fight it out," explained Robert. "[B]eing brothers, ... we can say things to each other that nobody else would take." They encouraged improvisation during a shoot, and Robert stood by on the set to handle revisions, often indulging in shouting matches with his brother "just for the hell of it," as Vincent Price told it, adding: "The Lees were fine, jovial fellows to work for, and very generous at soliciting our ideas as to how a scene should play out. They reserved the cuss-fights for one another—I do believe they enjoyed yelling back and forth—and we all found it more amusing than threatening."

Deciding in 1936 to tackle an English historical yarn, the brothers seized upon "the roughest, hard-boiled'est period of all time," as Robert said. "... I held out for Richard. These guys made our modern thugs look like sissies."

While in England to research *Tower of London*, Rowland also found the time to direct Rathbone in *Love from a Stranger* (1937), a takeoff on the Bluebeard and Brides-in-the-Bath murder cases, and was suitably impressed with the actor's projection of suave villainy. Back at Universal, Rowland directed Rathbone, Karloff, Bela Lugosi and Lionel Atwill in *Son of Frankenstein*, signaling the rebirth of a neglected horror genre. He and Rathbone then collaborated on *The Sun Never Sets* (1939), a British-boosterism patriotic yarn that Lee jazzed up by casting Atwill as a mad scientist.

For *Tower of London*, Universal granted the Lees an extraordinarily generous budget of $500,000, with an intended 36-day shoot. The construction of a replica of the Tower of London was a big-ticket item in itself, and costuming was required for 75 featured players and some 300 extras. Rathbone and Karloff, of course, were in the $5,000-a-week class. Rathbone was also at work during this time on Universal's *Rio*, portraying an embezzler serving a hitch in a swampbound prison.

Terror in the dungeon

The Tower of London is a conveniently oversimplified identity for a 13-acre compound of lesser towers, barracks and armories, surrounded by a moat and distinguished by a 90-foot keep known as the White Tower. Art director Jack Otterson, in a memo prepared for the Motion Picture Association's weekly radio program, *What's Happening in Hollywood*, explained that he began designing the movie version of the Tower with a warm-up period in which "I walked around and dreamed about it" while absorbing historical documents, then started making sketches that would demand a practical realism of Robert Lee's evolving script.

Otterson's collection of some 75 sketches ranged from charcoal roughs to watercolor paintings. "For the most part," he said, "they were accurate reproductions of the Tower, its torture chamber, council rooms and chapel. But some of the rooms, important to the story, no longer exist. Some passageways are too dark for the camerawork and had to be opened up; and, here and there, forced scaling was required to gain the true perspective before the cameras.

"Then came models, to line up the long shots and mass action," Otterson wrote, "and finally, of course, the blueprints." The gigantic set, standing 75 feet at points, was constructed on Universal's backlot, where hills, valleys and a dried riverbed provided room for camera placements and mobility, with vistas as much as 1,200 feet in length. (The elaborate re-creation of 15th Century architecture was coincidentally echoed in RKO-Radio Pictures' 1939 retelling of *The Hunchback of Notre Dame*. This bit of synchronicity prompted an arch but astute observation from Mrs. T.G. Winter of the Motion Picture Association's Community Service Office: "It is interesting that both the Cathedral of Notre Dame and the Tower of London, as they stood in the 15th Century, should be reproduced for pictures coming to the screen at about the same time. I think it was Mme. DeStael who said, 'Such moments are like continuous and stationary music.' Certainly, these two have thrown long shadows across history and witnessed much suffering and many dreams.")

Principal photography began on August 11 with virtually the same crew that had handled *Son of Frankenstein*. Camera chief George Robinson's gift for creating strong radial compositions and dramatic shadowplay was a critical factor. Lee and Robinson decided to avoid the sweeping crane shots that were commonplace in epic-scale productions, settling on a minimum of camera movement to achieve a maximum of seething intimacy.

The silent screen's Frank R Benson (in 1911) and Frederick Warde (in 1912) had exploited Richard's misshapenness to the fullest. John Barrymore, in 1929's *The Show of Shows*, wears a hump but moves gracefully. Sir Laurence Olivier, in the 1955 *Richard III*, augments the hunchbacked appearance with a size-12 honker. Sir Ian McKellan, in a 1995 *Richard III*, updates the character brilliantly as an agent of the Third Reich. Basil Rathbone's Richard is a robust man of action, scarcely burdened by a hunched left shoulder; his ambition to eliminate each heir-to-the-throne ahead of him is shared only with Karloff's Mord.

Mord is the one wholly fictitious character in *Tower of London*. With a shaved head, a hawk-like nose, mountainous shoulders, a twisted leg and a clubfoot—augmented by Karloff's inexplicable gift for looking larger than anyone else on view—Mord makes an admirably terrifying menace.

Tower does resemble the Shakespearean model, but Robert Lee's retelling is significantly streamlined, however augmented, and offers less florid dialogue. The story spans 1471-1485, predating the Battle of Tewkesbury and closing with Richard's undoing at the Battle of Bosworth. Richard is particularly incensed by the scheming of George, Duke of Clarence (Vincent Price), whose comeuppance for daring to outmaneuver Richard in the political arena is a drowning in a vat of wine. The slaying of the boy-king, Edward the Younger (Ronald Sinclair), and his younger brother (John Herbert-Bond) affords a particularly harrowing moment.

Ian Hunter, a burly South African-born artist on loan-out from MGM, offers a spirited and brutal portrayal of King Edward IV, whose policy is: "Marry your enemies and behead your friends." Vincent Price, recently arrived in Hollywood in the wake of a triumph on the New York and London stages in *Victoria Regina*, is splendid as the cowardly, blithering lush, Clarence. Nan Grey, a striking blonde from Texas, makes a pleasingly right Alice Barton, lady-in-waiting to Queen Elysabeth (Barbara O'Neil), even though Miss Grey affects no English accent.

The tale, boiled to an essence here for brevity's sake, finds Richard so infatuated with Anne Neville (Rose Hobart), wife of the Prince of Wales (G.P. Huntley, Jr.), that he arranges to kill the husband under the guise of battle. Richard's appetite for treachery grows ever stronger.

Behind the scenes on the set of *Tower of London*

King Edward IV dies, succeeded by his son (Ronald Sinclair)—to whom Richard is assigned as protector, which is rather like selecting a fox to guard a henhouse. Elysabeth, meanwhile, robs the treasury to help the exiled Henry Tudor (Ralph Forbes). The Tudors march upon England, and Richard is done away with.

Among all the intrigues that lend flesh to these bones of a story, the crucial duel-by-drinking business is the most beautifully played—and ad-libbed, per the Lee brothers' preference, according to Vincent Price. This tensely comical contest, with each man's political power at stake, turns deadly when Richard passes out from too much Malmsey and the alcoholic Clarence cackles delightedly over the apparent coup. Richard revives and attacks. Mord emerges, and the allies force Clarence into the vat, submerging him and slamming the lid.

During a lecture tour of the Southwest in 1974, Price was offered a Coca-Cola by a well-meaning waiter at a college-campus reception. He cringed, politely, and declined.

Later, he explained: "Well, now, for Basil Rathbone's and my drinking-binge scene in *Tower of London*, they used watered-down Coca-Cola for the wine, and Basil and I had to drink quarts of it and slosh around in it. I can't stand the stuff, to this day. Like a fool, I volunteered to do the drowning scene myself, rather than be doubled, y'know. Basil and Boris were kidding me beforehand and took great delight in throwing their cigarette butts and other trash into the vat. The stunt coordinator told me that when they dumped me into the vat and slammed the lid down, I was supposed to grab hold of the bar at the bottom and count to 10 before coming up. After I did all that, the lid was still closed! Then, I heard the crew breaking in with axes. Boris had sat on it, and Basil had leaned on it—and it got stuck. They managed to pull me out before I could drown." (Price would play Richard in Roger Corman's 1962 remake of *Tower of London*, a rough-hewn companion-piece to the more polished Corman-and-Price adaptations of Edgar Allan Poe.)

The murder of the children, which upset many picturegoers of 1939, is less graphic than in earlier tellings. Mord, horrified at what he must do, nonetheless proceeds to measure the boys' height to show his assassins the size of the graves they must dig. He regains his composure and pushes his minions forward. Concerns over censorship affected the staging of the battles, which the studio had been warned to keep free of bloodshed. Lee filmed Tewkesbury in a rainstorm and Bosworth in a cloak of fog, satisfying the censors' demands while yielding more picturesque visuals.

Technical problems and uncooperative weather threw the principal shoot 10 days over schedule and about $80,000 over budget. At a studio screening shortly before the announced release date, the well-publicized musical scoring by Charles Previn, Frank Skinner and Hans J. Salter—utilizing period instruments, with an almost dainty melodic sensibility—was declared unsuitably quaint by the front office and ordered replaced with a bombastic score. The composers hastily rearranged music taken, for the most part, from *Son of Frankenstein*. Scraps of the abandoned score remain. It all works well, but the highly recognizable recycled cues—which even then were being applied to serials and B-pictures—left a false impression that the picture must have been made on-the-cheap. Universal's publicity department insisted upon exploiting the shock-value angle ("Horror Sells!" was the catch-phrase in an elaborate pitch to the theatre trade), but several critics seemed more thoroughly impressed with the historical and romantic aspects.

Despite some dismissive reviews and a prevailing reputation as a lesser Universal entry, *Tower of London* has aged well enough to hold its own as a handsomely staged, beautifully enacted picture from a very good year overall for Hollywood.

CREDITS: Producer and Director: Rowland V. Lee; Screenplay: Robert N. Lee; Photographed by: George Robinson; Background Photography: Henry Shuster; Art Director: Jack Otterson; Associate: Richard H. Riedel; Assistant Director: Fred Frank; Editor: Edward Curtiss; Set Décor: R.A. Gausman; Gowns: Vera West; Music: Charles Previn, Frank Skinner and Hans Salter; Sound: Bernard B. Brown; Sound Technician: William Hedgcock; Technical Advisors: Maj. G.O.T. Bagley and Sir Gerald Grove Bart; Fencing Instructor: Fred Cavens; Running Time: 92 Minutes; Released: November 17, 1939

CAST: Basil Rathbone (Richard); Boris Karloff (Mord); Barbara O'Neil (Elysabeth); Ian Hunter (Edward IV); Vincent Price (Clarence); Nan Grey (Lady Alice); Ernest Cossart (Tom Clink); John Sutton (John Wyatt); Leo G. Carroll (Hastings); Miles Mander (Henry VI); Lionel Belmore (Beacon); Rose Hobart (Anne Neville); Ronald Sinclair (Edward); John Herbert Bond (Prince Richard); Ralph Forbes (Henry Tudor); Frances Robinson (Isobel); G.P. Huntley, Jr. (Prince of Wales); John Rodion [Rathbone] (Lord DeVere); Walter Tetley (Chimney Sweep); Donnie Dunagan (Infant Prince)

Lugosi makes much of a diminished role in *Black Friday*.

The 1940s & '50s

BLACK FRIDAY
(Universal Pictures Corp.; 1940)

And no, *Black Friday* is not any sequel to *Robinson Crusoe*. This higher point in the checkered résumé of director Arthur Lubin is the most melodramatically adventurous entry in Boris Karloff's long string of mad-scientist pictures—though hardly a star vehicle for the Great Man and even less of a showcase for the comparably grand Bela Lugosi.

No, the larger soul of *Black Friday* belongs to Stanley Ridges, who plays the hapless Jekyll-become-Hyde recipient of an experimentally desperate surgical procedure. Lugosi, whose truer stardom was on the point of lapsing to the minor-league studios of PRC and Monogram, had been promised a leading role in *Friday* but landed instead in a supporting bad-guy role with the saving grace of an extravagant comeuppance and death scene. Karloff, who had balked at handling the milquetoast-Jekyll/gangster-Hyde part that became one of Ridges' finer hours, wound up instead with the renegade-surgeon role that patently had been written for Lugosi. What the film lacks in that famous opposites-in-attraction energy between Karloff and Lugosi, it makes up for with a cracking good yarn and an imperishable split-personality portrayal by Ridges.

Karloff, en route to another execution

As Dr. Ernst Sovac (Karloff) is led to the death chamber at State Prison on a Friday the 13th, he hands a book—his diary—to a reporter whose coverage of the case has shown understanding. The diary yields the story in flashback:

On an earlier Friday the 13th: Small-town college professor George Kingsley (Ridges), his wife (Virginia Brissac), and their friends, Dr. Sovac and his daughter, Jean (Anne Gwynne), are celebrating Kingsley's appointment to a larger school when a car chase breaks out. Gangster Eric Marnay (Lugosi) and his henchmen gloat as the bullet-riddled auto of their rival, Red Cannon, crashes. Kingsley is struck down.

Sovac sees that Cannon is likely to survive. Kingsley is dying. At the hospital, Sovac impulsively transplants a portion of Cannon's brain into Kingsley. Cannon is assumed to have died of head injuries. Kingsley recovers, only to be plagued by headaches and nightmares.

Sovac learns of a hidden fortune in loot from a Cannon robbery. In need of financing to build a new hospital, Sovac seeks to awaken Cannon's memories in Kingsley. The mind of Red Cannon asserts itself, transforming the gentle professor into a figure of vengeful ferocity. Sovac persuades Cannon to cut him in on the stolen money.

But the mind of Kingsley also reasserts itself, and the professor tells Sovac of strange and horrible dreams—memories of Cannon's blood vengeance. Cannon resumes control, confronting his onetime paramour, Sunny (Anne Nagel), who is now involved with Marnay. Cannon's rampage continues even as he retrieves the hidden fortune. At length, he strangles Sunny and leaves Marnay to suffocate in a closet.

Cannon slaps a garrulous cab driver (John Kelly) en route to the New York hotel, Cannon's former home, where Sovac has sequestered the professor. Cannon dozes off and wakes as Kingsley hands the cabbie what Kingsley believes is a dollar bill, and collapses in his hotel room. Sovac conceals the money and makes ready to return home.

Stanley Ridges and Karloff

The taximan is arrested when he tries to spend the $1,000 bill Kingsley has handed him. The police question Kingsley, who reasonably explains that $1,000 is 'way beyond his means. The burly cab driver exonerates Kingsley: "Can you imagine *him* pushin' *me* around?"

Back home, Kingsley is addressing a class when he hears a distant wailing of sirens. He imagines he sees the ghosts of Red Cannon's victims rising from the students' chairs as the personality of Cannon comes again to the fore. He storms from the room in search of Sovac. Cannon is strangling Jean Sovac when Dr. Sovac enters and shoots him. Dying, Kingsley looks up at Sovac and asks: "Why?"

The diary's tale is told, and Dr. Sovac dies in the electric chair.

The inner-conflict portrayal worked well enough for Ridges that he replayed it, on a supernatural note, in Republic Pictures' *The Phantom Speaks* (1945). The Southampton, England-born Ridges served long and well as an all-'round character man from the middle 1930s until his death at age 59 in 1951, typically in authoritative, lead-challenging supporting roles—but seldom associated himself with horror pictures. The effective contrast between meekness and meanness that Ridges strikes in *Black Friday* would go unmatched until 1996, when Edward Norton would achieve similarly gripping results as an altar boy accused of murder in *Primal Fear*. Karloff generously yields control of *Black Friday* to Ridges' now-bravura, now-subdued performance. Lugosi, despite the marginalization of his role, managed to upstage both Karloff and Ridges with a publicity gimmick in which he allowed himself to be hypnotized for his death scene.

Arthur Lubin had been helming pictures competently but often unremarkably since 1934. Lubin's more conventional old-dark-house thriller, *Who Killed Aunt Maggie?*, dates from the same year as *Black Friday*. The following year, Lubin would weigh in as one of the savvier directors of the Abbott & Costello comedies, and in 1943 he would deliver his masterpiece of a long and uneven career: *The Phantom of the Opera*, with Claude Rains.

CREDITS: Associate Producer: Burt Kelly; Director: Arthur Lubin; Story and Screenplay: Kurt Siodmak and Eric Taylor; Suggested by: Sam Robins; Photographed by: Ellwood Bredell; Art Director: Jack Otterson; Associate: Harold A. MacArthur; Film Editor: Philip Cahn; Musical Score: Hans J. Salter, Frank Skinner, Charles Previn and Charles Henderson; Songs: "Almost," by Ben Oakland & Sam Lerner, "Heart of Harlem," by Frank Loesser & Irving Actman, "Ain't That Marvelous?" by Joe McCarthy & Harry Harris and "At the Palomar," by Frank Skinner & Ralph Freed; Gowns: Vera West; Set Décor: R.A. Gausman; Sound Supervisor: Bernard B. Brown; Technician: Charles Carroll; Special Photographic Effects: John P. Fulton; Effects Cameraman: David S. Horsley; Makeup: Jack P. Pierce; Hypnotism Consultant: Manly P. Hall; Running Time: 69 Minutes; Released: April 12, 1940

CAST: Boris Karloff (Dr. Ernst Sovac); Bela Lugosi (Eric Marnay); Stanley Ridges (Prof. George Kingsley); Anne Nagel (Sunny Rogers); Anne Gwynne (Jean Sovac); Virginia Bressac (Margaret Kingsley); Edmund MacDonald (Frank Miller); Paul Fix (Bill Kane); Murray Alper (Bellhop); Jack Mulhall (Bartender); Joseph King (Police Chief); John Kelly (Taxi Driver); James Craig (Reporter); Selmer Jackson (Doctor); Raymond Bailey (Devore); Jerry Marlowe (Desk Clerk); Willair Parker (Bystander); Marcel Dalic (Head Waiter); Harry Hayden (Prison Doctor); Frank Sheridan (Chaplain); Edwin Stanley (Surgeon); William Ruhl, Victor Zimmerman (Detectives at Hospital); Eddie Dunn, Emmett Vogan (Detectives at Marnay's); David Oliver (Second Cabbie); Kernan Cripps (Detective); Frank Jacquet (Fat Man)

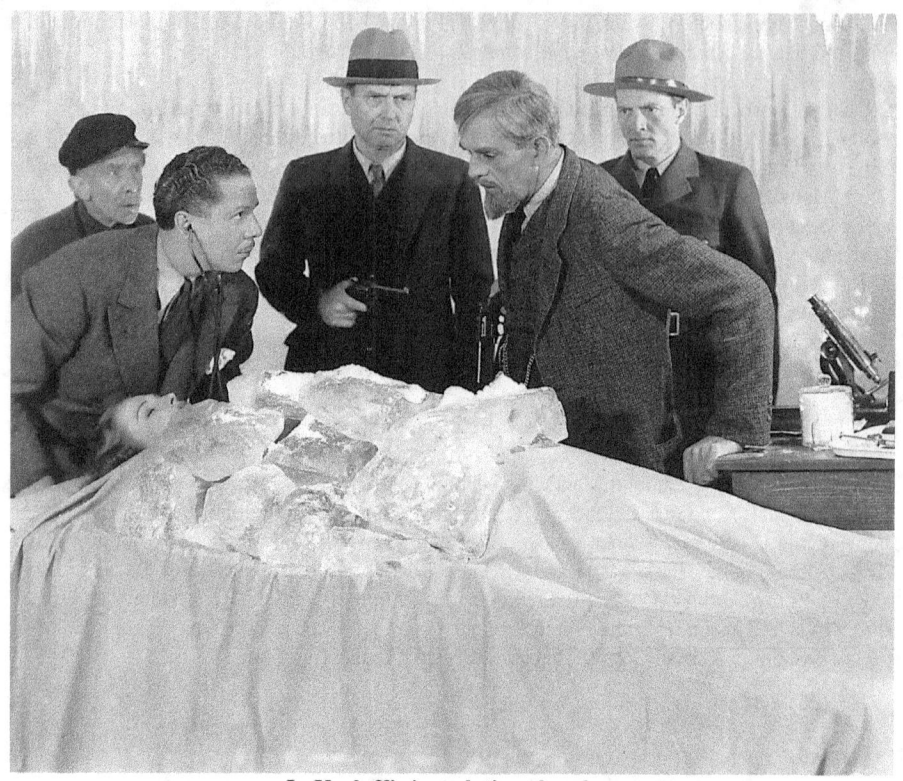

In Karloff's ice-o-lation chamber

THE MAN WITH NINE LIVES
(Columbia Pictures Corp.; 1940)

> Added to the many miracles... that have accounted for the saving of thousands upon thousands of human beings comes... frozen therapy.
>
> Estimates of how long frozen therapy can produce a state of suspended animation range from days to years. But on the fact that disease can be arrested—that life can be prolonged, by freezing human beings..., the medical world agrees.
>
> —From the Prologue

The "medical world" that "agreed"—terms used advisedly—upon the potential of "frozen therapy" existed only within the imaginations of such storytellers as Harold Shumate and Karl Brown, whose work on *The Man with Nine Lives* amounts nonetheless to an extraordinary prophecy of cryogenic research. The jury is, of course, *still* out on cryogenics, that notion of placing terminal patients on ice (whether literally or figuratively) until a cure proves forthcoming. This concept is not to be confused with the theory of frozen-therapy nose-jobs, also known as Cyranogenics. Just kidding.

Meanwhile, the deep-freeze treatment has long since proved effective in such smaller arenas as the removal of unwanted growths and the preservation of severed limbs pending reattachment. And never mind that the larger popular perception of cryogenics centers on a legend about the mortal remains of Walt Disney. One look at the tangled corporate intrigues and cultural compromises of times more recent within his namesake studio would only drive a thawed-out Uncle Walt back into the Frigidaire.

Boris Karloff in *The Man with Nine Lives* takes his own thawing more as a cause for jubilation, and he even seems pretty benevolent for a mad doctor. That is, until he realizes, first, that he will require laboratory animals to continue with the experiments he had been conducting prior to his subzero condition—and second, that he already *has* some ready-made laboratory animals in the fellow human beings sharing his quarters.

Karloff says as much in just one choice line of dialogue: "I *have* laboratory animals." The declaration conveys ideally the ambient chill of the film itself.

The adventure begins with a breakthrough discovery by Dr. Tim Mason (Roger Pryor). Tim's nurse and fiancée, Judith Blair (Jo Ann Sayers), praises his work, but Tim credits the long-ago accomplishments of Dr. Leon Kravaal—a radical scientist who "lived a hermit's existence at a place called Silver Lake." Tim and Judith undertake a search for the long-vanished Kravaal.

On Silver Lake, they learn that 10 years ago, Kravaal and a number of fellow citizens "rowed off to that island... ain't been seen since," as one of the locals helpfully informs them. Reaching a crumbling mansion on the island, Tim and Judith discover such niceties as an underground chamber—a skeleton—a cache of industrial-strength poisons—a doorway caked in ice—and the body of the fabled Dr. Kravaal (Karloff), who not only thaws out but also returns to life.

"Ten years?" ponders Dr. Kravaal. "It's yesterday afternoon to me... !" Kravaal explains: In 1930, his treatment of a wealthy patient was compromised by an intrusion from a distrustful posse. Kravaal threatened his accusers with a barrage of poisonous vapors.

"Why didn't it kill me?" Kravaal asks as his reminiscence ends. "I took nothing to keep myself from freezing to death—and yet I lived." He theorizes: "By sheerest accident, the fumes we inhaled were in perfect proportion." The others are removed from the ice. "We can all leave and announce this discovery to the world," Kravaal beams.

The reviving townsmen prove as cantankerous as ever. Kravaal turns deadly serious: "Nobody leaves this room until I've rediscovered the exact proportions of that formula." The body count escalates modestly until Kravaal realizes that Judith will make an ideal subject. Finally, Judith is established as "frozen but alive," vindicating the Great Experiment. Too late for Kravaal, who has been gunned down by his surviving enemies. Tim revives Judith, and they return to the world outside "to complete the great unfinished work of Dr. Kravaal."

Karl Brown was a fine scenarist for Karloff in the realm of characterizing dialogue, but a washout in the death-scene department. Gunplay represents such a mundane demise for so grand an actor that it's a wonder Karloff himself didn't object. Karloff, however, subscribed to the British attitude that "one mustn't grumble," and he told us in 1968 that Brown's contributions to *The Man They Could Not Hang* and *The Man with Nine Lives* and *Before I Hang* offered "some of the juiciest dialogue I've ever torn into."

Karloff clearly relishes the Kravaal role, for he also tears into the more brusque passages with generosity and zest. Few actors could read so much urgency into the simple "*Nurse*! Take his pulse!" that Kravaal fires off at Jo Ann Sayers while attempting to regain the momentum of a bygone quest. When demanding that Roger Pryor, as the intruding physician, must help find the flaws in a batch of formula, Karloff declares, "It's your *duty*," with such insistence as to make the outlandish situation believable. Karloff turns menacing with an equally persuasive abruptness, informing Pryor and Miss Sayers, "We need bodies with no poison in them. Bodies like yours—or *hers*."

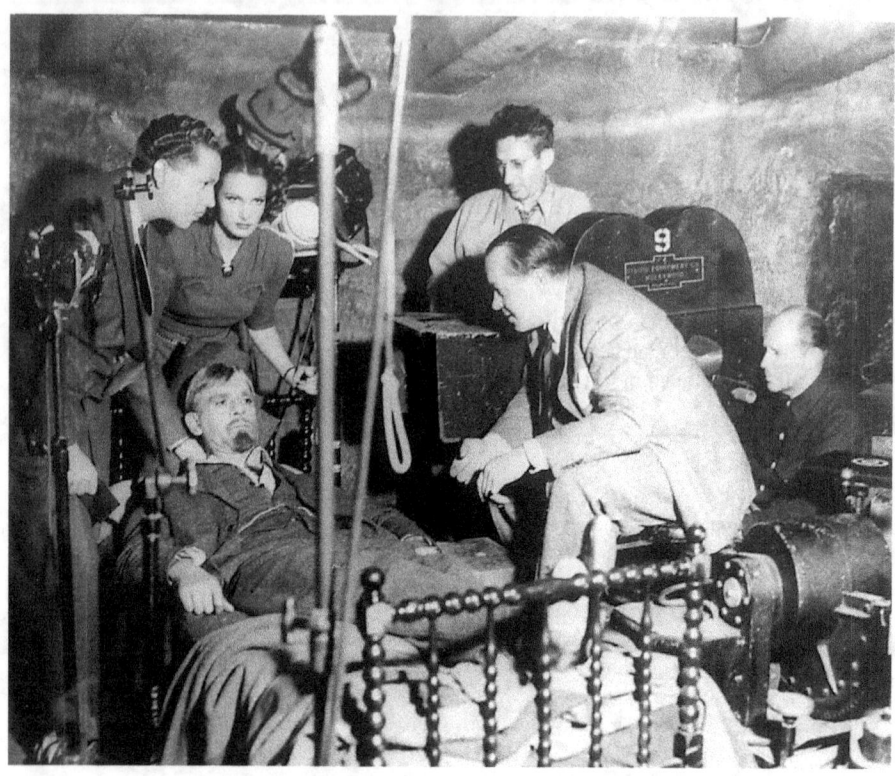

A shot is readied for *The Man with Nine Lives*

Lest we over-distinguish *The Man with Nine Lives* and its close-kin Columbias, it bears hammering here that the greater point of the Turner & Price collaborations has been to shed an unaccustomed appreciative light on pictures that were dismissed in their day as formulaic hackwork, or whose reputations have suffered from cheap-shot sniping in retrospect. (Our rediscovery of *The Man with Nine Lives* occurred in 1972—two years before the first hesitant outbreak of home video as a distinct industry—on a late-night Dallas television showcase bearing the snarky bourgeois-reactionary title of *One-Star Theatre*.) And yes, these pictures' origins lie entirely in fast-buck hucksterism: Irving Briskin's B-picture unit at Columbia had its *raison d'etre* in facile thrill-mongering, but Briskin had nothing to lose by allowing his assembled artists to come up with provocative ideas and impassioned portrayals, beyond the Betty Crocker plotting and child's-play resolutions. The upshot—amply well represented in these pages—was often a heady fusion of the Cinema of Ideas with the Cinema of Sensationalism. The Karloff Briskins are especially rewarding for their savvy science-fictional speculations, and for the immersion in character that distinguishes even Karloff's lesser work of those Depression-into-wartime years. The spirit, and even some of the letter, of these films would reassert itself in 1996, in *Unforgettable*, an uncompromisingly grim science-fiction/noir effort from director John Dahl.

(*Memo from George E. Turner: I was prowling about the Columbia backlot while stationed out West with the U.S.N. during the "Good War," as the revisionists insist on calling it, and found myself traversing a dark tunnel—kind of a quonset-hut sort of apparatus like they use for military barracks and rec halls—that had been dressed out to resemble a cave, rocky floor and all. It didn't take me long to realize that I was in good ol' Boris's ice-cave, left over from* The

Man with Nine Lives. *The silence was eerie, I mean to tell you, and* especially *eerie because I couldn't hear my own footfalls! I reached down to feel the ground, picked up a chunk of the rubble—and found that it was made out of cork. Of course! To keep things quiet for the microphones! I pocketed some of the stuff for a souvenir—still got a few pieces kicking around in the file cabinets.*)

CREDITS: In Charge of Production: Irving Briskin; Producer: Wallace MacDonald; Director: Nick Grinde; Screenplay: Karl Brown; Story: Harold Shumate; Photographed by: Benjamin Kline; Film Editor: Al Clark; Art Director: Lionel Banks; Technical Advisor: Dr. Ralph S. Willard; Musical Director: M.W. Stoloff; Musical Score: Dr. Karol Rathaus; George Parrish, Nico Gregor, Mischa Bakaleinikoff, Gregory Stone, Ben Oakland and Gerard Carbonara; Running Time: 73 Minutes; Released: April 18, 1940

CAST: Boris Karloff (Dr. Kravaal); Roger Pryor (Dr. Tim Mason); Jo Ann Sayers (Judith Blair); Stanley Brown (Bob Adams); John Dilson (John Hawthorne); Hal Taliaferro [a.k.a. Wally Wales] (Sheriff Stanton); Byron Foulger (Dr. Bassett); Charles Trowbridge (Dr. Harvey); Ernie Adams (Pete Daggett); Bruce Bennett [formerly Herman Brix] (Ranger); Ivan Miller (Sheriff Haley); Eddie Dew, Charles Miller, Landers Stevens (Doctors); Les Willard (Jasper Adams)

ISLAND OF DOOMED MEN
(Columbia Pictures Corp.; 1940)

Peter Lorre, the screen's greatest master of soft-spoken villainy, made several pictures during the early 1940s for Irving Briskin's B-picture unit at Columbia, the home of Boris Karloff's popular string of mad-scientist films. The first, and least readily remembered, of the Lorre Briskins is *Island of Doomed Men*, which was filmed and advertised initially as *Dead Man's Isle*. It was made in 12 shooting days for under $90,000.

Mark Sheldon (Robert Wilcox), a new undercover man with the F.B.I., learns of Dead Man's Island and its satanic master, Stephen Danel (Peter Lorre), who uses paroled convicts as slaves in his diamond mines. Brand (Don Beddoe), a henchman of Danel's, murders a senior agent and frames Sheldon straight into prison. Danel arranges for a parole—to Dead Man's Isle.

At first treating Sheldon cordially, Danel soon proves a menace. Sheldon is fascinated with Danel's wife, Lorraine (Rochelle Hudson), who though pampered is as much a victim as the workers. Danel torments Sheldon. Lorraine tries to meet with Sheldon but is thwarted by an electric fence. Sheldon gets a chance to escape when he is sent to the compound's drunken doctor (Kenneth MacDonald) after a lashing. Overpowering the doctor, Sheldon flees into the jungle. He is apprehended by Cort (Charles Middleton), the head guard. Cort agrees to leave Sheldon's manacles unlocked so that the two can steal Danel's diamonds.

At Sheldon's insistence, Lorraine steals the keys to the gate while Danel feigns slumber. Lorraine and Sheldon are recaptured. Sheldon and Cort are imprisoned, but they escape, killing Brand and a guard. Cort launches a rebellion.

Sheldon disables the electric fence. He enters, but Danel gets the drop on him. When Lorraine rushes to Sheldon's side, Danel decides to kill them both. Cort and the convicts intervene, but Danel kills Cort and regains the upper hand. Siggie (George E. Stone), an abused servant, stabs Danel—who retaliates. With the menace put down and ample evidence of his own innocence in hand, Sheldon looks forward to a new life with Lorraine.

The story differs little from any number of other penal-institution melodramas, but the diminutive, sad-eyed Lorre adds dimension. He is at his best here as a cultured, soft-spoken sadist who dotes on Chopin nocturnes (performed by his tormented wife) and who politely expresses his regrets to convicts he has ordered flogged: "I sincerely hope you will be more careful next time." Although he pretends to detest violence, occasionally he erupts savagely, as when he kills his servant's pet monkey. Rochelle Hudson, beautifully gowned in a series of seven Kalloch creations, is an asset as Lorre's bird in a gilded cage. Robert Wilcox, a sensitive actor whose promising career was lost in alcoholism and an early death, makes a memorably moody romantic lead. The picture benefits from such notables as Charles Middleton and Don Beddoe, as secondary villains, and George E. Stone, Addison Richards, Bruce Bennett and Earl Gunn.

Much of the exterior photography was done at Bronson Canyon, a granite quarry seen in hundreds of adventure pictures and located only a few miles north of Columbia's Hollywood studio. The plush exterior of the house and the adjacent jungle, as well as all interiors, were set up in sound stages at the Columbia Ranch in Burbank. The director, Charles Barton—better known for a run of Paramount's Zane Grey pictures of the 1930s and several of the sharper Abbott & Costello films of the 1940s—gets abundant atmosphere out of the sun-baked canyon and the shadowy jungle.

Expert photography and an unobtrusively weird musical score bolster the mood. Both factors propel a scene in which the lovers sneak past Lorre and the camera moves in to show his heavy eyelids opening. First and foremost, the picture gives Lorre control in a leading role—instead of having him play second fiddle to more glamorous stars, as was too often his lot.

CREDITS: Executive Producer: Irving Briskin; Associate Producer: Wallace MacDonald; Director: Charles Barton; Story and Screenplay: Robert D. Andrews; Photographed by: Benjamin Kline; Editor: James Sweeney; Art Director: Lionel Banks; Gowns: Kalloch; Music: M.W. Stoloff; Music: Gerard Carbonara; Assistant Director: Thomas Flood; Sound System: Western Electric; Running Time: 67 minutes. Released: May 20, 1940

CAST: Peter Lorre (Stephen Danel); Rochelle Hudson (Lorraine Danel); Robert Wilcox (Mark Sheldon); Don Beddoe (Brand); George E. Stone (Siggie); Kenneth MacDonald (Doctor); Charles Middleton (Cort); Stanley Brown (Eddie); Earl Gunn (Mitchell); Bruce Bennett (Hazen); Addison Richards (Agent 46); Forbes Murray (Chairman of Parole Board); Howard Hickman (Judge); Donald Douglas (Secret Service Officer); Walter Miller (Detective); Trevor Bardette (District Attorney); Richard Fiske (Convict); George McKay (Bookkeeper); Sam Ash (Ames); Eddie Laughton (Borgo); Al Hill (Clinton); John Tyrrell (Durkin); Ray Bailey (Mystery Man); Lee Prather (Warden); Bernie Breakston (Townsend); Harry Strang and Charles Hamilton (Policemen); William Gould (Parole Board Member)

Lorre gets a grip.

STRANGER ON THE THIRD FLOOR
(RKO-Radio Pictures, Inc.; 1940)

Two years before Val Lewton proved at RKO (with 1942's *Cat People*) that a tightly budgeted picture of skill and inventiveness could outclass the high-budget fare, a tiny film from that very studio achieved comparable excellence. *Stranger on the Third Floor* drew little critical attention and hardly advanced any careers.

Stranger is something more than the usual budget-bound production: It was given a full month's schedule, June 3-July 3 of 1940, with a negative cost of $171,192.

Struggling newspaperman Michael Ward (John McGuire) is in a lunchstand near his boardinghouse when the proprietor has a run-in with Joe Briggs (Elisha Cook, Jr.), a taxi driver. Later, Michael finds the owner slain. With Michael as the principal witness, Briggs is sentenced to death. Jane (Margaret Tallichet), Michael's fiancée, senses that Briggs is innocent. Michael begins to worry as the execution date nears. Michael and Jane, caught in a rainstorm one night, retreat to his quarters. Mr. Meng (Charles Halton), a crotchety neighbor, demands that the couple be evicted. Michael impulsively threatens to kill Meng.

Michael encounters an odd-looking stranger (Peter Lorre), who tries to enter the boardinghouse but leaves after Michael shuts the door in his face. Later on, in the hall, Michael encounters and pursues the stranger, who vanishes into the darkness. Michael notices that Meng's oppressive snoring has ceased. In a fitful sleep, Michael dreams of his own arrest and trial before a ghostly jury. He sees himself dragged toward the electric chair as Joe Briggs jeers at him.

Michael wakes with a start and finds the corpse of Meng. He packs and steals away. Jane pleads with him to call the police. Michael is convinced that both the diner man and Meng were slain by the stranger.

Jane prowls the neighborhood in hopes of finding the stranger. Late one evening, she encounters her suspect. While threatening Jane, the stranger is struck down by a street-cleaning vehicle. His dying confession clears both Michael and Briggs.

Producer Lee Marcus, a former executive at RKO, became impressed as early as 1936 with the possibilities of Frank Partos' story. Finally, he convinced the studio to buy the piece and hire Partos to write a script. A successful scenarist, Boris Ingster, was given a début as a director. (He did not have another directing job until *The Judge Steps Out* and *Southside 1-1000* of 1949-50, both successful but hardly artistically mounted films. These three titles represent the entire feature-directing résumé of Boris Ingster.)

Peter Lorre and Elisha Cook, Jr., are the only name-brand performers. Lorre received $7,000 for his brief participation; the other cast members found remuneration substantially less—more in line with their standing as in-house players. Marcus selected unknowns for the youth leads after studying the screen tests of several hopefuls. A former secretary at Paramount, Margaret Tallichet was discovered by Carole Lombard and had come within shouting distance of the Scarlett O'Hara role in 1939's *Gone with the Wind*. Marcus thought *Stranger* would make her a star, but no such luck. She married director William Wyler and retired from the screen. John McGuire had been a bit player before *Stranger*; he returned to (mostly) small roles.

Stranger is a prime example of intelligent filmmaking. Careful pre-production included 243 scene sketches and the sculpting-in-miniature of sets and characters. Lighting effects and camera angles were photographed in miniature before shooting began, enabling a high polish within the time limit. To find a more handsomely photographed picture of the period, one must resort to *Citizen Kane* or *The Long Voyage Home*. The cinematographer, Nicholas Musuraca, later worked with Val Lewton.

The *pièce de resistance* is a long dream sequence set in a fanciful courtroom—inspired, perhaps, by James Cruze's *Beggar on Horseback* (1925), but more fantastic in execution. Furnishings were built on mobile platforms so they could be rearranged and raised or lowered to permit bizarre camera angles and the casting of gigantic shadows on a gray cyclorama. Floors were brightly painted and lighted to give the impression that the players are walking in empty space. Among the remarkable props are a newspaper's front page with the word *MURDER* printed from 'specially made wooden type 19 inches tall, an outsized judge's bench, and a grotesque Justice figure—a skeleton brandishing a scythe in addition to the symbolic scales. Dazzling optics include a dissolve of the judge into the Justice image. The most harrowing moments are those in which the court refuses to believe the existence of the stranger even though the hero can see him climbing over the gallery chairs; and in which McGuire is being readied for execution, a barber working on him while a chaplain recites a prayer. Another impressive montage depicts Miss Tallichet's determined search.

The acting—from Lorre's beautifully underplayed man-from-nowhere, to the realistic portrayals of McGuire and Miss Tallichet, to the leering nastiness of Charles Halton—could scarcely be bettered. Many scenes are enacted on the RKO New York street—the same gloomy setting where Robert Armstrong chances upon Fay Wray in *King Kong* (1933). The ramshackle boardinghouse with its perilous stairways provides a perfect setting for despair and mayhem. A psychologically sound musical score by Roy Webb adds a great deal to this brilliant, underrated film.

Just how underrated *Stranger* was—and by its own company, yet—is evident in an RKO memorandum of 1949. A proposed remake was quashed with the words: "Must have been an effective 'B' and could be again, but see no real reason to remake it." Very belatedly, the picture has received popular and scholarly recognition as a cornerstone of the film noir movement.

Margaret Tallichet and Lorre

CREDITS: Producer: Lee Marcus; Director: Boris Ingster; Story and Screenplay: Frank Partos; Music: Roy Webb; Photographed by: Nicholas Musuraca; Special Effects: Vernon L. Walker; Optical Effects: Linwood Dunn; Art Director: Van Nest Polglase; Associate: Albert S. D'Agostino; Wardrobe: Renie; Sound: Bailey Fesler; Editor: Harry Marker; Running Time: 62 minutes; Released: August 16, 1940

CAST: Peter Lorre (The Stranger); John McGuire (Michael Ward); Margaret Tallichet (Jane); Charles Waldron (District Attorney); Elisha Cook, Jr. (Joe Briggs); Charles Halton (Meng); Ethel Griffies (Mrs. Kane); Cliff Clark (Martin); Oscar O'Shea (Judge); Alec Craig (Defense Attorney); Otto Hoffman (Police Surgeon); Charles Judels (Nick); Frank Yaconelli (Jack); Paul McVey (Lt. Jones); Robert Dudley (Postman); Frank O'Connor (Officer); Herbert Vigran, Robert Weldon, Terry Belmont and Gladden James (Reporters); Harry C. Bradley (Court Clerk); Greta Grandstedt (Chambermaid); Katherine Wallace (Woman); Bud Osborne (Bartender); Lynton Brent (Taxi Driver); Broderick O'Farrell (Minister); Emory Parnell, Jack Cheatham and Del Henderson (Detectives); Don Kelly (Cop); Henry Rocquemore (Boss McLean); Jane Keckley (Landlady); Bess Wade (Charwoman); Ralph Sanford (Truck Driver); James Farley (Policeman); Betty Farrington (Stout Woman); Ray Cooke (Drugstore Attendant); Donald Kerr (Man); William Edmunds (Janitor); Lee Phelps (First Taxi Driver); Max Hoffman (Second Taxi Driver); Bobby Barber (Italian); Frank Hammond (Second Janitor)

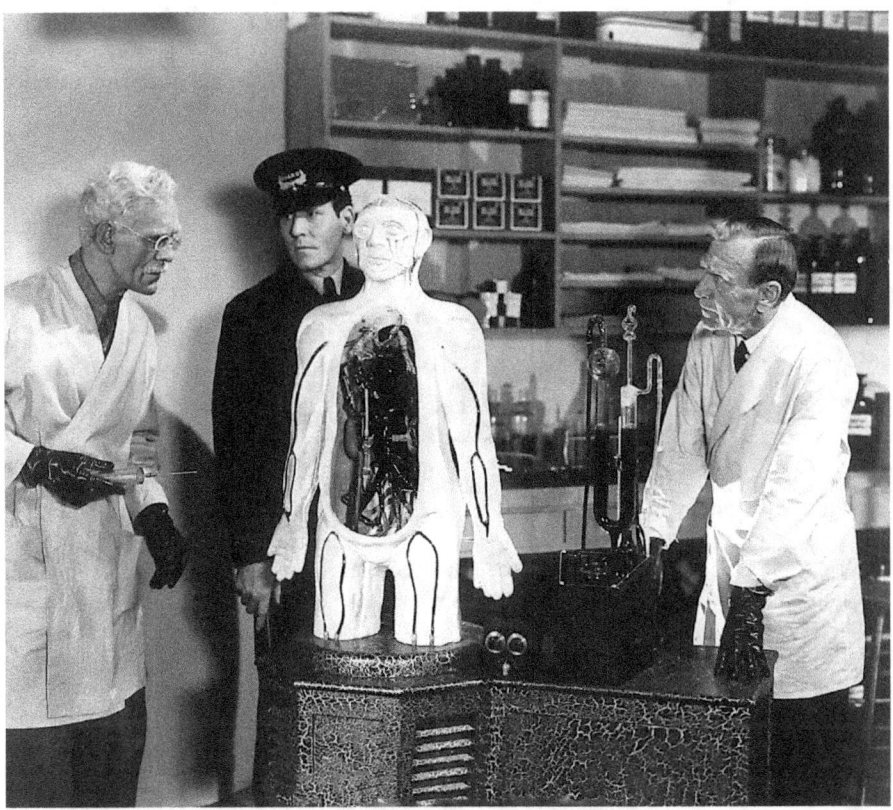

Laboratory privileges for jailbird Karloff

BEFORE I HANG
(Columbia Pictures Corp.; 1940)

Variations upon a theme: Maverick medico tries radical therapy but is undone by intolerant society. This prototypical High Concept is the reliable basis of Boris Karloff's handful of mad-doctor pictures—five of which issued from Columbia's B-picture unit. (And yes, even the comedy *The Boogie Man Will Get You* fits, if only just.) Nick Grinde's *Before I Hang* is the last of the more genuinely formula-bound entries, giving way to the cosmic necromancy and fatalistic film-noirisms of Ed Dmytryk's *The Devil Commands* (1941).

Before I Hang finds Karloff as Dr. John Garth, an elderly physician on trial for a mercy killing. Garth seeks to no avail to explain that his patient was dying of advanced age—which he considers a disease. Dr. Ralph Howard (Edward Van Sloan), the prison's surgeon, persuades the authorities to allow Garth to continue the experiments up to almost the moment of execution. Garth's serum requires fresh blood, and Howard agrees to use a cadaver fresh from the gallows as the source.

Garth tests the serum on himself, over Howard's objections. Garth's own death march is interrupted by word that the state has commuted his sentence to life. Garth collapses and wakes, unnaturally refreshed, in the prison hospital. "By every medical test," Howard declares, "you are at least 20 years younger..."

Karloff contemplates an assault upon the aging process.

Later, while preparing to treat Howard similarly, Garth is suddenly afflicted with a pained agitation. Howard comprehends: "There's *poison* in you—that *murderer's* blood!" Garth strangles Howard. Otto Kron (Frank Richards), a half-witted trusty, is killed by Garth after a savage fight. The warden (Ben Taggart) concludes that Kron killed Howard and attacked Garth, who then killed Kron. The state pardons Garth.

Among Garth's friends, an aging maestro (Pedro de Cordoba) consents to submit to the treatment, but Garth is gripped again by the strangling frenzy. Finally, Garth proposes to turn himself in. The doctor has begun a determined march through the fogbound night, arriving at last at the prison. A terrified guard (Richard Fiske) opens fire on the advancing Garth.

So here we have another garden-variety ballistics demise for Karloff, a thorough letdown from the larger-than-life tragedies on display here. (The title, *Before I Hang*, leaves rather a bit to be desired, too, when compared with the attention-grabbing name of the film as a work-in-progress: *The Wizard of Death*.) The film fairly exults in its larger melodramatic conceits, placing the viewer entirely on the side of Karloff's Dr. Garth—even when he berates his cronies for their reasonable belief that advanced age is an unquestionably natural state of being. Karloff's transformations are disturbingly realized without extravagant external devices, and his trek back to the prison packs the quiet relentlessness of a nightmare. Edward Van Sloan is as grand as ever as Karloff's custodial colleague, who realizes too late the damning flaw in a miraculous discovery: *The Hands of Orlac* has nothing on "that *murderer's* blood."

CREDITS: In Charge of Production: Irving Briskin; Producer: Wallace MacDonald; Director: Nick Grinde; Screenplay: Robert D. Andrews, from His Collaborative Story with Karl Brown; Photographed by: Benjamin Kline; Film Editor: Charles Nelson; Art Director: Lionel Banks; Sound: J.S. Westmoreland; Musical Director: M.W. Stoloff; Musical Score: George Parrish, Nico Gregor, Gerard Carbonara, Dr. Karol Rathaus, Gregory Stone, Ben Oakland and Leigh Harline; Running Time: 63 Minutes; Released: September 17, 1940

CAST: Boris Karloff (Dr. John Garth); Evelyn Keyes (Martha Garth); Bruce Bennett (Dr. Paul Ames); Edward Van Sloan (Dr. Ralph Howard); Ben Taggart (Warden Thompson); Pedro de Cordoba (Victor Sondini); Wright Kramer (George Wharton); Bertram Marburgh (Stephen Barclay); Don Beddoe (Capt. McGraw); Robert Fiske (District Attorney); Kenneth MacDonald (Anson); Frank Richards (Otto Kron); Richard Fiske (Gate Guard); Eddie Laughton (Laboratory Guard); Edward Earle (Prison Doctor); Lee Shumway (Lawyer); John Tyrell (Detective); George Magrill (Policeman); Frederick Burton (Governor); Ernie Adams (Sam)

Kay Kyser, in unlikely company

YOU'LL FIND OUT
(RKO-Radio Pictures, Inc.; 1940)

Pity the theatre manager who, when obliged to field questions of what was playing, had to answer, "*You'll Find Out*," and try to keep a straight face in the bargain. History has tended to lump together *You'll Find Out* and *The Boogie Man Will Get You* (1942) as waggish summit meetings of Hollywood's more famous horror-movie actors. The pictures are, however, distinct and unrelated products save for their shared teamings of Boris Karloff and Peter Lorre. Bela Lugosi further distinguishes *You'll Find Out*, completing the triumvirate of the talking-picture era's definitive bogeymen. *You'll Find Out* prefigures by a generation the gathering of Karloff, Lorre and Lon Chaney, Jr., for a peculiar episode of the early-'60s teleseries *Route 66*—in which Lorre plays a disorienting amalgamation of himself and Lugosi.

The larger point of *You'll Find Out* is to showcase the ersatz-jazz hokum of Kay Kyser & His Kollege of Musical Knowledge, a Columbia Records hitmaking act that had just completed *That's Right, You're Wrong* at RKO and would grace half-a-dozen other features during 1941-44. The cultural historian Phil Hardy goes so far as to declare Kyser the most horrifying thing about *You'll Find Out*.

"The word that fits Kyser to a *K* is *korn*...," reads a fan-magazine article from 1940. "*Hokum* was a good enough word for Grandpa but would never adequately describe Kay, Ginny Simms, Ish Kabibble, Harry Babbitt and the rest of Mr. Kyser's remarkable cross between a dance

Kyser distracts Lugosi.

orchestra, an amateur hour, a spelling bee and the grammar-school boys back in Rocky Mount, N.C. [Kyser's hometown], cutting up on Halloween with stolen corsets and kazoos.

"*You'll Find Out* gains no little of its charm from the presence of Bela Lugosi, Peter Lorre and Boris Karloff, who are almost as cute as Mr. Kyser's makes-you-want-to-dance music...," continues the piece. "[T]he audience is one minute scared out of its pants by Lorre, Lugosi and Karloff, and the next is soothed by Kyser's rippling Dixie drawl... " And enough of the fatuous hype, already.

The Lorre-Lugosi-Karloff combo is a delight, of course, holding forth in a classic-manner old-dark-house setting—where the Kyser orchestra has conveniently been engaged to perform—and plotting the murder of an heiress (Helen Parrish) for the customary reasons. The disclosure of each star's dire motivations comes but gradually: Karloff is a judge who knows the ins and outs of inheritance law; Lugosi, a bogus mystic who is fleecing the lady of the manor (Alma Kruger); and Lorre, a debunker of spiritualism who proves to be an accomplice. Not to give away too much, y'know.

Kyser even gets to play the hero, ordering a séance to smoke out the menace(s) and finally tackling Karloff when the badman resorts to gunplay. It all climaxes with imminent doom for Kyser and his ensemble, when Lorre lobs a bomb into their midst. A pet dog obligingly returns the explosive to its owners, blasting the would-be killers to smithereens. (And yes, the pooch gets away intact.)

Kyser is an acquired taste but a natural for the cameras—and a delight for those who have acquired the taste. The sprightly musical selections issue from the pop-composer team of Jimmy

McHugh and Johnny Mercer, mainstays of big-band swing and movie-themewriting. The unsprightly, downright ominous, settings and underscoring are the brilliant work of art director Van Nest Polglase, orchestral composer Roy Webb and camera aces Frank Redman and Vernon Walker, who provide as unnerving a haunted mansion, as foreboding an orchestral backdrop and as dark and stormy a night as ever graced any more straightforward chiller.

A word about Kyser's featured player Ish Kabibble: His real name was Merwyn Bogue, and he was very much the childlike stooge of the act, what with his pudding-bowl haircut and his prevailing air of childlike indignation. Bogue took his stage name from the Yiddish expression *Ische ga bibble?*—meaning, essentially, "What? Me worry?" This attitude was appropriated during the 1950s by *MAD* magazine as a motto for its Ish Kabibble-like fictitious mascot, Alfred E. Newman. The real Ish died in 1994.

CREDITS: Producer and Director: David Butler; Screenplay: James V. Kern; Story: David Butler and James V. Kern; Special Material: Andrew Bennison, Monte Brice and R.T.M. Scott; Photographed by: Frank Redman; Special Effects: Vernon L. Walker; Art Director: Van Nest Polglase; Assistant Art Director: Carroll Clark; Editor: Irene Morra; Set Décor: Darrell Silvera; Gowns: Edward Stevenson; Assistant Director: Fred A. Fleck; Music: Roy Webb; Orchestrations: George Dunning; Songs: "The Bad Humor Man," "I'd Know You Anywhere," "You've Got Me This Way," "Like the Fella Once Said" and "I've Got a One-Track Mind," by Jimmy McHugh & Johnny Mercer; Sound: Earl A. Wolcott; Sonovox Effects: Gilbert Wright; Running Time: 95 Minutes; Released: November 22, 1940

CAST: Kay Kyser (Himself); Peter Lorre (Prof. Carl Fenninger); Boris Karloff (Judge Mainwaring); Bela Lugosi (Prince Saliano); Helen Parrish (Janis Bellacrest); Dennis O'Keefe (Chuck Deems); Alma Kruger (Aunt Margo); Joseph Eggenton (Jurgen); Ginny Simms, Harry Babbitt, Ish Kabibble and Sully Mason (Band Members); Louise Currie (Marion); Mary Martha Wood (Georgia); Dorothy Moore (Penny); Mimi Montaye (Mimi); Joan Warner (Joan); Jeanne Houser (Jean); Mary Bovard (Mary); Jane Patten (Jane); Joe North and Eugenia Raffee (Servants); Frank Mills (Cabbie); Beulah Parkington (Mother); Guy Webster (Infant); Jeff Corey (Mr. Brown); Eleanor Lawson (Miss Crandall); Bill Telaak (Bus Driver); and Bess Flowers, Larry McGrath, Frank O'Connor

THE TELL-TALE HEART
(Metro-Goldwyn-Mayer Corp.; 1941)

The survival of any writer's work is due much more to chance than most critics care to admit.
—Hervey Allan, *Tales of Edgar Allan Poe*; 1944

For a talent long deceased before the earliest stirrings of motion-picture technology could come about, Edgar Allan Poe has exerted a profound influence upon the cinema. The truth is self-evident not merely in a storytelling sense, but in a kinetic urgency that foreshadows the very rhythm of a ribbon of film clacking through the projector-gate, pulsating in rapid bursts of light onto the screen while its accumulated length laps in measured surges from one reel onto another, barring a glitch in the pumping mechanism. The over-obvious metaphor thus hammered here lies in "The Tell-Tale Heart," a centuried favorite that needs no introduction but will receive one, anyhow. A good deal of history wants recapping before our chosen version of this famous story can have its due.

Eight years before his death, Edgar Allan Poe ran afoul of a predatory literary dilettante who would become not only Poe's most eagerly parasitic freeloader—but also his bitterest and most cowardly enemy, self-appointed and trivially motivated. Poe had experienced combative dealings with his foster father, but this new antagonist would prove more relentless by far.

The point is not to suggest that Poe accumulated all that many enemies during a short lifetime of troubled brilliance, but when occasionally he got crosswise with this or that party he tended to make the alienation stick. As a rule, that only meant quitting a job in disgust—over, for example, the stingy compensation and fatuous editorial content of Philadelphia-based *Graham's Magazine*—and then sticking around to gripe. But Poe's vexatious relationship with his adoptive father, the dour and resentful merchant John Allan of Richmond, Virginia, became a long-term exercise in reciprocal antagonisms and begrudging courtesies that ended with Allan's death in 1833.

Allan had written in 1833 that Poe's "talents are of an order than can never prove a comfort to their possessor," in the course of rejecting a plea for financial assistance from the struggling author, then 24. At the least, John Allan exhibited the graciousness to keep his opinions more-or-less to himself, via private correspondence.

Poe fared increasingly better over the course of the 1830s, but his burgeoning success as a writer and editor was leading him headlong into the clutches of the contemptible Rufus Wilmot Griswold. Griswold, a few years Poe's junior, usually appended a Reverend Mister title to his name as a misleading convenience: The foppish manipulator was a credentialed clergyman of the Baptist persuasion, but he busied himself chiefly as a self-promoting huckster in the guise of editor and literary agent.

In Philadelphia in 1841, the 32-year-old Poe was formally affiliated with *Graham's Magazine*, where he became a stationary target for the Rev. Mr. Griswold's opportunistic scheming. The bait was an anthology Griswold had announced, to be called *The Poets and Poetry of America*. Poe offered Griswold a variety of pieces and recommended other poets for consideration. Griswold took three of Poe's works—"The Coliseum,"

"The Haunted Palace" and "The Sleeper"—but paid nothing for their inclusion. He rejected Poe's list of other suggested contributors.

The following year saw Poe quit *Graham's* out of distaste for "the namby-pamby character of the magazine," only to remain on friendly terms with the publisher, George Graham, while serving as a freelance contributor: Work-for-hire paid more generously than a staff position. Poe's successor on staff was Rufus Griswold, who did not last long at the job because of what Graham characterized as an explosive disposition and an inability to work cordially with colleagues—including Poe.

Poe was not above the occasional conflict of journalistic interest, and when *The Poets and Poetry of America* appeared in 1842 he published a critique of the book in *The Boston Miscellany*, generally overpraising the project but lambasting Griswold's showcasing of some poets "too mediocre to entitle them to particular notice." This salient line enraged Griswold, whose backlash moved Poe to describe the book (in private correspondence) as "a most outrageous humbug."

There followed between Griswold and Poe "a sort of on-and-off friendliness," as a 20th Century scholar, Peggy Robbins, has put it in a splendidly detailed monograph from the National Historical Society, *Edgar Allan Poe: The Creation of a Reputation*. She notes that the men shared chiefly in common a suspicious outlook and a volatile temperament. Griswold suspected that Poe had been responsible for an anonymous and scathing later review of *The Poets and Poetry of America*. Griswold began spreading such defamatory rumors about Poe that George Graham found himself moved to declare that Poe's "nature... eludes the rude grasp of a mind so warped and uncongenial as Mr. Griswold's."

Curious, then, that Poe should have invited Griswold to serve as literary executor, should the author come to an untimely end. Which Poe did, on October 7, 1849, in Baltimore, at the age of 40.

Griswold could scarcely wait to begin a concerted campaign of slander as a prelude to assuming control of the published and yet-unpublished legacy of tales, poems and correspondence. He promptly placed an obituary notice in the New York *Tribune*, under cover of a pseudonym: "[F]ew will be grieved... The poet was known [internationally]; but he had few or no friends; and the regrets for his death will be suggested principally by the consideration that in him literary art has lost one of its most brilliant but erratic stars." This blindside hatchet-job emphasized "no moral susceptibility... and little or nothing of the true point of honor."

The point here was less to disparage Poe's character, however, than to sensationalize a body of work from which Griswold now stood to profit. The greater the massed perception of Edgar Allan Poe as a debauched madman—the slanders ranging from drug addiction to "criminal relations with his Mother-in-Law"—then the more extensively Griswold could lunch out on the work of an artist for whom he harbored only contempt. No published collection of Poe was considered complete for two generations to come without the inclusion of Griswold's bogus *Memoir*, which defined the popular view of Poe-as-reprobate despite protests from saner voices. Sarah Helen Whitman, who had contemplated marriage to the widowed Poe shortly before his death, wrote an eloquent rebuttal but refrained from publishing it during Griswold's lifetime—he died in 1857, and none too soon—because she feared retaliation from the antagonistic little *poseur*. This, according to an essay by John C. Miller, in that same *Creation of a Reputation*.

Rufus Griswold notwithstanding—and his calculated defamations, however lasting, took place over a very brief span of years—it was the American institution of the daily newspaper, in a day when newspapers actually were assembled for people who enjoyed reading, that kept Poe a vital presence over the longer haul. Here would lie Poe's chief posthumous forum until the cinema could emerge as a viable form of art and commerce as one century warped into another. The dailies presented Poe's more accessible poems and shorter stories repeatedly, free of the baggage of the Rev. Mr. Griswold's underhanded anti-homages.

Gradually, Poe could only become the deathless beating heart while Griswold became the undone assassin—although Griswold seems not to have suffered the pangs of conscience that would force a confession from his nearest literary counterpart in the Poe canon, the obsessive-compulsive killer of "The Tell-Tale Heart." (The resemblance is no doubt unintentional, but even so "The Tell-Tale Heart" first saw publication in 1843, the same year that saw Griswold's earliest escalations of the anti-Poe campaign.) Griswold left his own confession through plain damned-fool carelessness, like a murderer who neglects to obliterate the evidence, by neglecting to destroy the original Poe letters whose contents he had altered for publication in order to cast himself in a saintlier light.

"That Poe survived at all was largely due to continued newspaper re-publication of 'The Raven' and 'The Bells,'" as Poe's pre-eminent anthologist of the 20th Century, Hervey Allen, wrote in 1944. Such celebrated short stories as "The Gold Bug" and "The Tell-Tale Heart" became, likewise, beloved mainstays of the newspapers and the publishers of classroom textbooks. Poe's reputation outlasted even the Civil War, whose upheavals rendered obscure most other American authors of the antebellum era, and the French literary establishment embraced him during the second half of the 19th Century as not only an entertaining storyteller but also an inspiration.

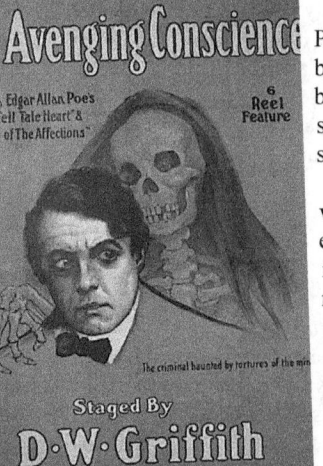

To say nothing of what the movies have made of Poe. "The Raven" may be the best known of the author's bids to examine the darker side of the Human Condition, but it is "The Tell-Tale Heart" that has figured most strikingly in the author's afterlife as a muse and ticket-selling mainstay of the motion-picture industry.

For in the tidal rhythms of the heartbeat lies the very soul of the cinema's distinctive imitation of life. If ever a story was ideally suited to the moving pictures, it is "The Tell-Tale Heart," whose kinetic, inexorable momentum and claustrophobic intimacy have proved irresistible time and again to generations of filmmakers. Loyalty to the source can only vary, of course, from picture to picture, but the spirit of Poe prevails in even the most liberal adaptation.

Most enthusiasts nowadays speak of Poe in the same breath with Vincent Price, the Grand Manner actor, and Roger Corman, the exploitation-film maestro of American International Pictures. Corman validated his entire career, fore and aft, with a succession of lavishly mounted Poe adaptations—most starring Price, none explicitly involving "The Tell-Tale Heart"—during the 1960s. Price's one-man touring shows, from the late '60s until only several years before his death in 1993, often included a beat-for-beat, word-for-word re-enactment of "The Tell-Tale Heart," and in 1972 he preserved this performance in a stagebound featurette, *An Evening of Edgar Allan Poe*, from American International's television branch,.

But Poe's words had begun informing and enlightening the motion-picture screen many years beforehand. "The Tell-Tale Heart," coupled with elements from the poem "Annabel Lee," provided the basis of D.W. Griffith's *The Avenging Conscience: Thou Shalt Not Kill* (1914), in which a youthful Poe aficionado (played by Henry B. Walthall) is driven to near-suicide after murdering his overprotective guardian uncle (Spottiswoode Aitken). Griffith, as writer-director, undermines the harsh resolution of the source—betrayal-of-self by an overwhelming guilt—and even pronounces the crime imaginary by giving the film a just-a-dream climax and a fairytale-happy ending.

In that same year of 1914, a rival studio adapted "The Murders in the Rue Morgue," adding the conceit of having a Poe-like character serve as the protagonist. A seafaring adventure called *Annabel Lee*, inspired by the poem, surfaced in 1921, compromising the mournful romanticism of Poe with a safe-and-sound upbeat finale.

Poe has graced most of his picture-show adaptations (and we use the word advisedly) more as a bankable name than as any literary standard. Robert Florey's *Murders in the Rue Morgue* (1932) draws perhaps more strikingly, and without attribution, upon H.P. Lovecraft's 20th Century pulp-magazine yarn, "Arthur Jermyn, or The White Ape," in its tale of trans-species tampering between human and simian. Among other such takeoffs, Roy Del Ruth's *Phantom of the Rue Morgue* (1954) trades more upon hypnotism and Pavlovian suggestibility in its account of a crazed zoologist (Karl Malden) who conditions an ape to kill upon command.

Various pictures traveling under the name of *The Black Cat* (from 1934, 1941 and 1966, as examples) have started out far from Poe and veered farther yet. (Our accompanying chapter on the '34 *Black Cat* covers the most significant of those bases, and Dwain Esper's notorious corruption of "The Black Cat" as an element of the 1934 *Maniac* figures in the first volume of our escalating *Forgotten Horrors* series.) Harold Hoffman's Texas redneck drive-in theatre version of 1966 takes pains, all the same, to re-create Poe's walling-up of a murder victim along with the noisy creature of the title—which is, really, a caterwauling (hence the term) literalization of the imagined rhythmic thumping of "The Tell-Tale Heart." "The Black Cat" first came into print a few months after "The Tell-Tale Heart," also in 1843. As Burgess Meredith would express it in Richard Attenborough's *Magic* (1978): "A pro never forgets his good lines."

We can skip over a great deal of the rest. The point, in any event, is not so much to inventory Poe as a sweeping cinematic influence as it is to bring to light one superb adaptation of "The Tell-Tale Heart" that has gone too long forgotten, along with kindred examples. The preamble is the appetizer—and herewith, the main course:

Metro-Goldwyn-Mayer cherished the short-subject idiom, though perhaps less because of any aesthetic potential than because the shorts allowed this wealthiest of the old-line major studios to fill out its programs with MGM-brand titles against the onslaught of the second-feature phenomenon that would become prevalent during the 1940s among theatre chains. The double-bill system, which offered the customer two feature-length attractions with a single admission, tended to showcase pictures of a lesser caliber. MGM handled the most polished shorts to be found: Hal Roach's knockabout comedies of the 1920s and '30s, including the *Laurel & Hardy* two- and three-reelers; MGM's own *Pete Smith Specialties* series of mocking documentary-like pieces and occasional dead-earnest items; Robert Benchley's droll dramatized monologues; the wonderful *Fitzpatrick TravelTalks*; musical vignettes as tuneful and eye-catching as any feature-length song-and-dance extravaganza; and the Harmon & Ising (or "Harmon-Ising") cartoons, which boasted colorful animation and fanciful fables to rival those of the Disney factory. MGM also handled the wonderful *Our Gang* comedies, but made the mis-step in 1938 of buying that trademark outright from Roach's independent production company and then transforming *Our Gang* from a natural-kid delight into a series of preachy, treacly moral lessons.

The short subject was crucial to any theatre's program, especially during World War II. Features had not yet been extended to the overlong running times that would become Standard Practice by the 1960s. The exhibitors were anxious to build crowd-pleasing programs consisting of a feature, a one-reel (seven to 10 minutes) cartoon, a one-reel news program and a two- or three-reel comedy, documentary, sporting event or travelogue.

Most distinctive among all the industry's outpouring of short subjects was a line of serious dramatic exercises developed at MGM under the supervision of Carey Wilson. These included such series-within-the-series as *Historical Miniatures*, *Carey Wilson's Miniatures*, *The Passing Parade* and *Crime Does Not Pay*. The Wilson pieces dealt with rustic Americana, patriotic boosterism and sociological issues and short fictional entertainments.

The lavish production values of the MGM shorts-as-a-class—yes, and even the later, lesser *Our Gang* abominations *look* great—stemmed from the use of elaborate standing sets that had been built and dressed for features, as well as the utilization of costumes from bigger pictures. The shorts offered a proving ground for up-and-coming directors. And the films could be cast with the same recognizable contract players who appeared in the supporting ensembles of MGM's top-of-the-line features.

Under the *MGM Specials* banner, there fell several adaptations of respected literary works. The finest is undoubtedly "The Tell-Tale Heart," to which the services of two brilliant actors, Joseph Schildkraut and Roman Bohnen (1898-1949), added considerable prestige. Neither had been associated with short subjects. Vienna-born Schildkraut (1895-1964) had landed an Academy Award for his portrayal of Capt. Alfred Dreyfus in *The Life of Emile Zola* (1937). Bohnen's busy character-actor résumé—often playing roles far beyond his actual age—included a show-stopping portrayal of a heartbroken old-timer in 1939's *Of Mice and Men*. Both men were so interested in the proposed filming of the Poe story that they volunteered to grace it despite the short-subject unit's lower pay scale. To his last days, Schildkraut cited "The Tell-Tale Heart" among his favorite assignments.

Director Jules Dassin impressed the studio so strikingly with "The Tell-Tale Heart" that he was promptly graduated to feature-film assignments, the first of which was 1942's *Nazi Agent*. Ahead lay a competent-to-extraordinary career, highlighted by the likes of *Brute Force* (1947), *Never on Sunday* (Greece; 1960) and *Topkapi* (1964). There was a detour to Broadway—and another to filmmaking in England, where he delivered a brilliantly rancorous film noir called *Night and the City*—during the 1950s after Dassin had found himself branded a Communist by the House Committee on Un-American Activities. His accuser was a fellow screen director, Edward Dmytryk, about whom more later (under *The Devil Commands* and *Obsession*).

Now, Dmytryk had himself been blacklisted arbitrarily (owing to his Ukrainian ancestry and perceived Russian-ness) and even jailed as a member of the defiant Hollywood Ten during that postwar witch-hunt. And Dmytryk wound up implicating Dassin, in a spiteful and random outburst, while flailing about in a futile and ill-reasoned bid to square himself with HUAC. Dassin denied the accusation to no avail and called Dmytryk's action a betrayal. But Dassin also refused to lower himself to Dmytryk's level by calling anybody else a Bolshevik. Thus the congressional agency accepted Dmytryk's hearsay over Dassin's denials. Both directors suffered from the effects of the purge, which obviously derived much of its momentum from an attitude of anti-Semitism, and both delivered some of their finer postwar work as self-exiles at large in the U.K.

But we digress. In 1968, during an interview occasioned by the opening of *Uptight*, his black-ensemble remake of John Ford's *The Informer* (1935), Dassin commented adversely on "The Tell-Tale Heart": "It was the springboard, the basis, of my career, but I consider it an overly arty little picture."

Poe's murderous narrator introduces his crime in these words: "Object there was none. Passion there was none. I loved the old man. He had never wronged me. He had never given me insult. For his gold I had no desire. I think it was his eye!… One of his eyes resembled that of a vulture—a pale blue eye, with a film over it…"

Doane Hoag's adapted screenplay overrides Poe from the outset, establishing a hateful relationship between the characters designated as the Young Man (Schildkraut) and the Old Man (Bohnen). Schildkraut plays an indentured servant in a small loom-weaving shop owned by Bohnen. Their opening encounter is overtly hostile, and although Bohnen sports a ghastly eyeball, it seems to have less bearing than his cruelties upon Schildkraut's festering hatred.

Schildkraut contemplates striking out on his own, but his master reminds him once too often of who is in charge here.

The murder in the dead of night is a foregone conclusion, but the lantern that Poe had employed to guide the killer to the offending eye serves here chiefly to justify an eerie lighting-and-composition effect by cinematographer Paul Vogel. The objective becomes that of showing Schildkraut stalking forth with the beam extended, which envelops the actor in a shimmering aura. The sequence suggests nothing so much as one of Virgil Finlay's famous scratchboard-and-ink illustrations of the simultaneous pulp-magazine era, brought to life.

The slaying is accomplished with efficiency and discretion, and the hiding of the corpse is only suggested by Schildkraut's gathering obsession with a certain patch of flooring. The perceived beating of the heart issues from a clock, from a faucet, from a rain-gathering pan—all of which are soon enough silenced. When the police (played by Oscar O'Shea and Will Wright) come calling, following up on a neighbor's complaint about a scream in the night, Schildkraut seems rational enough until the thumping resumes. His mental state deteriorates alarmingly. The discovery of the body comes in short order, although that is suggested rather than shown, and the lawmen take Schildkraut into custody.

Dassin's retroactive dismissal aside, the MGM version of "The Tell-Tale Heart" remains a powerfully affecting featurette, as satisfying for its efficiency as for its inventive variations upon Poe. *The Film Daily* likened it to "a swell and luscious bonbon coming suddenly out of a candy slot machine." Another movie-biz publication, *Showmen's Trade Review*, raved that the film "[elevates] the quality of the short subject beyond that of most features… a new standard in short-subject production, directing and acting. Indeed, a miniature masterpiece."

Dassin's "The Tell-Tale Heart" has been rescued from obscurity by the Turner Entertainment interests as part of a campaign to preserve the entire surviving output of MGM. The film shows at random intervals over the Turner Classic Movies cable network.

There are many other examples of how "The Tell-Tale Heart" has brought itself to bear upon the movies; hence this selective laundry-list:

- *The Tell-Tale Heart* (1934)—Brian Desmond Hurst's Anglo-American production stars Norman Dryden and John Kelt as the respective slayer and victim, along with an expanded cast including Yolande Terrell; Thomas Shenton, James Fleck, Colonel Cameron and Hevry Vasher. Hollywood's Fox Film Corp. helped to underwrite the English-based project of Clifton-Hurst Studios. The film was released in the United States as *Bucket of Blood*
- "The Tell-Tale Heart" (1939)—This British-made short-form adaptation for the still-experimental medium of television features Basil Cunard, Stuart Latham, Ernest Milton, Olaf Olsen and A. Harding Steerman.
- "Heartbeat" (1949)—This early-day television entry (for the General Television Enterprises syndicate) is the work of Frank Wisbar, the great German-émigré director whose larger career has been obscured by such conspicuously impressive low-budget American films as *Strangler of the Swamp* and *Devil Bat's Daughter* (both from 1946). The two-reel "Heartbeat," shot in 16-millimeter format, boasts a savvy job of film-cutting by Holbrook N. Todd, a busy editor with Old Hollywood's low-budget independent studios. Alan Wells plays the killer, Jack Davis the victim, and Don Pecano and Jack George serve as the Policemen.
- "The Tell-Tale Heart" (1950)—A busily nightmarish two-reel short for television, from Hal Roach's pioneering studio, this version boasts the striking pictorial design and emotionally charged directing style of William Cameron Menzies—who also was coming back into his own as a director (see our chapter on 1931's *The Spider*) from a long span of greater acclaim

as an art director. Menzies' last outpouring of directing assignments, including the misadventure of working with Howard Hughes on *The Whip Hand* and the more successful *Drums in the Deep South* and *The Maze* and *Invaders from Mars*, would follow during 1951-53.

- "The Tell-Tale Heart" (1953)—This inventive version from the cartoon-animation studio of John Hubley packs a memorable charge of terror, helped along by an evocative musical score by Boris Kremenliev. Stanley Baker provides the voice of Poe, and James Mason narrates.
- *The Tell-Tale Heart* (1960)—English director Ernest Morris' retelling, from a screenplay by Brian Clemens & Eldon Howard, opens up the story to encompass a plot motivated by jealousy. Laurence Payne offers a memorably tormented leading portrayal. An overwrought musical score is a debit. And speaking of overwrought, the film also has been issued under the proxy titles *The Hidden Room of 1,000 Horrors* and *The Horror Man*.
- "Edgar Allan Poe's 'The Tell-Tale Heart'" (1971)—Director Steve Carver's 26-minute adaptation boasts affecting performances from Sam Jaffe as the victim and Alex Cord as the murderer. The musical score is the work of Elmer Bernstein.
- *An Evening of Edgar Allan Poe* (1972)—Director Kenneth Johnson delivered this direct-to-television staging of a Vincent Price solo performance as a coda to the Corman/Price/Poe cycle of the prior decade. Price delivers classically impassioned readings of "The Tell-Tale Heart," "The Cask of Amontillado," "The Sphinx" and "The Pit and the Pendulum"—aided by rudimentary camera-and-lighting effects that belong more to stagecraft than to cinema.
- "The Tell-Tale Heart" (1973)—A Texas-made entry in the super-8 format, produced as part of a high-school term-thesis project by Mark Evan Walker and James Maynard. The telling benefits from the use of 400-ASA black-and-white film stock, which accommodates the moody lighting essential to a representation of Poe, with a visual basis in the German Expressionist classics *Nosferatu* and *The Cabinet of Dr. Caligari*. A brief color sequence "was primarily for shock-value," Walker has written, adding: "and it still works today." Walker and Maynard returned to Poe later in 1973 with a similarly styled version of "The Raven."
- *The Tell-Tale Heart* (1989)—A self-consciously artsy retelling, with psychological subtexts well beyond the provinces of simple obsession that Poe had staked out. Steve Barry directs from a screenplay by Rohanna Mehta and Carl Ruscica, and Matt Holland and Dennis St. John head the ensemble cast.
- *El Corazon Delator* (2002)—This 10-minute broadcast-Beta video production (in black-and-white) features Paul Naschy and Eladio Sanchez in a liberal adaptation involving a mental-institution fugitive nursing a vengeful grudge.

CREDITS FOR MGM'S 1941 "THE TELL-TALE HEART": Director: Jules Dassin; Screenplay: Doane Hoag; Based upon: "The Tell-Tale Heart," by Edgar Allan Poe; Musical Score: Sol Kaplan; Film Editor: Adrienne Fazan; Running Time: 20 Minutes; Released: During 1941 as an Added Attraction/Selected Short Subjects

CAST: Joseph Schildkraut (Young Man); Roman Bohnen (Old Man); Oscar O'Shea and Will Wright (Policemen)

Karloff peers into a deeper-than-usual abyss in *The Devil Command*s.

THE DEVIL COMMANDS
(Columbia Pictures Corp.; 1941)

Speaking of cornerstones of film noir—as we were, in the section on *Stranger on the Third Floor*—here is a striking candidate for belated preeminence within that very school of cinema. And yes, noir is where you find it, even in a horrific tale of science-fantasy.

Now, some devotees would define noir as a *genre* and confine it to a fixed period of WWII and-after time, thus narrowing its sweep severely. Others reckon noir a *style*, pluralizing its range of genres but requiring a certain fixed narrative-and-visual grammar. We are more inclined to let that overworked term, film noir, stand merely for an *attitude*, which accommodates all manner of styles and genres on condition that the story and its telling bespeak Doom-with-a-Capital-D—and preferably a Doom with an emotional, if not a spiritual, toll. It need not even be an Epic Doom: The intimate, Existentialistic cataclysms of a *Stranger on the Third Floor*, a *Devil Commands* or a *Double Indemnity* belong more to the noir tradition than a glitzy doom-to-the-world slam-banger like, say, 1998's *Armageddon*, which despite its prevailing ordained fatalism and intimate struggles is more of the neither-noir variety.

And yes, we digress. So what else is new?

Director Edward Dmytryk himself characterized *The Devil Commands* as crucial to the origins of film noir. In a series of interviews we conducted during 1977-78, while Dmytryk was holding a Distinguished Professorship at the University of Texas, the artist also spoke persuasively of an origin for the term *B-movie*—as to which, he should know.

Activating the vortex

"I loved working with Billy Pratt—Karloff, y'know—on *The Devil Commands*," said Dmytryk. "He was a lovely man. He's the only actor I ever knew who knew how to look *big*. He was really not a burly man, y'know, and though tall he was hunched over and kind of bandy-legged, at that, but he could *look* big. He had me read a play that had been offered him, and he asked me, 'Should I do it?' I said, 'Yes, by all means.' The play was *Arsenic and Old Lace*, a wonderful play." (Karloff proved such a knockout in the Broadway production of *Arsenic and Old Lace*, which afforded him a caricatured, self-joshing central role, that Columbia was able to exploit that success in its publicity campaign for *The Devil Commands*.)

"I had a very pleasant time on that picture," Dmytryk continued. "It was my first Columbia film. There was no front-office interference, none whatsoever. Irving Briskin's B-picture unit—and it was the *B* in *Briskin* that prompted the use of the term *B-unit*, and then, *B-picture*, at Columbia, although the *B* also came to stand for *budget*—was purely dedicated to invention and imagination, having little to lose and plenty to prove. So I experimented a lot, used different lenses and low-key lighting. Some of the film students say that my *Murder, My Sweet* [1944] is a seminal work in what they call film noir. I'm not sure, exactly, what they mean, because I don't think it's possible to come up with a blanket definition for film noir—but *The Devil Commands* was the beginning of *my* film noir stuff."

The mournful attitude, that sinking feeling of life-out-of-balance, is certainly here, from the very opening: No sooner has Dr. Julian Blair (Karloff) taken a reading of the brainwaves of his wife, Helen (Shirley Warde), than she is killed by a speeding auto while on an errand. Blair notices later that his laboratory devices are registering a graph identical to the patterns he had sampled from his wife. Obsessed with a campaign to communicate with the dead, Blair resigns his university chair and retreats to an isolated house on a seaside clifftop. His daughter,

Anne (Amanda Duff), and her fiancé, Dr. Richard Sayles (Richard Fiske), decline to involve themselves.

Blair recruits one Mrs. Walters (Anne Revere), who practices as a fortune-telling charlatan but has genuinely mediumistic abilities. She assists him for self-serving reasons. Blair's servant, Karl (Ralph Penney), submits to a test, which leaves him impaired in body and mind. Rumors circulate in the neighboring village that Blair has been robbing graves.

Blair's housekeeper (Dorothy Adams) snoops about and finds an imposing array of machinery, surrounded by half-a-dozen helmeted suits containing cadavers. Activating the power, she is crushed in some cosmic vortex. Blair and Mrs. Walters make it appear the maid has fallen from a cliff. The housekeeper's husband (Walter Baldwin) provokes unrest among the townspeople.

As the experiments escalate, Mrs. Walters dies in the vortex. A mob rushes the house. It dawns upon Blair that the most powerful readings have come when Anne was close by. Coercing Anne to take Mrs. Walters' place in the machine, he at last hears the ghostly voice of his wife, calling to him. Blair is pulled into the vortex to his death, but Anne survives to conclude that her father was no crackpot, after all.

The story bears no kinship to a 1933 Columbia picture, *As the Devil Commands*, but is rather an adaptation of a popular novel, William Sloane's *The Edge of Running Water*. Like the book, the picture moves deliberately to a bang-up finale, mingling renegade science, *Frankenstein*-like corpse-snatching and supernatural terrors to compelling effect. The laboratory sounds as dangerous as it looks.

Karloff dominates the proceedings as a man whose quest renders him ever bolder even as it ages him to a haggard condition. He receives able support from Anne Revere, as the sinister soothsayer. Amanda Duff, who narrates the film as an extended flashback, is very good in one of her few movie appearances. One of the best scenes has Miss Duff's longing face, in extreme close-up, fade into a view of the desolate house—a strategically genuine location, which Dmytryk said was reputed to harbor ghosts—overlooking a turbulent sea. Published reviews of *The Devil Commands* proved almost uniformly hostile, as if struck from a cookie-cutter template.

CREDITS: Executive Producer: Irving Briskin; Producer: Wallace MacDonald; Director: Edward Dmytryk; Screenplay: Robert D. Andrews and Milton Gunzburg; Based upon: William Sloane's 1939 Novel, *The Edge of Running Water*; Photographed by: Allen G. Siegler; Art Director: Lionel Banks; Assistant Director: George Rhein; Film Editor: Al Clark; Music: M.W. Stoloff; Running Time: 66 Minutes; Released: February 3, 1941

CAST: Boris Karloff (Dr. Julian Blair); Richard Fiske (Dr. Richard Sayles); Amanda Duff (Anne Blair); Anne Revere (Mrs. Walters); Ralph Penney (Karl); Dorothy Adams (Mrs. Marcy); Walter Baldwin (Seth Marcy); Kenneth MacDonald (Sheriff Willis); Shirley Warde (Helen Blair); Eddie Kane (Prof. Walt); Erwin Kalser (Prof. Kent); Wheaton Chambers (Dr. Sanders); Harrison Greene (Mr. Booth); John Tyrrell (Postmaster); Frank S. Hagney (Villager); Lester Alden (Dr. Van Den); Jacques Vannaire (Dr. Hartley); Earl Crawford (Johnson); Ernie Adams (Elam); George McKay (Station Agent); Al Rhein (Truck Driver); William Marion (Man); Minta Durfee [Mrs. Roscoe "Fatty" Arbuckle] (Woman).

THE MAD DOCTOR
(Paramount Pictures, Inc.; 1941)

'Twas ever thus that a hefty body of published film criticism should tell the reader more about the critics' communal (in)ability than about the topic. Of course, the larger reason-for-being of the society of critics is to engage one another in a game of one-upsmanship with snarky put-downs, and secondarily to overpraise selected films in hopes of getting blurbed in the advertising campaigns. It is a herd mentality, whichever direction the stampede takes. There are found an abiding tendency to judge a picture by its title; a refusal to divorce lurid subject matter from expectations of shoddy or sensationalized execution; and a contemptuous overuse/misuse of the industry term, *B-movie*, as though the letter represented some schoolmarmish scale of grading for quality. Such failings helped to scuttle prospects of popular acceptance for *The Mad Doctor* in its day—and have figured in the inaccuracy of its reputation these many years later. "Not a horror film," Leonard Maltin's hyper-bourgeois *TV Movies & Video Guide* ventures to explain, "but a polished B."

Call even that tolerant reference a B-as-in-*baloney*. No more a B-for-budget picture than its contributing talents are second-stringers, *The Mad Doctor* is a lavishly mounted, elegantly played psychological chiller, of prestigious origin and elaborate development. The film supplied director Tim Whelan with a fittingly classy return to Hollywood after a long span of activity in England, lastly as co-director on 1939's *The Thief of Baghdad*.

The Mad Doctor allowed Basil Rathbone a showy, cerebral role that should weight any argument for his supremacy among the movies' villains. It inspired a memorably brooding orchestral score from the great composer Victor Young. It showcased superb cinematography by future director Ted Tetzlaff. And it put paid—however belatedly and secretively—to a bizarre and brilliant working relationship that had existed between Paramount Pictures and the independent company of Ben Hecht and Charles MacArthur. And yet the New York *Times*' self-important Bosley Crowther, dissecting *The Mad Doctor* as a fresh release, declared it best not to wonder what misfortunes had placed such artistry at the service of such a motion picture.

In fairness, *The Mad Doctor* proves to have suffered as much from its own poor timing of production and distribution as from the generally unkind notices. The film reached the screen only after a long period of false starts, neglect, hurried and indecisive final preparation and postponed distribution. Its Valentine's Day release must have impressed many patrons as one sick joke.

Those madcap neo-Renaissance men, Hecht and MacArthur, had conceived the screenplay during the early 1930s as a star vehicle for John Barrymore, naming it *The Monster* in a sly reference to the wanton actor's nickname among his comrades. Later, Hecht and MacArthur rewrote the piece as *Destiny* for Noel Coward, who had just starred in *The Scoundrel* (1935) for their outfit at Astoria, Long Island. The Hecht-MacArthur films had proved unprofitable for Paramount, which provided financing and distribution, and the partners' company was dissolved. From the collapse, Paramount inherited *Destiny*—for which the big studio had already paid $50,000. Basil Rathbone at first nixed the picture, but with a title change and a new opening scene ordered by producer George Arthur, Rathbone took the job.

Retitled *A Date with Destiny*, the property was put into production on January 22, 1940. It was given preview showings more than a year later as *Destiny*, then finally was rechristened *The Mad Doctor*. The names of Hecht and MacArthur were dropped from the credits; in the realm of art-for-hire, corporate Hollywood often develops amnesia as to authorship.

Time lost between completion and playdates cost *The Mad Doctor* dearly in acceptance among fashion-conscious audiences of the day, who found the reappearance of 1940 hemlines, heels and hairstyles jarring in a new-for-1941 picture. The horror audience, drawn by the title and lulled into readiness by an ominous first reel, rankled at the subsequent leisurely pacing and sparse deployment of shock value and could not have been much help in the word-of-mouth department. The critical brethren—who had praised the commercially unsuccessful Hecht-MacArthur Paramounts—had no knowledge of source-authorship this time as a Pavlovian signal to start salivating with the superlatives.

But if *The Mad Doctor* appeared superficially behind the times in fashion sense or ill-matched to its exciting title, it was more cripplingly *ahead* of its time in subject matter and narrative style. Such painstakingly characterized psychological horrors would become quite the rage all during and following World War II, but *The Mad Doctor* emerged in first run as an anomaly.

Dr. Charles Downer (Ralph Morgan), the only practicing physician in the New England town of Midbury, learns that Dr. George Sebastien's (Rathbone) wife, Downer's patient, has died. Dr. Downer—fine name for a pill-pusher!—suspects Sebastien, a psychiatrist from Vienna, of murder.

The suspicion is well founded. Sebastien is in fact Dr. Frederick Langamann, a fugitive from an Austrian death sentence. Unhinged by his first wife's infidelity, he had slain her and her lover, then decided he must marry one monied woman after another and do away with them. The obsession has brought him to the United States and his latest victim. Sebastien's charm, good looks and knowledge of the mind serve him well in his campaign of Freudian Bluebeardism.

Moving to New York, Sebastien and his accomplice, Maurice Gretz (Martin Kosleck), find a ready clientele of neurotic rich women. The lovely Linda Boothe (Ellen Drew), an orphaned heiress beset with a suicidal urge, would seem an ideal victim.

Linda's former fiancé, Gil Sawyer (John Howard), is a conniving journalist who sets out bitterly to expose Sebastien as a charlatan. But Sebastien falls in love with Linda and chooses to pursue a normal life. Finding his plan endangered by Sawyer's nosing about, Sebastien makes haste to marry Linda.

Sawyer seeks out Dr. Downer and compares observations. An autopsy is ordered in the death of Sebastien's Midbury wife. Gretz hurries to empty the grave and kills a watchman while he's about it.

Sawyer arranges to bring Dr. Downer to New York. Downer telephones Linda and tells her of the matter of the prior Mrs. Sebastien. Linda hurries to meet Downer at a subway station. Sebastien, learning of the rendezvous, dispatches Gretz. Linda arrives just as Downer is pushed to his death under a train.

Returning home, Linda accuses her husband. Sebastien, resigned, calmly admits the truth and tells her that he must kill her. Sawyer arrives with the police in time to save Linda. Sebastien

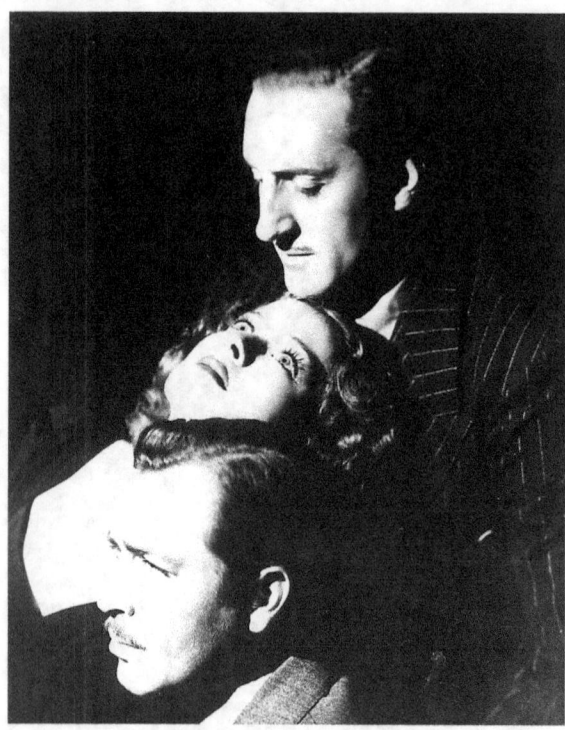

An uneasy encounter in *The Mad Doctor*

flees onto a ledge. As the law closes in, Sebastien takes a flying leap. "You should have seen his face," Linda tells Sawyer. "His eyes—so cruel, and yet so sad."

Taken without prejudice or false expectations, the film succeeds on practically all counts. What *The Hollywood Reporter* singled out as a "wildly hypnotic" main-title sequence (a rainstorm enhances the lettering's illusion of three dimensions, with water dripping from the words) gives way to creepy Martin Kosleck's dead-of-night summoning of a physician. Basil Rathbone is a study in forced dignity and restrained rage from his entrance until, after a show of mock-tenderness at a graveside ceremony, he begins letting the controls slip almost imperceptibly.

Railing about his late wife, Rathbone provokes this from Kosleck: "She's *dead*. Isn't that enough?" Rathbone snaps back: "*No*! I can never forgive her the eight months spent in this *cave* of romance!" (The "cave" is a mansion.) There surfaces the occasional suggestion of a tensely homosexual bond, culminating in some pointedly bitchy harshness as Rathbone dares to acknowledge his tender feelings toward Ellen Drew. "Has it ever crept into that aboriginal skull of yours," he rants to Kosleck, "a slight wonder as to why anyone so brilliant, so superior, as *I* should have gone through life like some—some medieval *mon*ster?" This element is patently a ghost of the script's having been tailored at one point to the more-or-less openly gay Noel Coward. Kosleck, for that matter, was of Old Hollywood's gay community.

Kosleck, as the subordinate Human Monster, accounts for the welcome occasional jolt of terrifying violence. Recalling by turns the polished menace of Peter Lorre and the feral presence of Dwight Frye, Kosleck tallies a moderate body count until an unsavory past literally catches up with him—in a rather clumsily contrived chance encounter—and he meets his doom in the stairwell of a subway depot.

Whelan, who would work again with Rathbone on 1941's *International Lady*, brings forth in the actor the combination of cruelty and pitiability that Ellen Drew finally puts into words. Even the bustling Manhattan social whirl, once Rathbone has arrived, turns cold and dark. A faint leavening of comic relief is desultory and forced, especially when a scatterbrained young matron pronounces Dr. Sebastien to be one of history's great minds. "What about Socrates?" asks John Howard. The reply: "Well, if Dr. Sebastien doesn't work out, we'll try *him*." This is a trademark bubblehead portrayal by the radio comic Barbara Allen, better known as Vera Vague.

Such attempts at humor at least demonstrate what easy marks Rathbone has selected. More convincing is the California-as-New York location work, especially a Coney Island montage comprising shots made at the now-extinct Ocean Park Amusement Pier. The body of water where Kosleck disposes of a snatched body is Lake Sherwood, site of the MGM *Tarzan* pictures and a portion of the 1931 *Frankenstein*. There are imposing large-scale process background shots by Farciot Edouart and several nifty matte shots by Gordon Jennings, blending a rooftop nightclub into the cityscape.

CREDITS: Producer: George Arthur; Director: Tim Whelan; Screenplay: Howard J. Green; Based upon a Screenplay by: Ben Hecht and Charles MacArthur; Photographed by: Ted Tetzlaff; Music: Victor Young; Art Directors: Hans Dreier and Robert Usher; Editor: Archie Marshek; Costumes: Edith Head; Sound: Harry Mills and John Cope; Special Photographic Effects: Gordon Jennings; Process Photography: Farciot Edouart; Interior Décor: A.E. Freudeman; Assistant Director: Joe Youngerman; Sound System: Western Electric; Running Time: 90 Minutes; Released: February 14, 1941

CAST: Basil Rathbone (Dr. George Sebastien); Ellen Drew (Linda Boothe); John Howard (Gil Sawyer); Barbara Allen [a.k.a. Vera Vague] (Louise Watkins); Ralph Morgan (Dr. Charles Downer); Martin Kosleck (Maurice Gretz); Kitty Kelly (Winnie); Hugh O'Connell (Lawrence Watkins); Hugh Sothern (Hatch); Howard Mitchell (Stationmaster); Charles McAvoy (Conductor); Billy Benedict (Mickey); Henry Victor (Dr. Thurber); Douglas Kennedy (Hotel Clerk); Frances Raymond (Librarian); Harry Hayden (Ticket Seller); Harry Bailey (Man with Newspaper); James Seay and John Laird (Interns); Ben Taggart (Motorman); Ned Norton (Passenger); Max Wagner (Taxi Driver); Edward Earle (Attendant); Jean Phillips, Kay Stewart and Wanda McKay (Girls); Betty McLaughlin and Dorothy Dayton (Cigarette Girls); George Chandler (Elevator Man); Norma Varden (Susan); Jacques Vanaire (Waiter); Laura Treadwell (Woman); William J. Kline (Butler); Larry McGrath (Photographer); William Wayne (Taxi Driver); Johnnie Morris (Newsboy); George Walcott (Chauffeur); Charles Hamilton (Cop); Dick Rich (Riley)

AMONG THE LIVING
(Paramount Pictures, Inc.; 1941)

Maxim Raden, hated owner of the defunct Radentown Mills, is lowered into his grave while millworkers crowd outside the private cemetery, wondering what their future might hold. At the grave is Maxim's son, John (Albert Dekker), who has been away for 25 years; John's wife, Elaine (Frances Farmer); and Dr. Ben Saunders (Harry Carey), a trusted friend. Watching from a distance is Pompey (Ernest Whitman), an aged black man who has guarded the family's secret for a quarter of a century. Strapped in a straitjacket in a hidden room at Radenhouse, the forbidding mansion at the edge of town, is John's twin brother, Paul (Dekker, again), reputedly long dead.

Later, Saunders explains to John that Paul is alive, a lunatic. Long ago, Paul had sought to defend his mother from the brutal Maxim and was hurled headlong against a wall. Paul's only lasting memory is that of his mother's agonized scream. Maxim had refused to consign Paul to an institution, bribing Saunders to falsify a death certificate. Pompey has looked after Paul all these years.

During an electrical storm, Paul becomes agitated and demands to visit the grave. Next day, John and Saunders find Pompey strangled, his hands clamped over his ears as if to shut out some horrible sound. Paul has dug up his father's grave, unwilling to let the body lie next to that of his mother. Afraid to inform the law, they search frantically.

Paul exults in his freedom. He falls in love with the first girl he meets, an unemployed mill worker named Millie Pickens (Susan Hayward). He wanders into a honky-tonk. Pretty, blonde Peggy Nolan (Jean Phillips) flirts with Paul. A fight erupts among the carousing mill hands. Paul chases Peggy into an alley. Next morning, her body is found.

Terror grips the town. A frenzy of greed follows when Saunders tricks John into offering a $5,000 reward for the killer's capture. Millie obtains a revolver and recruits Paul—who remembers neither murder—to go with her to Radenhouse. Bill Oakley (Gordon Jones), Millie's jealous sweetheart, follows. A mob also heads toward Radenhouse. Catching Paul in the act of strangling Millie, Oakley shoots Paul, who escapes into the great hall and encounters John. The twins struggle, and Paul exits through a window, leaving John unconscious. The mob arrives, and Millie identifies John as her attacker. The mob cries for a lynching. Elaine, who has learned the truth, pleads with Saunders to save John's life. The crowd accuses Saunders of concocting the story of the insane brother. John escapes the vigilantes and runs to the cemetery, where he finds the body of Paul lying across their mother's grave. Dr. Saunders surrenders to the sheriff (Frank M. Thomas).

Stuart Heisler had been a film editor for 24 years when he made a tentative stab at directing with *Straight From the Shoulder* (1936) for Paramount and handled the second-unit work for John Ford's *The Hurricane* (1937). He returned to the Moviola for another three years before Paramount entrusted him with the helming of a low-budgeter about a boy and his dog, *The Biscuit Eater* (1940), which to the studio's surprise proved to be a real sleeper, widely praised for its deft touches of atmosphere. Heisler followed through in 1941 with two moody horror films, *The Monster and the Girl* and *Among the Living*. Critical praise for *Living* catapulted him into the upper echelon. Although Heisler's bigger pictures include such gems as *The Glass Key* (1942), *Along Came Jones* (1945), *Tulsa* (1949) and *The Star* (1953), it is in *Among the Living* that his mastery of the medium is best exemplified. The picture ranks high among the outstanding psychological thrillers in terms of suspense, dramatic construction and sustained terror.

Albert Dekker's acting as Paul is sharply understated, avoiding the leering overstatement so often utilized in portraying madness. He builds sympathy for the beast, whose adventures bear more than a passing resemblance to those of the Monster in Universal's *Frankenstein* (1931), another dangerous innocent who kills his keeper, escapes from his chambers, kills one girl and terrorizes another and is pursued by a howling mob. That the script was written in part by Garrett Fort, co-scenarist of *Frankenstein*, may account for the similarity. There are many nice details to Dekker's characterization, such as a scene where Paul listens to the angry villagers raving that the unknown killer must be caught; tries to concentrate on the problem; becomes concerned; and finally nods in innocent agreement. The massively built Dekker also does well by the normal brother, an unusual characterization for an actor who had so recently become famous as the monstrous title character of *Dr. Cyclops* (1939).

Susan Hayward, poised on the threshold of stardom, is splendid as a small-town tart, a prototype for many such roles to come. Miss Hayward's Millie Pickens is cheap, flashy and vulgar, avaricious and gutsy enough to try to capture a maniac. "For $5,000, I'm not afraid of *any*thing, not even *death*," she tells the unsuspecting killer. "What're *you* scared of? He only *chokes* people. *We*'ve got a *gun*!" Needless to say, Millie turns against Paul just as readily.

Harry Carey, Ernest Whitman and Gordon Jones do good trouping in important roles, and Jean Phillips has a brief but telling sequence as a victim. The tragic Frances Farmer registers well as Dekker's confused but determined wife, although she said later that her mental state was such at the time that she hardly knew what she was doing. Maude Eburne, as Hayward's slovenly mother, contributes some scene-stealing lowbrow comedy: "Us Pickenses has always had a weakness for refinement," she says as she picks at her backside.

The photography by Theodor Sparkhul—a German cameraman who had found a niche in Hollywood after the rise of Hitler—heightens the menace without trickery. Sharply etched shadows, dramatic tonal patterns and hard-lighted close-in shots give the film a consistently forbidding visual style. The separate worlds of the mansion and the blue-collar town are delineated boldly throughout in purely visual terms, with a dividing fence in evidence from the first scene. Well-executed matte paintings of the mills and smokestacks are composited with live action to pleasing effect.

The most remarkable sequence finds Jean Phillips (who bears a strong resemblance to Ginger Rogers) dancing wildly to a jitterbug tune in a sweat-dripping, smoke-laden blue-collar juke joint. The angles and cutting become increasingly bizarre until an orgiastic frenzy is reached. The childlike murderer watches Miss Phillips' flashing legs, mesmerized. Inevitably, his arousal turns deadly. The camera witnesses the murder from a great distance, in a carefully framed composition that emphasizes deep perspective and black, angular shapes.

The kangaroo-court sequence is likewise bracing, on a par with its more celebrated counterparts in Fritz Lang's German masterwork, *M* (1930), and Cecil B. DeMille's *This Day and Age* (1933). The sequence is imaginatively edited, with nerve-jangling swish-pans from one agitated face to another. A somewhat impressionistic score by Gerard Carbonara adds to the burden of fear and unease.

CREDITS: Producer: Sol C. Siegel; Associate Producer: Colbert Clark; Director: Stuart Heisler; Screenplay: Lester Cole and Garrett Fort; Story: Brian Marlow and Lester Cole; Photographed by: Theodor Sparkhul; Art Directors: Hans Dreier and Haldane Douglas; Set Décor: A.E. Freudeman; Editor: Everett Douglas; Music: Gerard Carbonara; Western Electric Sound: Hugo Grenzbach; Assistant Director: Arthur Black; Running Time: 68 minutes; Released: December 19, 1941

CAST: Albert Dekker (Paul Raden and John Raden); Susan Hayward (Millie Pickens); Harry Carey (Dr. Ben Saunders); Frances Farmer (Elaine Raden); Gordon Jones (Bill Oakley); Jean Phillips (Peggy Nolan); Ernest Whitman (Pompey); Maude Eburne (Mrs. Pickens); Frank M. Thomas (Sheriff); Harlan Briggs (Judge); Clarence Muse (Waiter); Patti Lacey, Roy Lester, Ray Hirsch and Jane Allen (Jitterbug Dancers); and Dorothy Sebastian, Rod Cameron, Archie Twitchell, Ella Neal, William Stack, Lane Chandler, Catherine Craig, Eddy Chandler, Abe Dinovitch, Jack Curtis, Christian Frank, Bessie Wade, Delmar Watson, Richard Webb, Mimi Doyle, John Kellogg, Blanche Payson, George Turner, Harry Tenbrook, Ethan Laidlaw, Charles Hamilton, Frank S. Hagney, Lee Shumway, James Millican, Len Hendry

THE NIGHT HAS EYES
a.k.a.: TERROR HOUSE
(Pathé Films, Ltd./Associated British Productions/Producers Releasing Corp.; 1942)

But for a prevailing dramatic weakness in the supporting ranks, *The Night Has Eyes* might be mistaken for vintage Hitchcock. An old-fashioned Gothic in the vein of *Jane Eyre* and *Rebecca*, the film spotlights the best Byronic hero of the period, James Mason, as a dashing sort who might or might not be a mad killer. Mason's polished performance admirably achieves the proper balance of the sinister and the romantic. Matching his work are Wilfrid Lawson and Mary Clare, as an appealingly bucolic pair who—but let the story unspool itself:

Marian Ives (Joyce Howard), and a fellow schoolteacher named Doris (Ann Tucker McGuire) set out onto the Yorkshire moors to see if they can solve the disappearance of a friend of Evelyn's, all of two years ago. Losing their bearings in a storm, they find shelter in a gloomy mansion occupied by Stephen Deremid (Mason), a morose young composer. Stephen's servants, Sturrock (Lawson) and Mrs. Ranger (Miss Clare), arrive to take the girls back to the village.

Marian returns and, as she becomes intimate with Stephen, learns that he believes himself subject to violent lapses. Mrs. Ranger has been Stephen's nurse since the Spanish Civil War. Stephen reveals that he and the missing Evelyn had carried on an affair—and he wonders whether he had killed her during a blackout. Finally, it develops that the kindly servants have duped Stephen into believing himself dangerous, and that they had killed Evelyn and now plan to do away with Marian. It all has to do with a coveted inheritance. Suddenly, Stephen arrives in time to pull off a rescue. Forcing the servants into the swamp at gunpoint, he sees them safely onto a path to freedom. They stop to bicker, however, and fall into a quicksand bog, sinking before Stephen can so much as ponder a rescue.

The Night Has Eyes is an early directing job from Leslie Arliss, a scriptwriter since the early 1930s and a specialist in comedy. Following *The Night Has Eyes*, Arliss directed Mason in two much more popular romantic mysteries, *The Man in Grey* (1943) and *The Wicked Lady* (1945);

Stranded in a house of murder.

he remained in England after Mason resettled in Hollywood. Arliss kept directing for the big screen on into the early 1950s, then leapt to television.

The Night Has Eyes boasts grand scenic values on the stark moorlands (actually, built on a sound stage, for better fog control), and within a spectacular stone manor house. The four leads are splendid, but the backup cast is almost uniformly afflicted with self-consciousness and stilted delivery. The German-bred master cameraman, Gunther Kramph, cleverly hired midgets as stand-ins for the long shots, giving the moors a greater illusion of depth. Charles Williams' score, a pocket-concerto for piano and orchestra, possesses the same charm as Williams' "Dream of Olwyn" leitmotif from *While I Live* (1947). The shocking revelation of the servants' truer colors is heightened by stark lighting and a well-timed zinger from the orchestra.

The Night Has Eyes was saddled with an H Certificate (for horrific content) by the British Board of Film Censors. In its U.S. playdates as *Terror House*, the picture ran into complaints because of its frank portrayal of hanky-panky between a social outcast and an upstanding schoolteacher—to say nothing of the dialogue's liberal peppering with *hell*s and *damn*s.

CREDITS: Producer: John Argyle; Director: Leslie Arliss; Screenplay: Alan Kennington, from His Novel; Photographed by: Gunther Kramph; Art Director: Duncan Sutherland; Music: Charles Williams; Sound: Harris Benson and Albert Ross; Production Manager: Mannon G. Inglis; Editor: Flora Newton; Camera: Ronald Anscombe; Makeup: Bob Clark; Running Time: 74 Minutes; U.K. Release: During March of 1942; U.S. Release by Producers Releasing Corp. as *Terror House*

CAST: James Mason (Stephen Deremid); Wilfrid Lawson (Sturrock); Mary Clare (Mrs. Ranger); Joyce Howard (Marian Ives); Ann Tucker McGuire (Doris); John Fernald (Barry Randall); Dorothy Black (Mrs. Fenwick); Amy Dalby (Miss Miggs)

WHO IS HOPE SCHUYLER?
(20th Century-Fox Film Corp.; 1942)

Quick, slick and thick with suspense, *Who Is Hope Schuyler?* is a delightful example of the high-quality product from the 20th Century-Fox B-picture unit of the early 1940s. Photography, sets and sound are equal—if not superior—to comparable work in the general run of top-of-the-line pictures. The effective musical scoring is the work of David Raksin (of those celebrated scores for 1944's *Laura* and 1947's *Forever Amber*) and Emil Newman, later head of Samuel Goldwyn's music department. Direction, by the little-known Thomas Loring, has snap and style, building upon the mystery encoded in the title.

Special Prosecutor Tom Mason (Joseph Allen, Jr.) finds his case collapsing against District Attorney Anthony Pearce (Ricardo Cortez). Mason cannot find or even identify Hope Schuyler, Pearce's mistress and the go-between connecting Pearce with a fortunetelling-and-extortion racket. The court grants Mason 48 hours to produce the vital witness lest the case be dismissed. Mason rejects advice to drop the case from Rossiter (Charles Trowbridge), the politically prominent father of Mason's attractive assistant, Dianne (Mary Howard).

Courthouse reporter Lee Dale (Sheila Ryan) learns that Pearce has been subsidizing a small airport operated by one Bill Guerney (Eddie Acuff). Guerney receives a visit: The elusive Hope pitches a lighted cigarette into a gasoline spill. Investigator Carl Spence (Paul Guilfoyle) trails Pearce's secretary, Vesta Hadden (Janis Carter). He is murdered by Hope Schuyler.

Mason now believes that Hope Schuyler must be Vesta, Lee, Guerney's widow, Phyllis (Joan Valerie), or Pearce's wife, Alma (Rose Hobart). Three more prospective witnesses are done away with. Mason, Dianne and Lee find Vesta Hadden and Phyllis Guerney at Pearce's countryside house. By identifying a melted cigarette lighter found at the airport, Mason reveals that Hope Schuyler is Dianne Rossiter. Dianne draws a pistol. Alma Pearce arrives and opens fire on Dianne. Mason now is assured of Pearce's conviction.

Mayhem amid the search for Hope Schuyler.

Virgil Miller was a versatile cinematographer best known as a master of ominous lighting. He was Lon Chaney's favorite at Universal during the silent-screen years. Fox used Miller for some of the better *Charlie Chan* and *Mr. Moto* series entries, and Universal kept him busy on the *Sherlock Holmes* franchise. His work on *Who Is Hope Schuyler?* emphasizes forbidding tonal patterns and dense shadows to frazzling effect.

The cast, though hardly an assemblage of box-office names, is an unusually dependable ensemble: Ricardo Cortez stands out as a smooth villain (almost a repeat of his role in *The Walking Dead*), and Mary Howard earns praise as a menace hidden by her very prominence. Rose Hobart shines briefly in the crucial role of Cortez' crazed wife. Joseph Allen, Jr., and Sheila Ryan make a believably spirited romantic team. Janis Carter and Joan Valerie add both beauty and intrigue. The supporting cast of character actors is as strong as can be found in any big-budget movie.

CREDITS: Executive Producer: Sol M. Wurtzel; Director: Thomas Z. Loring; Screenplay: Arnaud D'Usseau; Based upon: Stephen Ransome's Novel; Photographed by: Virgil Miller; Art Directors: Richard Day and Chester Gore; Set Décor: Thomas Little; Editor: Louis Loeffler; Costumes: Herschel; Western Electric Sound: Oscar Lagerstrom and Harry M. Leonard; Technical Advisor: Detective Lt. Frank L. James; Musical Director: Emil Newman; Music: David Raksin; Running Time: 57 minutes; Released: April 17, 1942

CAST: Joseph Allen Jr. (Tom Mason); Mary Howard (Dianne Rossiter); Sheila Ryan (Lee Dale); Ricardo Cortez (Anthony Pearce); Janis Carter (Vesta Hadden); Joan Valerie (Phyllis Guerney); Robert Lowery (Robert Scott); Rose Hobart (Alma Pearce); Paul Guilfoyle (Carl Spence); William Newell (Perley Seymour); Pat Flaherty (Nash); Charles Trowbridge (Rossiter); Frank Puglia (Baggott); Edwin Stanley (Stafford); Edward Keane (Judge); Cliff Clark (Lt. Palmer); Jeff Corey (Coroner); Eddie Acuff (Guerney); Bud Geary (Policeman)

THE MAN WHO WOULDN'T DIE
(20th Century-Fox Film Corp.; 1942)

Michael Shayne, novelist Brett Halliday's genial private-eye character, made his film début in the person of Lloyd Nolan in January of 1941. *Michael Shayne, Private Detective* proved profitable for Fox, which had come to rely upon Sol Wurtzel's handsomely produced, moderately priced melodramas to compensate for losses incurred by big-budget flopperoos.

Over a three-year period, Wurtzel produced six more Nolan-as-Shane mysteries. The series-opener was based on a Halliday story, but the others would draw from novels by Raymond Chandler, Frederick Nebel, Richard Burke, Borden Chase, Jo Eisinger and Clayton Rawson. The fifth—and arguably, the best—of this generally excellent series is *The Man Who Wouldn't Die*, based upon a yarn by Rawson. Rawson's detective-hero was a magician called Merlini. In this adaptation, the detective work is accomplished by Shane, with Merlini making a token appearance.

The yarn packs suspense, rapid-fire action and hair-trigger wisecracking comedy: Lovely Catherine Wolff (Marjorie Weaver) finds her family's countryside estate haunted by an intruder with glowing eyes. Her father (Paul Harvey) finds her description of the prowler unnervingly similar to a body he has just had buried in secret. Catherine calls in fast-talking Michael Shayne (Nolan). The intruder crops up again, killing a participant in the burial. Apparently slain while fleeing, the menace is identified as Zorah Bey (Leroy Mason), an East Indian magician—and a longtime enemy of Mr. Wolff's. The murderer returns, and this time Shayne stops him for good. Turns out that Zorah Bey had learned to feign death through self-hypnosis, which affords but scant protection from a slug through the ticker.

Herbert I. Leeds' smooth direction should have earned him a kick upstairs to the high-budget shows, but no such luck. Nolan plays the wiseacre detective in an easygoing, realistic manner. Marjorie Weaver, a gifted light comedienne, brings a welcome sprightliness to the ingénue role. Helene Reynolds is convincing as a rich-bitch trophy wife. The excellent Henry Wilcoxson fares less well with an undemanding and expendable role. Neat comic touches beyond Shayne's banter include Billy Bevan as a Cockney servant, Jeff Corey as a coroner with a dark sense of humor and Francis Ford as a crotchety caretaker. Paul Harvey is appropriately nervous as a threatened millionaire. Leroy Mason dispenses a memorable chill as the title character.

The beautifully composed photography also includes such winning special effects as a teeth-rattling car crash and Mason's glowing eyeballs. David Raksin's musical score works surprisingly well for

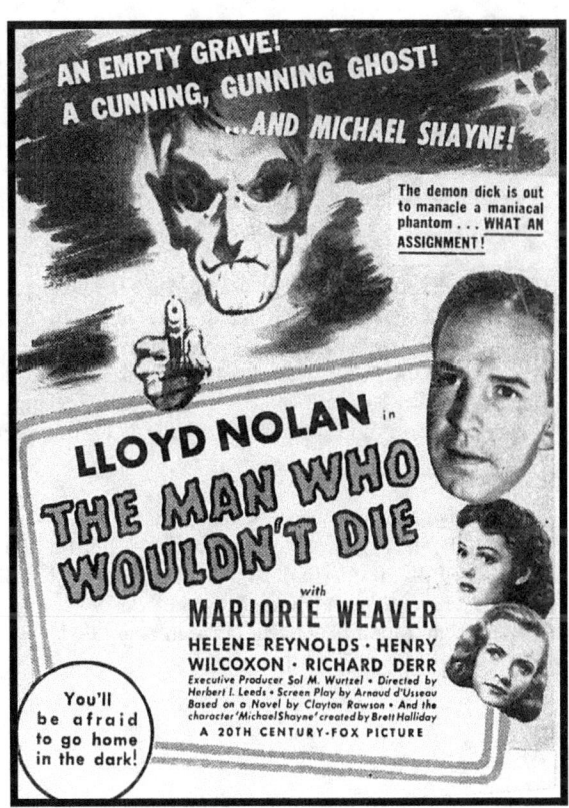

Lloyd Nolan and Marjorie Weaver.

its recycling into a picture of such overt witticisms; most of these cues had been composed to fit the somber renegade-science chiller *Dr. Renault's Secret* (1942).

And for the record, Fox's other *Michael Shayne*s: From 1941, *Dressed To Kill* and *Sleepers West*, in addition to *Michael Shayne, Private Detective*; from 1942, *Blue, White and Perfect* and *Just off Broadway*, in addition to *The Man Who Wouldn't Die*; and from 1943, *Time To Kill*. A PRC Pictures series of *Shayne*s, dating from 1946-47 and starring Hugh Beaumont, include *Blonde for a Day*, *Larceny in Her Heart*, *Murder Is My Business*, *Three on a Ticket* and *Too Many Witnesses*.

CREDITS: Executive Producer: Sol M. Wurtzel; Director: Herbert I. Leeds; Screenplay: Arnaud D'Usseau; Based upon: Brett Halliday's Character, Michael Shayne, and Clayton Rawson's 1942 Novel, *No Coffin for the Corpse*; Photographed by: Joseph P. MacDonald; Art Directors: Richard Day and Lewis Creber; Set Décor: Thomas Little; Editor: Fred Allen; Costumer: Herschel; Sound: Harry M. Leonard and Joseph E. Aiken; Technical Advisor: Det. Lt. Frank L. James; Musical Director: Emil Newman; Music: David Raksin; Running Time: 73 Minutes; Released: May 1, 1942

CAST: Lloyd Nolan (Michael Shayne); Marjorie Weaver (Katherine Wolff); Helene Reynolds (Ann Wolff); Henry Wilcoxson (Dr. Haggard); Richard Derr (Rodger Blake); Paul Harvey (Dudley Wolff); Billy Bevan (Phillips); Olin Howland (Chief Meek); Robert Emmett Keane (Alfred Dunning); Leroy Mason (Zorah Bey); Jeff Corey (Coroner Larson); Francis Ford (Caretaker); Charles Irwin (Merlini); and Ruth Warren, Mary Field, Harry Carter

MOONTIDE
(20th Century-Fox Film Corp.; 1942)

Frank Borzage's *Seventh Heaven* (1927) caused a sensation with its vivid combination of Germanic pictorialism and sentimentality, its daring placement of a delicate love story amid squalor. Emulations and outright imitations followed in short order and over the long term: These include *Street Angel* (1928), *Heaven on Earth* (1931), *Man's Castle* and *Zoo in Budapest* (both from 1933) and another *Seventh Heaven* (1937). Fox revived the theme emphatically in *Moontide*, from a sordid but beautifully written novel by the actor Willard Robertson. A working novelist, John O'Hara, wrote the screenplay, lightening the downbeat tone of the book by making the lovers less tawdry and the ending less tragic, but retaining the somber atmosphere. Veteran screenwriter Nunnally Johnson polished the script without credit.

Such a project would have been a natural for the great German director, Fritz Lang, who originally was assigned to *Moontide*. Lang, who had been suffering from a gall-bladder infection, withdrew after the fourth day of shooting. The same thing had happened with his previous assignment at the same studio, 1941's *Confirm or Deny*. In both instances, Lang was replaced by the versatile Archie Mayo. Like Lang, Mayo was a slave-driving genius who achieved terrific results but often at the cost of his alienation from the cast and crew.

Moontide provided an American début for Jean Gabin, who had come to the States the year previous. An established star in France, Gabin was a leader of the naturalistic school—anything but handsome in the matinee-idol sense, but very much the rugged and plain-spoken he-man. The American stars most like Gabin were Richard Dix and, especially, Spencer Tracy, a pioneer of un-prettified acting. Gabin was completely unlike previous Continental stars who had been transplanted to America; they tended to be boudoir-lover types such as Charles Boyer and Raoul Roulien and, of course, the pre-*Dracula* Bela Lugosi.

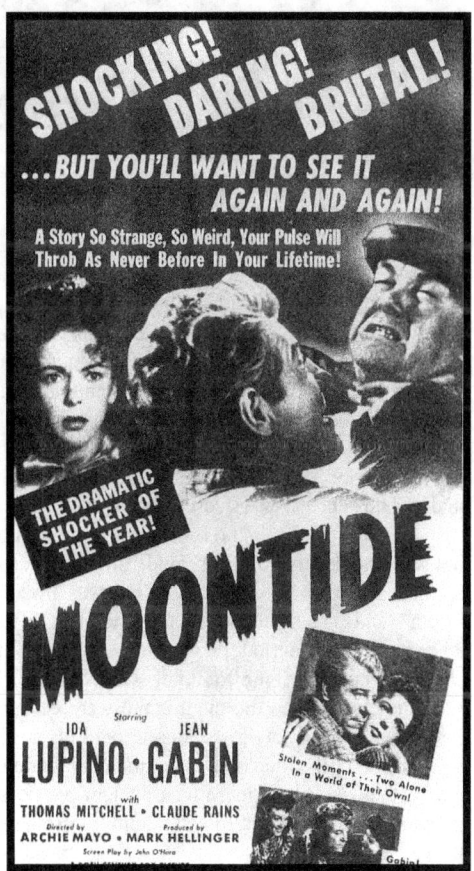

Fox honcho Darryl Zanuck placed Gabin in fine company: Ida Lupino posed the greatest challenge to Bette Davis' station as the screen's leading dramatic actress. Claude Rains and Thomas Mitchell were at once stars and versatile character players—a difficult combination to achieve.

The story finds Bobo (Gabin), a fun-loving dockworker at San Pedro, passing out from a drunken bender and waking with no immediate memory. Events pile up to leave Bobo wondering whether he has committed murder during a blackout. His surly pal, Tiny (Mitchell), believes they should leave town. Another friend, the philosophical Nutsy (Rains), destroys incriminating evidence.

Bobo rescues a destitute girl named Anna (Miss Lupino) from a suicide attempt. The two fall in love, infuriating the possessive Tiny. Finally Tiny betrays

Jean Gabin and Ida Lupino in *Moontide*.

himself as the killer when he attempts to rape Anna and beats her savagely. Bobo stalks the assailant, cornering him into a fatal fall.

Moontide abounds with top-notch portrayals. Gabin, in a role reminiscent of his work in 1938's *La Béte Humaine*, cannily underplays in contrast to Miss Lupino's volatile histrionics, while Rains quietly upstages both. Thomas Mitchell brings off the cleverest coup of all, moderating his role until the climax, when he reveals himself as a murderer and pervert. The colorful backup players score as waterfront grotesques.

Strong production values are evident in the elaborate studio settings designed by Fox's two most celebrated art directors, James Basevi and Richard Day. Charles Clarke's photography, featuring memorable night-lighting and fog effects, is marvelously evocative of the shifting moods. Clarke told us that the entire film—including the oceanside scenes—was shot in the studio. The score is an effective job of recycling, making fresh use of the ominous title music from *Swamp Water* (1941), by David Buttolph. Popular songs are utilized as romantic themes, and some honky-tonk tunes provide the right backdrop for Gabin's descent into drunkenness.

The Chinese actor Chester Gan was hired to play a sympathetic barge owner named Hirota—and is so listed in the cast roster. But by the time the picture was completed, World War II had erupted, rendering the good-guy Japanese character socially unacceptable in these United States. By an adroit bit of dubbing, Gan was rechristened Henry the Chinaman.

The critics liked the picture and were ecstatic about Gabin. The public, however, was as hostile as usual to foreign stars and paid his U.S. début little notice. (Most of what has been published over the long haul about the "tremendous" "popularity" of Garbo, Valentino, Dietrich *et al.* is the wishful exaggeration of celebrity-obsessed re-visionists.) Where the first advertising campaign had attempted to sell Gabin on grounds of sex appeal ("S-a-a-a-y, Girls! Come and meet Jean Gabin!"), a second promotional package tried a horror angle: "So Strange, So Weird,

Your Pulse Will Throb as Never Before... !" Nice try, but no particularly rewarding results.

Universal's *Imposter*, from 1943, met with no more success than *Moontide* had at selling Gabin to the English-speaking audience. Gabin soon returned to France and resumed his reign. He was still an important star, no thanks to America, when he died in 1976.

CREDITS: Executive Producer: Darryl F. Zanuck; Producer: Mark Hellinger; Director: Archie Mayo; Screenplay: John O'Hara; Script Revisions: Nunnally Johnson; Based upon: Willard Robertson's Novel; Photographed by: Charles G. Clarke; Art Directors: Richard Day and James Basevi; Set Décor: Thomas Little; Editor: William Reynolds; Costumer: Gwen Wakeling; Makeup: Guy Pearce; Western Electric Sound: Eugene Grossman and Roger Heman; Music: Cyril J. Mockridge and David Buttolph; Songs: "Moontide," by Alfred Newman & Charles Henderson, and "Remember the Night," by Irving Berlin; Special Effects: Fred Sersen; Running Time: 94 Minutes; Released: May 29, 1942

Anna and Bobo take on Henry (Chester Gan) in *Moontide*.

CAST: Jean Gabin (Bobo); Ida Lupino (Anna); Thomas Mitchell (Tiny); Claude Rains (Nutsy); Jerome Cowan (Dr. Brothers); Helene Reynolds (Woman on Boat); Ralph Byrd (Rev. Mr. Price); William Halligan (Bartender); Sen Yung (Takeo); Chester Gan (Hirota [Henry the Chinaman]); Robin Raymond (Mildred); Arthur Aylesworth (Pop Kelly); Arthur Hohl (Hotel Clerk); John Kelly (Mac); Ralph Dunn (Cop); Tully Marshall (Simpson); Tom Dugan (Waiter); and William Forrest, Blackie Whiteford, Pat McKee, Constantine Romanoff, Vera Lewis, Julian Rivero, Paul J. Burns, Thomas Mack, Forrest Dillon, Bruce Edwards, Max Wagner, William Forrest, Gertrude Astor, Marian Rosamond, Roseanne Murphy

THE BOOGIE MAN WILL GET YOU
(Columbia Pictures Corp.; 1942)

Boris Karloff had wrapped up his Monogram Pictures contract of 1938-40 by breaking from the *Mr. Wong* series' sleuth role to play a mad doctor in *The Ape*. He wrapped up his Columbia Pictures series by breaking from the (over)familiar mad-doctor persona to play—well, another mad doctor, albeit of a befuddled comical bent, in *The Boogie Man Will Get You*.

"I hadn't really considered myself to be exploring any particularly specialized type of role," Karloff told us in 1968. "And for that matter, Columbia wasn't even regarding my so-called mad-doctor pictures as any kind of formally delineated series, beyond a sequence of jobs for me to fulfill. We did what we knew would sell tickets, that's all. It was the fans, in those days—and, later, you chaps who sift through the bygones in search of patterns—who decided I must have been doing something on a grander scale than just a succession of assignments. One's career—really, now—is never as strategically well ordered as all that. One *works*, that's all."

For *Boogie Man*, Columbia raised the ticket-seller stakes conspicuously by putting Peter Lorre to work alongside Karloff. The teaming is purely pleasurable, although the picture itself belongs as much to the screwball, slapstick and war-propaganda schools as to any horrific traditions. Excepting the shared presence of Karloff and Lorre, *Boogie Man* is unrelated to 1940's *You'll Find Out*.

There is, however, a strikingly oblique kinship here with the Lindsay & Crouse Broadway production of Joseph Kesselring's *Arsenic and Old Lace*, in which Karloff had defined the menacing deadpan-comic role of Jonathan Brewster in early 1941. Frank Capra wanted Karloff for his Warner Bros. picturization of *Arsenic and Old Lace*—filmed during October-December of 1941, but not formally released until 1944—but the actor consented to stick with the play, as a courtesy to the producers, for what turned out to be a three-and-a-half-year run. He had the flexibility to tackle other pictures, of course, but the Broadway *Arsenic* had already lost Josephine Hull, Jean Adair and John Alexander (for the duration of shooting) to its movie version, and Karloff's presence clearly meant a great deal to the play's box office. Raymond Massey subbed admirably for Karloff in the film, which also wound up with Peter Lorre in the role of a cockeyed plastic surgeon.

Karloff's concession was hardly the only agreement struck to keep the film from diluting the play's popular appeal. Warner Bros. agreed not to release its *Arsenic* until the end of the Broadway run—which no one could have guessed would stretch to nearly 1,450 performances, and more than that, if one were to count the benefit matinees. Warners' thwarted release date was September 30, 1942, which compares interestingly with Columbia's October-of-'42 opening of *Boogie Man*. Anticipation was running high for *Arsenic and Old Lace* as a transcontinental big-screen attraction, and Columbia served up *The Boogie Man Will Get You* as more or less an imitation. Certainly, the yarns have a great deal in common—quaint setting, tense romantic situation, bodies galore and enough loonies at large to overload a loony-bin.

Karloff serves *Boogie Man* in distracted grandfatherly form as Prof. Nathaniel Billings, who during World War II is seeking to sell a ramshackle New England tavern that has been in his family since 1764. Billings is carrying on some peculiar experiments—"Relax, and just pretend you're in a steam room," he calls to a subject of his tests—even while holding open house. When Winnie Layden (Jeff Donnell) announces she will buy the place, Billings is overjoyed: Now he can rid himself of his pesky mortgage-holder, Dr. Lorentz. Winnie indulges Billings' request to stay on in the cellar so that he can finish "toying with a few physio-dynamics."

Billings' research proves as weird as anything on view in the more straightforward Karloff Columbias: His patient falls out of a cabinet. "Cold as a mackerel," says Billings. "Dear, dear, dear—I wonder what could have gone wrong *this* time?" He finds a monkey wrench in the victim's pocket. "No wonder! The rays were deflected!"

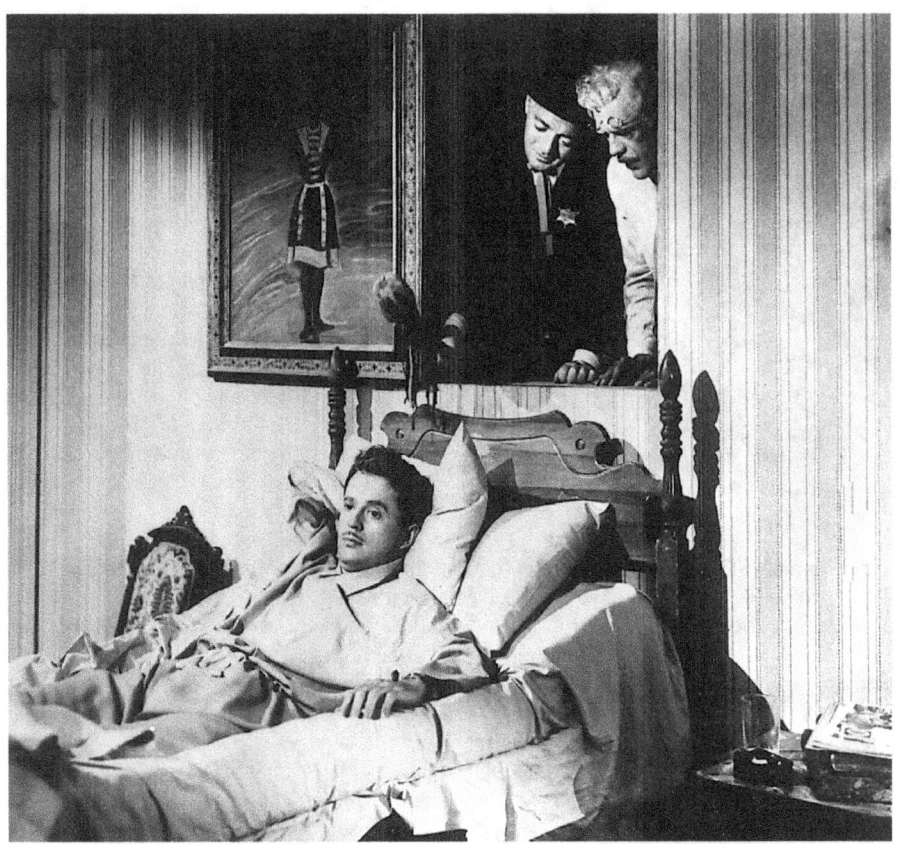

Lorre and Karloff go skulking, however absurdly, through *Boogie Man*.

Then comes Lorentz (Lorre)—a frock-cloaked undertaker and one-man political machine who serves as both mayor and sheriff. Bill Layden (Larry Parks), Winnie's former husband, intrudes and eventually finds the inert body of Billings' experimental patient. Billings insists that the victim is a martyr to a grand experiment to produce an army of supermen for the war effort. Billings also maintains that the inn is haunted by the ghost of Uncas, last of the Mohicans. Lorentz seems a menacing sort in his own right.

More guests arrive, and more mayhem ensues, including a couple of garden-variety knifings. A lunkheaded salesman named Maxie (championship boxer "Slapsie" Maxie Rosenbloom) tries to play along with Billings' experiments—but he can't be fitted with an electronic helmet because his scalp is ticklish, and he cannot respond to ether because his sinuses are blocked. The anesthetic does knock out Billings and Lorentz and Bill and Winnie, and Maxie decides he must be "a wholesale murderer."

A more overt menace barges in—Bacigalupi (Frank Puglia), a one-man Axis suicide squad, who has strapped dynamite about himself. Lorentz suggests that Maxie be given the superman treatment to dispose of Bacigalupi. Everything fizzles, including the bomb. The more mundane attacks are chalked up to two eccentric hired-hands (Maude Eburne and George McKay). Billings' five "martyrs" return to life, demonstrating his unintended success at inducing suspended animation. "But I did *so* want to make a superman," Billings complains. The police finally decide that everybody in the house must be removed to the state asylum. Which is okay with Lorentz, who is also the chairman of the board of that institution.

Further weird absurdities afoot in *Boogie Man*.

And of course, *The Boogie Man Will Get You* is no *Arsenic and Old Lace*. The picture transcends its imitative intentions, however, to deliver a wealth of lowbrow cornball yocks. The slight story would have worked as well if squeezed into one of Columbia's *Three Stooges* short-subject slapstickers. Supporting player Maxie Rosenbloom was, for that matter, a pal of the Howard-Howard-Fine Stooges and would later team with Billy Gilbert and Stooges co-founder Samuel "Shemp" Howard for a trilogy of ersatz-Stooges features at Monogram Pictures.

Karloff and Lorre are as amusing here as they are intimidating in most of their other pictures represented in these pages. (Miss) Jeff Donnell and Larry Parks make a lifelike estranged pair who haven't lost the spark of either romance or antagonism. Don Beddoe slices the ham generously as a purported ballet master. The truer murderous villainy falls to George McKay and grumpy Maude Eburne, as servants with strange ambitions and stranger habits.

Though a trifle in the greater scheme of Hollywood's horrors, *Boogie Man* grows ever more valuable with the passage of time—serving notice, alongside such sarcastic gems as the Lugosi-starrer *The Devil Bat* (1940) and John Carradine's self-parodying contributions to *Myra Breckenridge* (1970) and *Everything You Always Wanted To Know about Sex (But Were Afraid To Ask)* (1972), that the movies' favorite bogeymen never lost touch with their sense of humor.

CREDITS: Executive Producer: Irving Briskin; Producer: Colbert Clark; Director: Lew Landers; Assistant Director: Seymour Friedman; Screenplay: Edwin Blum; Adaptation: Paul Gangelin; Story: Hal Fimberg and Robert B. Hunt; Photographed by: Henry Freulich; Art Director: Lionel Banks; Associate: Robert Peterson; Editor: Richard Fantl; Interior Décor: George Montgomery; Music: M.W. Stoloff; Sound: John Goodrich; Running Time: 66 Minutes; Released: October 22, 1942

CAST: Boris Karloff (Prof. Nathaniel Billings); Peter Lorre (Dr. Arthur Lorenz); Maxie Rosenbloom (Maxie); Larry Parks (Bill Layden); Jeff Donnell (Winnie Layden); Maude Eburne (Amelia Jones); Don Beddoe (J. Gilbert Brampton); George McKay (Ebenezer); Frank Puglia (Silvio Bacigalupi); Eddie Laughton (Johnson); Frank Sully (Officer Starrett); James Morton (Officer Quincy)

Margaret Landry cringes from a make-believe cat shadow in *The Leopard Man*.

THE LEOPARD MAN
(RKO-Radio Pictures, Inc.; 1943)

Cornell Woolrich's *Black Alibi* is an episodic, rather sadistic novel with marvelous characterizations and a brilliantly sustained aura of dread and melancholy. The Val Lewton–Ardel Wray adaptation, which the studio christened *The Leopard Man* as a touchstone to Lewton's 1942 hit *Cat People*, captures well the unique vision of the author. This is so despite a number of changes—the most conspicuous being a shift of setting from Latin America to New Mexico and a shift of blame from the chief of police to a mild-mannered—but don't let's spill everything at once.

To draw popular attention to nightclub singer Kiki Walker (Jean Brooks), publicist Jerry Manning (Dennis O'Keefe) hires a black leopard from an Indian trainer, Charlie How-Come (Abner Biberman). Making a spectacular entrance at the club with the beast on a leash, Kiki upstages a temperamental dancer, Clo-Clo (Margo). The dancer lunges at the leopard, rattling her castanets, and the startled beast breaks free, disappearing into the desert night.

On the outskirts of town, the cat stalks Teresa Delgado (Margaret Landry), a girl returning from an errand, and kills her just as she reaches her family's *hacienda*. Next to die is Consuela Contreras (Tula Parma), who has found herself stranded within the walls of a cemetery. Jerry wonders about blaming the cat in this latest case because the predator "doesn't eat what it kills." Clo-Clo soon becomes the third victim. Jerry, Kiki and Raoul Belmonte (Richard Martin), Consuela's sweetheart, pursue the possibility of a human killer and finally unmask the soft-spoken Dr. Galbraith (James Bell), curator of the local museum, apprehending the madman within a religious procession of hooded monks.

Galbraith admits that something within him was unleashed when he saw the results of the leopard's attack on Teresa. Galbraith had tracked and killed the leopard and made a weapons of its claws. "I didn't want to…," he attempts to explain, "but I *had* to." Galbraith is shot to death by the crazed Raoul.

Dennis O'Keefe and Jean Brooks in *The Leopard Man*.

The Leopard Man is the third in a sharply defined series of 11 moderately budgeted films made at RKO during 1942-46. These are the work of a special unit headed by Val Lewton, a Russian-born novelist previously employed in various capacities at MGM and Selznick-International. Each entry was granted about $150,000—somewhat higher than the average B-picture but well below prestige product. An artistic, literary producer, Lewton was given considerable creative leeway. All but two of the entries turned out as horror pictures of one stripe or another, saddled by the head office with lurid, exploitable titles.

Lewton's first inflexible title was *Cat People*. In March of 1942, while searching for stories to fit, Lewton encountered *Black Alibi* and urged his boss, Lou Ostrow, to purchase it. "To my mind, this is still the best horror story I have been able to uncover," Lewton wrote in a memorandum. "It seems particularly good to me because it has the cat element [with] the most chilling sequences I have read in recent fiction." RKO bought the rights for $5,175, but Lewton decided to use an original story for *Cat People*. He saved *Black Alibi* for a third mandated title: *The Leopard Man*.

Lewton, whose distinctively detail-conscious touch is evident in each of his films, chose to utilize the power of suggestion and implied menace conveyed through a frightening atmosphere rather than horrific makeups or (with certain rare exceptions) gruesome scenes. His use of sound to intensify dread and to provide startling punctuation was most imaginative—and has been widely imitated.

The first two Lewtons, *Cat People* and 1943's *I Walked with a Zombie*, are prime examples of the poetic possibilities of supernatural and/or psychological horror, however slim the cost or horrendous the title. The director of these, Jacques Tourneur (son of the great French filmmaker, Maurice Tourneur), also helmed *The Leopard Man* as his last collaboration with Lewton before a promotion to big-budget pictures. *The Leopard Man* was filmed entirely at RKO-Radio and Pathé Studios in just under a month, during February and March of 1943. The New Mexico location was suggested by sets and props based upon photographs that Ardel Wray had shot during a visit to Santa Fe. Although he does not receive a writing credit, Lewton prepared the adaptation in story form and crafted the final shooting script, which retains the curious episodic structure of the book. One segment, the stalking of a girl on holiday, was dropped. So was Woolrich's terrific ending in which the killer is trapped in his lair, a torture chamber beneath an ancient church.

Unlike the first two Lewtons, *The Leopard Man* contains several explicitly gruesome scenes that the producer later repudiated as a betrayal of his generally subtle approach. Only once did he return to the ambivalence of *The Leopard Man*: in the extremely popular *The Body Snatcher* (1945), 10th of the RKO series.

Tourneur's directing is a wonder; it is easy to see why the studio wanted him in charge of more important (economically, at least) projects. But hindsight is particularly revealing here: None of the supposedly classier Tourneur pictures (and some are excellent, including this volume's *Nightfall*) has any sort of reputation by comparison with his work for Lewton. There are numerous scenes with what Lewton called "black patches—shadows, to be filled in with whatever menace the spectator's mind can conjure." Typical of the expert cinematographers who worked with the Lewton unit, Robert de Grasse achieves throughout the suggestion of unseen menace.

Augmenting the disturbing images of light and shadow are equally unnerving sounds: Castanets clatter in deserted streets and in darkened rooms; leaves rustle in a graveyard; a locomotive rumbles overhead; the big cat hisses at the least expected moment. The castanets, representative of the temperamental and tragic dancer played by Margo, form almost a leitmotif. They are heard during the title music, then continue through the opening scenes and recur in other key sequences. After the character's death, the castanets' relentless clacking is used to unnerve the murderer.

Most unforgettable is the first killing, by the actual leopard. The extended stalk and chase—the sudden appearance of a train roaring overhead in an arroyo—the girl's terrified pounding and screaming at the door—the mother's callous refusal to believe there is anything amiss—the sudden silence, followed by the rivulet of blood over the threshold—all add up to the most memorable scene in any Lewton film, one of the most memorable in the genre as a class. The episode in the cemetery packs almost as great a charge.

The characterizations are rich, though secondary to atmosphere. Dennis O'Keefe is ideal as a flashy promoter with a soft heart, and Jean Brooks is equally so as a nice girl trying to succeed in a dehumanizing racket. The Mexican-born Margo (who was between marriages at the time, respectively to Francis Lederer and Edward Albert) is by turns brittle and touching as a brassy entertainer struggling to overcome her peasant origins. Tula Parma, the refugee Finnish actress, etches a touching portrait of the victim in the cemetery, and lovely Margaret Landry does likewise as the villager who falls prey to the leopard. The fatalistic theme is emphasized by the observations of a sad-eyed fortuneteller, played with her usual skill by Isabel Jewell. Equally right is the philosophical gatekeeper at the graveyard, played by that venerable stage actor, Brandon Hurst. "Time is strange," he muses. "A moment can be as short as a breath or as long as eternity."

James Bell, a low-key actor somewhat reminiscent of Harry Carey, renders the murderer deliberately sympathetic—an outwardly gentle, pipe-smoking dreamer. He establishes the philosophy of the picture when he indicates a sphere tumbling in the jet of a fountain and observes, "We know as little of the forces that move us and move the world around us as that empty ball." Later, he registers an opinion of the murderer's nature: "He'd go about his business calmly except when the fit to kill was on him." When trapped, he declares: "...I was going to help..., and then I saw her white face... *Fear*, that was it!"

Roy Webb's music, though less arresting than his score for *Cat People*, adds materially to the artistry of this weirdly beautiful production.

A cat's-paw murder weapon had figured just the year previous in RKO's release of the independently produced *Scattergood Survives a Murder*, part of the folksy *Scattergood Baines* series. Columbia's *The Devil's Mask* (1946) also would utilize the theme of a leopard-man killer. Then in Mexico in 1948, *The Leopard Man* was virtually remade as *Han Matado a Tongoléle* (*They Have Killed Tongoléle*).

And apropos of almost nothing: Devotees of inadvertently humorous typographical errors will get a kick out of a reference to *The Leopard Man* that appeared during the 1960s in a Texas newspaper's television listings: *The Leotard Man*. On other occasions, that same publication gave 1956's *The Black Sleep* as *The Black Sheep* and 1964's *Where Love Has Gone* as *Where Has Louie Gone?*—and once listed the back-to-back showing of two popular teleseries as *Leave It to Lucy* and *I Love Beaver*. When shown these various gaffes, the paper's city editor would remark, "Yeah—the proofreader's seeing-eye dog must've been off-duty that day."

CREDITS: Producer: Val Lewton; Director: Jacques Tourneur; Screenplay: Ardel Wray; Based upon: Cornell Woolrich's 1942 Novel, *Black Alibi*; Additional Dialogue: Edward Dein; Photographed by: Robert de Grasse; Art Directors: Albert S. D'Agostino and Walter E. Keller; Set Décor: Darrell Silvera and Al Fields; Music: Roy Webb; Musical Director: Constantin Bakaleinikoff; Sound: John C. Grubb; Assistant Director: William Dorfman; Optical Effects: Linwood Dunn; Running Time: 66 Minutes; Released: May 8, 1943

CAST: Dennis O'Keefe (Jerry Manning); Margo (Clo-Clo); Jean Brooks (Kiki Walker); Isabel Jewell (Maria); James Bell (Dr. Galbraith); Margaret Landry (Teresa Delgado); Abner Biberman (Charlie How-Come); Richard Martin (Raoul Belmonte); Tula Parma (Consuela Contreras); Ben Bard (Chief Robles); Ariel Heath (Eloise); Feli Franquelli (Rosita); Robert Anderson (Dwight); Jacqueline DeWit (Helene); Bobby Spindola (Pedro); William Halligan (Brunton); Kate Drain Lawson (Sra. Delgado); Russell Wade (Man in Black Car); Ottola Nesmith (Sra. Contreras); Jacques Lory (Phillipe); Margaret Sylva (Marta); John Dilson (Coroner); Charles Lung (Manuel); Brandon Hurst (Gatekeeper); George Sherwood and Joe Dominguez (Policemen); Eliso Gamboa (Sr. Delgado); Mary McLaren (Nun); Betty Roadman (Clo-Clo's Mother); Rosarita Varella (Clo-Clo's Sister); Rene Pedrina (Injured Waiter); Tom Orosco (Window Cleaner); John Tettemer (Minister); John Piffle (Flower Vendor); Rose Higgins (Indian Woman); Dynamite (Leopard)

Jean Brooks and Feodor Chaliapin in *The Seventh Victim*.

THE SEVENTH VICTIM
(RKO-Radio Pictures, Inc.; 1943)

Not all of Val Lewton's celebrated psychological thrillers were hits in their day. His fourth, *The Seventh Victim*, inspired the hatred of critics and customers alike. Bad timing only worsened the situation, for war-era moviegoers demanded the robust escapism that dominated the schedules at all the studios. Horror pictures of a more traditional stripe were, for some, as exhilarating as a Betty Grable musical—but so deeply philosophical and morbid a work as *The Seventh Victim* hardly fit any pop-thriller traditions. Even the critics, despite an often-professed desire to see weightier fare, snubbed the picture, several going so far as to admit they were confused by the story and the less wide-awake crix griping that the title had nothing to do with the picture. It remains, all the same, that *The Seventh Victim* is a defining masterpiece of film noir—and the title could hardly be a more straightforward summation.

The story concerns the disappearance of a New York cosmetics manufacturer named Jacqueline Gibson (Jean Brooks). Her finishing-school sister, Mary (Kim Hunter), sets out to find Jacqueline but stumbles, instead, into a bohemian netherworld of Satanism. Jacqueline, secretly a member, is accused of betraying the cult, which answers disloyalty with murderous torments. Along the way, Mary manages to fall in love with Gregory Ward (Hugh Beaumont), a lawyer who is married, if only in the technical sense, to Jacqueline. The devil-cultists finally receive a good chewing-out. Jacqueline fares less favorably, finding herself at last driven to suicide.

"The picture's appeal, like that of its predecessors, is based upon three fundamental theories," Lewton told the press. "First is that the audience will people any patch of darkness with more horror, suspense and frightfulness than the most imaginative writer could ever dream up. Second, and most important, is that extraordinary things happen to very ordinary people. And third is to

Kim Hunter, with a nervous Lou Lubin.

use the beauty of the setting and camerawork to ward off an audience's laughter at situations which, when less beautifully photographed, might seem ludicrous."

Lewton also took a jab at the competition, Universal Pictures' lucrative *Frankenstein/Dracula/Wolf Man, etc.*, franchises: "Up to the advent of the new RKO horror school, the characters in the run-of-the-mill weirdies were usually people very remote from the audiences' experiences. European nobles of dark antecedents, mad scientists, man-created monsters and the like cavorted across the screen. With the thought that it would be much more entertaining if people with whom audiences could identify were to be shown in contact with the strange, the unusual and the occult, we made it a basic part of our work to show normal people—engaged in normal occupations—in our pictures."

The Seventh Victim has fewer normal people than most other Lewtons, inasmuch as it is set in Greenwich Village, where bourgeois normalcy is hardly, well, *normal*. The orphaned heroine—beautifully played by Kim Hunter, David O. Selznick's 20-year-old discovery, in her début—is almost a modern-day Jane Eyre. The cultists are superficially ordinary types, such as one might expect to meet in any larger city. There are bracing hints of lesbianism in the female-dominated cult (anything stronger than a hint would have been quashed by the Legion of Decency), and a couple of the men are less subtly deranged than the others. The overall impression is that of misfits who feel betrayed by life and turn to evil: Call it the Original Revenge of the Nerds, if not an outright foreshadowing of the *Dungeons & Dragons* and *Magic: The Gathering* plagues of mock-occult nerdism of times more recent.

DeWitt Bodeen wrote the first story treatment from Lewton's idea about murders around a Los Angeles oilfield. Lewton then sent Bodeen to New York to research a forthcoming project called *Curse of the Cat People*. While there, Bodeen received word that Lewton and Charles O'Neal were working on a different approach to *The Seventh Victim*. A subsequent letter instructed Bodeen to infiltrate, or at least observe, a Satanist meeting. Through the efforts of RKO's New York office, Bodeen was admitted as a silent watcher at a cult gathering. He told us, years after the fact, that he found the members to be unassertive "chinless-wimp" sorts who knitted and sipped tea while casting spells against Hitler. "One might find more hellfire dynamism in a Pentecostal tent-revival," Bodeen said.

Thus did Bodeen contribute important, realistic details. The film's cultists bear no resemblance to the robed, Latin-chanting cultists of *The Black Cat* (1934) and in fact anticipate the bourgeois Satanists who bedevil Mia Farrow in the William Castle–Roman Polanski production of *Rosemary's Baby* (1968). There are no ominous rituals, no sacrificial posturing and no thrilling raids on, or routings of, the cultists—only a matter-of-fact exposure of their treacheries and a severe dressing-down.

Prominent among the cultists, and establishing most effectively the idea of twisted intelligence, are a one-armed former dancer, played with venomous zest by Evelyn Brent; a study in melancholy despair by Isabel Jewell; and a mannish boss-lady, invested with a stewing malevolence by Mary Newton. Ben Bard's portrayal is precisely the grim sort of fanatic one finds in the vanguard of extremist political groups—a man who smiles often, but without humor.

The most curious element lies in Tom Conway's repetition of his *Cat People* role, the enigmatic but courageous Dr. Louis Judd. Never mind that Dr. Judd gets killed at the climax of that first Lewton entry; no doubt *The Seventh Victim* is what we'd call a prequel—irritating anti-word, that—nowadays. Anyhow, Judd surfaces in *Victim* as a more sympathetic presence, even though he is still a philanderer and there remains a suggestion of menace in his suave cynicism.

Hugh Beaumont, a Methodist preacher who financed his ministry with acting roles, deadpans the part of the lawyer. It is an unfortunate cultural hangover that few people can watch Beaumont in *anything* today without feeling compelled to remark on the player's larger identification with the TV sitcom *Leave It to Beaver*. Erford Gage lends but little credibility to the part of a failed poet who fancies himself a kindred soul of Cyrano (as did Lewton). Lou Lubin is wonderful as a sleazy, nervous private eye—anticipating the work of Walter Matthau in *Mirage* (1965)—and Marguerite Sylva, a celebrated operatic star of the turn of the century, is cast fittingly as a once-famous singer. Chef Milani, a famed culinary expert and radio personality, is right at home as the proprietor of a restaurant that bears the ominous name of Dante.

Most haunting is Jean Brooks' portrayal of the doomed Jacqueline. Her exchange with a dying neighbor (played by Elizabeth Russell) is at once poignant and harrowing. Miss Brooks' delineation of a fragile beauty, doomed by her own irreconcilable distractions, is so true to life as to strike a painful chord in the breast of anyone who has known such a person. It is Miss Brooks who embodies the John Donne quotation that opens and closes the film: "I run to Death, and Death meets me as fast/And all my Pleasures are as Yesterdays."

The Seventh Victim boasts the directing debut of Mark Robson, who had edited the prior Lewtons. Juggling artistry and efficiency with solid results, Robson brought the picture in within its budget in only 24 days. Robson directed four additional Lewtons before his promotion to bigger productions. Camera boss Nick Musuraca photographed five of the Lewtons; Musuraca's command of composition and chiaroscuro helps immeasurably with the mood of *The Seventh Victim*. There is one interesting, undetectable optical composite in the picture: Only the left side of the hallway of Jacqueline's apartment was constructed, and the right half was reproduced photographically for certain scenes.

The quality of sound matches the photography, with long silences shattered by sudden noises, and subtly integrated music of a superior kind.

CREDITS: Producer: Val Lewton; Director: Mark Robson; Screenplay: Charles O'Neal and De-Witt Bodeen; Photographed by: Nicholas Musuraca; Editor: John Lockert; Art Directors: Albert S. D'Agostino and Walter E. Keller; Optical Effects: Linwood Dunn; Effects Cameraman: Harry Underwood; Set Décor: Darrell Silvera and Harley Miller; Music: Roy Webb; Musical Director: Constantin Bakaleinikoff; Orchestrations: Maurice De Packh; Costumes: Renié; Sound: John C. Grubb; Assistant Director: William Dorfman; Dialogue Director: Jacqueline DeWitt; Running Time: 71 Minutes; Released: August 21, 1943

CAST: Jacqueline Gibson (Jean Brooks); Tom Conway (Dr. Louis Judd); Isabel Jewell (Frances Fallon); Kim Hunter (Mary Gibson); Evelyn Brent (Natalie Cortez); Erford Gage (Jason Hoag); Ben Bard (Bruns); Hugh Beaumont (Gregory Ward); Chef Milani (Romari); Marguerita Sylva (Mrs. Romari); Mary Newton (Mrs. Redi); Wally Brown (Durk); Feodor Chaliapin (Leo); Eve March (Miss Gilchrist); Ottola Newmith (Mrs. Lowood); Edythe Elliott (Mrs. Swift); Milton Kibbee (Joseph); Marianne Mosner (Miss Rowan); Elizabeth Russell (Mimi); Joan Barclay (Gladys); William Halligan (Radeau); Lou Lubin (August); Dewey Robinson (Conductor); Lloyd Ingraham (Watchman); Kernan Cripps (Policeman); Sara Selby (Miss Gottschalk); Betty Roadman (Mrs. Wheeler); Ann Summers (Miss Summers); and Tiny Jones, Eileen O'Malley, Lorna Dunn, Cyril Ring

THE MAD GHOUL
(Universal Pictures Co., Inc.; 1943)

Whoever said arrogance is an inverse function of competence must never have caught George Zucco's act. In his mastery of a narrow range, the Manchester-born character man could radiate a confidence to rival Errol Flynn, a calculating obsessiveness on a par with Lionel Atwill and a full-of-himself caliber of stubborn pride that dresses up even such lesser efforts as *The Black Raven* (1943) and *Fog Island* (1945). Portly and balding, Zucco addressed the camera with a matinee idol's bearing and spent a 20-year career in film as a dependable—customarily villainous—stealer of scenes. His outthrust profile and huge, radiant eyes abetted the thefts, and so did his nuanced readings of predatory dialogue.

Zucco's big set-piece in *The Mad Ghoul* is a polite drawing-room scene, well removed from the film's ticket-selling grisly business. "Don't you suppose that I know how a woman should look at a man when she loves him?" the 57-year-old Zucco asks of the 25-year-old Evelyn Ankers. Having persuaded her to admit she wants out of an engagement to boyish David Bruce, Zucco presses the issue: "It's perfectly natural, now, that you should turn to a more sophisticated man... who knows the book of life—and can teach you to read it." Miss Ankers' response dovetails exquisitely with Zucco's escalating come-on to create a sequence that almost could have been lifted from one of the period's sophisticated bedroom farces. She is agreeing to matters quite apart from what he is suggesting, and his arrogance renders him as vulnerable as her innocence renders her.

The film, which was shot under the cumbersome title *The Mystery of the Mad Ghoul*, finds Prof. Alfred Morris (Zucco) wresting the secret of living death from the traces of some prehistoric civilization—and to what use would *you* put such a discovery? Morris lusts after Isabel Lewis (Miss Ankers), whose singing career is about to blossom. Her possessive fiancé, Ted Allison (Bruce), is an assistant to Morris. Certain that Isabel can be his if Ted is put out of the way, Morris infects the youth with the life-in-death formula. Ted's only hope of restoration—temporary, at best—requires a freshly extracted human heart. The resulting serial-murder case follows Isabel's concert-tour schedule, until

The Definitive Edition

Robert Armstrong gets the drop—however temporarily—on George Zucco.

Morris is accidentally exposed to the chemical. Ted is gunned down as he barges in on one of Isabel's performances. Dr. Morris dies while trying to claw open a grave.

David Bruce, who seldom graced films of this sort, fits the title role superbly—a robust but insecure character, and easy prey for Zucco's machinations. Mysterious-looking Turhan Bey, already a veteran of high-octane adventure serials and mystery-and-horror features after only two years in Hollywood, has unaccountably little to do here as the pianist who becomes Miss Ankers' lover. Milburn Stone, likewise a dependable of the B-pictures, also keeps an unusually low profile as a cop who pegs Bey as a suspect. *King Kong*'s Robert Armstrong serves *The Mad Ghoul* memorably as a news reporter whose plot to crack the case backfires fatally. No one diverts much attention from Zucco, whose forceful performance here is topped only by another of his professor-type roles—Moriarty in 1939's *The Adventures of Sherlock Holmes*.

Zucco's aloof elegance is complemented throughout by Universal's customary attention to production design and the camerawork of one of the studio's top-notchers, Milton Krasner. As effective camouflage for the picture's low-budget essence, the climactic concert-hall sequence was photographed on the *Phantom of the Opera* stage, with strategic panning and in-the-camera cropping to create the illusion of a full house of dress extras. The only laughable aspect—unless some crank cares to ridicule the deliberately far-fetched yarn—is the big-nose/big-foot cartoon style of the mock-ancient paintings that illustrate Zucco's obsession.

Director James P. Hogan pursued two distinct careers in film, helming almost 30 features during the 1920s and then returning in 1936 after patiently accustoming himself to talking-picture grammar and technique. He averaged four movies a year from that point, including many of the *Bulldog Drummond* and *Ellery Queen* series entries. *The Mad Ghoul* was Hogan's final assignment, released a week after his death.

CREDITS: Executive Producer: Joseph Gershenson; Associate Producer: Benjamin Pivar; Director: James P. Hogan; Screenplay: Brenda Weisberg and Paul Gangelin; Story: Hans Kraly; Photographed by: Milton Krasner; Art Directors: John B. Goodman and Martin Obzina; Sound: Bernard B. Brown; Technician: Jess Moulin; Set Décor: R.A. Gausman and A.J. Gilmore; Music: Hans J. Salter; Editor: Milton Carruth; Gowns: Vera West; Songs: "I Dreamt I Dwelt in Marble Halls," by M.W. Balfe, "Our Love Will Live" (from Tchaikovsky's *Piano Concerto in A*), with Lyrics by Everett Carter, and "All for Love" (from Mozart's *Minuet in A*), with Lyrics by Milton Rosen; Running Time: 65 Minutes; Released: November 12, 1943

Attention to evocative lighting and production design elevates *The Mad Ghoul* **a notch or two.**

CAST: David Bruce (Ted Allison); Evelyn Ankers (Isabel Lewis); George Zucco (Prof. Alfred Morris); Robert Armstrong (Ken McClure); Turhan Bey (Eric Iverson); Milburn Stone (Macklin); Andrew Tombes (Eagan); Rose Hobart (Della); Addison Richards (Gavigan); Charles McGraw (Garrity); Gus Glassmire (Caretaker); Lillian Cornell (Singing Voice for Miss Ankers); Gene O'Donnell (Radio Announcer); Lew Kelly (Stagehand); Gibson Gowland (Detective); Isabel LeMal (Maid); Hans Herbert (Attendant); William Ruhl (Stagehand No. 2); Bess Flowers and Cyril Ring (Theatre Patrons)

THE SOUL OF A MONSTER
(Columbia Pictures Corp.; 1944)

> Into the lives of many come strange realities—into the lives of others come... weird dreams that shape and guide their destinies. You may have lived or perhaps dreamed the story you are about to see. To many of you, it may be a grim reality; to others, perhaps, just a dream.
> —From the Prologue

Once in a great while at the major studios, a producer dared to tackle a bizarre, provocative idea along highly stylized lines. Very few such efforts actually went into production—Columbia's own *The Devil Commands* is a striking example, what with its significant departure into metaphysics from the other Karloff-as-mad-doctor thrillers. Comparatively few gained favorable notice, such as a majority of the Val Lewton-at-RKO pictures. Most, however, were either ignored by the critics or subjected to ridicule. Such was the fate of *The Soul of a Monster*, which the New York *Times* dismissed as "a cheap way to go nuts."

The Soul of a Monster is hardly a classic, but it deserves a longer glance. It contains sharp dialogue; neat touches of direction; an imaginative photographic treatment; sophisticated utilization of Euro-classical and American jazz themes; and solid ensemble playing by freelancers George MacReady and Rose Hobart, backed by a splendid cast of contract players. The story emphasizes religion (unusual outside the Biblical epics), as befits a modern-dress *Faust*. Paramount later tried something along similar, larger-scaled lines with *Alias Nick Beal* (1949), but *The Soul of a Monster* is the more adventurous picture.

MacReady plays Dr. George Winson, physician and philanthropist, who lies near death as the picture opens. His wife, Ann (Jeanne Bates), rejects the counsel of a clergyman friend, Fred Stevens (Erik Rolf), and offers up a prayer to Satan for Winson's recovery.

The prayer summons Lilyan Gregg (Miss Hobart), who announces: "He'll live, but not if he's left in the hands of self-appointed saviors and friends." Winson rallies, but he becomes a menacing shadow of himself—alienating friends and family, recoiling at sight of a crucifix, stalking Stevens with murderous intent and refusing to perform a life-saving operation on a trusting colleague (Jim Bannon). Finally, Winson comprehends his wretched state; he approaches Lilyan to buy back his soul but then forces her into a fatal fall as she opens fire on him.

The ordeal proves to have been Dr. Winson's dream, brought on by his wife's prayer to Satan. He regains consciousness and halts her.

Edward Dein had co-written *The Leopard Man* for Val Lewton. His other work included Universal's *Inner Sanctum* series-opener, *Calling Dr. Death* (1943). Director Will Jason was better known as a popular tunesmith; most of Jason's movie work consisted of second-feature musicals and comedies.

The influence of Lewton is unmistakable: There is the pretentious Foreword (equally so, an Afterword), plus emphasis upon ominous shadowplay, and a tendency among even the lesser characters to interject archly philosophical remarks. A long sequence in which the bedeviled doctor quietly pursues the young parson through weirdly lighted streets is of a piece with the furtive stalks in *Cat People* and *The Seventh Victim*. There are startling interruptions (a noisy sidewalk elevator, a sudden intrusion from a cop), and a strategic use of the soundtrack and lighting to *suggest* rather than *demonstrate*.

Dein's dialogue, though often preachy and over-intellectualized, plays almost like natural conversation between MacReady and Jim Bannon, as the worshipful associate. There is a moving reference to a siren as "the cry of a distressed city." The opening scene, in which the grief-crazed wife rebukes the preacher, seems almost a reversal of the stern confrontation of the devil-cultists in *The Seventh Victim*: "Prayers are *cheap*... Someone once put them down so stupid fools like you would have something to cling to... I've never prayed to the devil... Maybe he's been done an injustice." A surge of storm clouds and surreal imagery underscores her blasphemy.

The only-a-dream device usually strikes us as a cheat. This odd picture dares hint at its intentions from the start, though, and the very *immediacy* of the menace pulls the viewer into the fevered mind of the dreamer. That mind is highly imaginative, with MacReady seeing himself as a zealous convert—and demanding at one point that a recital pianist perform Liszt's *The Mephisto Waltz* as accompaniment for a thunderstorm.

Rose Hobart and George MacReady in *The Soul of a Monster*.

(The presentation of the familiar melody is distinctive.) Elsewhere, a boogie-woogie piano solo by the great actor-composer, Dr. Clarence Muse, lends dramatic irony to a tense meeting between the Satanized MacReady and holy man Erik Rolf.

The tight budget (around $80,000) is well concealed by high-grade photography and optical effects. The story has its loose ends, but these are fairly explicable in light of the all-in-your-mind context. The ending is more ambiguous than outright happy, with the question of MacReady's recovery left hanging.

Rose Hobart is coldly effective as the visitor from Hades, her stern visage enhanced by a hairdo—of her own design, so she told us—that suggests concealed horns. MacReady brings a masterful understatement to the role of the good doctor who becomes a walking dead man. Backup principals Rolf, Jim Bannon and Jeanne Bates were veterans of radio drama, and their voices are particularly memorable. Rolf is especially winning in a role that could have come across as unbearably pompous.

Burnett Guffey's expert photography creates an atmosphere of the fantastic on ordinary backlot streets and in standard-issue, knocked-together stage sets.

CREDITS: Producer: Ted Richmond; Director: Will Jason; Screenplay: Edward Dein; Photographed by: Burnett Guffey; Editor: Paul Borofsky; Art Directors: Lionel Banks and George Brooks; Set Décor: Far Babcock and Robert Priestley; Musical Director: Mischa R. Bakaleinikoff, Utilizing Compositions from Dr. Karol Rathaus, Mario Castelnuevo-Tetesco, George Antheil, Nico Grigor, Ernst Toch, George Parrish, Daniele Amfitheatrof, Frederick Hollander, John Leipold, Robert Stringer, Ben Oakland and Gerard Carbonara; Incidental Music: "Boogie-Woogie Special," by Saul Chaplin & Walter Samuels, "Ain't That Just like a Man?" by Don Ray & Gene DePaul, Franz Liszt's *Spanish Rhapsody* and *The Mephisto Waltz*, Mozart's *Sonata No. 8*, Schubert's *Ave Maria* and Handel's "Awake, My Soul"; Running Time: 61 Minutes; Released: August 17, 1944

CAST: Rose Hobart (Lilyan Gregg); George MacReady (Dr. George Winson); Jim Bannon (Dr. Vance); Jeanne Bates (Ann Winson); Eric Rolf (Rev. Fred Stevens); Ernest Hilliard (Wayne); Clarence Muse (Pianist); Al Hill (Waiter); Edith Evanson (Mrs. Jameson); Ida Moore (Mrs. Kirby); Milton Kibbee (Driver); Harry Strang and John Tyrrell (Cops); Al Cross (Crippled Man); Charles Sullivan (Man in Bar); Howard Negley and Byron Shores (Reporters)

DARK WATERS
(Benedict Bogeaus Productions/Dark Waters Productions, Inc.; 1944)

An elite cast, a popular *Saturday Evening Post* serial and some unusual bits of Real World topicality combined in their day to make *Dark Waters* one of the most popular Gothic chillers of the World War II years.

Merle Oberon plays Leslie Calvin, the traumatized survivor of a seagoing Japanese attack. Sent for a rest cure to her kinfolks' plantation in Louisiana's swampy Cajun-Creole country, Leslie meets—for the first time—Aunt Emily and Uncle Norbert (Fay Bainter and John Qualen). Also in residence are Mr. Sydney (Thomas Mitchell) and Mr. Cleeve (Elisha Cook, Jr.). Everyone on hand seems secretive if not downright creepy, and Leslie senses two distinct possibilities: Either she's cracking up, or there's a plot afoot to make her believe she's cracking up.

Pearson (Rex Ingram), a handyman better known for his furtive moves than for being particularly handy about the place, is slain after he attempts to warn Leslie of some pressing danger. In rapid order, Aunt Emily and Uncle Norbert prove to be hirelings of Mr. Sydney, who had murdered Leslie's relatives. It all has to do with the usual scam to gain control of an estate. Weasly accomplice Cleeve gets in Sydney's way and is mowed down in the swamp. Leave it to the local doctor (Franchot Tone) to save the day. The bogus aunt and uncle get away Scot-free, if only because there aren't all that many Scots roaming at large in the bayou country.

Dark Waters was produced independently by Benedict Bogeaus, a Chicago real estate broker who in 1941 had purchased the very site of the film's production, the Metropolitan Studio at 1040 Las Palmas in Hollywood. The presentation is remarkably lavish, taking into account the government's defense-effort obsession with conserving construction materials.

Most of the work was done at the studio, with process plates and insert footage made in Louisiana, home of the darkest waters in these Continental United States. New Orleans and the nearby Teche County Bayou, Three Rivers, St. Tamminy Parish and the Cherfuncta River provide vivid scenic values. The swamp itself only looks authentic; it was constructed on three acres of the backlot, with a tank in which submerged fixtures were mounted on submerged dollies. This invention allowed the crew to move trees and foliage about for varied settings. The jungle area outside the water measured 110 by 150 feet.

The ghostly mansion was based upon a Louisiana landmark called Homeland, which had burned several years earlier.

Elaborate interiors, built on sound stages, are spacious but seem emotionally confining. These menacing settings are just right for the story, which receives further impetus from a now-somber, now-upbeat musical score, tricky lighting and gloomy fog effects that pass nicely for the genuine article.

André de Toth had been a cameraman and director in Hungary, then came to America to get shed of the Nazis. He started out small in Hollywood, then promptly leapt to the big-budgeters with *None Shall Escape* (1944), followed by *Dark Waters*. De Toth is best remembered today for his extremely popular 3-D chiller, *House of Wax* (1952), starring Vincent Price.

Joan Harrison, associate producer of the well-received *Phantom Lady* (1944), performs double-duty on *Dark Waters*, as both associate producer and co-screenwriter. Miss Harrison had started out with Alfred Hitchcock in England in the 1930s; she would at length become producer of the Hitchcock teleseries. (In the Price & Turner collection is a bound copy of *Dark Waters*' magazine serialization, bearing Miss Harrison's signature, rubber-stamp address and marginal notes.)

The acting in *Dark Waters* is all that could be desired, with Merle Oberon doing a virtuoso job of conveying high-strung distraction and mounting hysterics without overplaying. Thomas Mitchell, wearing a pasty-faced makeup and dressed all in white, manages to seem terrifying without raising his voice or indulging in any impassioned histrionics. Franchot Tone makes a convincingly intelligent hero. The supporting villains are splendid: Elisha Cook, Jr., in his specialty as a hungry-looking sneak; Fay Bainter, in a turnabout from her usual motherly roles; and John Qualen, the downtrodden little twerp of many a John Ford production. Rex Ingram, Nina May McKinney and Alan Napier lend distinguished assistance in sympathetic and/or tragic roles.

For the most part, the melodramatics are of the well-bred variety, with only the occasional shocker—a severed arm afloat, for example, and a dead man's face framed by the undergrowth. Miklos Rosza's music also incorporates melodic bits of Cajun heritage, though without the proper traditional instruments.

CREDITS: A Benedict Bogeaus Production; Executive Producer: James Nasser; Associate Producer: Joan Harrison; Director: André de Toth; Screenplay: Joan Harrison and Marian Cockrell; Based upon; Frank & Marian Cockrell's *Saturday Evening Post* serial; Additional Dialogue: Arthur T. Horman; Photographed by: Archie Stout and John Mescall; Music: Dr. Miklos Rosza; Production Associate: Arthur Landau; Assistant to Producers: Carley Harriman; Art Director: Charles Odds; Set Décor: Maurice Yates; Editor: James Smith; Costumer: René Hubert; Sound: Frank Webster; Assistant Director: Joseph Depew; Choreographer: Jack Crosby; Properties: Kenny Wagner; Special Effects: Harry Redmond; Second Unit Director: John W. Boyle; Dialogue Director: Herbert Farjeon; Running Time: 89 Minutes; Released: November 10, 1944

CAST: Merle Oberon (Leslie Calvin); Franchot Tone (Dr. George Grover); Thomas Mitchell (Mr. Sydney); Fay Bainter (Aunt Emily); Elisha Cook, Jr. (Mr. Cleeve); John Qualen (Uncle Norbert); Rex Ingram (Pearson Jackson); Odette Myrtil (Mama Boudreaux); Alan Napier (Doctor); Eugene Borden (Papa Boudreaux); Eileen Coghlan (Jeanette); Nina May McKinney (Florella); Rita Beery (Nurse); and Gigi Perreau, Peter Miles, Louise Kerbrat, Alice Kerbrat, Fleurette Zama, Diana Martin and Diana Dubois (Children)

THE MISSING JUROR
(Columbia Pictures Corp.; 1944)

Oscar "Budd" Boetticher, Jr., has become something of a cult-of-personality figure, thanks to a series of rip-snorting Randolph Scott Westerns he directed during the late 1950s, and to a fascination with bullfighting that he indulged in such films as *The Bullfighter and the Lady* (1951) and *Arruza* (1972). Boetticher had been both a bullfighter and an assistant director—the jobs have rather a great deal in common—before he began his own directorial career with Irving Briskin's B-unit at Columbia. Boetticher's first effort on his own is a comedy-mystery in the *Boston Blackie* series, 1944's *One Mysterious Night*. His second, *The Missing Juror*, is a taut suspenser that advanced George MacReady to the ranks of memorable movie villains. Rising conspicuously above its humble origins, *Juror* attracted more attention than the usual double-bill second feature and assured MacReady of steady work playing psychopathic intellectuals, including the plum role of Rita Hayworth's sadistic husband in *Gilda* (1946). *Juror* also enabled Janis Carter's promotion to high-budget pictures and proved a worthwhile heroic vehicle for Jim Bannon.

Bannon is news reporter Joe Keats, who is keeping track of deaths among the members of a jury that had sent an innocent man to Death Row. The body count to date is five; Keats begins to sense a pattern. Keats dictates a memoir, rendering a flashback inescapable: Playboy Harry Wharton (MacReady) was patently innocent in a murder case, but a crooked private eye (George Lloyd) swayed the jury. Later, when ambushed by gangsters, the detective cleared Wharton in a dying confession.

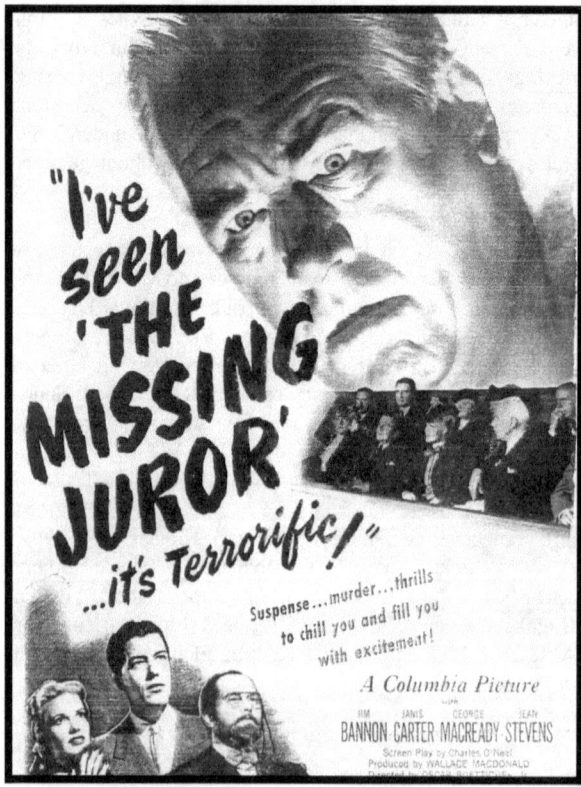

The ordeal has shattered Wharton's mind, but he still has enough on the ball to fake a suicide and escape from an asylum in order to get cracking on his campaign of vengeance. Keats' journalistic interference only causes Wharton to escalate. Finally, a cleverly disguised Wharton attacks Keats and lures jury member Alice Hill (Miss Carter) to a date with a hangman's noose. Keats may be just a bit too late getting there, for the reporter gets thrown into the hoosegow by mistake just as Wharton is carrying out his dirty business. The suspense stays cranked to the bitter end, tearing the absorbed viewer between an uneasy sympathy with MacReady's Wharton and an urgency to learn what new horrors can transpire next.

"I was just learning on those five pictures I directed at Columbia," Boetticher told us in 1989. "[Studio chief] Harry Cohn called them 'fillers'—they were put with more important pictures to fill out a double bill. Each was made in 12 days, for about $100,000.

"But, now, *The Missing Juror*—that was the one I liked, the *good* one," added Boetticher. "I have fond memories of George MacReady, a fine actor and fun to work with. Janis Carter was wonderful. I believe she could have been a top star if she'd wanted to be. She was too nice and too smart to play the game. Columbia's B-unit allowed us plenty of room to invent and experiment."

Jim Bannon spoke admiringly of MacReady and Miss Carter but told us that "some of the supporting players were real *prima donnas*... I suspect that Budd had less trouble fighting *el toro* than in trying to direct some of the actors in that film." Bannon was too much the gentleman to name any names, except when complimenting his colleagues.

The story resembles Columbia's own *The Ninth Guest* (1934) and *The Man They Could Not Hang* (1939), with an echo of Fox's *Almost Married* (1932). Scripter Charles O'Neal, co-author of *The Seventh Victim*, develops the picture as a whodunit until about the halfway mark, then reveals (to the audience only) the killer's identity and maintains suspense thereafter by convincing the viewer of the perils hovering about Miss Carter and Bannon.

Boetticher's style, even so early in the game, shows a precipitous momentum. The hard-lighted, calculatedly dramatic camera angles and extensive musical scoring—most of it from the Columbia library—contribute to a foreboding atmosphere that makes MacReady's outlandish machinations pressing, if hardly plausible. Notable among the supporting players is the mountainous wrestler, "Iron Mike" Mazurki, as a masseur who recites Oscar Wilde's "The Ballad of Reading Gaol" while plying his trade.

CREDITS: In Charge of Production: Irving Briskin; Producer: Wallace MacDonald; Director: Oscar Boetticher, Jr.; Screenplay: Charles O'Neal; Story: Leon Abrams and Richard Hill Wilkinson; Photographed by: L. William O'Connell; Film Editor: Paul Borofsky; Art Director: George Brooks; Set Décor: George Montgomery; Musical Director: Mischa Bakaleinikoff; Assistant Director: Ivan Volkman; Sound: John Goodrich; Running Time: 65 Minutes; Released: November 16, 1944

CAST: Jim Bannon (Joe Keats); Janis Carter (Alice Hall); George MacReady (Harry Wharton); Jean Stevens (Tex Tuttle); Joseph Crehan (Willard Apple); Carole Matthews (March); Mike Mazurki (Colly); Cliff Clark (Inspector); John Tyrrell (Sgt. Regan); William Newell (Wally); George Lloyd (George Szazbo); Forbes Murray (District Attorney); Charles Wilson (Mack); Edwin Stanley (Warden); Ernest Hilliard (Doctor); Harry Strang (Sgt. Newton); Edmund Cobb (Deputy)

GUEST IN THE HOUSE
a.k.a.: SATAN IN SKIRTS
(Guest in the House, Inc. [Hunt Stromberg Productions]/United Artists Corp.; 1944)

Hunt Stromberg produced more than 100 films in 20 years as an executive at MGM. He won 45 formidable awards, including *Fame* magazine's coveted designation as Champion of Champions Producer, over a 10-year period. Stromberg quit MGM in the spring of 1942, vowing to seek greater creative freedom as an independent. United Artists contracted with him to make five pictures with an average budget of $700,000 each, with UA obligated to take part in the financing. The arrangement got off to a terrific start: *Lady of Burlesque* grossed about $2 million. The second entry, *Guest in the House*, was a favorite with the critics but proved only mildly profitable, clearing about $50,000. In an industry that champions moneymaking crowd-pleasers over artistry, five subsequent box-office duds brought a distinguished career to a dismal close.

In a telegram to United Artists in January of 1944, Stromberg wrote: "*Guest in the House*... is a sensational Broadway stage hit whose theme combines appeal of three of my most popular box-office champions, *The Thin Man*, *Night Must Fall* and *Guilty Hands*. Elliott Paul, author of famous bestseller *The Last Time I Saw Paris*, is now completing most distinguished, exciting script. Will announce director next week—he's a top-notcher."

Anne Baxter, a lovely young actress whose career was blooming at Fox, was borrowed to head a splendid ensemble cast. Ketti Frings, an acclaimed writer of dialogue, performed considerable doctoring on Paul's script before production began. The result proved only basically similar to the play, which had run 45 weeks on Broadway. The director proved a top-notcher, indeed: Lewis Milestone, of *All Quiet on the Western Front* (1930), *The Front Page* (1931) and *Of Mice and Men* (1939).

Milestone got things under way, but an attack of appendicitis cut short his work. André de Toth took over for about two weeks but was called away for military duty. John Brahm was borrowed from Fox to complete the film—a wise choice. Brahm had just completed a brilliant study of a murderous psychopath, *The Lodger*. Brahm's Germanic style and Lee Garmes' unusual photographic technique dominate *Guest in the House*.

Evelyn Heath (Anne Baxter), under care for a heart condition, is brought by her fiancé, Dr. Dan Proctor (Scott McKay), to his family's seacoast home. Evelyn meets Dan's older brother, Douglas (Ralph Bellamy), a magazine illustrator; Douglas' wife, Ann (Ruth Warrick), and their daughter, Lee (Connie Laird); Aunt Martha (Aline MacMahon); Miriam (Marie MacDonald), Douglas' model-in-residence; and the servants, John (Percy Kilbride) and Hilda (Margaret Hamilton). The family is won over by Evelyn's sweet manner. Dan and Evelyn plan on living in during her recovery.

Evelyn wakes the household with screams of terror, occasioned by the discovery of a pet canary in her room. Douglas, first to arrive at her bedside, unwittingly arouses Evelyn's predatory appetites.

Evelyn makes herself increasingly a recluse, unnerving the household with endless playings of a recording of Liszt's "Liebestraum." She nurtures rumors that Miriam is undermining Douglas' marriage. Lee begins to imitate Evelyn's hypochondria. The canary dies unaccountably. No one suspects Evelyn is responsible for the venomous atmosphere, but a wise friend, Hackett (Jerome Cowan), pegs the visitor as a dangerous misfit.

The torments escalate, and finally Douglas storms out of the house to lose himself in a drunken bender. Evelyn orchestrates a scene that causes Ann to leave. Aunt Martha, realizing the truth at last, undertakes to undo Evelyn's plot—playing upon the schemer's fear of birds to convince her that the house is filled with the creatures. Screaming in terror, Evelyn races outside and plunges over a cliff to her death. None too soon to suit the Proctor family.

Anne Baxter is unnervingly true-to-life as a manipulative bitch masquerading as an innocent. She keeps this showy central role subdued except when bravura playing is called for. Her grasp

Ralph Bellamy and Marie Mac Donald in *Guest in the House*.

of the crucial psychologies—the use of failing health and soft-spoken shyness to disarm her intended victims—helps to overcome her appearance as one too physically fit for a role better suited to, say, Ida Lupino. Ralph Bellamy's artist-as-hero portrayal is robustly sensitive; toward the climactic moments, he delivers one of the most convincing drunk scenes ever filmed.

The highly publicized beauty, Marie "the Body" MacDonald, graces the scene as a semi-intelligent and entirely sympathetic innocent who finds herself among Miss Baxter's targets. Jerome Cowan seems a real friend in time of need. The austerity of the rockbound coastline is reflected in the faces and voices of the accomplished Aline MacMahon, Percy Kilbride (the future Pa Kettle of a long-running comedy series) and *The Wizard of Oz*'s Margaret Hamilton. Scott McKay and the moppet, Connie Laird, are convincingly naïve as they succumb to the wiles of the houseguest. As the victimized wife, Ruth Warrick—an Orson Welles discovery—matches Bellamy's realism.

Strictly a sound-stage creation, *Guest* was made on small but imposing sets, with the exteriors suggested by props, painted backdrops and photographic enlargements. Low ceilings made the house difficult to light, Garmes told us. The camera chief's solution was to custom-design a system of illumination so perfectly controlled as to sparkle like sunshine.

The horror grows without recourse to Gothic props or freakish shadows. Wide-angle lenses, deep focus and slightly lowered camera angles lend somewhat of a *Citizen Kane* look. Most scenes are enacted in an outwardly cheerful environment, which takes on its ominous shadings unobtrusively as the visitor's scheming becomes more and more pernicious. For the final breakthrough into madness, hard shadows and angular compositions take over: The clincher is a striking overhead shot of Miss Baxter whirling about in terror. Garmes said he devised this stunner in homage to Lillian Gish's trapped-in-a-closet ordeal in *Broken Blossoms* (1919).

A hysterical accusation.

Werner Janssen's memorable score, built in part upon Liszt, deserves much of the credit for dramatic impact. Though somewhat overlong for such heavy emotional going, *Guest in the House* is nonetheless an engrossing film—fully worthy of the producer of that pioneering classic of psychological horror, *Night Must Fall* (1936), the director of *The Lodger* (1944) and the photographer of that most pictorially beautiful of the early talkers, *Zoo in Budapest* (1932).

CREDITS: Producer: Hunt Stromberg; Director: John Brahm; Additional Direction: Lewis Milestone and André de Toth; Adaptation: Elliott Paul and Ketti Frings; Based upon: the Play by Hagar Wilde and Dale Eunson; Photographed by: Lee Garmes; Musical Score: Werner R. Janssen, Conducting the Janssen Symphony Orchestra of Los Angeles; Art Director: Nicolai Remisocc; Associate Art Director: Richard Irvine; Supervising Film Editor: James Newcomb; Film Editor: Walter Hanneman; Gowns: Natalie Visart; Assistant Director: Sam Nelson; Running Time: 121 Minutes; Released: December 8, 1944

CAST: Anne Baxter (Evelyn Heath); Ralph Bellamy (Douglas Proctor); Aline MacMahon (Aunt Martha); Ruth Warrick (Ann Proctor); Scott McKay (Dan Proctor); Jerome Cowan (Hackett); Marie MacDonald (Miriam); Percy Kilbride (John); Margaret Hamilton (Hilda); Connie Laird (Lee Proctor)

DRAGONWYCK
(20th Century-Fox Film Corp.; 1946)

> I did a wonderful villain in a marvelous picture called *Dragonwyck*. I'd have to say it was my favorite.
> —Vincent Price, From a Marathon Conversation with Price & Turner; 1974

Any time a work of fiction cracked the bestseller charts, in those bygone days of hard-earned honest bookstore sales, 20th Century-Fox's Darryl F. Zanuck could be counted on to bid aggressively for the movie rights. Among the many romantic novels that Zanuck brought to the screen, *Dragonwyck* ranks high in terms of spectacle and emotional resonance. Ernst Lubitsch produced (but did not direct) the film, and he ordered his name removed from the title cards. Vincent Price, who steals the show, told us that Lubitsch clashed bitterly with Zanuck all during the production, and that "Zanuck called Mr. L. a 'son-of-a-Lubitsch'—a pretty good pun, considering that Mr. Zanuck was more the humorless sort—right to his face." *Dragonwyck* provided a directing début for the distinguished writer Joseph Manckiewicz, launching him onward to the likes of *A Letter to Three Wives* (1949), *No Way Out* (1950), *All About Eve* (1950), *Julius Caesar* (1953) and *Suddenly, Last Summer* (1959).

Manckiewicz made no secret of his dislike for Anya Seton's *Dragonwyck*, complaining of the source-novel's insipid romanticism and lapsed opportunities for flamboyant villainy—but sensing a potential for development along bolder lines of malice and mayhem. The opening shots establish a deliberate pace that Manckiewicz sustains throughout, biasing his adaptation in Price's favor but never over-emphasizing the horrors of madness and murder. As an adaptation of a book that owes its inspiration to Edgar Allan Poe, *Dragonwyck* is an explicit foreshadowing of the Roger Corman–Vincent Price series of interpretations of Poe of the 1960s.

In the Hudson River Valley in 1844, Miranda Wells (Gene Tierney) braves the disapproval of her religious-fanatic father (Walter Huston) to leave for Connecticut and a job at the grand manor of Dragonwyck as governess to little Katrine Van Ryn (Connie Marshall). Miranda is awed by the grandeur of the place, and of its master, Nicholas Van Ryn (Vincent Price). He is the territorial Patroon, a feudal landlord. Miranda feels only sorrow for Johanna (Vivienne Osborne), Nicholas' ailing wife, and she senses the approach of tragedy. Nicholas insists the manor is haunted.

During a ceremonial tribute to the Patroon, an angry farmer tries to assassinate Van Ryn, who is

Walter Huston challenges Vincent Price's intentions.

saved by Jeff Turner (Glenn Langan), a local doctor. Nicholas rather unsubtly makes known his designs on Miranda even as his wife hovers between recovery and death. When Johanna dies, Nicholas proposes marriage before the funeral bells are silenced. Miranda flees to Connecticut, but he lures her back.

A son is born to Nicholas and Miranda, but the infant dies at christening. Nicholas disappears into the estate's tower, where at last Miranda finds him a wreck—crazed by drugs and superstition. Finding her threatened, Jeff overpowers Nicholas and tells Miranda of his belief that Nicholas poisoned Johanna with an oleander plant.

Nicholas has meanwhile ascended to his ceremonial throne, behaving in a threatening and deranged manner. A disgruntled sharecropper shoots Nicholas, this time with the desired results. Nicholas, arrogant to the end, tells all within earshot: "Take off your hats in the presence of the Patroon."

A magnificent group of sets serves as the manor house of the title. The vast exteriors were built on one sound stage, with a four-inch layer of earth that was landscaped to represent the shifting seasons. The mighty hall, including a carved-oak staircase, filled another stage, and the bedroom wings took up a third. Camera boss Arthur Miller experimented exhaustively during preproduction, seeking a style of lighting that would serve the romantic and eerie aspects of the story with equal emphasis. This was achieved with a simulation of candlelight. Subtle changes in the intensity of illumination make the photographic tone flow smoothly from one mood to another. Alfred Newman's musical score, containing some of the most exquisite passages ever heard in a movie theatre, helps to unify the rambling story.

That rambling nature itself, of course, helps to disguise a genuinely boneheaded lapse in the editing: Connie Marshall, who plays the daughter of the manor lord, disappears utterly. Hers is a necessary part, being the factor that draws Gene Tierney to the accursed mansion—and yet the film never mentions her sudden vanishment. A lesser character, a strange servant played by

Spring Byington, also pulls an inexplicable fade. (We've always suspected the kid and the maid became fertilizer for Vincent Price's poisonous garden.)

Dragonwyck was promoted heavily in terms of Gene Tierney, a leading ticket-seller for Fox since her début there in 1940. Miss Tierney's performance justifies the emphasis. There is equally strong work from Walter Huston, who toplines the supporting cast despite the brevity of his role. Coloradan Glenn Langan, the drive-in cinema's *Amazing Colossal Man*-in-waiting, seems born to *Dragonwyck*'s rock-jawed heroic role of a town doctor. Third-billed Price is the dominant presence. In an exceptional performance, handily the best of a vibrant career, Price earns sympathy and hatred, by turns, through subtly disciplined shadings of character. He is persuasive in equal measure as a dashing romancer; as a cool-headed murderer who cultivates deadly oleanders (shaped by the prop department from the twisted branches of a manzañita and oleander blooms and foliage); and as a crazed addict.

In the first of many lengthy visits spanning almost 20 years, Price told us: "A villain represents conflict, but he need not be a drab fellow." (In the typo-laden 1995-96 edition of this book, from a since-defunct publishing house, this establishing sentence came out as: "… he need not be a drag fellow." The authors scarcely knew whether to be amused at the accidental Freudianism or infuriated at the sloppiness of the typesetting.)

But Vincent Price has the floor: "According to Aristotle, [the villain] can be a man of great culture and high station. That makes him all the more interesting because the audience is fascinated that such a person can come to this. Our job is to make the unbelievable *believable*. We have to con you into thinking maybe we could not be so bad as you think.

"[In *Dragonwyck*,] I was an extraordinary villain... who believed in survival of the fittest. Anything that didn't live up to his standards—well, it just simply shouldn't *live*, that's all there was to it.

"I did a lot of research, trying to understand him, and I finally found the key in the front of the very book that we were making into the movie. Anya Seton quoted this poem, 'Alone,' in her foreword."

And here, Price delivered a profoundly *knowing* interpretation of the poem, from its haunting assertion that "From childhood's hour, I have not been/As others were—I have not seen/As others saw…," to its harrowing disclosure of "a demon in my view."

"Edgar Allan Poe wrote that," Price continued, "and it has to be one of the most revealing autobiographical poems ever written, for Poe was indeed born with a demon within."

Price's affection for the picture notwithstanding, he still had some *kvetches*: "Censorship was a problem then. We had to leave out some of the best business in the book, including the ending where Van Ryn reformed. We had to kill the poor guy, instead, because 'evil must be paid for,' per those sour killjoys who ran the Legion of Decency. On top of everything else, I didn't know *how* I was supposed to die because Mr. Manckiewicz wouldn't tell me. He thought an actor's knowledge of his fate would psychologically type the performance. Which is hardly *my* style, but it seems to have worked."

The production was "tremendously lavish," Price said. "The sets were gigantic, and we had an unusually long schedule, about five months. I loved it, for the most part. It was in those days when pictures were really produced beautifully."

CREDITS: Executive Producer: Darryl F. Zanuck; Producer: Ernst Lubitsch (Unacknowledged in Screen Credits); Director and Screenwriter: Joseph L. Manckiewicz; Based upon: Anya Seton's Novel; Photographed by: Arthur Miller; Art Directors: Lyle Wheeler and Russell Spencer; Set Décor: Thomas Little; Associate: Paul S. Fox; Music: Alfred Newman; Orchestrations: Edward Powell; Film Editor: Dorothy Spencer; Costumes: René Hubert; Makeup: Ben Nye; Special Effects: Fred Sersen; Choreography: Arthur Appel; Sound: W.W. Flick and Roger Heman; Propmaster: A.E. Lombardi; Assistant Director: Johnny Johnson; Running Time: Given Variously as 103 and 110 Minutes; Released: Following New York Opening on April 10, 1946

CAST: Gene Tierney (Miranda Wells); Walter Huston (Ephriam Wells); Vincent Price (Nicholas Van Ryn); Glenn Langan (Dr. Jeff Turner); Anne Revere (Abigail); Spring Byington (Magda); Connie Marshall (Katrine); Harry Morgan (Kass Bleeker); Vivienne Osborne (Johanna); Jessica Tandy (Peggy O'Malley); Trudy Marshall (Elizabeth Van Borden); Reinhold Schunzel (Count de Grenier); Jane Nigh (Tabitha); Ruth Ford (Cornelia Van Borden); David Ballard (Obediah); Scott Elliott (Tom Wells); Boyd Irwin (Thompkins); Maya Van Horn (Countess de Grenier); Keith Hitchcock (Mr. McNabb); Francis Pierlot (Dr. Brown); Edwin David and Selby Bacon (Dancers); John Challot (French Count); Virginia Lindley (Helena); Nanette Vallon (French Countess); Mickey Roth (Nathaniel); Jamie Dana (Seth); Betty Fairfax (Mrs. McNabb); Douglas Wood (Mayor); Steve Olsen (Vendor); Grady Sutton (Hotel Clerk); Charles Waldron (Minister); Gertrude Astor (Nurse); Larry Steers, Tom Martin, Wallace Dean, Arthur Thompson and Al Winter (Servants); Ruth Cherrington and Elizabeth Williams (Ladies); and Ted Jordan, William Carter, George Ford, Alexander Sacha, Nestor Eristoff, Trevor Bardette, Walter Baldwin, Robert Malcolm, Harry Humphrey, Tom Fadden, Arthur Aylesworth, Addison Richards and Clancy Cooper (Farmers and Townsmen)

Steven Geray and Eugene Borden in *So Dark the Night*.

SO DARK THE NIGHT
(Darmour, Inc./Columbia Pictures Corp.; 1946)

"I am the Whistler. I know many strange tales," intones an ominous voice at the start of each of nine Larry Darmour productions, derived from J. Donald Wilson's long-running radio series, *The Whistler*. Each picture is a self-contained hair-raiser, but *So Dark the Night* stands quite apart; one surviving cut eliminates the *Whistler* trappings altogether and is diminished none by the removal.

A nervous breakdown threatens the Sûreté's ablest detective, Henri Cassin (Steven Geray), who is sent to the village of St. Margot for a rest. The resort there is operated by Pierre Michaud (Eugene Borden) and his wife (Ann Codee). Their daughter, Nanette (Micheline Cheirel), is engaged to marry Léon Archaud (Paul Marion), a young farmer. Mama Michaud persuades Nanette to consider the wealthy, middle-aged detective instead. Nanette trains her wiles upon Henri, and they become engaged despite the objections of Pierre and Léon. At the announcement party, Léon angrily declares that no other man will have Nanette. Léon and Nanette go missing.

Days later, Nanette is found strangled. Henri can find no clues. Then, Léon, the key suspect, turns up croaked. Henri makes a cast of a footprint found beneath the body. Mama Michaud is next to die.

In Paris, Henri is astonished to find that he resembles a forensic reconstruction of a likely perpetrator. A psychiatrist determines that Henri is subject to homicidal fugues. The great sleuth is locked away but escapes and returns to St. Margot. A police commissioner (Gregory Gay) follows, arriving just as Henri is strangling Pierre Michaud. A bullet saves the innkeeper. Henri, dying, regards himself in a mirror and then smashes the glass, declaring: "Henri Cassin is no more. I have caught him and killed him."

The Definitive Edition

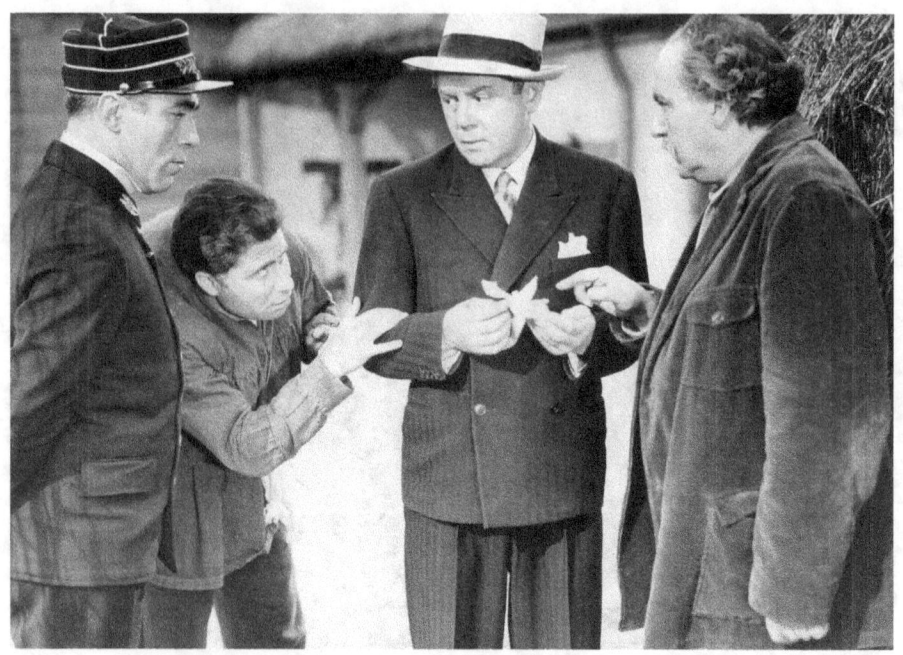

Geray is on the case—but so is his murderous subconscious mind.

Director Joseph H. Lewis learned the movie business from the bottom up, beginning as a camera boy at MGM; becoming chief film editor on the Mascot and Republic serials during the 1930s; and directing second-unit work and quick-and-cheap Westerns for years at a stretch. Lewis served with the U.S. Signal Corps during World War II. Returning to Hollywood, he made an impressive entry in RKO's *Falcon* series (*The Falcon in San Francisco*, from 1945) and won a berth as a contract director for the B-picture unit at Columbia. His first Columbia, a mystery called *My Name Is Julia Ross* (1946), delivered so much high artistry on a low budget as to raise Lewis' status overnight. He made one more B-programmer, *So Dark the Night*, before finding himself kicked upstairs to direct *The Jolson Story* (1946). Such was Lewis' long, deliberate path toward the major leagues; over the next dozen years, he delivered such highly regarded gems as *Gun Crazy* (a.k.a. *Deadly Is the Female*; 1950) and *The Big Combo* (1955).

Although it showcases Lewis' familiar expertise, *So Dark the Night* attracted vastly less attention than *My Name Is Julia Ross*—probably obscured by the blanket mystery-series identity, which many critics and customers took as a keep-away sign. *So Dark* cannot match its predecessor for popular appeal, for Czech-born Steven Geray is more an actor for the sake of the craft than he is any kind of prepossessing star player (he oftener handled overtly villainous roles), and the nearest thing to a pretty girl on view is more of an angular type who is done away with early on. The film also falls short in the high-tension department, developing slowly with an ominous mood but little exciting punctuation.

So Dark the Night is, however, a remarkable study of a soul-in-torment, with a nuanced and soulful performance from Geray as the detective who is unknowingly tracking himself. (This narrative gimmick would figure again in Boris Karloff's starring picture of 1958, *Grip of the Strangler* [a.k.a. *The Haunted Strangler*], and yet again in Alan Parker's supernatural thriller of 1987, *Angel Heart*.) The effectiveness of Geray's acting was demonstrated by default in 1955, when the more famous Joseph Schildkraut tackled the same role with less happy results for an installment of *Lux Television Theatre*.

The story is based upon a documented case from mid-1930s Europe. The presentation is realistically well dialogued. The sets, which had seen service in some elaborate war films, are properly dressed to suggest prewar France. Many of the shots are made through windows, a distancing effect that makes the viewer as much an outsider as the visiting detective. Hugo Friedhofer's musical score, as conducted by Morris Stoloff, is a powerfully moving work. Both Friedhofer and Stoloff won Oscars that year, for *The Best Years of Our Lives* and *The Jolson Story*, respectively.

The radio-spin-off series of which *So Dark the Night* is (technically) a part had started in 1944 with *The Whistler*, a nerve-wracker starring Richard Dix as a bereaved husband harboring a death wish and J. Carrol Naish as a schemer intent upon frightening Dix into an early grave. There followed *The Mark of the Whistler* (1944), from a Cornell Woolrich story; *The Power of the Whistler* and *Voice of the Whistler* (both from 1945); *Mysterious Intruder* and *The Secret of the Whistler* (both from 1946, bookending *So Dark the Night*); *The 13th Hour* (1947); and *The Return of the Whistler* (1948), from another Woolrich yarn. Dix was steadily involved, though not as a recurring character, and William Castle honed his chops as a pretender to Alfred Hitchcock's Master-of-Suspense tag as a contributing director within the series.

CREDITS: Producer: Ted Richmond, for Larry Darmour Productions; Director: Joseph H. Lewis; Screenplay: Martin Berkeley and Dwight Babcock; Story: Aubrey Wisberg; Suggested by: J. Donald Wilson's Radio Series, *The Whistler*; Photographed by: Burnett Guffey; Camera Operator: Gert Anderson; Art Director: Carl Anderson; Editor: Jerome Thoms; Assistant Director: Chris Beute; Décor: William Kiernan; Musical Score: Hugo Friedhofer; Musical Director: Morris W. Stoloff; Theme Song: "The Whistler," by Wilbur Hatch; Sound: Frank Goodwin; Re-Recordist and Effects Mixer: Russell Malmgren; Music Mixer: Edwin Wetzell; Research: Marie Deramie and Vera Mikoll; Running Time: 71 Minutes; Released: October 10, 1946

CAST: Steven Geray (Henri Cassin); Micheline Cheirel (Nanette Michaud); Eugene Borden (Pierre Michaud); Ann Codee (Mama Michaud); Egon Brecher (Dr. Boncouri); Helen Freeman (Widow Bridelle); Theodore Gottlieb (Georges); Gregory Gay (High Commissioner); Jean Del Val (Dr. Manet); Paul Marion (Léon Archard); Emil Rameau (Pere Cortort); Louis Mercier (Jean Duval); Billy Snyder (Chauffeur); Frank Arnold (Antoine); Adrienne d'Ambricourt (Newspaper Lady); Marcelle Corday (Proprietor); Alphonse Martel (Bank President); André Marsaudon (Postmaster); Francine Bordeaux (Flower Girl); Esther Zeitlin (Peasant); Cynthia Gaylord (Shoeshine Woman)

THE DARK MIRROR
(Inter-John, Inc./Nunnally Johnson Productions/
Universal-International Pictures Co., Inc.; 1946)

"This is it—my best to date," declared director Robert Siodmak upon viewing *The Dark Mirror* as a newly finished product. The point is arguable, even when one considers Siodmak's intimacy with the material, for his *Suspect*, *The Spiral Staircase* and *The Killers* (1945-46) surpass *The Dark Mirror* in most respects. Even so, the picture is a charming, even delicate, chiller that managed a freshness of approach at a time when psychological melodramas were running a dime-a-dozen in Hollywood.

Although the familiar opening logo bespeaks a Universal-International identity, *The Dark Mirror* is not a product of that company. Free agent Nunnally Johnson produced the film in association with International Pictures, Inc. It was scheduled at first to be an RKO-Radio release. Upon the merger in 1946 of Universal and International, the film became International's first contribution.

Johnson, whose writing credits include 1940's *The Grapes of Wrath*, 1944's *The Woman in the Window* and 1950's *The Gunfighter*, provided *Mirror* with a script laden with unusual twists, clever dialogue and well-spaced humor. The piece is surprisingly naïve at times, however, and it lacks the agreeable earthiness that is found in most of Johnson's writing. The story moves rapidly under the German-trained Siodmak, who makes the most of the pivotal set of twins who seem more or less evenly matched—but for the hidden beast in one.

A society physician is found knifed to death in his apartment. Detective Stevenson (Thomas Mitchell) learns that the victim had gone out on a date with Ruth Collins (Olivia de Havilland), who works in the building where the doctor maintained a clinic. Stevenson builds a case against Ruth until he learns that she has an identical twin, Terry Collins (Olivia de Havilland). One—but which?—has a workable alibi. They have habitually subbed for one another on dates and jobs, and neither will reveal the truth.

Stevenson enlists Dr. Scott Elliott (Lew Ayres), a mental-case specialist, to determine which sister might be capable of murder. Both seem cooperative, and each takes a romantic interest in Elliott.

Ruth, the quieter sister, appears emotionally disturbed and predisposed to hallucinations. Terry is the more aggressive and self-assured. Elliott becomes enamored of one of the sisters, but their tricks confuse him as to which is which. One contemplates stabbing Elliott. He feels that one girl is in danger from the other. It develops that Terry has undertaken to drive Ruth to a breakdown.

Finally, triumphant in the belief that Ruth has killed herself,

Terry acts the part of the good sister until she sees Ruth's reflection in a mirror. Terry flies into a murderous rage and is taken into custody. Ruth finds solace in Elliott's arms.

Olivia de Havilland restrains both performances until the climax, when she pulls out all the stops in depicting the mental disintegration of the evil sister. The portrayal is splendidly surprising, given as the sweet-faced actress' popular identification with such highly sympathetic portrayals as Maid Marian in 1938's *The Adventures of Robin Hood* and Melanie Wilkes in 1939's *Gone with the Wind*. Lew Ayres, back at work following a four-year conscientious-objector stint as assistant to an Army chaplain, is a persuasively capable psychiatrist. Thomas Mitchell provides sturdy support, close to leading-man caliber, as a no-nonsense enforcer with a sense of humor and a reasonably high boiling point.

The special-effects sequences in which the twins interact are among the most sophisticated of their kind, rivaled during the period only by those of Danny Kaye in *Wonder Man* (1945) and Bette Davis in *A Stolen Life* (1946). The use of complex separations, opticals, strategic doubling and traveling mattes enables Miss de Havilland to roam the full breadth of the screen, cross in front of herself, walk arm-in-arm with herself and even embrace herself. The effects are so flawless as to suggest an ahead-of-its-time case of cloning. Amelita Ward, a leading lady with the B-picture departments at Universal and RKO, stands in as one twin; when both are required in a scene, Miss de Havilland's face is matted in seamlessly with Miss Ward's body.

A highly emotional score by Dimitri Tiomkin points up the action a bit too much at times, but the music generally fits the mood. Miss de Havilland re-created her dual role for a 1950 radio broadcast in the *Screen Directors Playhouse* series.

CREDITS: Executive Producers: Leo Spitz and William Goetz; Producer and Screenwriter: Nunnally Johnson; Director: Robert Siodmak; Based upon: Vladimir Poznir's Serialized Novel; Photographed by: Milton Krasner; Music: Dimitri Tiomkin; Production Designer: Duncan Cramer; Special Photographic Effects: J. Devereaux Jennings and Paul Lerpae; Costumes: Irene Sharaff; Editor: Ernest Nims; Makeup: Norbert Miles; Hair Stylist: Mary Freeman; Sound: Fred Lau and Arthur Johns; Set Décor: Hugh Hunt; Dialogue Director: Phyllis Loughton; Assistant Director: Jack Voglin; Running Time: 85 Minutes; Released: Following New York Opening on October 18, 1946

CAST: Olivia de Havilland (Terry Collins and Ruth Collins); Lew Ayres (Dr. Scott Elliott); Thomas Mitchell (Detective Stephenson); Richard Long (Rusty); Charles Evans (District Attorney Girard); Garry Owens (Franklin); Lester Allen (George Benson); Lela Bliss (Mrs. Didriksen); Marta Mitrovich (Miss Beade); Amelita Ward (Double for Miss de Havilland); Lane Chandler (Orderly); Jack Gargan (Waiter); Rodney Bell (Fingerprint Man); William Halligan (Sgt. Temple); Ida Moore (Mrs. O'Brien); Barbara Powers (Girl); Jack Cheatham (Cop); Ralph Peters (Dumb Cop); Charles McAvoy (Janitor O'Brien); Lane Watson (Mike); Ben Erway (Police Lieutenant); Jean Audren (Secretary)

THE LOCKET
(RKO-Radio Pictures, Inc.; 1946)

A bizarre and artistically mounted film by John Brahm, *The Locket* was all but buried in the avalanche of psychological thrillers that followed World War II. Once this pattern had caught hold, the critics grew increasingly cold to such yarns, meting out the same rubberstamp harshness they had long accorded pictures about monsters and mad scientists. Nor was *The Locket* a popular favorite: Many viewers reacted to its complex structure in the same way moviegoers of 1916 had recoiled from the convolutions of *Intolerance*. However intolerant the response to it, though, *The Locket* is a virtuoso noir in which Brahm's gift for imagery and his understanding of "the love that harms"—to borrow a line from a kindred (but much more recent) song by John Hiatt—assume full control. The film is an equally fine showcase for the brilliant cameraman, Nick Musuraca, whose contributions to this style in the Val Lewton productions are definitive.

During a party heralding the wedding of John Willis (Gene Raymond) and a delicate beauty named Nancy (Laraine Day), Dr. Harry Blair (Brian Aherne) arrives, uninvited, and demands to speak to Willis. Seems Blair is a disappointed former husband of Nancy's, and his story opens a veritable Chinese box-puzzle of flashbacks.

Blair relates that he and Nancy had been happy, until one day an artist named Norman Clyde (Robert Mitchum) approached Blair with a strange story—which constitutes a flashback-within-the-flashback: Nancy had introduced Clyde to a wealthy patron named Bonner (Ricardo Cortez), from whose mansion Nancy later stole a valuable bracelet. Confronted, Nancy revealed a sad story of misplaced blame from her childhood, further compounding the flashback. Later, Clyde had found Nancy with the body of Bonner, who had been murdered. Clyde shielded her, and an innocent man took the rap. After the execution, Clyde returned to Blair's office, outwardly calm, and then committed suicide.

Blair and Nancy visited London as guests of a household whose fabulous collection of jewels Nancy admired. In the Nazi Blitzkrieg, Blair's apartment was bombed, and the rubble yielded evidence of a theft. Blair's mind snapped, and only now has he begun to trail Nancy in hopes of halting her quietly methodical rampage.

John Willis refuses to believe Blair's story. The wedding proceeds, and John's mother (Katherine Emery) presents Nancy with an heirloom—which the bride recognizes as the very object that she, as a child, had been accused of stealing. John's mother had been the girl's accuser. Nancy lapses into a passive state and at length must be committed to an asylum.

Sheridan Gibney's scenario (the outline treatment was called *What Nancy Wanted*) requires an intense concentration: Brian Aherne's tale contains Robert Mitchum's account, which in turn contains Laraine Day's recollection of a traumatic experience. The viewer who settles in after the picture is even barely under way has little hope of picking up the threads. The transitions are garnished with the superb optical effects that had become an RKO trademark. Roy Webb's brooding musical score embellishes the visuals and helps to unify the various narrative voices and points of view.

Mitchum's suicide scene is singularly memorable: He leaves the doctor's office. The doctor hears the shattering of glass and rushes to the waiting room. The camera takes in the room and its several horrified occupants—then moves toward the smashed window—proceeds through the break—and finally tilts downward to show a crowd gathering about a body on the sidewalk. Although this appears to be one continuous shot, forcing the viewer to retrace the fatal plunge, it is actually a seamless composite of sequences, welded together through ingenious optical work. Opticals also intensify Miss Day's climactic breakdown, imparting a surreal quality through carefully planned distortions. The soundtrack responds with the appropriate dissonances.

Miss Day keeps up a cool front until the shattering climax, bolstering the premise than none of her victims can consider her anything but angelic. Aherne is ideally convincing as a self-assured psychiatrist driven to madness but determined to rescue whomever he can from his lethal former wife. Mitchum gives a robust portrayal of a working artist, quite unlike the ivory-tower stereotype. Raymond is just as believable in his reading of a wealthy man bedazzled by beauty and feigned innocence. Katherine Emery is more flamboyant as the lesser predator, a cruel society matron. Sharyn Moffett gives a sensitive reading of the misunderstood child, lending weight to the argument that an ordeal in youth can rebound in hideous ways over the long haul. Helene Thimig, the widow of Max Reinhardt, offers a touching cameo as Nancy's mother. Ricardo Cortez, Henry Stephenson, Reginald Denny, Fay Helm and Queenie Leonard stand out among the many top-shelf backup players who distinguish this engrossing exercise in the macabre.

CREDITS: Executive Producer: Jack J. Gross; Producer: Bert Granet; Director: John Brahm; Original Story and Screenplay: Sheridan Gibney; Photographed by Nicholas Musuraca; Music: Roy Webb; Musical Director: Constantin Bakaleinikoff; Special Effects: Russell A. Cully; Optical Effects: Linwood Dunn; Art Directors: Albert S. D'Agostino and Al Herman; Set Décor: Darrell Silvera and Harley Miller; Editor: J.R. Whittredge; Sound: John L. Cass and Clem Portman; Gowns: Michael Woulfe; Assistant Director: Harry D'Arcy; Dialogue Director: William E. Watts; Running Time: 85 Minutes; Released: December 20, 1946

CAST: Laraine Day (Nancy); Brian Aherne (Dr. Harry Blair); Robert Mitchum (Norman Clyde); Gene Raymond (John Willis); Sharyn Moffett (Nancy at Age 10); Ricardo Cortez (Bonner); Henry Stephenson (Lord Wyndham); Katherine Emery (Mrs. Willis); Reginald Denny (Wendell); Fay Helm (Mrs. Bonner); Helene Thimig (Mrs. Monks); Nella Walker (Mrs. Wendell)

IVY

(Inter-Wood Productions/Universal-International Pictures Co., Inc.; 1947)

Although best known for her great novel of psychological horror, *The Lodger*, Marie Belloc Lowndes wrote other memorable tales of murder with a greater stress on the Why than on the Who. Foremost of these is *The Story of Ivy*, a 1928 effort, which reached the screen as a triumph of elegant production and pictorial design.

The picture is, like *Dragonwyck*, a prime example of the elaborate films made in post-World War II Hollywood. Given a 120-day shooting schedule and a budget of $1.5 million—of which $30,000 was allotted for a magnificent wardrobe for the title character—producer William Cameron Menzies and director Sam Wood beat the deadline by 20 days. This accomplishment can be attributed to Menzies' careful designing of each shot, and to Wood's habit of staging long sequences without interruption after thorough rehearsals.

In London just after the turn of the century, Ivy Lexton (Joan Fontaine) is fed up with her weakling husband, Jervis (Richard Ney), who has squandered an inheritance. Ivy is superstitious to the point of fanaticism—and frustrated because a seer cannot tell her what to expect from life. Recklessly fashioning her own fate, Ivy carries on a secret affair with a fashionable young physician, Roger Gretorex (Patric Knowles), who is unresponsive to her hints that he should kill Jervis. Ivy steals poison from her lover's clinic and hides it in a compartment within the clasp of her purse. Jervis does not suspect that Ivy is tainting his brandy.

Ivy's greed outstrips Gretorex's means. The wealthy Miles Rushworth (Herbert Marshall) is next to fall under the spell. Rushworth gives Jervis a job and moves the couple into a fine apartment. When Jervis dies, Inspector Orpington (Sir Cedric Hardwicke) suspects murder. An autopsy turns up poison, which is traced to Gretorex. The doctor, too much the gentlemanly fool to implicate Ivy, finds himself indicted for murder. Then, scandalous disclosures cause Rushworth and his community of aristocrats to abandon Ivy. Orpington, certain that Ivy is responsible, finds the incriminating purse. Ivy tries to flee but falls to her death in an elevator shaft.

Wood's command of nuanced tight-ensemble work makes for fine viewing—an impeccably enacted movie that is made all the more watchable by Menzies' flair for design. Menzies may, in fact, be the greatest production designer in the history of filmmaking. The artists had collaborated before as director and designer, their *magnum opus* being *Kings Row* (1941), another elegantly mounted horror yarn.

Screenwriter Charles Bennett invests *Ivy* with a remarkable balance between tension and leisurely pacing, faithful to the novel's lavish amplification of an elemental and simply resolved tale. Bennett, also known for his novels and plays, scripted many influential examples of suspense cinema, notably in league with Alfred Hitchcock during 1934-40 on such memorable works as *The Man Who Knew Too Much*, *The 39 Steps*, *Young and Innocent* and *Foreign Correspondent*. The more conspicuous elements are the photography by Russell Metty and a rich orchestral score by Daniele Amfitheatrof, who used the eerie tones of a Theremin—electronic descendant of the primitive musical saw and ancestor, in turn, of the keyboard synthesizer—as a mood-building solo instrument. *Ivy* is rather a bit long, its almost languorous development being appropriate to the period and the subject matter, but at the sacrifice of the anxiety that a speedier pace would have generated.

Olivia de Havilland was originally scheduled to play Ivy, but she balked at tackling another murderess so soon after *The Dark Mirror*. Her sister (and bitter rival), Joan Fontaine, stepped in willingly and proved ideal. Usually seen as a shy girl in the likes of Hitchcock's *Rebecca* and Robert Stevenson's *Jane Eyre*, Miss Fontaine is very much the center of attention here. (Incidentally, she told us many years later that she despised *Ivy* and was uncomfortable with Wood's inflexible directing style.) There is good support, particularly from the Grand Manner actor Sir Cedric Hardwicke as a cold-eyed Scotland Yard man, from the genteel Herbert Marshall as Ivy's most affluent admirer and from Richard Ney as a pathetic if likable boozer.

An interesting, not entirely marginal, sequence involves preparations for a flight of a primitive Curtiss-Wright aircraft across the English Channel. Hoagy Carmichael wrote a song, "Ivy," to promote the film; it surfaces as a secondary theme within the dramatic scoring, but the tune *per se* is not heard in the film. The Carmichael piece was recorded intact by such hitmakers as Dick Haymes, Woody Herman, Vaughn Monroe and Jo Stafford.

In 1956, Martha Hyer starred in a television adaptation of *Ivy*, for the *Lux Video Theatre* portmanteau series.

CREDITS: Producer: William Cameron Menzies; Director: Sam Wood; Screenplay: Charles Bennett; Based upon: Marie Belloc Lowndes' 1928 Novel, *The Story of Ivy*; Photographed by: Russell Metty; Music: Daniele Amfitheatrof; Art Directors: John B. Goodman and Richard H. Riedel (under Supervision of William Cameron Menzies); Set Décor: Russell A. Gausman and T.F. Offenbecker; Film Editor: Ralph Dawson; Special Photography: David S. Horsley; Assistant Director: John F. Sherwood; Theme Song, "Ivy," by Hoagy Carmichael; Orchestrations: David Tamkin; Sound: Charles Felstead; Technician: William Hedgecock; Gowns: Orry-Kelly; Hair Stylist: Carmen Dirigo; Running Time: 97 Minutes; Released: Following New York Opening, Week of June 26, 1947

CAST: Joan Fontaine (Ivy); Patric Knowles (Roger Gretorex); Herbert Marshall (Miles Rushworth); Richard Ney (Jervis Lexton); Sir Cedric Hardwicke (Orpington); Lucile Watson (Mrs. Gretorex); Sara Allgood (Martha Huntley); Henry Stephenson (Judge); Rosalind Ivan (Emily); Lillian Fontaine (Lady Flora); Molly Lamont (Bella Crail); Una O'Connor (Mrs. Thrawn); Isobel Elsom (Mrs. Chattle); Alan Napier (Sir Jonathan Wright); Paul Cavanaugh (Dr. Berwick); Sir Charles Mendl (Sir Charles Craig); Gavin Muir (Sergeant); Mary Forbes (Lady Crail); Al Ferguson (Bailiff); Alan Edmiston (Harpsichordist); James Logan (Pilot); C. Montague Shaw (Stevens); Bess Flowers (Set Rehearsal); Robert Cory (Deck Officer); James Fairfax and Wally Scott (News Vendors); Elsa Peterson (Guest); J.C. Johnston, John Peters and Nigel Horton (Mechanics); Clive Morgan (Assistant King's Counsel); Wyndham Standing (Assistant Chief Justice); Manuel Paris (Cook's Tours Guide); Herbert Evans (Deck Officer); Normain Ainsley, Al Ferguson and Dave Dunbar (Ushers); Schuyler McGuffin and Harry Evans (English Gentlemen); Charles Knight and Frank Tomlinson (Solicitors); Eric Wilson (Steward); James Logan (Aviator); Herbert Clifton (Bates); Lois Austin (English Lady); Leon Lenoir, Jack Boyjan and Albert Morin (Dock Workers); Art Foster (Constable); Dave Thursby (Groves); and Lumsden Hare, Norma Varden, Matthew Boulton, Lydia Bilbrook, Harry Hays Morgan, Holmes Herbert, Gerald Hamer, Colin Campbell, Jean Fenwick, Claire duBrey, Art Foster, David Cavendish, Jack Bolan, Alberto Morin, Jack Perrin, David Ralston, Eric Wilton, Norman Ainslee, Ella Etheridge, William Mind, Beauregard Bonifacio, Robert Hale, Renée Evans, Judith Woodbury

A WOMAN'S VENGEANCE
(Universal-International Pictures Co., Inc.; 1948)

Hell hath no fury like—well, *you* know. That venerable truism about a woman scorned (and never mind whether the scorn is genuine or merely perceived) is the elemental springboard of Aldous Huxley's "The Giaconda Smile," centerpiece of the great philosopher-storyteller's 1922 anthology, *Mortal Coils*.

Huxley also was making literary hay off a Real World murder case, in which a Welsh lawyer was acquitted, following a lengthy due-process ordeal, in connection with the poisoning of his wife. The vengeance here has nothing to do with setting right any miscarriages of justice, nor with squaring any scores for murder—and everything to do with a neighborly spinster's indignation at not being chosen to succeed the defunct lady of the manor. The setting forth of that vengeful woman is the splendid work of London-born Jessica Tandy.

The popular view of Miss Tandy today hangs on her touchingly spirited big-screen work as an outspoken Southern Jewish widow in *Driving Miss Daisy* and as an aged sprite of a Scheherazade in *Fried Green Tomatoes*, among other crowd-pleasers and critics' darlings of the late 1980s and early '90s. Her work in film was sporadic over the long haul, being subordinate to a distinguished Broadway career (often in collaboration with her husband, Hume Cronyn) that included the defining 1948 portrayal of Blanche DuBois in Tennessee Williams' *A Streetcar Named Desire*.

A Woman's Vengeance was whipped into cinema during July-September 1947 by Huxley himself and Zoltan Korda. Korda had come to Hollywood from England early in the decade to work with his brothers, producer Alexander Korda and art director Vincent Korda, on *The Jungle Book*. Zoltan weighed in as a producer—that budget-minding chore usually fell to Sir Alex—on *A Woman's Vengeance*, performing double-duty as director, his usual berth.

The result is one of the most nearly perfect products of the Universal-International coalition, almost suggesting a bigger-budget Val Lewton–RKO picture in its seething understatement and its stormy atmosphere of gathering miseries. Camera chief Russell Metty, who had assisted Gregg Toland with the photography of Orson Welles' *Citizen Kane* (1941) as one of RKO's unwitting preludes to the style and the attitude of the Lewtons, brings to bear a similarly angular darkness on *A Woman's Vengeance*. The put-upon air of leading man Charles Boyer; the aggressive friend-turned-foe portrayal of Miss Tandy; even the sense that no home in their upper-crust English community seems free of disease or embittered resentment—all combine to convey a crushing fatalism. The rather pretentious intellectualism of Huxley (who delivered the shooting script), as earnestly filtered through such worldly-wise and bigger-than-life players as Charles Boyer and Sir Cedric Hardwicke, is of a piece with the noirish near-Existentialism of Lewton.

Henry Maurier (Boyer) treats his invalid wife, Emily (Rachel Kempson), with all the patience he can muster, but she responds with vile ingratitude. After a quarrel involving Emily's parasitic brother, Robert (Hugh French), Henry turns to a friendly neighbor, Janet Spence (Miss Tandy, whose character's very surname suggests an old-maid state of being), to help him patch matters up with the missus. Janet understands the situation—after all, she has spent the better portion of her life caring for her crippled father (Cecil Humphreys). Janet finds Emily unyielding, and she hears ugly things about Henry from Emily's man-hating nurse, Caroline Braddock (Mildred Natwick).

Henry has been carrying on in secret with Doris Mead (Ann Blyth). Robert spots the couple at a nightclub and confronts Henry with a threat of blackmail. Emily dies of apparently natural causes. Henry promptly embarks on a voyage. When he returns, Janet musters the courage to tell him she has loved him for years. She withdraws the assertion, pretending to have been joking, after Henry tells her he has married Doris.

Miss Braddock is angered when Doris winds up in possession of a piece of jewelry that the nurse had coveted. Miss Braddock blabs her suspicions that Henry had poisoned Emily. An inquest proves sufficiently incriminating, and Henry is sentenced to hang.

Janet grows prone to sleeplessness as the date of execution nears. The Maurier household's physician, Dr. James Libbard (Sir Cedric Hardwicke), believes Henry innocent and suspects Janet. Just before the hanging is to take place, Janet visits Henry and coldly informs him she committed the slaying in hopes that he would marry her. Henry tries to report this disclosure but cannot obtain a hearing. Finally, Dr. Libbard plays upon Janet's haggard condition. She breaks down and reveals her crime in exchange for a sleeping potion. Libbard stops Henry's execution, none too soon.

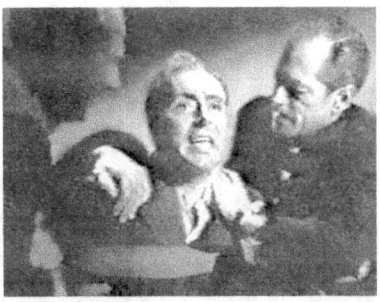

In *A Woman's Vengeance* Charles Boyer cracks under pressure.

Third-billed Miss Tandy steals the show decisively as the embodiment of wrongheaded revenge, conveying ideally an attractive, even reassuring, presence with a withered soul that asserts itself with a—what else?—vengeance. Her breakdown approaches by measured degrees until she confronts Boyer with heartless impunity and then pulls a crash-and-burn for the final encounter with Hardwicke. It defies reason that *A Woman's Vengeance* did not trigger a bidding war between Hollywood and Broadway for Miss Tandy's services. She found herself back on camera only belatedly, in 1951's *September Affair* and *The Desert Fox*, and even then hardly for keeps.

Boyer underplays cunningly to convey Henry Maurier's weariness at the pageant of insults his life has become. Lord Hardwicke uses all the Royal Academy training at his disposal to make the heroic physician-turned-sleuth the very soul of English persistence and fighting spirit. Ann Blyth is touchingly effective as the one bright spot in Boyer's benighted orbit, a sensitive sort who is driven to attempt suicide by the treacheries of Miss Tandy and Mildred Natwick, as the resentful repressed-lesbian nurse. Boyer's adulterous affair with Miss Blyth comes across as a perfectly sensible response to the glacial atmosphere of his household.

In a film of little built-in kineticism, Korda keeps things moving on an emotional fast track, plunging the viewer headlong into the waking nightmare that looms ahead of Boyer. The gloomy mansion settings give way strategically at points to the upbeat environment of a Real World location, Santa Monica's Riviera Country Club. The rather lengthy running time fairly zips past.

Later on in 1948, Boyer and Miss Blyth repeated their roles in a *Lux Radio Theatre* version, and Huxley re-adapted his tale for the London stage.

CREDITS: Producer and Director: Zoltan Korda; Screenplay: Aldous Huxley, from His Story, "The Giaconda Smile"; Photographed by: Russell Metty; Art Directors: Bernard Herzbrun and Eugene Lourié; Assistant Director: Horace Hough; Editor: Jack Wheeler; Set Décor: Russell Gausman and T.F. Offenbecker; Costumer: Orry-Kelly; Music: Miklos Rosza; Sound: Leslie I. Carey and Corson Jowett; Hair Stylist: Carmen Dirigo; Makeup: Bud Westmore; Assistant to Mr. Korda: Fred Pressburger; Running Time: 95 Minutes; Released: Following New York Opening on January 29, 1948

CAST: Charles Boyer (Henry Maurier); Ann Blyth (Doris Mead); Jessica Tandy (Janet Spence); Sir Cedric Hardwicke (Dr. James Libbard); Mildred Natwick (Caroline Braddock); Hugh French (Robert Lester); Rachel Kempson (Emily Maurier); Valeris Cardew (Clara); Carl Harbord (Coroner); John Williams (Prosecutor); Leland Hodgson (Warder); Ola Lorraine (Maisey); Harry Cording (McNabb)

THE SIGN OF THE RAM
(Columbia Pictures Corp.; 1948)

Susan Peters had every reason to live in 1944. At 23, hers was a blossoming career, and she was happily married to the writer-director-actor Richard Quine. A hunting accident on January 1, 1945, changed everything: A bullet shattered Miss Peters' spine, paralyzing the lower portion of her body. For more than two years, she struggled to resume her career. Help came at last from a surprising source: Harry Cohn, ostensibly that most despotic of movie moguls, approved Miss Peters for the starring role in a high-budget film about an invalid young matriarch-turned-tyrant.

Miss Peters told the press that she herself had chosen *The Sign of the Ram* as a story property, "because the central character... seemed real to me. At the beginning, she is a sweet, thoughtful, kind girl who suffers an accident and afterwards is confined to a wheelchair. From then on, the fear of being left alone haunts her, and her affections become distorted. Possessiveness grows, and... she almost ruins the lives of everyone within her reach."

The courageous actress makes the role such a powerhouse of subtle villainy as to keep the rest of a noteworthy cast in her shadow. The finer backup performances, overshadowed or not, belong to Alexander Knox, Phyllis Thaxter and Peggy Ann Garner.

Sherida Binyon (Miss Thaxter) reports to a cliffside mansion along the Cornish coast, where she has hired on as secretary to Leah St. Aubyn (Miss Peters), a popular writer. Sherida is surprised to learn that Leah goes about in a wheelchair. Leah seems almost savagely devoted to her family, which includes husband Mallory (Knox) and his three children from a prior marriage. Leah was paralyzed two years earlier while rescuing two of the youngsters, Logan (Ross Ford) and Jane (Allene Roberts), from drowning.

Logan is engaged to marry a minister's daughter (Diana Douglas), and Jane has become infatuated with a local doctor (Ron Randell). Teen-age Christine (Peggy Ann Garner) is slavishly dedicated to Leah—whose benevolence hides an attitude of malignant martyrdom. She subtly causes a rift between Jane and her sweetheart, and her psychological assaults drive Logan's fiancée to attempt suicide. Sensing an attraction between Mallory and Sherida, Leah inspires Christine to flirt with murder. Mallory finally grasps the truth. Leah wheels herself to the edge of the cliff and plunges over.

Shot almost entirely on sound stages in 36 days, *The Sign of the Ram* unfolds at a leisurely pace in tasteful, exquisitely lighted surroundings. The screenplay, by Hitchcock associate Charles

Bennett, makes no concessions to sensationalism except for an attempt—taken directly from the popular source-novel—to explain Leah's despotism in terms of astrology. Such star-gazing quackery associates Aries, the Ram, with an obstinacy of character that can lead to disaster.

Director John Sturges graduated here to top-of-the-line pictures after several years' apprenticeship in Columbia's low-budget division. His work is subtle and rich in characterizing touches. Even the studio's publicity department picked up on this quality, calling Sturges "a believer in understated performances." Sturges' fancier term was "inferential acting." He told us he liked to "build an emotional scene carefully and let it be enacted with... a restraint that engenders reality. The strange events will have a greater impact... if they are enacted in a way so natural that they appear likely to occur to anyone in the audience."

Hans Salter, longtime house composer at Universal who had become a freelancer after the Universal-International merger, cued the musical score's many ominous surges and stings to a wealth of sound effects, including the pounding of breakers and a thunderstorm. This detailed sound design adds greatly to the suspense.

The Sign of the Ram was both comeback and swan song for Susan Peters, who died on October 23, 1952, without having made another film.

CREDITS: Producer: Irving Cummings, Jr.; Director: John Sturges; Screenplay: Charles Bennett; Based upon: Margaret Ferguson's Novel; Photographed by: Burnett Guffey; Music: Hans J. Salter; Song: "I'll Never Say, 'I Love You,' to Anyone but You," by Allan Roberts & Lester Lee; Art Directors: Stephen Goosson and Sturges Carne; Editor: Aaron Stell; Set Décor: Wilbur Menefee and Frank Tuttle; Sound: Jack Goodrich; Assistant Director: James Nicholson; Makeup: Clay Campbell; Hair Stylist: Helen Hunt; Gowns: Jean Louis; Operative Cameraman: Gert Anderson; Script Supervision: Rose Loewinger; Grips: Ray Rich and Eddie Blaisdell; Stills: William Avery; Running Time: 84 Minutes; Released: During March of 1948

CAST: Susan Peters (Leah); Alexander Knox (Mallory); Phyllis Thaxter (Sherida); Peggy Ann Garner (Christine); Ron Randall (Dr. Simon Crowdy); Dame May Whitty (Clara Brastock); Allene Roberts (Jane); Ross Ford (Logan); Diana Douglas (Catherine Woolton); Margaret Tracy (Emily); Paul Scardon (Perowen); Gerald Hamer (Woolton); Doris Lloyd (Mrs. Woolton); Gerald Rogers (Station Master)

THE QUEEN OF SPADES
(Associated British/Pathé, Ltd./Wellwyn Studios; 1949)

Here we find not only the most elegant of all English-made horror films, but also the least known. Adapted from Alexander Pushkin's *The Queen of Spades*, the film was produced with lavish care by Anatole de Grunwald and directed with a ferocious attention to detail and nuance by Thorold Dickinson. It compares most favorably with the adaptations of *Great Expectations* and *Oliver Twist* that David Lean directed during that same Golden Age of post-WWII British cinema.

Queen's terrifying centerpiece is the ancient Countess Ranevskaya, as played by Dame Edith Evans—one of the last holdouts among the U.K.'s great stage stars to appear in a talking picture. She is entirely convincing as a creature who has dodged death long after her contemporaries have fallen to dust. Hopelessly frail, fawned over by a retinue of ladies-in-waiting, buried in layers of silken clothing whose rustlings become a motif within the dramatic context, the character would seem to be an object more of pity than of revulsion. There is, however, an air of undeniable wickedness about this living mummy.

In the inner sanctum.

St. Petersburg, 1906: Herman Suvorin (Anton Walbrook), a downright fool for gambling, learns of how a Russian countess had sold her soul in exchange for the secret of winning at Faro. The countess (Lady Evans) still lives, and Suvorin seduces a ranking servant (Yvonne Mitchell) as a means of infiltrating the inner circle. He finally confronts the ancient noblewoman with a plea that she share her forbidden knowledge. The countess dies of fright.

Later, Herman fancies he receives a message of forgiveness from the countess, along with a code for a foolproof progression of three cards. In a gambling duel with a former friend (Ronald Howard), Herman runs the stakes unreasonably high—until what he thinks is a crucial ace turns out to be the Queen of Spades. The face on the card is that of the countess. Herman suffers a crack-up on the spot.

The only player not overwhelmed by Lady Evans is the brilliant Anton Walbrook, who offers an obsessed schemer as memorable as his famously fanatical ballet-master in *The Red Shoes* (1949). Here, too, like the countess, is a character who might be expected to elicit a sympathetic response: He is an impoverished sort, surrounded by aristocrats who throw money about like so much confetti. Instead, Walbrook's Herman becomes more despicable by the moment, using seduction, subterfuge and armed threat in his attempts to learn the forbidden secret. At last, the young woman who had loved him admits that, when she met his gaze, "It was like looking into the eyes of Satan."

Yvonne Mitchell is particularly good as the victimized sweetheart, and likewise for Anthony Dawson as a cynical officer, Mary Jerrold and Athene Seyler as confidantes of the countess and Ivor Bernard as a sinister book-merchant. A flashback sequence features Pauline Tennant as the beautiful young countess, Yusef Ramart as her faithless lover and Valentine Dyall—the popular

Man in Black of British radio and an early-in-the-game Hammer picture of that same title—as a member of a necromancer's cult.

Thorold Dickinson (1903-1984) had worked in films since 1926 as an actor and writer, but not until 1938 did he begin directing, with *The High Command*. Seven more features over the next 13 years would include the excellent *Gaslight* (1941) and *The Secret People* (1951). Thereafter, Dickinson became an administrator of London University. *The Queen of Spades* is Dickinson's best of a fine lot, even though he had originally stepped in merely to rescue the project from a false start under director Rodney Ackland.

Much of the picture's effectiveness derives from the sets and costuming designed by Oliver Messel. Messel's résumé includes *The Private Life of Don Juan* and *The Scarlet Pimpernel* (both from 1934), and *Romeo and Juliet* (1936), as well as a Tony-winning job on the Broadway production of *House of Flowers* (1955) and a return to film with *Suddenly, Last Summer* (1959). In 1945, *Caesar and Cleopatra* had placed Messel in the front ranks of film designers. For *The Queen of Spades*, Messel delivered a fancifully caricatured Russia of baroque décor so rich as to seem almost suffocating. The set is as prominent as the talent in a terrifying sequence where Suvorin returns to search the countess' rooms while her disembodied eyes seem to follow him.

Otto Heller's lighting brings out the urgency inherent in the settings, and the almost ceaseless camera movement is smooth and unobtrusive. The musical score is as redolent of Imperial Russia as anything by Tchaikovsky or Borodin; it is the work of the pure-film composer Georges Auric, who also scored *Dead of Night* (1945), *La Symphonie Pastorale* (1946) and *La Belle et la Bete/Beauty and the Beast* (1946).

A Russian filming of *The Queen of Spades*, directed by the prolific Yakov Protazanov with a screenplay by director-to-be Fedor Ozep, dates from 1916.

CREDITS: Producer: Anatole de Grunwald; Director: Thorold Dickinson; Screenplay: Rodney Ackland and Arthur Boys; Based upon: Alexander Pushkin's Story; Photographed by: Otto Heller; Operative Cinematographers: Gus Drisse and Val Stewart; Settings and Costumes: Oliver Messel; Sets/Costumes Assistant: Ann Wemwyss; Editor: Hazel Wilkinson; Music: Georges Auric; Musical Director: Louis Levy; Art Director: William Kellner; Production Manager: Isobel Parciter; Sound: Frank McNally; Dubbing: L.H. Shilton and Audrey Bennett; Assistant Director: John Gaudioz; Continuity: Marjorie Owens; Makeup: Robert Clarke; Hairdressers: Frank Cross and Betty Cross; Set Dresser: Phillip Stockford; Period Adviser: Dr. Baird; Wardrobe Advisor: W. Smith; Fabrics Advisor: Scot Slimon; Furrier: Dean Fields; Choreography: David Paitinghi; Running Time: 96 Minutes; U.K. Release: During April of 1949

CAST: Anton Walbrook (Herman Suvorin); Dame Edith Evans (Aged Countess); Yvonne Mitchell (Lizaveta Ivanova); Ronald Howard (Andrei); Mary Jerrold (Old Varvarushka); Anthony Dawson (Fyodor); Miles Malleson (Tchybukin); Michael Medwin (Iliovaisky); Athene Seyler (Princess Ivashin); Ivor Bernard (Bookseller); Maroussia Dimetrevitch (Gypsy Singer); Violetta Elvin (Gypsy Dancer); Pauline Tennant (Young Countess); Jacqueline Clarke (Milliner's Assistant); Yusef Ramart (Countess' Lover); Valentine Dyall (St. Germain's Messenger); Gordon Begg (General Velchelnikoff); Gibb McLaughlin (Bird Seller); Drusilla Wills (Aged Servant); Aubreu Mallalieu (Fedya); George Woodbridge (Vassili); Pauline Jameson (Amayatka); Hay Petrie (Herman's Servant); Brown Derby (Footman); Geoffrey Dunn (Hairdresser); Ian Colin, Clement McCailin, John Howard, Aubrey Woods and David Palenghi (Officers)

Robert Newton and Sally Gray in *Obsession*.

OBSESSION
a.k.a.: THE HIDDEN ROOM
(Independent Sovereign Films, Ltd./Pinewood Studios/
J. Arthur Rank/General Film Distributors; 1949)

"The intelligence of a civilized husband is insulted," declares Dr. Clive Riordan (Robert Newton), a right and proper Englishman, after his wayward wife, Storm (Sally Gray), finally brings home one interloper too many. This newest trespasser is Bill Kronin (Phil Brown), an American diplomat, whom Riordan kidnaps and chains in a cellar.

Riordan intends to keep his victim alive and healthy until the disappearance has passed unsolved. Then, Riordan will dispose of Kronin. Capturing Storm's pet Poodle, Kronin trains the animal to drain the tub where Riordan is collecting acid. A Scotland Yard man (Naunton Wayne) becomes sufficiently interested to mount a nick-of-time rescue.

So runs the tale of *Obsession*, an extraordinary U.K. production that served, in its day, as something more than a droll thriller. Exiled director Edward Dmytryk insisted the film was as significant in a behind-the-scenes sense as in entertainment value. (Dmytryk found himself working in England at the same time that Jules Dassin, a casualty of Dmytryk's random finking before the House Committee on Un-American Activities, was in London, preparing to direct *Night and the City* for U.S.-based 20th Century-Fox.)

"There's one important thing *Obsession* did," Dmytryk told us in 1978. "It helped kill a movement in England that could have been disastrous."

Seems that studio chief J. Arthur Rank "had bought into a system of making pictures against process backgrounds—a system called Independent Frame," Dmytryk explained. "But Rank evolved the crackpot idea of breaking down a story into exactly timed scenes and then putting it onto a conveyor belt, so to speak. Automation is never a good idea, to begin with, because it takes the soul out of the experience, and the automation of the creative impetus is a *particularly* bad idea.

"So anyhow, a crew would go out and shoot all the backgrounds, and then, separately, they'd shoot the foreground action as interiors with a simple foreground set, such as the featured actors with a table and chairs. *Terrible.* Everything had to be timed to the second with a stopwatch and a little bell. It made things unbearable for *everybody*, but in theory a picture could be made much more efficiently and cheaply.

"They work slowly in England," said Dmytryk. "Much more slowly in England than in the States. The Hollywood crews are superior to any of the world, and they work together better. [In England,] they were taking [as long as] 48 days to make their Independent Frame productions, and they thought they were doing great. For *Obsession*, we set a schedule of 30 days, stuck to it, finished on time—and had a much better film. The other J. Arthur Rank units, working with Independent Frame, had scheduled a slate of 12 pictures and made about four of them. But when they saw what *we'd* done, organically and without Rank's robotic process system, they gave it up in disgust. Not a *one* of the Independent Frame productions was a success."

Obsession is a curiously nonconformist work—cleverly written, beautifully performed and directed with wit and skill. The principals all manage to strike sympathetic notes, even though one is a wife-stealer, another a chronically faithless wife and the third a murderer-in-the-making. These, plus Naunton Wayne's vaguely concerned investigator and a rambunctious lap-dog, are the only performers of consequence in a story that takes on its momentum with deceptive ease, suddenly reaching a high pitch of suspense during the final moments. The music by Nino Rota, then Italy's most celebrated composer-for-the-screen, is unusually melodic. Duncan Sutherland's camera placements keep the settings claustrophobic, as befits the situation, but visually interesting.

Robert Newton and Phil Brown are on screen most of the time as kidnapper and victim. Here is one of Newton's less fiery performances—and one of his best: Few other actors could make so fiendish a character so winning.

Dmytryk told us that Newton "had a tremendous drinking problem. In fact, he had to post £20,000 bond on this picture. He was a sweet man when sober, but when drunk he was mean—very, very nasty. But he lasted through the picture, and on the last day of shooting he started at lunchtime to have some ale and was beginning to glow at 5 o'clock, when we finished."

Brown was an American method-style actor—seen memorably as a psychopath in 1942's *Calling Dr. Gillespie*—who, like Dmytryk, had suffered a blacklisting in the U.S. government's commie-buster purges. Dmytryk considered Brown a fine, technically oriented talent and used him as an assistant on *Give Us This Day* (1949). As the blatantly faithless wife, Sally Gray seems precisely the type to lure a chap hither or thither—and to inspire a husband to contemplate murder. Naunton Wayne does well as the bemused detective, although it is a bit disorienting to see him working solo without his familiar comedy-team partner, Basil Radford. The Wayne-Radford combo—seen to best advantage in Hitchcock's *The Lady Vanishes* (1939), Carol Reed's *Night Train to Munich* (1940) and the anthology picture *Dead of Night* (1945)—was a tremendous influence upon the partnership of Ronnie Corbett and Ronnie Barker, better known to U.K. television audiences as The Two Ronnies. Admirers of the much later Gothics from Hammer Films will be delighted to spot Christopher Lee in a tiny role as a police officer.

Canadian-born Edward Dmytryk was 14 when he started working after school at Paramount in 1923. He became a film editor there at 22, and a fully fledged director at 31. Dmytryk had built a reputation as a maker of taut thrillers—from *The Devil Commands* in 1941 to *Crossfire* in 1947—when he ran afoul of the House Committee on Un-American Activities and attempted to mollify that agency by accusing others of purportedly Communistic leanings. *Obsession* is the first of several pictures Dmytryk made abroad while blacklisted. Later, he returned to America to direct such memorable entries as *The Caine Mutiny* (1954), *Raintree County* (1957), *The Young Lions* (1958), *Warlock* (1959) and *Mirage* (1965).

As to his blacklisting, Dmytryk told us: "I never could figure out which was the bigger crock—Communism itself, or the anti-Communist lunatic John Bircher fringe. Congress was, of course, so hell-bent on persecuting us curious souls who'd attended a few pinko-faction meetings or who had Russian- or Jewish-sounding names, that they never got around to weeding out many real Bolshevik villains. If there ever were many such monsters lurking amongst us, to start with. The real enemies were upstanding, all-American bigots and thugs.

"So I finked on some colleagues for no good reason other than to placate the Committee," Dmytryk admitted. "As if there were any hope of placating that mob. But that was the desired effect of HUAC—to divide and conquer, to turn us against one another—and I played right into their hands because I allowed 'em to intimidate me. Cost me some respect, too, and it cost me some self-respect, in the bargain.

"Truth is, *all* systems of government are a crock," he continued, "and the moronic notion of a Free World vs. some Godless Evil Empire is the biggest crock of all, calculated to make us fearful enough that we'll accept bogus heroes. All due respect, y'know." Dmytryk, a delightfully grouchy, outspoken maverick to the last, died in 1999.

CREDITS: Presented by: J. Arthur Rank; Producer: N.A. Bronsten; Director: Edward Dmytryk; Screenplay: Alec Coppel, from His Novel *A Man about a Dog*; Photographed by: C. Pennington-Richards; Music: Nino Rota; Musical Director: Louis Levy; Assistant to the Producer: Kenneth Horne; Art Director: Duncan Sutherland; Dialogue Director: Alec Coppel; Running Time: 98 minutes (U.S., 93 Minutes); U.K. Release: During July-August of 1949

CAST: Robert Newton (Dr. Clive Riordan); Sally Gray (Storm Riordan); Phil Brown (Bill Kronin); Naunton Wayne (Supt. Finsbury); Monty [Dog] (Monty); Ronald Adam (Opinionated Clubman); Michael Balfour (American Sailor); Betty Cooper (Miss Stevens); Olga Lindo (Miss Hampshire); Russell Waters (Flying Squad Detective); Roddy Hughes, Allan Jeays and Lyonel Watts (Clubmen); Christopher Lee (Policeman)

IN A LONELY PLACE
(Santana Productions/Columbia Pictures Corp.; 1950)

For years, Humphrey Bogart carried on a running feud with his boss, Jack L. Warner, chief executive of Warner Bros. This epic clash led eventually to the Santana-Columbia production of *In a Lonely Place*, which represents Bogart's finest job of work while away from his longtime home base at Warners.

By 1947, after almost a dozen years under Warners contract, Bogart had become, at $400,000 a year, the industry's highest-paid actor. Bogart was, however, something of a grump who protested most of his assignments and referred to Jack Warner as "the creep." Bogart was determined to break away, and so with his business manager, A. Morgan Maree, he formed a company to make a picture a year for Mark Hellinger Productions, an upstart studio.

Some of Bogart's better Warners pictures, including the hard-boilers *They Drive By Night* and *High Sierra*, had been produced by Mark Hellinger, a husky, hard-living sort who had labored as a crime journalist, war correspondent, newspaper columnist and radio personality. After leaving Warners as a first step toward launching his own company, Hellinger had made *The Killers*, *Brute Force*, *Swell Guy* and *Naked City* for Universal.

Bogart's new deal ended abruptly in December of 1947, when Hellinger died of a heart attack at age 44. Bogart and Maree then teamed with the writer-producer Robert Lord to purchase Hellinger's assets. On April 12, 1948, they organized Santana Productions—named after Bogart's beloved yacht—with headquarters at Columbia Pictures in Hollywood. Columbia contracted to release Santana's pictures and agreed to provide studio facilities for 25 percent of production costs.

Santana made five features in six years, all starring Bogart. The first, *Knock on Any Door*, had borrowed the able but rebellious young director Nicholas Ray from RKO-Radio Pictures. *Knock on Any Door*, which set sail during August of 1948, starred Bogart and introduced John Derek. Ray was the proverbial nervous wreck on the set, worrying himself sick over each day's work and seeking solace in alcohol and drugs. Bogart thought at first that Ray was crazy, but the artists soon found much in common.

Santana once again borrowed Ray for its fourth and finest production, *In a Lonely Place*, based upon a novel by Dorothy B. Hughes. The source-story concerns one Dixon Steele, a young, war-battered serial killer who preys on women around Santa Monica. By the time the tale

A tense interlude from *In a Lonely Place*.

had been adapted by Edmund H. North and scripted by Andrew Solt, it had undergone drastic revisions and was given the working title of *Behind This Mask*. It had become a Hollywood-on-Hollywood yarn in which Steele, now transformed to a screenwriter, was not a murderer—not just yet, at any rate. Solt called him "a portrait of a future killer." The role was no longer suitable for a smooth-faced player like Derek; it now demanded a cynical, middle-aged man with a lived-in face—Bogart.

Solt reminisced in 1982 that he was worried at first about Bogart's being both star and boss: "I'd had experience with star-producers. In the final stage, it was always the star whose personal interests had to be served... Bogart said, 'I have one very important request—something I absolutely insist upon.'

"So my inner voice says to me: 'Here it comes: the star's request that will ruin the whole thing.' But then, he told me about an old actor friend who was very nice to him when he had first started on Broadway: 'Now he is out here, struggling, living on canned beans, too proud to accept my help. I want you to write him a part in the picture—one that will give him a few weeks' work.'" Thus was created the pivotal character of Charlie Waterman, a boozy, down-and-out thespian.

The supposedly struggling actor was Robert Warwick, star of the 1922 play *Drifting*, in which the nervous greenhorn Bogart had a supporting role. At that time, Warwick was a movie topliner as well, starring for several East Coast studios. Although he had a superb voice for the newfangled talkies, he had been reduced to supporting roles by 1931, when he appeared in Fox Film Corp.'s George O'Brien Western *A Holy Terror*. Here again, Warwick proved helpful to the far-from-stardom Bogart, who had landed the role of a villainous ranch foreman. Warwick was actually working steadily in Hollywood at the time of *In a Lonely Place*, but only in lesser roles.

The role of Bogart's menaced lover had been intended for his wife, Lauren Bacall, who had teamed with him with great success at Warner Bros. in her first movie, *To Have and Have Not* (1945), and then in *The Big Sleep* (1946). She was under contract to Warners, and it is no stretch to imagine the satisfaction Jack Warner must have derived from refusing to loan Mrs. Bogart to her own husband. Conceding the round, Bogart sought out Ginger Rogers. She was willing, but Ray couldn't conceive of her handling the role and argued against it.

In 1948, Ray had married a blonde actress with an ability to project the insolent sex appeal that had worked so well for Miss Bacall. She was Gloria Grahame, as eccentric and talented as her husband and also under contract to RKO. Howard Hughes, owner of RKO, balked at a loan-out, but Columbia honcho Harry Cohn finagled Hughes into a deal: Miss Grahame was placed at the services of Santana for $3,750 a week, with an eight-week guarantee. The Ray marriage was coming apart by the time production commenced on October 25, 1949. The Rays managed to keep their estrangement a secret, lest the actress be replaced.

Cinematographer Burnett Guffey had been an outstanding second cameraman for a generation, working anonymously on such pictures as John Ford's *The Iron Horse* (1924) and *The Informer* (1934) and Alfred Hitchcock's *Foreign Correspondent* (1940). After filming *Cover Girl* (1944) at Columbia, Guffey was designated a director of photography, and for three years he did superior work for the studio's B-picture unit. He was elevated to the A-list category via his expertise with mystery lighting on *The Soul of a Monster*, *I Love a Mystery* and *My Name is Julia Ross* (1944-45) and *Night Editor* and *So Dark the Night* (both from 1946). Even then, Guffey's most eye-catching work during 1947-48 involved such moody films as *Framed*, *Johnny O'Clock* and *The Sign of the Ram*. He had done fine work on Santana's *Knock on Any Door*. After *In a Lonely Place*, Guffey moved ahead to many additional top-shelf pictures, including the Academy Award champs *From Here to Eternity* (1953) and *Bonnie and Clyde* (1967).

Composer George Anthiel had scored half a dozen movies, delivering a fine rhapsody of cowboy themes for Cecil B. DeMille's *The Plainsman* (1937) and the ballet accompaniment for Ben Hecht's *The Specter of the Rose* (1946). Anthiel was a colorful Hollywood character who, in his spare time, was a practicing psychoanalyst.

In basic outline, *In a Lonely Place* is quite uncomplicated. The complexities lie in the careworn characterizations and the brusque dialogue. Following a nightclub brawl, Dixon Steele (Bogart), a mercurial screenwriter whose renown has faded since combat duty in World War II, brings hat-check girl Mildred Atkinson (Martha Stewart) to his home to tell him the story of a terrible popular novel he has been asked to adapt. His neighbor, a struggling actress named Laurel Grey (Miss Grahame), sees Mildred leave. The next morning, Mildred's body is found in Benedict Canyon—thrown from a moving car after having her throat crushed.

Laurel furnishes an alibi for Dix. Police Capt. Lochner (Carl Benton Reid) is convinced of Dix's guilt, but Detective Brub Nicolai (Frank Lovejoy), Dix's war buddy, believes otherwise. Dix and Laurel fall in love, and she begins typing his screenplay. Their idyllic relationship begins to crumble under the weight of his violent temper. She soon realizes that he *is* capable of murder, and her fears are amplified when she learns that Nicolai's wife (Jeff Donnell) is afraid of Steele. When Laurel attempts to flee, the night before they are to be married, Dix begins strangling her. He is interrupted by the telephone; it is Nicolai, notifying him that Mildred's murderer has confessed. Dix, knowing he has lost Laurel, walks out of her life. (In the version originally shot, Laurel was killed, but this scene was reworked almost spontaneously as a brilliant afterthought before the cameras.)

Bogart's performance is at least the equal of his work in such more popular films as *The Maltese Falcon* and *Casablanca*. His Dixon Steele is arrogant, caustic, bitter and aggressive. No other actor could project rage and the potential for violence more convincingly. Even the love scenes have a threatening quality as his hands caress the face and neck of his sweetheart. His sense of humor is dark: "I could never throw a lovely body from a moving car. It would offend my artistic sense." These qualities are made all the more real by the equally compelling moments of tenderness with Miss Grahame, as well as scenes illustrating Dix's fondness for his agent, Mel (Art Smith), and a solicitous concern for Warwick's Charlie Waterman, who is shunned by everyone else.

There is a relentless buildup to the likelihood of a killing urge. The opening titles show Steele's ferocious eyes reflected in the rearview mirror of his car as it prowls the darkened streets. A convertible pulls up alongside, revealing a glamorous blonde actress riding with an unsightly man. A former sweetheart of Dixon's, she speaks to him, whereupon the man snarls at Dix to leave his wife alone, then orders Dix to pull over. Steele leaps furiously into the street and demands: "Why not right here?" The convertible speeds away. (This scene can only provoke a sobering onrush of genuine Hollywood melancholia: The unbilled bit-actress is June Vincent, who had been the acclaimed star of Universal's *The Black Angel*, only four years earlier.)

Steele arrives at a nightclub, where he insults a famous director and beats up an obnoxious second-generation studio boss who has slighted Waterman. For a while, we are allowed to see a better side of Steele, but his dark self emerges again: During a beach party with the Nicolais, Dix gleefully describes how Mildred's murder must have taken place. Then, upon learning he is still a suspect, he takes Laurel on a terrifying nocturnal ride over Mulholland Drive. In the wake of a collision, Steele beats the other motorist unconscious; Laurel intervenes when Dixon picks up a rock. Eventually, Dix lashes out at even the worshipful Mel—and ultimately comes close to strangling Laurel.

Lauren Bacall undoubtedly would have made a memorable Laurel, but Miss Grahame proved an excellent foil, her coolness standing in fine dramatic contrast to Bogart's nervous energy. Miss Grahame was in fact a more realistic, down-to-earth performer than the glamorous Miss Bacall, a definite advantage in putting across so hard-edged a story. She reminds one of Miss Bacall when she dodges Dix after telling him that she likes his face, remarking: "I said I *liked* it. I didn't say I wanted to *kiss* it." There is sturdy support from Lovejoy and Jeff Donnell, who plays Lovejoy's frightened wife. Both continued to do well in movies, and even better on television. Carl Benton Reid (without his trademark mustache) makes an unyielding Nemesis. In tense scenes with Miss Grahame, Reid's close-ups are lighted for diabolical effect, with eyes and lower face veiled in deep shadows.

Martha Stewart, an RCA Victor recording artist and former dancer on Broadway, does a neat job of setting forth the pretty and hopelessly naïve murder victim, who describes an epic as "a picture that's real long and has a lot of things going on." Adding to the gathering darkness with expert performances are Morris Ankrum, as a crass but successful director, and Steven Geray as the boss of a Sunset Strip nightclub. The nightspot's real owner, Mike Romanoff, appears in a bit part.

In a key piano-bar sequence, the lovely, deep-voiced Hadda Brooks plays and sings "I Hadn't Anyone 'til You," a moody number written for the occasion by the British-born bandleader Ray Noble. Miss Brooks recalled that Nicholas Ray became angry when she experienced difficulty in lip-synching the song, which she had recorded separately. (The problem is evident in the close-ups.)

Art Smith lends a touching quality as Dix's gentle, protective agent, a role said to be based upon the studio executive and agent Sam Jaffe. It is the agent alone who really understands his client. An active Communist, Smith later was blacklisted during the purges of the House Committee on Un-American Activities.

A real asset is Robert Warwick's portrayal of the alcoholic ex-star, who maintains his dignity even while tottering about in a stupor. The imposing, long-neglected actor is superb, displaying a profound Shakespearean voice as well as a marvelous range of body language and facial expression. The mutual respect between Bogart and Warwick is evident, and their shared scenes do much to impart a warm dimension to Steele.

One unnervingly strange passage finds Laurel receiving a massage from a grim, mountainous woman named Martha (Ruth Gillette), who commands, "Now, turn over," as the scene opens. Laurel settles down, face close to the camera, her chin resting on her arms, while Martha hovers eerily. The low camera angle keeps Laurel's body out of sight. Martha is as explicit a lesbian as the censors of the day would permit. Trying to pry Laurel away from Steele, the masseuse mentions Dix's former lover, Frances Randolph (played by Alice Talton): "I used to take care of her," Martha declares. "He beat her up, broke her nose. Someday, you'll realize who your friend is. I only hope it isn't too late... You'll beg me to come back when you're in trouble—and you will, angel, because you don't have anybody else."

Nicholas Ray and Gloria Grahame separated in November, about halfway through production, just as the climactic murder scene was scheduled to be filmed (out of continuity, of course). Realizing that Bogart and Lord would be horrified at the effect the split could have on their picture, Ray pretended that he needed to sleep in a dressing room for the remainder of production so he could work late on preparations. Miss Grahame cooperated with the charade, and no one suspected. Amid this tense atmosphere, the murder sequence was filmed as written, beginning on November 15: When Dix realizes that Laurel is about to run away, he pushes her onto the bed. Morning finds Dix hunched over his typewriter. The cleaning woman, the masseuse and a deliveryman all arrive and go past Dix into the bedroom. Somebody screams. Brub Nicolai and a crew of policemen arrive. Dix says, "Just a second, Brub. I'm finished." Brub finds Laurel's corpse. He takes the paper out of the typewriter and reads the last lines of Dix's script, echoing words Dix had spoken to Laurel:

> I was born when she kissed me, I died when she left me,
> I lived a few weeks while she loved me.

Ray, under the stress of his own situation, was horrified at the scene he had helped to write. When it had been completed, he sent most of the personnel away and reshot the last part of the sequence. In this partly rewritten, partly improvised version, Dix is strangling Laurel when the ringing of a telephone interrupts him. (Or *is* he? Actually, he appears to wilt an instant before the phone rings.) The caller is Brub, reporting that Henry Kesler (Jack Reynolds), Mildred's sweetheart, has confessed to her murder and tried to commit suicide. (The killer's name is also that of the associate producer.) Lochner takes the phone and begins to apologize. Dix, emotionally destroyed, hands the telephone to Laurel, saying, "A man wants to apologize to you." She listens and replies, "Yesterday, this would have meant so much to us. Now it doesn't matter. It doesn't matter at all." In extreme close-up, as she watches Steele go down the stairs, Laurel murmurs tearfully, "I lived a few weeks while you loved me. Goodbye, Dix." The picture fades out on a high-angle view of Dix walking across the desolate patio.

Lord and Bogart decided they preferred Ray's revised ending and retained it for the final cut.

Burnett Guffey's photography is more subtle than his work on previous film noir assignments. There is less of the customary shadow-play, with fewer hard-lighted close-ups and low angles. The picture's scenes of domestic normalcy are also rendered in a more naturalistic lighting, a look that differs little from the style favored for lighthearted romantic movies. The film is made up entirely of carefully designed scenes with little camera movement to alter the compositions, few moves by the actors, no fancy crane or dolly shots, and only an occasional pan to follow action. The compositions have almost a subliminal effect, becoming increasingly claustrophobic as they mirror Laurel's fears of confinement—of being pent up in cars and tiny rooms, or imprisoned by the alternately loving and menacing hands of Dix and the suffocating attentions of Martha and Lochner.

Guffey admirably captures the gray look of dawn in Beverly Hills when Dix leaves the police station—and where else could there be a precinct house that looks like the Taj Mahal?—and roams the streets. These scenes have a magical quality reminiscent of the celebrated early-morning sequence in *The Lost Weekend* (1946).

Anthiel's music adds considerably to the prevailing atmosphere of unease. Most of it is based on a smooth, emotionally neutral leitmotif that sometimes gives way to a bittersweet love theme. The latter is introduced meaningfully when Dix and Mildred are talking on the patio between the apartments. As Laurel enters and walks between them, the love theme rises, effectively signaling the end of any plans Dix might have had for Mildred. It is a key moment, thanks largely to Antheil. The two themes are sometimes combined and enlarged upon for dramatic effect, most notably as a terrifying accompaniment for the wild ride over Mulholland Drive.

To best appreciate *In a Lonely Place*, it is necessary to harbor some understanding of the enigmatic Steele. Most of us know someone rather like him—a person who is generally disliked or even feared, but is understood and defended by a few real friends. The long-suffering Mel expresses it well when Laurel tells him, "Dix doesn't act like a normal person. I'm *scared* of him, I don't *trust* him. Why can't he be like *other* people?"

Mel replies angrily: "'Like other people!' Would you have liked him if he was like everybody else? You *knew* he was always dynamite! He's *Dixon Steele*—and if you want him, you've got to take it all, the bad with the good!"

CREDITS: Producer: Robert Lord; Associate Producer: Henry S. Kesler; Director: Nicholas Ray; Screenplay: Andrew Solt; Adapted by: Edmund H. North; Based upon: Dorothy B. Hughes' Novel; Photographed by: Burnett Guffey; Musical Score: George Antheil; Musical Director: Morris W. Stoloff; Song: "I Hadn't Anyone 'til You," by: Ray Noble; Art Director: Robert Peterson; Set Decor: William Kiernan; Film Editor: Viola Lawrence; Sound: Howard Fogetti, Western Electric Recording; Costumes: Jean Louis; Makeup: Clay Campbell; Hair Stylist: Helen Hunt; Technical Advisor: Rodney Amateau; Assistant Director: Earl Bellamy; Special Effects: Don Glouner; Operative Cameraman: Gert Anderson; Gaffer: William Johnson; Grip: Walter Meins; Stills: Irving Lippman; Script Supervisor: Charlsie Bryant; Running Time: 94 Minutes; Released: May 17, 1950

CAST: Humphrey Bogart (Dixon Steele); Gloria Grahame (Laurel Gray); Frank Lovejoy (Brub Nicolai); Carl Benton Reid (Capt. Lochner); Art Smith (Mel Lippman); Jeff Donnell (Sylvia Nicolai); Martha Stewart (Mildred Atkinson); Robert Warwick (Charlie Waterman); Morris Ankrum (Lloyd Barnes); William Ching (Ted Barton); Steven Geray (Paul); Hadda Brooks (Singer); Alice Talton (Frances Randolph); Jack Reynolds (Henry Kesler); Ruth Warren (Effie); Ruth Gillette (Martha); Guy Beach (Swan); Lewis Howard (Junior); Mike Romanoff (Mike); Arno Frey (Joe); Pat Barton (Second Hat Check Girl); Cosmo Sardo (Bartender); Don Hamin (Young Driver); George Davis (Waiter); Billy Gray (Young Boy); Melinda Erickson (Tough Girl); Jack Jahries (Officer); David Bond (Dr. Richards); Myron Healey (Post Office Clerk); Robert Lowell (Airline Clerk); June Vincent (Actress); Charles Cane (Her Husband); Robert Davis (Janitor); and Frank Marlowe, John Mitchum, Tony Layng, Laura K. Brooks, Jack Santoro, Evelyn Underwood, Allen Pinson, Oliver Cross

M

(Superior Films/Columbia Pictures Corp.; 1951)

Comparatively few remakes stand out in an industry where such pictures are most often gratuitous. William Wyler's studied avoidance of schmaltz in *Hell's Heroes* (1930)—drawn from a sentimental yarn by Peter B. Kyne—sets it apart from not only two adaptations before but also three after. John Huston weighed in formidably as a director in 1941 with the third filming in just over a decade of *The Maltese Falcon*, perceiving that Dashiell Hammett's exercise in detection and deception must possess grander possibilities than could be found in either Roy Del Ruth's *The Maltese Falcon* (a.k.a. *Dangerous Female*; 1931) or William Dieterle's *Satan Met a Lady* (1936). Henry Hathaway delivered in 1951 a Western that invites regard as a classic, *Rawhide* (later shown as *Desperate Siege*, to avoid confusion with the teleseries *Rawhide*), by rethinking the gangster yarn told in George Marshall's *Show Them No Mercy!* (1935).

In this light, a reappraisal of Joseph Losey's *M*, which came nearly a generation after Fritz Lang's imperishable German version, proves the remake to possess a distinctive vision that transcends competence. The reworked *M* was widely reviled and repressed in its day because of its explicit handling of the psychosexual subject matter—not to mention a controversy over the radical-left political bearings of Losey, writers Norman Reilly Raine and Waldo Salt, and cast members Howard da Silva and Karen Morley, among others. The remake was banned outright in eight of these United States and in seven foreign countries; censored into varying conditions of incoherence in those regions where it wasn't banished from view; picketed and railed against by people who, of course, couldn't be bothered with actually *watching* the thing; and, in general, made to feel about as welcome as King Farouk at a Passover Seder.

Such hysterics having lapsed during the long stretch intervening, the film has suffered from other forms of reactionary-ism: an inaccurate reputation as "almost an exact remake," and one prominent cheap-shot dismissal as "an extremely minor film." Which amount to so much film-snob hogwash.

There are, of course, fundamental elements in common with the original: The producer, New York-born Seymour Nebenzal, had worked with Lang in Berlin until the rise of Naziism provoked their departure during the early 1930s. The source-story remains that of Thea von Harbou, Lang's wife and collaborator of the lapsed glory days in Berlin. Each version makes its locale as crucial as its characters, and each version situates its murders off-screen. The *Threepenny Opera*-like gangland fellowship of the original is reworked especially well into an American milieu of uneasy camaraderie among thieves. (Both Losey and Lang reckoned that the remake was weakened by the fact that the underworlds of Berlin and Los Angeles were entirely unalike.) Once more, the voice of a mother calling for her missing daughter echoes in a stairwell, but in a larger sense the 1951 film is quite different, visually and emotively, from its predecessor. In both films, a tune is rendered by the murderer in anticipation of the next crime. In the Lang *M*, Peter Lorre whistles Grieg's "In the Hall of the Mountain King." In the Losey version, David Wayne plays on a pennywhistle an original tune written by the composer of the overall modernistic score, Michel Michelet.

It is that pennywhistle that opens the film, luring a girl named Elsie (Robin Fletcher) to become the fifth victim of a maniac-at-large. Inspector Carney (Howard da Silva) orders Lt. Becker (Steve Brodie) to get cracking on a list of newly discharged mental patients. One of the names thereon belongs to Martin Harrow.

Harrow (David Wayne), alone in his lodgings, fondles the laces of his victims' shoes, noodles about on his tin flute and shapes in clay an image of his mother. He admires the figure, then crushes it. In another tense sequence, Harrow stalks a bird.

Carney's investigation has disrupted the orderly flow of commerce within the city's criminal rackets. Mob boss Charles Marshall (Martin Gabel) engineers a vigilante campaign to dispose of the killer. Meanwhile, Harrow begins trailing a sixth victim. A blind vendor (John Miljan) recognizes the pennywhistle melody and associates it with a prior victim; he informs a mobster, who chalks the letter *M* onto Harrow's back.

Marshall's gangsters track Harrow to a storeroom within the cavernous Bradbury Building and take him to face a mock-trial. Harrow is assigned a disgraced lawyer (Luther Adler) as counsel for his defense but astonishes the massed crooks by begging for punishment. A lynching seems imminent, but the police arrive in time to take Harrow into custody.

This *M* finds in the intimidating vastness of Los Angeles as oppressive a setting as the Lang film had located in the claustrophobic stuffiness of Berlin. Much of the action occurs in the then-decaying northern downtown area among the tall, wooden apartment buildings that stood on Bunker Hill above the Hill Street Tunnel. A long sequence occurs on the since-extinct Angel's Flight, a tramway along a steep hill. Streets, saloons, cafés, streetcars and a barbershop are used in important scenes.

Losey's adventurous embel-lishments are countered somewhat by a loyalty to the letter of the original story. The departure has most notably to do with a film noir style, which translates into a near-documentary narrative approach and the physical darkness that Losey and camera chief Ernest Laszlo ascribe to Los Angeles. Losey gave much of the credit for the look of the picture to John Hubley, a cartoon animator who made numerous conceptual drawings.

Peter Lorre in the original *M*.

But the quality of reinvention hinges most strikingly on the title portrayal by David Wayne, who brought a more advanced age—at 37—to the murderer's role than Peter Lorre had, at 27, to the Lang film. Extraordinarily long scenes are deployed throughout, with the most remarkable being Wayne's speech before the kangaroo court; this hypnotic sequence was filmed in a single take, with an immobile camera.

A brooding sadness anchors both the Lorre and Wayne performances, planting in the viewer a forbidden sympathy at odds with the automatic response of revulsion. Lorre had conveyed an energetically controlled rage, which in turn defined for many years the cinema's vision of sexual psychopaths. Wayne's performance is more one of apprehensive world-weariness, his fatigue punctuated by unnervingly explicit surges of erotic pleasure. On his wall is a poster that asks: "Did you write your mother?" Shortly before his death in 1984, Losey told us that he envisioned Harrow as "a mother-dominated, closeted homosexual... He fancied himself on a divine mission, but was being crushed by a burden of guilt."

Perhaps because of the picture's enforced obscurity, Wayne never found himself typecast as a deranged sort. A 13-year veteran of the stage by the time he had come to film during the 1940s, Wayne found in *M* "an intriguing test of the outer limits of my range," as he told us. Wayne forged a career in both comedy and drama from this point.

(Peter Lorre's whereabouts at this time are significant: Lorre was back in Germany, at work on his only project as a director, *Der Verlorene/The Lost One* [1951], in which he plays a physician consumed by the killing urge. The paths of Lorre and Wayne would cross six years later, when both supplied pleasing relief from Jerry Lewis' tiresome star turn in *The Sad Sack*. And enough of the Six Degrees of Separation ritual.)

Strong tensions between the police and the underworld, combined with Wayne's dominant performance, create a triangle of inexorably shifting dimensions. Howard da Silva's boss cop is a study in surly efficiency, suggestive of a beefier and more driven Jack Webb. His counterpart among the lawless is the commandingly sinister Martin Gabel—an Orson Welles crony who became better known as a *What's My Line?* quiz-show panelist. Jowly Luther Adler is impressive as the disbarred, alcoholic lawyer. Steve Brodie makes a suitably rugged No. 2 detective. Among the gangsters are some wonderful character actors: Hefty Raymond Burr (pre-*Perry Mason*), sweaty Glenn Anders, the intense Norman Lloyd and the nervous Benny Burt. Veteran character man John Miljan creates a memorable presence as the balloon-peddler.

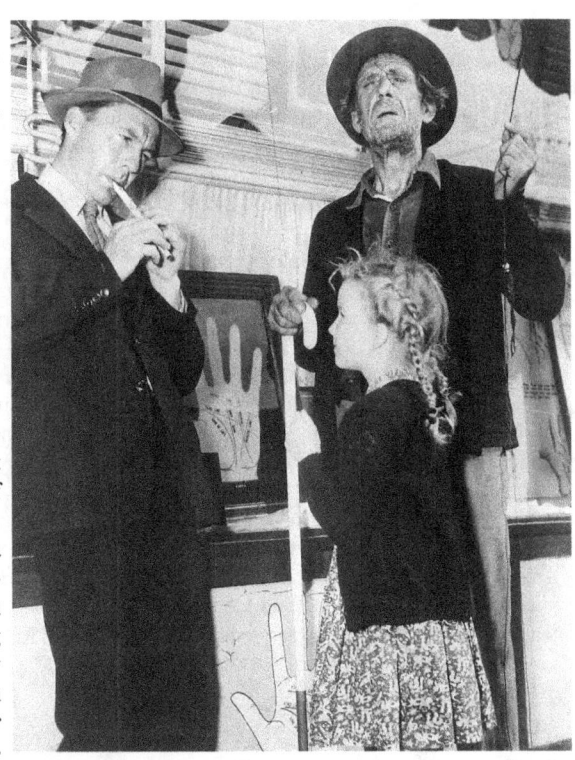

David Wayne, John Miljan and Janine Perreau in *M*.

Losey, a former drama critic who had helped in 1932 to make Radio City Music Hall a showcase for ensemble productions, studied under Sergei Eisenstein in Moscow before coming to the American cinema in 1938 as a specialist in short subjects. His string of notable stage productions climaxed with a 1947 collaboration with the playwright and film theorist Bertolt Brecht, on *Galileo Galilei*. That success led Losey to a shot at feature-film directing, with the social-tolerance fable *The Boy with Green Hair*. His five Hollywood pictures in three years—*M* was the third—averaged an efficient three weeks' shooting per title and signaled the arrival of a tremendous talent for pessimistic character-study drama, preoccupied with emotional vulnerability and the failures of society.

As *M* was coming into release, Losey was at work in Italy on *Imbarco a Mezzanotte/Stranger on the Prowl* when summoned to testify before the House Committee on Un-American Activities. He declined, reluctant to delay the Italian project, and returned to America after the shoot—only to learn that he had been blacklisted as a Communist. Losey retreated to Great Britain, and even there he was obliged to work under such pseudonyms as Joseph Walton, Terence Hanbury and Alec Snowden. His identity restored on *Time without Pity* (England; 1956), Losey gradually crystallized his interests and abilities into a pretentious, over intellectualized style that would serve nicely on such imaginative oddities as *These Are the Damned* (England; 1961), *Modesty Blaise* (England; 1966) and *The Go-Between* (England; 1971). This style, of course, also yielded such disastrous self-indulgences as *Boom!* (England-U.S.; 1968) and *Figures in a Landscape* (England; 1971).

Its hidden state and its inaccurate reputation notwithstanding, the Losey *M* has proved influential among filmmakers concerned with the portrayal of destructive madness. The film exercises particular bearing upon the overall tone and central portrayals of two pictures by William Lustig, the notorious *Maniac* (1980) and the more popularly well-received *Relentless* (1989). Shortly before his death in 1982, John Belushi told us of his plan to take on the title role in a third filming of *M*.

CREDITS: Producer: Seymour Nebenzal; Associate Producer: Harry Nebenzal; Director: Joseph Losey; Screenplay: Norman Reilly Raine and Leo Katcher; Additional Dialogue: Waldo Salt; Based upon: the 1931 Screenplay by Thea von Harbou (from Her Story) and Paul Falkenberg, Adolph Jansen, Karl Vash and Fritz Lang; Photographed by: Ernest Laszlo; Musical Score: Michel Michelet; Orchestra Conducted by: Bert Shefter; Art Director: Martin Obzina; Set Décor: Ray Robinson; Production Layout: John Hubley; Sound: Leon Becker; Re-Recording: Mac Dalgleish; Makeup: Ted Larsen; Production Supervisor: Ben Hersh; Assistant to Mr. Losey: Robert Aldrich; Editor: Edward Mann; Script Supervisor: Don Weis; Assistant to Mr. Nebenzal: Jorja Curtright; Running Time: 88 Minutes; Released: June 10, 1951

CAST: David Wayne (Martin Harrow); Howard da Silva (Inspector Carney); Luther Adler (Langley); Martin Gabel (Charles Marshall); Steve Brodie (Lt. Becker); Raymond Burr (Pottsy); Glenn Anders (Riggert); Karen Morley (Mrs. Coster); Norman Lloyd (Sutro); Walter Burke (MacMahan); John Miljan (Blind Man); Roy Engel (Regan); Benny Burt (Jansen); Lennie Bremen (Lemke); Jim Backus (Mayor); Janine Perreau (Girl); Robin Fletcher (Elsie Coster); Bernard Szold (Watchman); Jorja Curtright (Mrs. Stewart)

NIGHTFALL
(Copa Productions/Columbia Pictures Corp.; 1957)

Ever since the Price & Turner identity first cropped up in print and on the air, usually calling popular attention to undeservedly obscure films, we've found ourselves on the receiving end of any number of messages such as this one: "I can't remember what was the name of this movie, like, but it was about, like, this guy, y'know, and he was, like, out in the countryside, somewhere, and it was in the winter, like, and there was this other guy, y'know, and this other guy, he was tryin' to, like, y'know, grind up the first guy under this snowplow, and..."

Say no more. The picture is *Nightfall*, a neglected gem if ever there were one, that holds up among the noir-est of the noirs. The tale issues from David Goodis, as tormented an intellect as ever cast his lot with the sleazy paperback-novel racket of the post-World War II years. Goodis' book, *The Dark Chase*, is the basis here, as adapted by the prolific scenarist and all-'round filmmaker Stirling Silliphant and directed by former Val Lewton associate Jacques Tourneur. (Tourneur's near-perfect homage to Lewton, *Night of the Demon* [a.k.a. *Curse of the Demon*], also dates from 1957.)

Random misfortune and gathering paranoia, all heaped upon the burly but vulnerable Aldo Ray, combine to make *Nightfall* a feast of torments. Ray plays Jim Vanning, a commercial artist, who is on a hunting trip with Dr. Edward Gurston (Frank Albertson) when their reverie is interrupted by an auto accident nearby. Hastening to render aid, the friends are taken captive by the car's occupants, John (Brian Keith) and Red (Rudy Bond), who are fleeing the law after a bank robbery. Having slain Dr. Gurston and leaving Vanning mortally wounded—or so they believe—the bandits travel on but mistakenly take the doctor's satchel instead of the valise containing their loot.

John, who acts out his more violent impulses through Red, backtracks to pursue Vanning, who is meanwhile sought by the law in connection with Gurston's murder. A chance acquaintance with Marie Gardner (Anne Bancroft), promises a momentary relief, but Vanning grows to wonder whether she might be in cahoots with John. Marie finally proves as innocent as Vanning, and together they go on the lam. An insurance investigator, Fraser (James Gregory), also trails Vanning, but at length rules him out as a suspect in the heist and offers help.

Now, Vanning must return to the scene of the tragedy to retrieve the money from where he had hidden it. But John and Red have already reclaimed the bag. Red

The Definitive Edition

kills John, then commandeers a snowplow and attacks Vanning and Marie. Red falls to his death under the blades of the snowplow.

The initial perils are mundane and coincidental, which makes their escalation to a state of siege all the more unsettling for Aldo Ray and Anne Bancroft. There are no Dark Secrets, no crimes unpaid-for and no festering resentments, in Jim Vanning's past. Jim is already susceptible to self-doubt, however, desperate adventure or no. Just before the encounter with the killers, he had been searching for the right words to tell his murdered friend about an adulterous temptation posed by the friend's wife. Vanning is a plain-spoken, hard-working guy who happens to have been in the wrong place at the wrong time, and the film makes less of the pressing dangers than it does of Ray's futile struggle to comprehend. The brilliant distinction here is that Ray looks like a guy who could take care of himself plenty well, if only he could shake the "Why me?" obsession. Miss Bancroft is ideally cast as a tender-hearted and determined not-quite-floozy who might be the best friend Ray could find in such a situation.

Brian Keith, son of the distinguished playwright and actor Robert Keith, paid his dues generously as a bad-guy specialist before his emergence during the 1960s as a sympathetic leading man and character actor. *Nightfall* is Keith's richest showcase for villainy—a bully who prefers to let his brutal accomplice carry out the uglier deeds. The teaming with Rudy Bond, who plays Red as more-or-less apelike, foreshadows the pairing of suave Roy Scheider and loose-cannon Adam Baldwin in Eric Red's neo-noir gem of 1989, *Cohen and Tate*. Frank Albertson, in a welcome return to pictures after a decade's absence, contributes a winning turn as Ray's doomed friend. A haunting main-title song, "Nightfall," is crooned by Al Hibbler, a Duke Ellington Orchestra vocalist gone solo; Hibbler's blindness lends a poignant subtext to his perception of the concept of nightfall. (A rain barrel-resonant voice and a mannered, exaggerated-British delivery once prompted the Los Angeles jazz critic Leonard Feather to dub Hibbler "the Boris Karloff of the blues"—a peculiar moniker that bears mentioning within this book's context.)

Bond's rampage with the snowplow is a hair-raiser, all right, serving both to literalize the crush of dire happenstance that has befallen Aldo Ray and to provide a sustained episode of edge-of-the-seat terror. The sequence is as memorable as the wail-from-the-crypt business in *Murder by the Clock*; the corpse-as-store-window-dummy sequence of *Cross Country Cruise*; the hellacious first attack in *The Leopard Man*; and the vortex-from-beyond climax of *The Devil Commands*—even if one has forgotten the title or the greater dramatic thrust of the movie itself.

CREDITS: Producer: Ted Richmond; Director: Jacques Tourneur; Screenplay: Stirling Silliphant; Photographed by: Burnett Guffey; Sound: Ferol Redd and John Livadary; Music: George Duning; Orchestra Conducted by: Morris Stoloff; Orchestrations: Arthur Morton; Song: "Nightfall," by Sam M. Lewis (Lyric) and Peter DeRose & Charles Harold (Melody, Inspired by a Paul Whiteman Orchestra Tone Poem); Vocalist: Al Hibbler, Courtesy of Decca Records; Art Director: Ross Bellah; Set Décor: William Kiernan and Louis Diage; Costumes: Jean Louis; Makeup: Clay Campbell; Hair Stylist: Helen Hunt; Assistant Director: Irving Moore; Editor: William A. Lyon; Running Time: 80 Minutes; Released: January 23, 1957

CAST: Aldo Ray (James Vanning); Brian Keith (John); Anne Bancroft (Marie Gardner); Jocelyn Brando (Laura Fraser); James Gregory (Ben Fraser); Frank Albertson (Dr. Edward Gurston); Rudy Bond (Red); George Cisar (Bus Driver); Eddie McLean (Cabbie); Lillian Culver and Maya Van Horn (Women); Orlando Beltran and Maria Belmar (Mexican Couple); Walter Smith (Bootblack); Monty Ash (Clerk); Art Bucaro (Cashier); Arline Anderson (Hostess); Gene Roth (Barkeep); Robert Cherry (Man); Winifred Waring (Fashion Show Announcer); Jane Lynn, Betty Koch, Lillian Kassan, Joan Fotre, Pat Jones and Annabelle George (Models)

THE TATTERED DRESS

(Universal-International Pictures Co., Inc.; 1957)

Screen heartthrob Jeff Chandler, in a fan magazine pin-up from around the time of *The Tattered Dress*.

Jeff Chandler was in the prime of a tragically brief career during the middle 1950s, when his ruggedly handsome profile found the striking adornment of a prematurely white shock of hair. As almost a prototype for the reasserted stardom of Richard Gere during the 1990s, Chandler proved just right for morally compromised leading roles, with the air of heroism about him but little of the fiber: Chandler's best such turns came as a suspect romantic interest for Joan Crawford in the noir-shaded soap opera *Female on the Beach* (1955), and as a lawyer who must confront his own lapsed ethical sense in *The Tattered Dress*. Both issue from a branch of Universal-International run by the producer Albert Zugsmith, whose strange fusion of class-and-crass is in a broad sense definitive of the very climate of mid-century American moviemaking. With the Chandler-starrers, in their shrilly explicit struggles between human dignity and sleazy urgencies, Zugsmith was inadvertently warming up for what would become his *meisterverk* in collaboration with Orson Welles, *Touch of Evil*. Chandler was, for that matter, an early prospect for the *Touch of Evil* role that wound up with Charlton Heston.

Chandler serves *Dress* as a spellbinding lawyer named James Gordon Blane, all style and no substance, who arrives in a posh desert-resort village to defend a wealthy grouch, Michael Reston (Philip Reed), in a murder case. The generally well-liked victim supposedly had assaulted Reston's wife (played by Elaine Stewart), a slut-and-proud-of-it. Despite these odds, Blaine nails a not-guilty verdict by undercutting the testimony of Sheriff Nick Hoak (Jack Carson).

Hoak retaliates with an accusation of bribery against Blaine. The lawyer's estranged wife (Jeanne Crain) rejoins him in this crisis, and Blaine—who is innocent of the charge—accepts the truth about his failed sense of justice. Mounting a passionate defense of himself, Blaine is cleared. But his truer exoneration lies yet ahead: Carol Morrow (Gail Russell), the juror who had supposedly fielded a bribe, is revealed to be Hoak's mistress. Enraged, Miss Morrow opens fire on the sheriff at the entrance to the courthouse. Seldom has a late-occurring act of murder turned out to be so (melo)dramatically fulfilling.

Much like Richard Gere in the 1996 neo-noir *Primal Fear*, Jeff Chandler develops a streak of common decency rather late—and even then, only because of the sorry mess in which his contempt for society has landed him. Chandler continued through a procession of romantic, heroic and even Biblical assignments until 1962, when he died at age 42 of blood poisoning following surgery to treat a chronic back ailment.

A more deeply layered character, and of course the truer Human Monster on display here, is the beefy sheriff, as played with deep currents of genuine pathos and bullying bluster by Old Hollywood's perennial glad-handing buffoon, Jack Carson. Carson's expressive face, at this weathered late stage, is ideal for a self-appointed, secretly crooked Nemesis for Chandler's hot-stuff citified lawyer. As the embodiment of Carson's own bad karma, Gail Russell seems the soul of scorned vengeance in the abruptly climactic scene.

Most fascinating in the larger scheme is director Jack Arnold's use of the California desert vistas to render *The Tattered Dress* of a piece with his more celebrated—not to mention, blatantly fantastic—pictures, *It Came from Outer Space* (1953) and *Tarantula* (1955). Though hardly any conscious trilogy, these films establish in Arnold an understanding of the vast landscape as a place of healing, almost spiritual, magnificence. His implicit take on civilization, by striking contrast, is that it has no business visiting its petty corruptions on such natural grandeur.

CREDITS: Producer: Albert Zugsmith; Director: Jack Arnold; Screenplay: George Zuckerman; Photographed (Technicolor and Cinemascope) by: Carl E. Guthrie; Sound: Leslie I. Carey and Robert Pritchard; Music: Frank Skinner; Musical Director: Joseph Gershenson; Art Directors: Alexander Golitzen and Bill Newberry; Set Décor: Russell A. Gausman and John P. Austin; Assistant Director: Dale Silver; Editor: Edward Curtiss; Running Time: 93 Minutes; Released: March 14, 1957

CAST: Jeff Chandler (James Gordon Blane); Jeanne Crain (Diane Blane); Jack Carson (Nick Hoak); Gail Russell (Carol Morrow); Elaine Stewart (Charleen Reston); George Tobias (Billy Giles); Edward Andrews (Lester Rawlings); Philip Reed (Michael Reston); Edward C. Platt (Ralph Adams); Paul Birch (Frank Mitchell); Alexander Lockwood (Paul Vernon); Edwin Jerome (Judge); William Schallert (Clerk); Joseph Granby (Foreman); Frank Scannell (Cal Morrison)

A menacing Orson Welles in *Touch of Evil.*

TOUCH OF EVIL
(Universal-International Pictures Co., Inc.; 1958)

A policeman's job is only easy in a police state. That's the whole point, Captain. Who's the boss—the cop, or the law?
—Charlton Heston to Orson Welles in *Touch of Evil*

Universal's facile and often-invoked promise to swear off making B-as-in-budget movies was a great deal like the ease with which Mark Twain could give up cigars or W.C. Fields could forgo strong drink: "It's *easy*," as Fields would put it, appropriating a line from Twain. "I've done it a *thousand* times."

Universal had meant business, certainly, when it declined to release its own production of *The Brute Man* (1946), unloading that final starring picture for the tragically deformed Rondo Hatton onto tiny Producers Releasing Corp. But economic realities prevailed, and Universal-International—so rechristened in a merger occasioned by a pinched postwar economy—soon leapt back into the cheap-and-easy sensationalism. The company became ever more strongly identified during the postwar years with lowbrow comedies (including the *Francis the Talking Mule* and *Ma and Pa Kettle* series) and a new outpouring of horror-fantasy attractions including the *Black Lagoon* series.

It can only have been with B-product ambitions that Universal-International purchased Whit Masterson's lurid paperback novel, *Badge of Evil*. The assignment of the property to producer Albert Zugsmith's slate, however, bespoke a somewhat higher ambition. U-I had once again sworn off making the B-unit programmers, but the studio kept Zugsmith busy in a cautiously bigger-budget category because the former publisher and broadcaster specialized in lucrative exploitation pictures. These made money because of their startling qualities more so than any extravagant production values or artistic strivings. Most (though hardly all) of Zugsmith's pieces served in their day as potboilers. And certainly, such Zugsmiths as *Female on the Beach* (1955) and *The Incredible Shrinking Man* and *The Tattered Dress* and *Written on the Wind* (all from 1957) are nothing to shame a major studio.

Of course, a teaming of Zugsmith and Welles would seem as aberrant as a blend of Worcestershire sauce and ice cream. But Zugsmith intended to Make Some Serious Art here, insofar as he understood Art as opposed to mere Commerce. Given an almost-generous budget of just under $900,000 and a five-week shooting schedule, Zugsmith went all-out to gather a prestigious cast. He first signed Welles as an actor, thus spurring the interest of Charlton Heston, who was in the spotlight on account of his portrayal of Moses in Cecil B. DeMille's religious epic of 1956, *The Ten Commandments*. (Jeff Chandler had been a candidate for a pivotal lawman role, but Heston's greater keenness upon working alongside Welles landed Heston the offer.) Then Zugsmith approached the increasingly popular Janet Leigh. Heston okayed Paul Monash's script, but he said his commitment would hinge upon who was chosen to direct. Then, Heston dropped the hint that Welles himself was a pretty fair director.

Now, Welles had not directed a movie in the United States since Republic Pictures' troubled production of *Macbeth* in 1948. Welles had recently returned from Europe to produce *King Lear* on Broadway and was intent upon re-establishing himself in American cinema. Zugsmith recalled that Welles asked him what pending project had the weakest screenplay; the producer replied that it probably was *Badge of Evil*. Welles said he would direct the picture if he could have two weeks to rewrite the script. Zugsmith gave Welles the writer-director job—without extra pay for the scripting chore—as manipulative leverage to cinch Heston and Leigh.

Welles changed the locale from San Diego to the fictitious border town of Los Robles, a decayed dumping ground for the scum of the earth. The book's hero, an Anglo detective with a Mexican wife, became lantern-jawed Mike Vargas (Heston), chairman of the Pan-American Narcotics Commission, whom we meet as he is honeymooning with his Anglo bride, Susan (Leigh). The Latinate role works for Heston because the character, as reconceived by Welles, has been thoroughly Americanized in the course of his career—and because of "a strategic bronzing I received, courtesy of the makeup department," as Heston told us. "Max Factor's Egyptian 24, I believe it was, and a darkening of the hair."

Mr. and Mrs. Vargas are walking on the U.S. side of the border when they see a millionaire and a blonde stripper blasted to smithereens by a car bomb. Vargas unofficially joins a famed American police captain, Hank Quinlan (Welles), and Quinlan's worshipful assistant, Pete Menzies (Joseph Calleia), in the sleuthing. When Vargas realizes that Quinlan is framing a Mexican youth to take the rap, he undertakes to expose the corrupt cop. Schwartz (Mort Mills), an assistant district attorney, assures Vargas that Quinlan, an embittered bigot, has used manufactured evidence to nail numerous suspects.

Gangleader Uncle Joe Grandi (Akim Tamiroff), who despises Vargas, connives with Quinlan against the upstanding investigator. As Vargas becomes enmeshed in the quest, Grandi's goons terrorize Susan, injecting her with sodium pentothal to make her appear a junkie, and deliver her to a sleazy rented room. Quinlan strangles Grandi and leaves the body on Susan's bed.

But even the faithful Menzies turns against Quinlan after he finds the captain's walking-stick near Grandi's body. Torn by conflicted emotions, Menzies wears a hidden microphone and accompanies the now-drunken Quinlan on a nocturnal prowl. Vargas follows and records their conversation. Wising up to the scam, Quinlan opens fire on his sidekick. He is about to kill Vargas as well, but the dying Menzies manages to gun down Quinlan.

Instead of using Universal's backlot border town, Welles and art directors Alex Golitzen and Robert Clatworthy chose to transform the colorful oceanfront city of Venice into Los Robles.

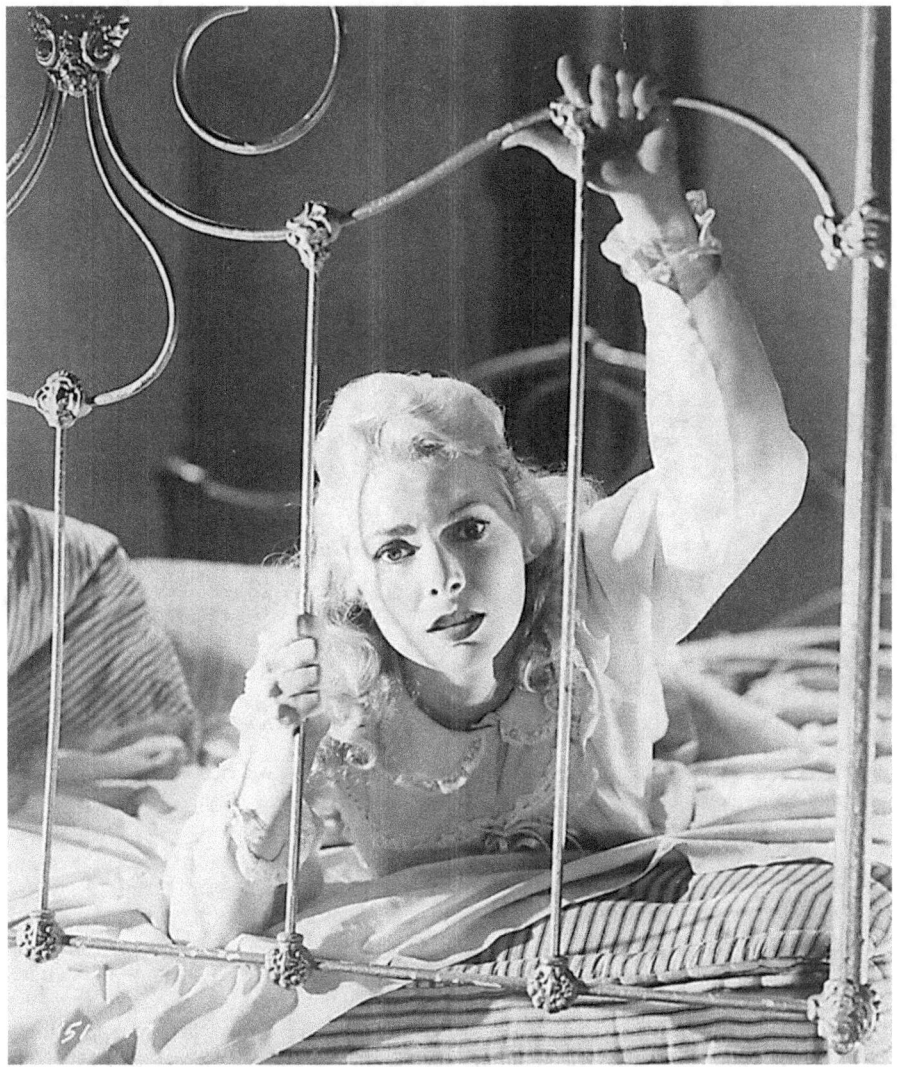

Janet Leigh is a frightened victim in *Touch of Evil*.

A beautiful panorama built to resemble its Italian namesake—complete with Mediterranean architecture, canals and gondoliers—Venice had fallen on hard times as a run-down crime zone. Because most of the exteriors were shot night-for-night, the city also posed a gigantic challenge to the lighting crew: There are many deep-focus shots down long streets past a landmark series of arches. To heighten the sense of place, technicians dumped trash everywhere to be swirled about by wind machines.

Russell Metty, who was on staff at Universal-International, had photographed Welles' 1946 effort *The Stranger*. The burly, cigar-smoking cinematographer was just the man to put Welles' wildest notions onto film.

The most remarkable feat is a lengthy opening scene, which Welles once told us was inspired by Alfred Hitchcock's more exhaustive use of extremely long takes in *Rope* (1948) and *Under Capricorn* (1950). This unbroken crane shot ordinarily would have been cut together from many separate shots. The action covers several blocks from an amazing array of angles, including

Charlton Heston and Orson Welles face off in *Touch of Evil*.

close-ups, low tracking shots, very long shots and bird's-eye views. It is further complicated by being elaborately night-lighted, and there is abundant detail and activity. Metty gave much of the credit for this display of virtuosity to camera operator Phil Lathrop, who soon became a distinguished director of photography in his own right. The camera fairly floats through the action, gliding in all directions, with nary a glitch.

The sequence begins with a close-up of a time bomb as its clock is being set. The camera swings up as the culprit looks to see if the coast is clear; pulls back as he runs to the right; and follows his shadow to a parked Cadillac convertible. The man deposits the bomb in the trunk and runs away as a doomed couple emerges from a nightclub. Drawing away, the car circles behind the building as the camera moves to a high angle. The camera then races far ahead of the car, swooping to eye level and turning back as the car draws near. Vargas and his wife cross in front of the car, and the camera closely follows them. The camera again moves ahead. The checkpoint guard and the driver chat with Vargas, congratulating him for cracking a case, while a passenger (Joi Lansing) complains of a ticking noise. After the auto passes, the camera moves in close as Vargas says to his new bride, "Do you realize I haven't kissed you in over an hour?" The explosion occurs off-screen, left. Only then is there a cut, to the Vargases' view of the shattered convertible.

Equally elaborate and difficult, but on a much smaller scale, is the scene where Quinlan interrogates a suspect in a tiny apartment, then plants dynamite to frame him. Heston recalled that the cast rehearsed during the night. By morning, Heston said, Welles and Metty had "laid out a master shot that covered the whole scene. It was a very complicated setup, with walls pulling out of the way as the camera moved from room to room [on a crab dolly], and four principal actors plus three or four bit players working through the scene." This single take covers 12 pages of script in almost five minutes, creating the impression of about 60 setups, yet somehow never calls attention to itself.

In another unusual location shot, the camera follows Vargas and five men into a building, where the investigator puts the others and the viewer, personified by the camera, aboard a tiny elevator. With its operator crouched in a corner, the camera records the shaky ride.

One of the most harrowing sequences is the murder of Grandi. The cramped room is barely illuminated by a flashing neon sign. Quinlan, a drunken ogre, pounces on the much smaller Grandi, and the fight rages all around the unconscious Susan. Garotting his victim at last, Quinlan drapes the corpse over the brass bedstead. A shock-value scene comes later, as Susan wakes and we see, from her vantage, an upside-down close-up of the dead man's contorted face and bulging eyes.

Most of the picture consists of hard-lighted night scenes with jagged, opaque shadows and, toward the end, a few strategically placed tilts. Daytime exteriors were done without fill lights. A few automobile interiors were filmed on the process stage, but most were done on location with the camera mounted on the car. The hard-edged style is broken inside the dramatically crucial setting of a brothel—the only place where the music is sweet, the lighting diffused, the shadows soft and the camera angles resolutely normal.

Welles brought in several friends and associates for major supporting roles: Akim Tamiroff, Marlene Dietrich and Zsa Zsa Gabor (whose fondness for Welles led them to accept guest-star billing), Ray Collins and Harry Shannon. Collins and Shannon portray, respectively, a district attorney and a police chief, glad-handing politicos who owe their popularity to Quinlan's success at nailing murder convictions.

Welles—his substantial bulk padded out grotesquely, eyes rheumy and heavily bagged, nose expanded—is barely recognizable. Ever embarrassed about what he called "this insignificantly small schnozzola of mine," Welles usually enlarged it with putty when performing. He makes Quinlan an almost completely despicable character, allowing faint provocation for sympathy, such as when the captain speaks of the slaying of his wife by a "half-breed," as he puts it, whom he was unable to bring to justice. (This is Quinlan's rationale for a comprehensive hatred of Mexicans.) Quinlan also takes on a more nearly human aspect while lounging within the brothel, where his venom subsides until he must return outside.

Many people today misperceive the Heston-Welles working relationship in light of a dramatically effective but patently bogus scene in Tim Burton's *Ed Wood* (1994), where a conveniently fictionalized Orson Welles (played by Vincent D'Onofrio) speaks disdainfully of Heston's involvement with *Touch of Evil*. In fact, the director was grateful for Heston's pro-Welles lobbying, and for the actor's immersion in character here. Heston is remarkably convincing as the idealistic crime buster. His exchanges with Welles are pointedly unpleasant, as when Heston remarks, "I don't think a policeman should work like a dogcatcher." Heston swings formidably into action when he tears into the Grandi boys and wrecks a saloon in the process. Miss Leigh's delicate beauty and vulnerability, combined with her witty handling of tart and defiant dialogue, set her well above the screen's typical lady-in-distress type.

Tamiroff sets forth ideally the vulgar narcotics kingpin whose dirty work is carried out by a corps of vicious, leather-jacketed nephews. Grandi is at once menacing and comical, qualities that Tamiroff brought to many roles. A short, rotund, wild-eyed schemer, Grandi wears a heavy toupee that is meant to look false: It continually goes askew. Tamiroff's Moscow Art Theatre accent comes through amusingly on occasion, as when he addresses Susan as "Mrs. Wargas."

Miss Dietrich, German diction intact, wears a black wig and smokes cigars as a hard-eyed madam. She initially fails to recognize Quinlan when he wanders into her refuge, which he had frequented in better days. She is by-and-large dispassionate, coldly informing her former client, "You're a mess, honey. You'd better lay off those candy bars," and then telling him, after consulting a deck of Tarot cards, "Your future is all used up." Yet at last, when she divines that Quinlan is in danger, she runs outside calling his name. She soon meets prosecutor Schwartz, who is looking down at Quinlan's corpse lying in a pool of oily water. "You really liked him, didn't you?" Schwartz asks the madam. Without apparent emotion, she replies memorably, "The

On the very night that Welles saw the studio's cut of *Touch of Evil*, he penned a 58-page memorandum detailing some 50 changes that he felt would improve the picture.

cop did, the one who killed him. He *loved* him. He was *some* kinda *man*. What does it *matter* what you say about people? *Adios*."

Miss Gabor, speaking Hungarian-tinged English, looks as glamorous as ever in her brief scenes as proprietress of the Rancho Grande, where the murdered girl had belonged to a troupe billed as Twenty Gorgeous Strippers. A number of Welles' other chums also leapt in for cameos. Billy House, a rotund old-time stage comedian, and Gus Schilling, one of Welles' Mercury Theatre players and a star of Columbia's two-reel comedies, play highway construction men. Mercedes McCambridge plays a sadistic lesbian in black leather who joins the boys converging on Janet Leigh in the motel while two girlfriends watch. Keenan Wynn and John Dierkes contribute unobtrusively to the oppressive ambiance. Joseph Cotten, as a grouchy, cigar-smoking medical examiner with a rube hat and a toothbrush moustache, shows up at the scene of the bombing. When the police chief comments that the big-shot victim had held the town in his control just an hour beforehand, Cotten adds: "Now, you could strain him through a sieve." When Heston's Vargas says he wants to meet Quinlan, Cotten growls: "No, you don't." Later, outside Susan's jail cell, he rants about "articles of clothing, half-smoked reefers, needle marks—you can *smell* the stuff on her."

More conspicuous is Dennis Weaver, then an obscure Universal contract player on the verge of television stardom, who takes an eccentric turn as the twitchy, half-witted night-manager of the desert motel. A raw-nerved religious fanatic, woman-hater and shrieking coward, the character is fascinating but overly flamboyant—almost a template for the edgy grotesques who would people David Lynch's weird-crime pictures of a generation and a half later.

Even among these performers, one man's sincerity stands out. Joseph Calleia, the veteran actor from Malta, makes Menzies the most realistic and touching character. Throughout the first three-quarters of the movie, Menzies frisks around Quinlan like a faithful dog—or even

Marlene Dietrich returns to the silver screen as a madam in *Touch of Evil*.

like Luis Alberni to John Barrymore's Svengali—barking at anyone who crosses his boss. It is heartbreaking to see Menzies' eyes well up as he watches Quinlan, influenced by Grandi, return to the bottle after years on the wagon. Even after he comprehends that his friend is a monster, Menzies tries to defend him, recalling how Quinlan once saved his life by taking a crippling bullet meant for Menzies. Upon realizing at last that he must betray Quinlan, Menzies becomes tormented beyond endurance. His agony is the truer touchstone of the film.

Principal photography wrapped within five weeks, on April 1, 1957, and Welles delivered a rough-cut version the following month. Musical director Joseph Gershenson assigned the scoring to Henry Mancini, who at that time was a staff composer, working anonymously in the shadows of fully fledged musical directors. Welles had requested what he called "musical color" incorporating Afro-Cuban rhythms and traditional Mexican music, mixed with contemporary rock-and-roll, most of it blaring from such on-screen sources as jukeboxes, car radios, cheap gramophones, loudspeakers and a player piano. The director demanded "sustained washes of sound, rather than a tempestuous, melodramatic or operatic style of scoring."

Mancini responded with a densely textured score that is launched by brief, jarring chords over the studio logo, followed by a percussive melodic pattern overlying a strong *Latino* beat that pulses through the title sequence until the explosion. The layered "washes of sound" continue throughout, always rhythmic and often as purposefully coarse as the visuals. The one lyrical theme is "Pianola," a lilting piece played in the brothel, which leavens those few scenes that lend Quinlan a hint of humanity.

Welles insisted that the incidental music should sound as raw and tinny as it would in reality. Toward this end, Mancini deliberately degraded music supposedly heard over outdoor speakers or in the motel by re-recording it from cheap playback units under lifelike conditions. Welles enjoyed bombarding his audiences with grating noises, a tactic that dates from his

A ceremonial gathering of punks.

Mercury Theatre of the Air radio broadcasts. (Moviegoers complained *en masse* about the screeching bird in *Citizen Kane*, and about the cracked phonograph record and persistently beeping telegraph in *Journey into Fear*.)

Touch of Evil propelled Mancini into the front ranks. One admirer was the producer-director Blake Edwards, who promptly hired Mancini to compose a jazz theme and incidental music for a noir-ified television series called *Peter Gunn*. The show was a hit, due in large part to the music, which Mancini told us he based upon a rumbling bass-clef piano riff used by a New Orleans barroom entertainer named Pleasant "Cousin Joe" Joseph. *Peter Gunn* begat a run of best-selling record albums from RCA Victor. The success of further Blake-Mancini collaborations—such as network television's *Mr. Lucky*, the big screen's *Experiment in Terror* and the *Pink Panther* features and one-reel cartoons—led to an extraordinary career for the young composer, whom RCA promptly dubbed "Our Man in Hollywood," promoting the shy and bookish Mancini with the same zeal it had applied to such more flamboyant artists as Elvis Presley, Van Cliburn, Harry Belafonte and Sam Cooke.

Welles originally cut *Touch of Evil* with editor Virgil Vogel. Dissatisfied with the result, Welles recut the footage from scratch with Aaron Stell, shuffling elements frantically, playing fast-and-loose with continuity and becoming increasingly unnerved. The narrative became rough-edged and nonlinear, with cross-cutting as disorienting as the labyrinthine patterns that D.W. Griffith had employed four decades earlier on *Intolerance*. True to form, Welles did not stick around for post-production. He and Tamiroff headed for Mexico to get cracking on an abortive movie version of *Don Quixote* that eventually would evolve into an Italian teleseries. (A patchwork attempt at reconstructing the feature-film project surfaced in Spain in 1992 as *Don Quijote de Orson Welles*.)

When Welles returned to screen the studio's cut of *Touch of Evil*, he found that some material had been dropped and several brief transitional scenes had been developed from scratch

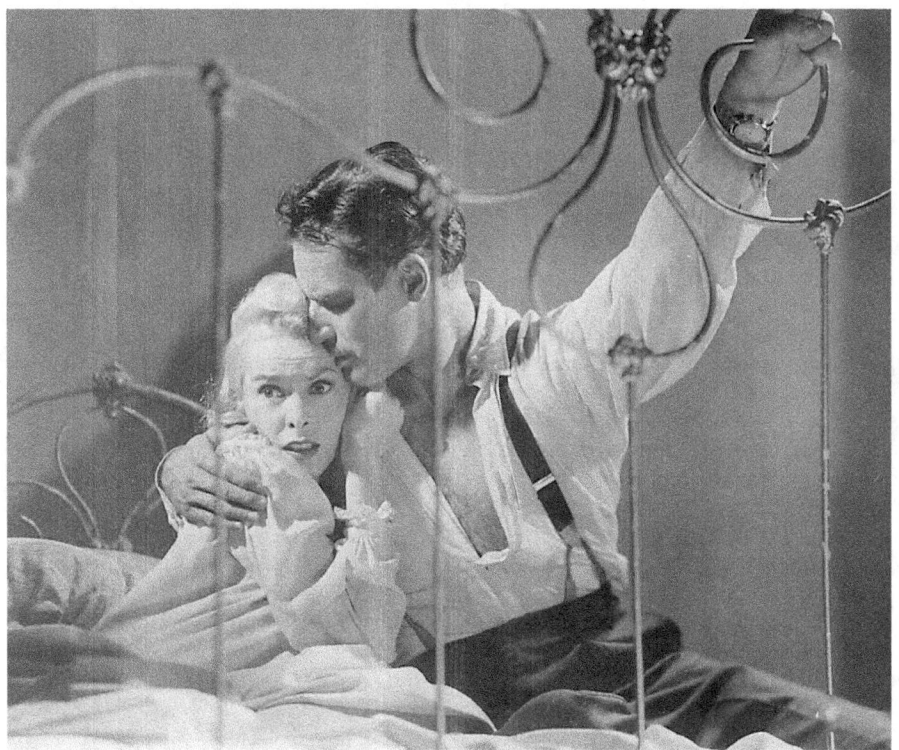

Leigh and Heston.

to lend a more straightforward continuity. The lengthy opening shot had become a title sequence, with credits superimposed. The added scenes were written and directed by Harry Keller and filmed in "less than half a day," according to Heston, who told us that the new bits of business "didn't vastly enhance, or particularly hurt, the film. They were there to help the progression of the story." Both Heston and Russell Metty maintained that Welles' concept was followed closely in the final cut, and that Keller's scenes did not replace any of Welles' footage. Janet Leigh has agreed, but as she told us: "Although the changes weren't blatant, unfortunately they were just enough to take away the film's jagged edge—which had been its entire point."

After a preview, the picture was shortened by about 10 minutes. It opened quietly, without a premiere or even much in the way of promotion. *Touch of Evil* was a box-office flop, but a jury of international filmmakers awarded it the Grand Prix at the Brussels World's Fair.

It was the last picture Welles would direct in the United States.

However: On the very night that he saw the studio's cut, Welles penned a 58-page memorandum detailing some 50 changes that he felt would improve the picture. This document is good-humored and friendly, although the sense of heartbreak bleeds through. Several suggestions were implemented. Most were not.

Then, after 40 years, *Touch of Evil* found itself recut—following Welles' memo to the letter. Sponsored by Universal and released during 1998-99 by October Films, the new edition was produced by Rick Schmidlin and edited by Walter Murch, a fine occasional director in his own right (as in 1985's *Return to Oz*) who as an editor earned an Oscar for his work on 1997's *The English Patient*. Bob O'Neil was in charge of picture restoration. The soundtrack was reconstructed under Universal's Bill Varney, a winner of Academy Awards for *The Empire Strikes Back* and *Raiders of the Lost Ark*.

Cinematographer Allan Daviau, who first read the Welles memo in the fall 1992 issue of *Film Quarterly*, credits UCLA Film Archives founder Bob Epstein with finding the missing footage. Daviau told us that Epstein had suspected as early as the mid-1980s that Universal must have a print of the authentic cut. Requesting to screen every available print, Epstein discovered a preview version containing the title-free opening shot and later-deleted scenes. This print supplied the footage required for the restoration *per* Welles' memo. (Daviau and Steven Spielberg had undertaken a similar quest some years earlier, to no avail.) A new digital restoration process from Pacific Title Mirage was employed to repair damage and decomposition in the source-negative. "One part looks as though the negative must have lain on the floor with people walking on it," O'Neal reported.

The serpentine opening shot is most strikingly altered by its return to Welles' concept. The overprinted titles of earlier editions (which still exist, of course) will pose an obstacle for anyone trying to absorb the dense concentration of detail, and even more of an annoyance for those few patrons who attempt to read the credits. (To this day, titles keep getting dumped onto opening sequences—and it's *still* a bad idea.) The restoration of ambient sound effects adds immeasurably to the vulgar atmosphere, and even prefigures the characterizations. The only regrettable aspect of the redone sequence is the necessary loss of Mancini's fine opening music. Film restoration, like the march of civilization, sometimes demands a step backward in exchange for two steps forward.

Schmidlin had done several years' research before the picture went back to the cutting room. The editing team worked for two months, incorporating both the release negative and the print of the longer preview version. "The film not only plays beautifully, but looks and sounds the way the Master himself wanted it to," Schmidlin told us. "That's what people really want from this film."

CREDITS: Producer: Albert Zugsmith; Screenwriter and Director: Orson Welles; Based on Whit Masterson's Novel, *Badge of Evil*; Photographed by: Russell Metty; Music: Henry Mancini; Musical Director: Joseph Gershenson; Art Direction: Alexander Golitzen and Robert Clatworthy; Set Décor: Russell A. Gausman and John P. Austin; Sound: Leslie I. Carey and Frank Wilkinson; Film Editors: Virgil W. Vogel, Aaron Stell and Edward Curtiss; Gowns: Bill Thomas; Makeup: Bud Westmore; Assistant Directors: Phil Bowles and Terry Nelson; Production Manager: F. D. Thompson; Camera Operators: Philip H. Lathrop and John Russell; Additional Direction: Harry Keller; First Screenplay: Paul Monash; Sound System: Westrex; Running time: 96 Minutes (1958 Release), 108 Minutes (MCA/Universal Home Video Edition), 111 minutes (1998 Re-Edit); Previewed during February of 1958; Released: May 21, 1958

CREDITS FOR 1998 RE-EDIT: An October Films Release; Mr. Welles' Requested Editorial Changes Produced by: Rick Schmidlin; Edited by: Walter Murch; Re-Recording: Bill Varney, Peter Reale and Walter Murch; Picture Restoration: Bob O'Neil; Consultant: Jonathan Rosenbaum; Assistant Editor: Sean Cullen; Supervising Sound Editor: Richard LeGrand, Jr.; Sound Effects Editors: Harry Snodgrass, Robert McNabb and William Hooper; Title Design: Deborah Ross, Digital Restoration Services Titles; Optical Effects: Pacific Title Mirage; Laboratory Services; YCM Laboratories; Negative Restoration, Cutting and Timing: Eric Aijala; Restored by: Universal Studios Restoration Services

CAST: Charlton Heston (Ramon Miguel Vargas); Janet Leigh (Susan Vargas); Orson Welles (Hank Quinlan); Joseph Calleia (Pete Menzies); Akim Tamiroff (Uncle Joe Grandi); Joanna Moore (Marcia Linnekar); Ray Collins (District Attorney Adair); Dennis Weaver (Night Manager); Victor Milian (Manolo Sanchez); Lalo Rios (Risto); Valentin de Vargas (Pancho); Mort Mills (Schwartz); Wayne Taylor, Ken Miller, Raymond Rodriguez (Gang Members) Michael Sargent (Pretty Boy); Phil Harvey (Blaine); Joi Lansing (Lita); Harry Shannon (Chief

Gould); William Tannen (Lawyer); Rusty Wescoatt (Casey); Dan White (Border Guard); Arlene McQuade (Ginnie); Domenick Delgarde (Lackey); Jennie Dias (Jackie); Yolanda Bojorquez (Bobbie); Eleanor Dorado (Lia); Joe Basulto (Young Delinquent); Marlene Dietrich (Tanya); Zsa Zsa Gabor (Nightclub Owner); Joseph Cotten (Police Surgeon); Mercedes McCambridge (Gang Leader); Billy House (Construction Chief); Gus Schilling (Eddie Farnum); Keenan Wynn (Bit Man); John Dierkes (Detective)

THE BIG COUNTRY
(Anthony-Worldwide Productions/United Artists Corp.; 1958)

The big news from United Artists in 1958 had less to do with the completion of William Wyler's massive new pageant of borderlands corruption—after nearly a year and a half of shooting and post-production polishing—than with the announcement that UA was poised to sock $2 million into the film's promotion. UA disclosed to the press only that *The Big Country* was "a multimillion-dollar production" (final cost of the film itself was $4.1 million, vs. an original budget of $3 million), but made patent what a whopping wad of cash had been set aside for exploitation. Star player Gregory Peck toured eight key cities to herald the opening, setting aside an embittered alienation from Wyler that had arisen from their combative partnership as producers of *The Big Country*.

The upshot was that *The Big Country* grossed $5 million in theatrical play, finishing 11th among 1958's top-performing box-office attractions without actually earning its keep. Burl Ives won the Best Supporting Actor Oscar for his show-stopping portrayal of relentless orneriness—which is the greater point of the inclusion here of this epic-scale, ostensibly pacifist, Western. Call it *How the West Was Scum*.

Ives is, of course, hardly the only menace on view, given producer-director Wyler's insistence upon presenting *The Big Country* as a polemic with the frontier myth of strength-through-violence. Ives is the most elementally ferocious, and the most memorable, of a memorably vicious lot that also includes Charles Bickford, Charlton Heston and Chuck Connors. In far hindsight, it turned out to be the bad-guy players who would remember *The Big Country* most fondly, where leading man Gregory Peck would recall the project more as "a heck of a trying time, emotionally and physically."

Peck is James McKay, a sea captain from Baltimore who finds himself at large in a hostile settlement on the Southwestern Plains. Bound for a reunion with his fiancée, Patricia Terrill (Carroll Baker), Peck finds himself confronted straightaway by her ranch's surly foreman, Steve Leech (Heston). Leech advises McKay: "I don't know as I'd wear that [derby] too long around here. One of these wild cowboys might... shoot it *off* you." More a promise than a threat, Leech's remark heralds an attack by Buck Hannassey (Connors). Buck is the son of Rufus Hannassey (Ives), sworn enemy of Patricia's father, Maj. Henry Terrill (Bickford).

Standing between Hannassey and Terrill is schoolmarm Julie Maragon (Jean Simmons), who owns crucial water-bearing land but refuses to sell it, certain that either rancher would use the real estate to destroy the other. Buck lusts after Julie, taunting her thusly: "I *like* a woman that's afraid of me."

McKay attempts to halt a Terrill raid onto Hannassey's land. The assault provokes an oath of vengeance from Rufus: "You set foot in Blanco Canyon once more, and this country's gonna run red with blood 'til there ain't one of us *left*!" Leech, considering the peaceable McKay unfit for Patricia, attempts to goad him into a public fistfight; McKay refuses, so humiliating Patricia that she rejects him as marrying material. Later, McKay and Leech slug it out in isolation—a marathon battle that settles nothing.

As the land-grabbing hostilities build toward an eruption, Rufus saves McKay from an ambush by gunning down his own son. The war is settled as Hannassey and Terrill go one-on-one in a mutually lethal showdown.

Wyler's running commentary on the insignificance of human struggles makes excellent use of the Technicolor/Technirama widescreen process. This pictorial splendor—often achieving a three-dimensional illusion, with scenic grandeur and elaborate stuntman choreography—is at the service of the argument that little matters in a society where brute force resolves all disagreements.

The persuasiveness of *The Big Country* lies in the historical record itself: Civilization *did* largely subdue that tribalistic element of warring lawlessness among white settlers. There is a compelling appeal in Peck's calmly heroic portrayal—which Heston has insisted "foreshadows Greg's work in *To Kill a Mockingbird*"—but even so, *The Big Country* remains an anomaly among Westerns: A good guy unwilling to deal with barbaric antagonists on terms they can comprehend is not likely to survive long enough to impose his more humane values. John Wayne would never have stood for such a bullyragging as Peck takes from Chuck Connors at the start of the film, and Wayne would have thrashed the beejeezus out of Heston in that dead-of-night slugfest. (Consider the fate of the gentlemanly stockman played by Terence Stamp in 1988's *Young Guns*.)

Peck's likable dude seldom even appears in sufficiently urgent danger. The climactic showdown between the vicious geezers is more inevitable than merely predictable, but other predictabilities abound: Chuck Connors' animalistic Buck Hannassey *will* attempt to rape Jean Simmons' level-headed schoolmarm, and Peck's romantic loyalties *will* shift from Carroll Baker to Miss Simmons, no *if*s or *but*s about it. Such a telegraphing of crucial developments can only be the result of on-the-spot dramatic contrivances forced by the lack of a finely honed shooting script. The truer saving graces are the degrees and types of villainy represented by the treacherous, almost feudal, land-grabber Charles Bickford; his impulsive enforcer, Heston; loose-cannon sociopath Chuck Connors; and ill-tempered but honest Ives.

"That meanness just came naturally to us, under the circumstances," Burl Ives told us in 1989. "Not because we were necessarily mean folks, I mean, but because—well, there we were, literally stranded on location, out in the Mojave, with a script that hadn't been completely written, a great director who also happened to be a dictator and proud of it, and the pressure to wrap it up and get back to civilization with a picture that'd already been hawked about Hollywood as a Great Film a-borning." Gregory Peck and William Wyler became estranged over a simple disagreement—Peck wanted a certain scene of his re-shot, and Wyler wouldn't accommodate him—that festered until they buried the hatchet nearly two years later during an Academy Awards ceremony. "I worked on the balance of *The Big Country* without speaking to Willy, except to take direction," Peck told us. "And of course, even after we shook hands and made up, I wouldn't have cared to work as equals with him again."

Then, too, Peck had insisted upon hiring Bickford and Ives. Ives got along well with Wyler—who since 1925 had forged a career of ticket-selling artistry and demeaning intimidation—by indulging the director's none-too-subtle manipulations. Bickford, who had clashed viciously with Wyler while making *Hell's Heroes* (1930), took the land-baron role only under pressure from Peck. In his 1965 autobiography, *Bulls, Balls, Bicycles and Actors*, Bickford ascribes to Wyler an emotional range of sullenness and rage.

Chuck Connors, Burl Ives and Gregory Peck in *The Big Country*.

"Willy liked those multiple takes of a scene," Peck said, "and Charlie liked to deliver a *fixed* performance, not varying it at all, no matter *how* many takes. Willy would tell me, 'I want Charlie to loosen up.' But all he'd tell Charlie was, 'I want you should do it *better*, Charlie.' So Charlie would storm off the set, cussing, have a couple of jolts of Jack Daniel's, and come back and do his scene exactly as he had been doing it all along." (Wyler finally modified Bickford's performance in the editing room, by jigsawing together bits and pieces of various takes.)

Ives said the original script for *The Big Country* "was awful!... The relationship between Charlie Bickford and me [in that version] was best described as a couple of old women, quarreling over the back fence." Ives mustered the gumption to complain to Wyler, who replied: "Of *course*, it's terrible. There'll be a new script up to you in five minutes." Ives said he grew to believe that Wyler was using such encounters to maneuver him into a mood that would be right for the character—"and his trickery won me an Oscar, so you *bet* I was grateful."

Connors said he found Wyler "scary, but brilliant... He told me, 'You've got the part, but I want you should grow a mustache.' So there I was, coming to this great filmmaker straight from a little bitty ol' Allied Artists picture—*Death in Small Doses*, it was called—and he says, okay, so I've got the part, but on a condition I didn't particularly care for. So what'm I to do?

"Well, I didn't want to wear a mustache," Connors continued, "but I grew it, anyway, because a supporting part for Mr. William Wyler would be a big leap upward from a starring part at Allied Artists. And so as uncomfortable as I felt wearing that mustache, it was right—because I was responsible for playing a real uncomfortable, edgy sort of character." Later, Connors received a backhanded greeting from the gossip columnist Hedda Hopper: "I'm not certain that I like you, sir... Nobody could do that part and not be really evil." Connors reflected: "That hurt me, I mean, to the *heart*! And yet, the old bat was really paying me a compliment."

Heston said he fared well with Wyler, for the actor came to the project with both big-league credentials and a reverence for the director's long range of accomplishments. They would work together in immediate follow-through, on the vastly more successful *Ben-Hur* (1959).

"The *good* thing about Willy, just to counterbalance a lot of the stuff about him that bothered people," said Heston, "is that the man had no vanity, himself. If an approach wasn't working, he was man enough to abandon it and try a new tack. [He'd say:] 'Oh, well—I was wrong.'

"Working with Willy, entrusting your abilities as an actor to his genius as an artist, was kind of like getting the works in a Turkish bath: You'd damn' near drown, but you'd come out smelling like a rose!"

CREDITS: Producers: William Wyler and Gregory Peck; Associate Producer: Robert Wyler; Director: William Wyler; Screenplay: James R. Webb, Sy Bartlett and Robert Wilder; Adaptation: Jessamyn West and Robert Wyler; Based upon: Donald Hamilton's *Saturday Evening Post* Serial, *Ambush in Blanco Canyon*; Photographed (Technicolor and Technirama) by: Franz F. Planer; Production Manager: Tom Andre; Assistant to Mr. Wyler: Clarence Marks; Art Director: Frank Hotaling; Set Décor: Edward G. Boyle; Costume Design: Emile Santiago and Yvonne Wood; Costumers: Eddie Armand and Neva Raines; Hair Stylist: Joan St. Oegger; Makeup: Dan Greenway and Harry Maret; Second Unit Directors: Robert Swink and John Waters; Second Unit Cinematographer: Wallace Chewning; Assistant Director: Ivan Volkman; Second Assistant Director: Ray Goswell; Second Unit Assistant Director: Henry Hartman; Script Supervisor: Sam Freedle; Location Manager: Carl P. Benoit; Titles Designed by: Saul Bass; Casting: Dorothy Witney; Supervising Editor: Robert Swink; Editors: Robert Belcher and John Faure; Musical Score: Jerome Moross; Music Editor: Lloyd Young; Sound Effects Editor: Del Harris; Sound Engineers: John Kean and Roger Heman; Running Time: 166 Minutes; Released: August 14, 1958

CAST: Gregory Peck (James McKay); Jean Simmons (Julie Maragon); Carroll Baker (Patricia Terrill); Charlton Heston (Steve Leech); Burl Ives (Rufus Hannassey); Charles Bickford (Maj. Henry Terrill); Alfonso Bedoya (Ramon Gutierrez); Chuck Connors (Buck Hannassey); Chuck Hayward (Rafe); Buff Brady (Dude); Jim Burk (Cracker); Dorothy Adams (Hannassey Woman); Chuck Robertson, Bob Morgan, John McKee and Jay "Slim" Talbot (Terrill Cowboys)

Afterword
Vincent Price and the Villains
That Still Pursued Him

Vincent Price, in a character study from the stage-touring years.

Once was never enough for those devoted audience members who sat through Vincent Price's one-man stage programs of the 1960s into the early 1990s. My cousin Vinnie's death in 1993 left a singular void on the lecture circuit. Whether discussing Old World artistic finery or Third World tribal sculpture, gourmet cookery or home décor, impersonating Edgar Allan Poe or Oscar Wilde, or holding forth on the rewards of unbridled make-believe wickedness, the *bon vivant* and fine Grand Manner actor crammed enough oscamazoola into a single performance to account for half-a-dozen shows. And yet he never ran dry of fresh material, with which he made each show distinctive. Price was a master of rapid-fire stream-of-consciousness rambles—"so I digress; so shouldn't we *all*?"—to say nothing of asides delivered in a stage-whisper tailored to reach past the balcony; a stand-up comic intensity to rival a Lenny Bruce or a Chris Rock; and an underlying *scholarliness* that was commanding simply because it had plenty to say and nothing to prove.

"You never seem to take yourself too seriously," I said to Vincent backstage one late evening in 1986, after he had completed one such presentation, an extraordinarily generous staging of his lecture, *And the Villains Still Pursue Me* (the title is a variant on that of a 19th Century melodrama), at Texas Christian University.

"Listen, Cousin," he replied, invoking our several-times-removed Welsh-Colonial ancestral kinship: "If a fellow takes his *craft* seriously and honors it by putting it to use, then it in turn frees him from the shackles of self-consciousness. Lenny Tristano said the secret to great piano-playing is to become so confident with your technique that you can let sheer *feeling* run roughshod over all that technique and never look back. Or as Oscar Wilde put it: 'Life is too important a thing ever to talk seriously about.'

"Now, most of the movie stars who have come up in the years since *my* turn in the spotlight, *they* take themselves so seriously that none of the rest of us should have to take them at all. And that seems to be the standard anymore. I've got my stories that I feel compelled to tell, and so where would I be if not for the audiences that seem to want to hear me tell them? I'm just grateful for the opportunity to get out there and run my mouth for an hour or two"—nearly *three hours* was more like it, in this instance—"and then to hear them calling for more.

"I'm still doing it, making the whistle-stops and blathering on about Art and Literature for as many people as seem willing to listen, because I like it. If the pleasure of doing so should even fade—why, *then* I'd quit."

On this particular occasion, during a period of severe conflict over his choices of movie roles, Price had delivered a spirited historical survey of dramatic and literary villainy. He had done the obligatory Q&A with an audience of perhaps 800 souls. He had taken a curtain call with a to-the-letter recitation of Poe's "The Raven." And he had taken yet another curtain call with a recitation of his rhyming spiel (and who dares to dismiss it as a *rap*?) from Michael Jackson's hit recording of "Thriller." He was fatigued but not beyond endurance, and he had received a stream of perhaps 200 well-wishers backstage in the university theatre's Green Room. He was 75 years old.

Price had long lectured on the appreciation of art when, during the 1960s, it occurred to him to ask an audience whether they might be interested in hearing about "my favorite aspect of my career, villainy." The response was sufficiently enthusiastic to convince him to draft the program he would call *And the Villains Still Pursue Me*, which of course he varied wildly from performance to performance. He never ran short of anecdotal material, but his presentation was so fundamentally scholarly that many colleges—his primary venues—offered class credit to students who would attend.

"I don't get at all bored with the monsterish business," he declared. "Horror abounds in life, and so why should we not confront it in our art?

"And I'm not the least bit disappointed that I'm remembered primarily for my horror roles. Boris [Karloff], Basil [Rathbone] and Peter [Lorre] and I—we all knew we weren't doing *Hamlet*, but we did know that we were making some marvelous entertainments."

One of Price's favorite yarns had to do with "this lady who comes up to me, while I'm minding my own business, which I do pretty well, and she says: 'You *are*! *Aren't* you?'"

"And I says, 'Oh, I don't know about that.'"

"And she says, 'Oh, yes, you *are*! *I* know all about you movie actors. You don't like to be recognized. You *are* Boris Karloff, *aren't* you?'"

"So, well, I says—and I'll swear, I'm *not* making this up!—'No, Madame, I promise you, I am *not* Boris Karloff.'"

"She says, 'Oh, come *on*! Why don't you admit it?'"

"And says I, 'I'm not Boris Karloff. Boris Karloff is dead.'"

"And she says, 'Well, then, who the hell are *you*?' But then she flounced off in a huff before I could tell her I was Christopher Lee."

The point of his mentioning this exchange, Price said, was this: "Fame doesn't matter, not one whit. It really doesn't."

What does matter, he said, is the savoring of life: "I lead a kind of a double life. I'm really a pretty nice guy, I think—very good citizen. Very normal and ordinary, once removed from the eccentricities of movie casting. I vote. Doesn't matter *what* you vote for: Just *vote*. And I'm a very good husband—have been, in fact, two or three times."

"But then, I really *love* villains, which is why I intend to do them some kind of justice in this *very serious* and scholarly lecture on villainy," he said, launching into a sustained discourse. "My own villainous assignments have connected me with some really wonderful people—Edward G. Robinson, Jimmy Cagney, Basil Rathbone, Peter Lorre, my dear friend Boris Karloff, and the list goes on—and I love the villains because *they* go on and on, really. They *last*. The hero, the minute he gets that double chin and the bags underneath his eyes and his hair recedes, he's finished. Not so, the villain, *no*! The more wrinkled and crevassed he gets, the better you're going to *like* him!

"Not to mention that the villain has this enormous appeal for the women. The ladies may try to reform the villain once they've captured him and married him—but it's the villain they want to marry.

"But we were talking about the dramatic thrust of villainy, weren't we? I think a lot of people don't realize how necessary the villain is. He is, in many instances, *more necessary* than the hero, because it is the villain's job to keep up the suspense. He has to be a man who keeps you guessing, and who keeps the good guys guessing, all the time.

"Sometimes, I've been cast as a red herring—*you* know, that means the character who's too fishy to be caught red-handed—because some know-it-all producer will say, 'Oh, yeah, put Vincent Price in it, and everybody will think he's the villain, and then we can surprise 'em when it turns out to be somebody else.' I did a picture one time, a big circus picture called—guess what?—*The Big Circus*, around 1959 or thereabouts, and Peter Lorre and I were in it. Well, once the mayhem started, everybody thought it was either one or both of us who'd turn out to be responsible. Because that's what, y'know, we *do*. But Peter and I weren't the villains at all. It turned out to be David Nelson, Ozzie and Harriet's boy—Ricky's big brother. Which *really* was a surprise, because *nobody* suspected *any* one of those Nelsons of being a villain, or even of being an actor! You've got to keep people guessing.

"It's our job to make the unbelievable, *believable*. To make the despicable, *delectable*. Now, in the sort of modern drama that we associate with Marlon Brando and Jimmy [James] Dean and all those other Method people, their job was to make the *believable*, believable. I suspect, however, that more often they made the believable, *unbelievable*. I never met a man in real life who talked like Marlon Brando, nor would I care to, because the style is unintelligible. And the job of the actor, especially the conflicted or villainous actor, is to make himself thoroughly *intelligible*. To make himself understood, for what he is trying to do. Which is to sustain the conflict, the suspense.

"I started my career playing some of the 'goodest' people known to history—like Prince Albert in *Victoria Regina*, with Helen Hayes. How do you play somebody who's just-plain *good*? Well, so I did some research and found, to my great relief, that there were certain elements of humanity in Albert—after all, he and Victoria had nine children—that included a hell of a temper when he'd get riled, plus the very humanizing fact that he was not all that nice to his son, Edward VII. And on human frailties, you can hang a cloak of character, a cloak of *acting*.

"One of the things about playing a historical character is trying to look like him. Prince Albert really did *fool* me. Every statue or painting, every tobacco can he's pictured on, he looks to be absolutely *unbending*! Helen's and my director in London kept saying, 'Mr. Price! Vincent! You know, you really do have the accent, you *look* like Prince Albert, but you're a *slob*!' I couldn't stand up that straight for any long stretches—I really *couldn't*.

"So I went over to the Victoria & Albert Museum, and it was there that I had one of those silly little revelations that hit you smack in the face when you're least expecting it: I asked the curator, there, I said, 'I'm an American slob—I mean, *actor*—and I'm playing Prince Albert on the stage, and I need to know: *Where did he get that ramrod posture?!?*'

"So I was shown to some of Albert's uniforms. They looked like he was still *in* them. I touched one, with permission, of course, and suddenly I knew why the old boy was so *unbending*: He braced his uniforms with a steel corset-like apparatus, like a backbone and rib cage, right from under his armpits all the way down his hipbones. So I thought, 'If it's good enough for Albert, it's good enough for V.P.'

"So then I went to this athletic store, y'know, and I bought one of those little half-corsets that middle-aged men wear on the golf course to keep everything from falling out. Slipped it on, laced it up, and—*voila*: instant Albert! Of course, I felt like I had a boa constrictor wrapped around me.

"And so I went back to the theatre, started to rehearse. Director says: 'Ah, *now*, Vincent! Now you have it. Now, you really *look* like Albert. You sound like Albert. You *are* Albert!'

"And so I said, 'Yes, well, thank you very much'—and passed out cold."

Price told hundreds of versions of his *Victoria Regina* story over the years, each consistent with the others in essence but each distinguished with subtle grace-notes of incident and inflection. As the scholars of folklore say: All versions are true, if you know all versions.

For his role as Oscar Wilde, Price said he "stepped into the character with as little artifice as possible. Orson Welles loves false noses, because Orson fancies his own nose lacking in character. I am perfectly happy with my own schnozzola, and apart from doing something with the hair and the facial expressions, my Oscar Wilde is essentially just me taking on something of Wilde's attitude.

"There was a time when actors were scared of certain roles," Price added. "In the studio days, they told you what roles you would play and then required you to do so. Oscar Wilde is a challenge, but hardly a daunting one. If I had met him in real life, I think I would have loathed him. Some people are terrifying because they are so witty."

Just as the actor declined to discriminate between the fine and commercial realms of art, or between the primitive and the sophisticated, he told us that he often felt hard-pressed to name a favorite among the villains he had defined—because he loved playing the crazed sculptor of *House of Wax* and the drug-addicted aristocrat of *Dragonwyck* as much as he loved playing the Shakespearean incarnation of Richard III. "From the classical realm to the popcorn cinema," Price said, "is too great a leap for most folks to take. And yet Shakespeare exerted as vast a popular appeal in his day as our movies do in *our* day. It is only the stuffy moderns who have taken Shakespeare out of the populist arena and stuck him up in the ivory tower. Which is *their* problem, of course, but it is *our* challenge as actors and arbiters of taste, y'know, to show our children and *their* children that Shakespeare can be as much fun as a good thrilling movie."

Price in *The Pit and the Pendulum*.

Apart for an overriding fondness for the overreaching villainy of Satan—"Beelzebub, Satan, Mephistopheles, Old Scratch; call him what you want, just don't call him late for Judgment"—and especially for the Satan of G.B. Shaw's *Man and Superman*, Price reserved a singular affection for Richard III.

"A terrible thing has happened to poor Richard, not to be confused with *Poor Richard's Almanack*," Price would say during 'most every staging. "This hideous little book called *The Daughter of Time*, by one Josephine Tey, a mystery writer who should have stuck to the perfectly respectable butler-did-it potboilers, pretended some years ago to have proved that Richard III was but a victim of one of the greatest hoaxes in history, that he wasn't a villain, oh, no, not at all. That he was a *nice guy*. Feh! Blamed it all on those dreadful Tudors, who of course were a pretty flawed lot in their own right but in fact rather put an end to Richard's epic troublemaking. A terribly influential treatise—emphasis on the *terrible*." (Josephine Tey often is hailed, backhandedly, as a mystery writer for people who despise mysteries. In other words: Why bother? *The Daughter of Time* concerns a police inspector who becomes fascinated by an official portrait of King Richard III and concludes that such a pleasant-looking man could never have committed all those dreadful deeds. As Vincent Price put it on another occasion: "What a crock!")

"But before all these new-made geniuses started trying to iron the kinks out of our man Richard's deliciously bad reputation, Shakespeare, that extraordinary genius of so few short centuries ago, posed the question without prejudice: Was Richard a villain, or *was*n't he? Now, there's an extraordinary scene in Shakespeare's *Richard III* where—right on the eve of the Battle of Bosworth—Richard is trying to catch a few winks and, suddenly, the ghosts of all those people he has murdered on the way to the throne appear to him: the little princes, smothered to death; Clarence, drowned in his favorite variety of wine; Buckingham, Richard's best friend, beheaded. And so Buckingham's ghost tells him, "Dream on, Richard. Dream on of bloody deeds and death... "

"Whereupon, of course, Richard wakes, telling himself—and let's condense things a tiny bit, here, shall we?— 'Alack, I love myself. Wherefore... Oh, no! Alas, I rather hate myself, for hateful deeds... My conscience hath a thousand sev'ral tongues, and ev'ry tongue brings in a sev'ral tale, and every tale condemns me for a villain... There is no creature loves me, and if I die no soul will pity me. And wherefore should they, since that I myself find in myself no pity to myself?'

"And there you have it," Price said. "*My* kind of villain. And so why the *blazes* can't these eggheads and revisionists leave him alone for all the rest of us to enjoy?!"
—Michael H. Price
From Newspaper Articles
Spanning 1974-1986

About the Authors

George E. Turner (1925-1999) and Michael H. Price first assembled *Human Monsters* during 1977-80 as a villain-centric sequel to the first edition of their watershed genre study, *Forgotten Horrors*. The demise of their original publishing-house and the peculiar disappearance of the original typescript left *Human Monsters* orphaned until 1995-96, when a reconstructed interim edition appeared. Times more recent have seen more direct sequels to *Forgotten Horrors*—including a revamped *Forgotten Horrors: The Definitive Edition* and (not to put too fine a point on it) additional *Forgotten Horrors* collections as well as a posthumous expansion of Turner's *Spawn of Skull Island*, all from Luminary Press and Midnight Marquee Press. When it proved necessary to cannibalize several sections of *Human Monsters* for the newer *Forgotten* volumes, Mike Price overhauled this survey of moving-picture villainy with additional materials compiled during his long-running association with Turner.

Michael H. Price served as an apprentice to George Turner during the preparation of Turner's seminal film-history book, *The Making of King Kong*, during 1968-75. Their numerous collaborations began in earnest during 1975-79 with the development of the *Forgotten Horrors* project. Combining Turner's rough notes and partial manuscripts with his own continuing research, Price has carried on with this revamp of *Human Monsters* while preparing subsequent entries in the *Forgotten Horrors* series and retooling *The Making of King Kong* into the revised and expanded *Spawn of Skull Island*. Price is founding president of Texas' Lone Star Film Festival, a lecturer and programmer for the Amon Carter Museum and the Modern Art Museum of Fort Worth, and critic-at-large with *The Business Press* of Fort Worth. As a recording artist, engineer and producer, Price has delivered such roots-music albums as *The Self-Righteous Bros.* (2003; with guitarist/vocalist Greg Jackson), *Cemetery Toons* (2001), *From Hell to Texas* (2000), and three volumes of *Bruton & Price Swingmasters Revue* (1995-2003; with guitarist Sumter Bruton). Price also contributes the occasional scrofulous novelty to syndicated radio's TM Century Comedy Network and *The Dr. Demento Show*.

George Eugene Turner moved from prominence as a Texas newspaperman to an internationally distinguished career in Hollywood as a cartoon animator, special-effects and scenic-design technician, storyboard artist, occasional character actor and scenarist and historian-in-residence at the American Society of Cinematographers. Turner's movie-town work includes the main-title sequence of Carl Reiner's *Dead Men Don't Wear Plaid*; the storyboarding and on-location directing of many episodes of network television's *Friends*; and a starring role in the European-made 70mm superscreen horror picture, *Dangling Death*. Turner had begun work on *Forgotten Horrors 2, et Seq.*, shortly before his death.

Also by Michael H. Price & George E. Turner:

Spawn of Skull Island
Forgotten Horrors: The Definitive Edition
Forgotten Horrors 2: Beyond the Horror Ban
Forgotten Horrors 3: Dr. Turner's House of Horrors (with John Wooley)
Southern-Fried Homicide (with John Wooley et al.)
Aw-Shucks Suspense Stories: Mo' Southern-Fried Homicide
V.T. Hamlin's Collected Alley Oop, Vols. No. 2 & 3
The Cinema of Adventure, Romance & Terror
The Spider (with Timothy Truman et al.)
Roy Crane's Collected Wash Tubbs & Captain Easy, Vol. No. 10
Al Capp's Collected Li'l Abner, Vol. No. 6
Forgotten Horrors: Early Talkie Chillers from Poverty Row (Two Prior Editions)

Also by Michael H. Price:
Forgotten Horrors IV: Dreams That Money Can Buy
   (In Preparation, with John Wooley)
Fishhead (with Irvin S. Cobb and Mark Evan Walker)
The Screen Archives/Screen Classics Series of Original Soundtrack Albums:
   HUK! — Kronos — Tokyo File 212 — The Big Country
   The Proud Rebel — The Wild Bunch
A Century of Fantastic Cinema
Selected Volumes in the Midnight Marquee Actors Series (Contributing Author)
It's Christmas Time at the Movies (Contributing Author)
Lex Eicon and the Numerologist (with Jerome McDonough)
The A-to-Z Encyclopedia of Serial Killers (Contributing Illustrator)
Krime Duzzin't Pay!
Cartooning Texas
The Guitar in Jazz (with James Sallis et al.)
R. Crumb: The Musical (with Robert Crumb)
The 50 Greatest Cartoons (with Jerry Beck et al.)
Michael H. Price's Hollywood Horrors
Electrified! (with Timothy Truman)
Bloody Visions, Vols. I-III

INDEX

-A-

Abbott & Costello 197
Absent-Minded Professor, The 163
Academy Awards 48, 72, 74, 99, 299, 302
Ace Ventura: Pet Detective 90
Adair, Jean 232
Adam Had Four Sons 89
Adams, Dorothy 215
Adams, Ernie 172
Adamson, Al 43
Addams, Dawn 100
Adler, Luther 284, 285
Adventures of Robin Hood, The 151, 263
Aherne, Brian 264-265
Ainslee, Mary 174
Ain't Misbehavin' 97
Aitken, Spottiswoode 208
Alba, Maria 73-74
Alberni, Luis 40, 41, 62-64, 297
Albert, Eddie 237
Albertson, Frank 287, 288
Alexander, J. Grubb 40, 65-66
Alexander, John 232
Alexander, Max 108
Alf's Button Afloat 74
Alias Nick Beal 246
All about Eve 255
All Quiet on the Western Front 252
Allan, Elizabeth 98-100, 129-133
Allan, John 206
Allen, Barbara 218
Allen, Joseph, Jr. 225, 226
Allen, Robert 136-137
Almost Married 15, 72-74, 251
Along Came Jones 220
Always Goodbye 72
Amazing Colossal Man, The 257
Amfitheatrof, Daniele 267
Among the Living 220-222
Ancient Mariner, The 15, 29-31
And the Villains Still Pursue Me 306
Anders, Glenn 285
André, Gwili 87-89
Andy Hardy Gets Spring Fever 50
Angel Heart 260
Angel, Heather 124-128
Ankers, Evelyn 243
Ankrum, Morris 280
Annabel Lee 208

Ansélme, L.E. 87
Antheil, George 279, 281
Ape, The 158, 232
Arachnophobia 170
Aratow, Paul 43
Arbuckle, Roscoe "Fatty" 35, 168
Arlen, Richard 134-135
Arliss, George 176
Arliss, Leslie 223-224
Armageddon 213
Armetta, Henry 60, 96
Armstrong, Robert 199, 244
Arnold, Jack 290
Arsenic and Old Lace 213, 232
Arthur, George 216
Arthur, Jean 121
"Arthur Jermyn, or the White Ape" 209
As the Devil Commands 215
As You Desire Me 37
Ashton-Wolfe, H. 87
Associated Press, the 14
Astaire, Fred 137
Asther, Nils 87, 110-113
Astor, Mary 117-119
Atlas, Leopold 124
Attenborough, Sir Richard 36, 209
"Attic of Terror, The" 15, 166-169
Atwill, Lionel 11, 17, 90-92, 120-123, 129-133, 184, 243
Auer, Mischa 60
August, Joseph 70
Aurelius Smith, Detective 171
Automaton 76
Avenging Conscience: Thou Shalt Not Kill, The 208
Awful Truth, The 74
Ayres, Lou 95-97, 262-263

-B-

Babbitt, Harry 203
Bacall, Lauren 279, 280
Bader, David 124
Badge of Evil 291, 292
Baggott, King 24
Bainter, Fay 248-249
Baker, Carroll 302, 303
Balderston, John L. 124, 156, 160
Baldwin, Adam 288
Baldwin, Walter 214

Bancroft, Anne 287-288
Banner, Jill 170
Bannon, Jim 246-247, 250-251
Bard, Ben 241
Barker, Ronnie 275
Barnum, P.T. 51
Barrault, Louis 24
Barry, Steve 212
Barrymore, Ethel 82
Barrymore, John 15, 20-26, 40-44, 49, 62-64, 65, 82, 150, 185, 216, 297
Barrymore, Lionel 48-50, 82, 129-133, 176
Bart, Jean 121
Barthelmess, Richard 154-155
Bartholomew, Freddie 147
Barton, Charles 197
Basevi, James 230
Bat, The 52
Bates, Jeanne 246, 247
Baxter, Anne 252-253
Beau Geste 94
Beaumont, Hugh 239, 241
Beauty and the Beast 107
Becky Sharp 121
Beddoe, Don 234
Bedlam 162
Beddoe, Don 196-197
Beebe, Ford 172, 174
Beethoven, L. von 197
Before I Hang 177, 193, 201-202
Beggar on Horseback 199
Behind the Mask 16, 68-69
Belafonte, Harry 298
Belasco, David 127
Bell, James 235, 237
Bellamy, Ralph 72-74, 252-253
Belle et la Bete, La 107, 273
Belloc Lowndes, Marie 266
Bells, The 158
Belushi, John 286
"Ben Bolt" 42
Ben-Hur 304
Benchley, Robert 87, 169
Benham, Harry 24
Benighted 76
Benson, Frank R. 185
Bennett, Bruce 197
Bennett, Charles 266, 270-271
Bennett, Chester 30-31
Bennett, Joan 122
Beresford, Harry 90, 93-94
Bergerman, Stanley 102

Bernstein, Elmer 212
Berryman, Michael 18
Best Foot Forward 97
Best Years of our Lives, The 261
Béte Humaine, La 229
Betz, Mathew 135
Bevan, Billy 227
Bey, Turhan 244
Biberman, Abner 235
Bickford, Charles 302-305
Big Circus, The 308
Big Country, The 15, 302-305
Big Sleep, The 279
Big Trail, The 70
Birell, Tala 76
Birth of a Nation, The 168
Biscuit Eater, The 220
Bishop, Julie (see: Wells, Jacqueline)
Black Alibi 235-238
Black Angel, The 280
Black Cat, The 17, 101-109, 171, 209, 241
Black Day, Blue Night 18
Black Dragons 182
Black Friday 188-191
Black Magic 89
Black Raven, The 243
Black Room, The 136-137, 172
Black Scorpion, The 121
Black Sleep, The 238
Blankfield, Mark 21
Blazing Saddles 116
Blind Husbands 36
Blondell, Gloria 173
Blondell, Joan 173
Bluebeard 76, 108
Bluyth, Ann 268-269
Bodeen, DeWitt 240-241
Body Snatcher, The 237
Boetticher, Oscar "Budd," Jr. 250-251
Bogart, Humphrey 15, 141, 277-282
Bogeaus, Benedict 248
Bogue, Merwyn (see: Kabibble, Ish)
Bohnen, Roman 210
Boleslavski, Richard 82
Bolton, Guy 72
Bond, Lillian 75-80
Bond, Rudy 287-288
Bonnie and Clyde 279
Boogie Man Will Get You, The 201, 203, 232-234
Books: Nonfiction Reference
    Cinema of Adventure, Romance & Ter-

ror, The 11
Edgar Allan Poe: The Creation of a Reputation 207
Forgotten Horrors (series) 11, 13, 17, 179
Human Monsters 11, 12-18
Making of King Kong, The 13
Matinée Idols, The 40
Poets and Poetry of America, The 206-207
Spawn of Skull Island 11, 13
Boom! 285
Borden, Eugene 259
Borland, Carol 129-133
Borzage, Frank 229
Boston Blackie (series) 250
Bow, Clara 29-31
Bowery at Midnight 182
Bowery Blitzkreig 174
Boy with Green Hair, The 285
Boyd, Bill "Cowboy Rambler" 138
Boyd, William "Hopalong Cassidy" 45, 138-140
Boyd, William "Stage" 44-47, 138
Boyer, Charles 229, 268-269
Brabin, Charles 82
Brahm, John (Hans) 154-155, 252, 264-265
Brahms, Hannes 107
Branagh, Kenneth 147
Brando, Marlon 308
Breakdown 18
Brecher, Egon 103
Breese, Edmund 65
Brendel, El 52
Brenon, Herbert 24
Brent, Evelyn 241
Brentano, Lowell 54
Bride, The 26
Bride of Frankenstein 124, 136-137
Briskin, Irving 196-197, 213, 250
Brissac, Virginia 189
British Board of Film Censors 181, 224
Brodie, Steve 285
Broken Blossoms 16, 154-155, 253
Bronte, Emily 16
Brooks, Hadda 280
Brooks, Jean 235, 237, 239, 241
Brooks, Mel 116
Brophy, Edward 141-143
Brown, Karl 176-178, 192-195
Brown, James S., Jr. 173
Brown, Phil 274-276

Brown, Russ 110
Browning, Tod 27, 129-133
Bruce, David 243, 244
Bruce, Virginia 134-135
Brute Force 210, 277
Brute Man, The 291
Buckingham, Tom 76
Bulldog Drummond 59, 244
Bullfighter and the Lady, The 250
Burke, Kathleen 90-92
Burke, Richard 227
Burke, Thomas 154-155
Burr, Raymond 285
Burt, Benny 285
Burton, Tim 295
Busch, Mae 27
Buttolph, David 230
Buzzell, Eddie 95-97
Byington, Spring 256-257
Byron, Arthur 118
Byron, Walter 77

-C-

Cabinet of Caligari 75
Cabinet of Dr. Caligari, The 75, 212
Cabot, Bruce 134-135, 141-143
Caesar and Cleopatra 273
Cage, Nicolas 143
Cagliostro 76
Cagney, James 94, 134, 141, 307
Cain, Paul (see: Ruric, Peter)
Caine Mutiny, The 275
Calhern, Louis 117-119
Calleia, Joseph 292, 296-297
Calling Dr. Gillespie 275
Calthrop, Donald 161
Cameron, James 79
Campeau, Frank 70
Cancel My Reservation 74
Cansino, Rita (see: Hayworth, Rita)
Capps, Edward 167-169
Capra, Frank 68, 232
Captain Blood 151
Captain Midnight 174
Carbonara, Gerard 222
Carew, Arthur Edmund 43
Carey, Harry 220, 221, 237
Carmichael, Hoagy 267
Carnegie Hall 108
Carrel, Dr. Alexis 152
Carroll, David 40
Carson, Jack 289-290

Carter, Janis 225-226, 250-251
Carver, Steve 212
Casablanca 279
Castle, William 79, 241, 261
Cat and the Canary, The 52, 78
Cat People 198, 235, 241, 246
Cavanaugh, Hobart 93-94, 164
Cavanagh, Paul 72
Cavern, The 108
Cellier, Frank 161-162
Chambers, Dudley 88
Chandler, Jeff 289-290, 292
Chandler, Lane 173
Chandler, Raymond 171, 227
Chandu the Magician 53, 72
Chaney, Lon 15, 26-28, 32, 76, 129, 130, 226
Chaney, Lon, Jr. 123, 203
Chang 145
Charge of the Light Brigade, The 151
Charlatan, The 15, 32-34
Charlie Chan (series) 226
Charlie Chan Carries On 70
Charteris, Leslie 171
Chase, Borden 227
Chase, Charley 36
Chauvel, Charles 144-146
Cheating Cheaters 111
Cheirel, Micheline 259
Cherniavsky, Josef 33
Chick Carter, Detective 174
Chopin 42
Churchill, Marguerite 151
Citizen Kane 64, 199, 268, 298
Clare, Mary 223-224
Clarence, Oliver B. 180
Clarke, Charles 157, 230
Clarke, Mae 118
Cliburn, Van 298
Clive, E.E. 126, 127, 157
Coasters, The 65
Cobb, Eddie 114, 172
Cobb, Lee J. 176
"Cobweb Hotel, The" 170
Codee, Ann 259
Cohen and Tate 288
Cohn, Harry 250, 270, 279
Colbert, Claudette 93-94
Coldewey, Anthony 118
Coleridge, S.T. 15, 29-31
Coll, Vincent "Mad Dog" 143
Collins, Ray 295
Colman, Ronald 33, 59-61, 99

Compson, Betty 35-39, 168
Conan Doyle, Sir Arthur 16, 124
Condemned 59
Confirm or Deny 229
Connell, Richard 16
Connors, Chuck 302-305
Conway, Jack 27, 70
Conway, Tom 241
Cook, Donald 63
Cook, Elisha, Jr. 198-200, 248-249
Cooke, Sam 298
"Corazon Delator, El" 212
Corbett, Benny 114
Corbett, Ronnie 275
Cord, Alex 212
Cording, Harry 103
Corey, Jeff 227
Corman, Roger 187, 208, 255
Corn Is Green, The 154
Cornish, Dr. Robert 152
Corrigan, Lloyd 165
Corsican Brothers, The 89
Cortez, Ricardo 117-119, 151-152, 225, 226, 264
Cotten, Joseph 296
Cotton Club, The 143
Courant, Curt 154
Cousin Joe (see: Joseph, Pleasant)
Cover Girl 278
Covered Wagon, The 35, 178
Cowan, Jerome 252-253
Coward, Noel 216
Coxen, Ed 115
Craig, Davina 148
Crain, Jeanne 289
Crash Dive 41
Crawford, Joan 289
Creature from the Black Lagoon (series) 291
Crime Club (series) 98
Crime without Passion 120
Crimes at the Dark House 149
Crisp, Donald 40, 41, 154-155
Crocodile Dundee (series) 144
Cronyn, Hume 268
Cross Country Cruise 15, 95-97
Crossfire 275
Crowley, Alastair 102-103
Crowther, Bosley 216
Cruze, James 24, 35-39, 93-94
Cummings, Constance 69
Cummings, Rose 22-24
Cunningham, Jack 102

Curse of the Cat People 240
Curse of the Demon (see: Night of the Demon)
Curtis, Dick 176
Curtiz, Michael 62-64, 150-153

-D-

da Silva, Howard 283, 285
Dahl, John 193
D'Agostino, Albert 121, 124
Darby O'Gill and the Little People 163
Dark Chase, The 287
Dark Eyes of London 179-182
Dark Mirror, The 262-263
Dark Tower 117, 118
Dark Waters 248-249
Darmour, Larry 259
Darro, Frankie 63
Darwell, Jane 96
Dassin, Jules 210, 211, 274-276
Date with Destiny, A (see: Mad Doctor, The)
Daughter of the Dragon 82
Daughter of Time, The 309
Daviau, Allan 299-300
David Copperfield 124
David Harum 36
Davis, Bette 229, 263
Davis, Cullen 14
Davis, George 103
Dawson, Anthony 272
Day, Josette 107
Day, Laraine 264-265
Day, Richard 230
De Brulier, Nigel 29-31
de Cordoba, Pedro 202
de Grasse, Robert 237
de Grunwald, Anatole 272
de Havilland, Olivia 262-263, 267
de Marigny, Bernard 26
De Mille, Cecil B. 138, 222, 279
De Mille, Katherine 137
de Toth, André 248-249, 252
Dead Don't Dream, The 140
Dead of Night 36, 273, 275
Deadly is the Female (see: Gun Crazy)
Dean, James 308
Death in Small Doses 304
Dein, Edward 246
Dekker, Albert 220-222
Del Ruth, Roy 209, 283
Denny, Reginald 265
Derek, John 277, 278

Desert Fox, The 269
Desperate Siege (see: Rawhide)
Destination Unknown 76
Destiny (see: Mad Doctor, The)
Destry Rides Again 142
Detour 108
Devil Bat, The 164, 174, 182, 234
Devil Bat's Daughter 211
Devil Commands, The 201, 210, 213-215, 246, 275, 288
Devil Doll, The 36
Devil To Pay, The 59
Devil's Triangle, The 72
Diaboliques, Les 130
Dibdin-Pitt, George 148
Dick Tracy 170, 173
Dickens, Charles 124
Dickey, Basil 172
Dickinson, Thorold 272, 273
Dierkes, John 296
Dieterle, William 283
Dietrich, Marlene 87, 295
Digges, Dudley 65
Dillon, Jack 69
Dinehart, Allan 73, 95-97, 110, 112
Dirigible 68
Disney, Walt 193
Dix, Richard 229, 261
Dmytryk, Edward 201, 210, 213-215, 274-276
Doll Family (see: Earles, Harry)
Doll, Harry (see: Earles, Harry)
Donizetti 42
Donlevy, Brian 94
Donne, John 241
Donnell, Jeff 232, 234, 279, 280
D'Onofrio, Vincent 295
Doomed To Die (see: Smoking Guns)
Doran, Ann 173
Double Indemnity 213
Doublemint Gum 137
Douglas, Donald 35-39
Douglas, Melvyn 11, 75-80
Dove, The 74
Dr. Cyclops 221
Dr. Jekyll & Mr. Hyde 15, 20-26, 35, 40, 44, 51, 53, 124
Dr. Renault's Secret 227
Dr. X 150
Don Quixote 298
Dracula 44, 51, 124, 130, 131, 179
Dragonwyck 255-258, 266, 309

Drew, Ellen 217, 218
Driving Miss Daisy 268
Drums in the Deep South 74, 212
Drums of Fu Manchu 172
du Maurier, George 40, 42
Dudgeon, Elspeth 75-80
Duff, Amanda 214, 215
Duffy, Jesse A. 174
Duncan, Anna 104
Duncan, Isadora 104
Duncan, Kenneth "Kenne" 172, 173, 174
Dunn, Michael 26
Dunsany, Lord 127
Dupont, E.A. 102
Dyall, Valentine 272-273

-E-

Eagle and the Hawk, The 127
Eagle's Brood, The 138-140
Earle, Edward 173
Earles, Daisy 26
Earles, Harry 26-28
Earth vs. the Spider 170
Eason, B. Reeves 174
East of Borneo 51
East of Java 183
Eburne, Maude 221, 233, 234
Ed Wood 295
Edeson, Arthur 79
Edge of Running Water 215
Edouart, Farciot 218
Edwards, Blake 298
Edwards, J. Gordon 170
Eight Legged Freaks 170
Eisenstein, Sergei 285
Eisinger, Jo 227
Ellery Queen (series) 244
Ellington, Duke 288
Elliott, Wild Bill 174
Ellison, Jimmy 139
Emery, Katherine 264
Empire Strikes Back, The 299
Endore, Guy 130
English Patient, The 299
Epstein, Bob 299-300
Eran Trece (see: *Charlie Chan Carries On*)
Ernest, Georgie 125, 127
Esper, Dwain 209
Evans Dame Edith 272-273
Evans, Madge 48-50
Everson, William K. 29, 44

Everything You Always Wanted To Know about Sex (But Were Afraid To Ask) 234

-F-

Face at the Window, The 149
Fairbanks, Douglas 168, 171
Falcon (series) 260
Farmer, Frances 220, 221
Farnum, William 139
Farrow, Mia 241
Fatal Lady 121
Faust 246
Fawcett, Jane 167
Feather, Leonard 288
Featherston, Eddie 173
Fellows, Rockcliffe 32-34
Female on the Beach 289, 292
Fenton, Leslie 29-31, 65-66
Field, Alexander 180
Fields, W.C. 147, 291
Fighting with Buffalo Bill 173
Figures in a Landscape 285
Finlay, Virgil 211
Fisher, Terence 24
Fiske, Richard 172, 202, 215
Fithian, Ted 76
Fitzmaurice, George 59
Fitzpatrick Travel Talks (series) 209
Fix, Paul 135
Flaherty, Robert 145
Flash Gordon (series) 71, 84, 107, 164, 173
Fleming, Ian 171
Fletcher, Bramwell 40, 41
Fletcher, Robin 283
Flight 68
Florey, Robert 209
Flynn, Errol 243
Fog Island 243
Fontaine, Joan 266-267
Foolish Wives 104
Forbes, Ralph 98-100, 186
Forbstein, Leo 66
Ford, Francis 227
Ford, John 70, 173, 220, 279
Ford, Ross 270
Foreign Correspondent 266, 279
Forever Amber 225
Fort, Garrett, 221
Foster, Jodie 43
Foxe, Earle 53,
Fox Movietone Follies of 1929 37

Framed 279
Francis, Kay 48-50
Francis the Talking Mule (series)
Frankenstein 44, 51, 76-78, 79, 84, 94, 179, 215, 218, 220-221
Frankenstein Meets the Wolf Man 136
Freaks 81
Frederick, Pauline 170
Free Soul, A 48
French, Hugh 268
Friderici, Blanche 44-47, 65
Fried Green Tomatoes 268
Friedhofer, Hugo 261
Frings, Ketti 252
From Here to Eternity 279
Front Page, The 59, 252
Frye, Dwight 218

-G-

Gabel, Martin 284, 285
Gabin, Jean 229-231
Gabor, Zsa Zsa 295, 296
Gadd, Renee 110, 112
Gage, Erford 241
Gan, Chester 230
Garbo, Greta 37, 87, 96
Garmes, Lee 252, 253
Garner, Peggy Ann 270
Gaslight 273
Gasway, Sam 13
Gaudio, Gaetano "Tony" 82, 118
Gay, Gregory 259
Gelbfisz, Schmuel (see: Goldwyn, Samuel)
Geluka, Abner J. 76
Genet, Ira 167
Geray, Steven 259-260
Gere, Richard 289
Geronimo 71
Gershenson, Joseph 297
Gerstad, Merritt 121
Get Cracking 74
Ghost Breakers, The 142
Ghoul, The 158, 160
"Giaconda Smile, The" 268
Gibbons, Floyd 166-169
Gibney, Sheridan 264
Gieb, Joe 26
Gift of Gab 102
Gilbert, Billy 234
Gilda 250
Gilks, Al 88

Gillette, Ruth 280
Gilliat, Sidney 160
Gish, Lillian 154-155
Give Us This Day 275
Glasmon, Kubec 141
"Glass Eye, The" 36
Glass Key, The 220
G-Men 134, 142
Go-Between, The 285
Goetz, Harry 93
Goldfish, Samuel (see: Goldwyn, Samuel)
Goldner, Orville 11, 13
Goldwyn, Samuel 18, 59-61, 99
Golem, The 76
Gombell, Minna 95-97
Gone with the Wind 18, 170, 263
Goodis, David 287
Goodwin, Harold 114
"Goofy Goat" 37
Gorilla, The 52
Gould, Dorothy 32-34
Gould, William 114
Goya, Mona 159
Grable, Betty 239
Graham, George 207
Grahame, Gloria 279, 280, 281
Grandee, George 37
Grant, Cary 127
Grant, Lawrence 59, 61, 82-86, 122
Grapes of Wrath, The 262
Grass 145
Gray, Lorna 177
Gray, Sally 274-276
Great Gabbo, The 20, 35-39
Great Expectations 124, 127, 180, 183, 272
Great Impersonation, The 79
Greed 36
Green Archer, The 174
Green Goddess, The 157
Green Hornet, The 173-174
Green Hornet Strikes Again, The 174
Gregory, James 287
Grenier, Mme. Hilda 125
Grey, Nan 185
Grey, Zane 197
Griffith, D.W. 50, 93, 138, 154-155, 168, 178, 208, 298
Grinde, Nick 176-178, 201-202
Grip of the Strangler 260
Griswold, Rufus Wilmot 206-208
Grossman, Eugene 72

Grot, Anton 40, 63, 65
Guard, Kit 60, 173
Guest in the House 17, 154, 252-254
Guffey, Burnett 247, 279, 281
Guilty Hands 13, 17, 29, 48-50, 252
Gun Crazy 260
Gunfighter, The 262
Gunga Din 70
Gunn, Earl 197
Gwenn, Edmund 151
Gwynne, Anne 189
Gynt, Greta 180

-H-

Haas, Dolly 155
Hagney, Frank 173
Hall, Charles 77
Hall, Thurston 136-137
Haller, Ernest 91
Halton, Charles 198-200
Hamilton, Margaret 252
Hamlet 307
Hammett, Dashiell 171, 283
Hamper, Geneveive 170
Hands of Orlac, The 202
Hangover Square 154
Harbou, Thea von 283
Hardwicke, Sir Cedric 147, 266, 267, 268-269
Hardy, Phil 158-159, 203
Hare, Lumsden 40, 41
Harlan, Kenneth 151
Harrie, Elmer 95
Harrison, Joan 249
Harvey, Forrester 70-71, 100
Harvey, Paul 151-152, 227
Hatchet Man, The 16, 17, 29, 65-67
"Hatchet Man, The" 65
Hathaway, Henry 283
Hatton, Rondo 291
Haunted Strangler, The (see: *Grip of the Strangler*)
Haupt, Ulric 60
Hawks, Howard 142
Hayden, Charles J. 21-22
Hayes, George "Gabby" 139
Hayes, Helen 99, 308
Haymes, Dick 267
Hayward, Louis 24, 156-157
Hayward, Susan 220, 221
Hayworth, Rita 132, 250

He Snoops To Conquer 74
He Who Gets Slapped 32
Hearn, Edward 173
"Heartbeat" 211
Heaven on Earth 229
Hecht, Ben 36, 59, 216-219, 279
Heisler,. Stuart 220
Hell's Heroes 283, 303
Helldorado 36
Hellinger, Mark 277
Heming, Violet 72-74
Hemmings, David 24
Henabery, Joseph 167-169
Hendrian, Oscar "Dutch" 173
Herbert, Holmes 32-34, 129-133
Herbert-Bond, John 185
Herman, Babe 51
Herman, Woody 267
Herrmann the Great 51
Hersholt, Jean 82-86, 129-133
Heston, Charlton 289, 292, 294, 295, 299, 302-305
Hibbler, Al 288
Hickok, Rodney 127
Hickox, Sid 66
High Command, The 273
High Sierra 277
Hills Have Eyes, The 18
Hinds, Samuel S. 164-165
Hitchcock, Alfred 36, 76, 160, 223, 266, 267, 270, 279, 293
Hoag, Doane 210
Hobart, Rose 185, 225, 226, 246-247
Hobson, Valeris 124-128
Hoey, Dennis 144-146
Hoffman, Harold 209
Hogan, James P. 244
Hogan, Paul 144
Holland, Billy 148
Holland, Cecil 83-84
Hollywood 35
Holt, Jack 68-69
Holy Terror, A 278
Hopalong Cassidy (series) 138-140
Hopper, Hedda 304
Hopton, Russell 77-78
Horne, James W. 172, 173
Hour of 13, The 100
House, Billy 296
House Committee on UnAmerican Activities 210, 274-276, 280, 285

House of Glass 111
House of Wax 248, 309
House That Shadows Built, The 46
Howard, David 70
Howard, John 217, 218
Howard, Joyce 223-224
Howard, Mary 225, 226
Howard, Ronald 272
Howard, Samuel "Shemp" 234
Howe, James Wong 55, 104, 131
Howell, E. Gilbert 144
Hubley, John 212
Hud 131
Hudson, Rochelle 141-143, 196-197
Hughes, Dorothy B. 277
Hughes, Howard 37-38, 212, 279
Hull, Henry 124
Hull, J. Warren 151, 164, 170-175
Hull, Josephine 232
Human Monster, The (see: *Dark Eyes of London*)
Humbug, The 111
Humphreys, Cecil 268
Hunchback of Notre Dame 124, 185
Hunter, Kim 239, 240
Huntley, G.P., Jr. 185
Hurricane, The 220
Hurst, Brandon 237
Huston, Walter 255-257
Huxley, Aldous 268-269
Hyer, Martha 267
Hymer, Warren 60-61, 141-143
"Hypnotist, The" 130

-I-

I Cover the Waterfront 13, 16, 36, 93-94
I Love a Mystery 279
I Walked with a Zombie 236
"I'm Laughing" 36
In a Lonely Place 15, 277-282
Ince, Ralph 65
Incredible Shrinking Man, The 292
Indiana Jones (series) 81
Informer, The 70, 210, 279
Ingram, Rex 248-249
Inner Sanctum (series) 246
Intermezzo 89
International Lady 218
Intolerance 168, 264, 298
Invaders from Mars 52, 74, 212
Invisible Ghost 38

Invisible Man, The 71, 76, 82, 107, 120, 123
Invisible Ray, The 158, 180
Ireland, Anthony 159
Iron Claw, The 23
Iron Horse, The 279
Island of Doomed Men 16, 196-197
It Came from Outer Space 290
Ives, Burn 302-305
Ivy 17, 266-267

-J-

Jackman, Fred 40
Jackson, Michael 307
Jaffe, Sam 212
James, Alan 114, 173
James, Thomas 124
Jane Eyre 163, 267
Janssen, Werner 254
Jarry, Ashton 144-146
Jason, Will 246
Jekyll & Hyde... Together Again 21
Jennings, Gordon 218
Jewell, Isabel 237, 241
Johnny O'Clock 279
Johnson, Kenneth 212
Johnson, Noble 70-71
Johnson, Nunnally 229, 262
Jolson Story, The 260, 261
Jones, Buck 70, 116
Jones Family (series) 125
Jones, Gordon 134-135, 220, 221
Joseph, Pleasant 298
Journey for Margaret 50
Journey into Fear 298
Journey's End 77
Juggernaut 158-159, 160
Julius Caesar 255
June, Ray 94
Jungle Book, The 268
Jungle Jim (series) 37
Jungle Menace 172
Jungle Terror (see: *Jungle Menace*)

-K-

Kabibble, Ish 203, 204
Kami, Virginia 110
Karloff, Boris 15, 16, 17, 51, 63, 68-69, 75-80, 81-86, 94, 101-109, 118, 124, 134, 136-137, 150-153, 158-159, 160-163, 164-165, 172, 176-178, 179, 180, 181, 184, 185, 186, 188-191, 192-195, 201-

202, 203-205, 213-215, 232-234, 246, 260, 288, 307
Kassel, Shirley 103
Katz, Ephraim 74
Katzman, Sam 37
Kaufman, George S. 117
Kaye, Danny 263
Keith, Brian 287-288
Keller, Harry 299
Kelly, John 189
Kelly, Paul 110, 112
Kempson, Rachel 268
Kent, Robert E. 172
Kesselring, Joseph 232
Kilbride, Percy 252-253
Killer, The 70
Killers, The 262, 277
Kilpatrick, Tom 102-103
Kindred, The 18
King, Bradley 124
King, Claude 69
King, George 148
King, Henry 94
King Henry VI 183
King, Joseph 151
King Kong 11, 199
King Lear 292
King, Rufus 87
Kings Row 266
Kingsford, Walter 125, 127, 157
Kirke, Donald 135
Kirkland, Alexander 72-74
Kiss of Death 141
Kline, Benjamin 176-178
Knight, June 95-97
Knock on Any Door 277, 279
Knowles, Patric 266
Knox, Alexander 270
Koenekamp, Hans 40
Kongo 81
Korda, Alexander 268
Korda, Vincent 268
Korda, Zoltan 268
Korff, Arnold 87
Kosleck, Martin 217, 218
Krafft-Ebing 81
Kramph, Gunther 224
Krasner, Milton 244
Krueger, Kurt 57
Kruger, Alma 204
Kuhn, Irene 82
Kurten, Peter 15-16

Kyne, Peter B. 283
Kyser, Kay 203-205

-L-

L.A. Law 26
Lackaye, Wilson 42
Lady of Burlesque 252
Lady Vanishes, The 275
Laemmle, Carl 32, 76, 79, 101, 107, 121, 124
Laemmle, Carl Jr. 76, 77, 115-116
Lafayette, Andrée 43
Laird, Connie 252-253
Landau, David 117
Landry, Margaret 235, 237
Lang, Fritz 16, 99, 222, 229, 283
Langan, Glenn, 257
Lansbury, Angela 18
Lansing, Joi 294
LaRocque, Rod 87
Last Performance, The 32
Last Time I Saw Paris, The 252
Last Warning, The 32
Laszlo, Ernest 284
Lathrop, Phil 294
L'Atlantide 108
Laughton, Charles 75-80, 147
Laura 225
Laurel & Hardy 274, 209
Lawford, Peter 100
Lawson, Wilfrid 223
Lawton, Frank 124
Laye, Evelyn 42
Lean, David 180, 272
Leather Burners, The 168
Leave It to Beaver 241
Lederer, Francis 237
Lee, Anna 160-163
Lee, Christopher 275, 307
Lee, Kendall 87, 89
Lee, Lila 27
Lee, Robert N. 184, 185
Lee, Rowland V. 183-187
Leeds, Herbert I. 227
Legion of Decency (see also: Motion Picture Producers & Distributors Association) 101-102, 103, 118, 164, 240, 257
Leiber, Jerry 65
Leigh, Janet 292, 293, 295, 299
Leigh, Vivien 170
Leni, Paul 112
Leonard, Queenie 265
Leopard Man, The 17, 235-238, 246, 288

Let 'Em Have It 16, 134-135
Letter to Three Wives, A 255
Levy, Benn W. 77-78
Lewis, Jerry 285
Lewis, Joseph H. 260
Lewis, Sheldon 15, 22-24
Lewton, Val 162, 198, 199, 235-238, 239-242, 268, 287
Life and Death of King Richard III, The 183
Life of Emile Zola, The 210
Life Returns 152
Lights of New York, The 141
Lindbergh, Charles A. 152
Linden, Eric 134-135
Lindsay, W.W. Jr. 72
Linow, Ivan 27
Lister, Eve 148
Liszt, Franz 107
Little Caesar 141
Livingston, Margaret 32-34
Lloyd, George 250
Lloyd, Norman 285
Loder, John 160-163
Lombard, Carole 127
Lodge, John 90-92
Locket, The 154, 264-265
Lodger, The 154, 252, 254, 266
Lom, Herbert 118
Lombard, Carole 199
London after Midnight 129-130
Long Voyage Home, The 199
Lord, Robert 277, 281
Loring, Thomas 225
Lorre, Peter 196-197, 198-200, 203-205, 218, 232-234, 284, 285, 307, 308
Losey, Joseph 16, 283-286
Lost City, The 170
Lost Empress, The 87
Lost One, The (see: *Verlorene, Der*)
Lost Weekend The 281
Love Begins at 20 174
Love Captive, The 16, 110-113, 183
Love from a Stranger 184
Lovecraft, H.P. 209
Lovejoy, Frank 279, 280
Lowe, Edmund 51-58
Loy, Myrna, 81-86, 97
Lubin, Arthur 188-191
Lubin, Lou 241
Lubitsch, Ernst 255
Ludwig, Edward 121
Lugosi, Bela 17, 51, 101-109, 129-133, 147, 164, 179-183, 184, 188-191, 203-205, 229
Lupino, Isa 229-230, 253
Lustig, William 286
Lux Radio Theatre 269
Lux Television Theatre 260
Lux Video Theatre 267
Lyon, Ben 93-94, 118
Lyons, Harry Agar 82

-M-

MacArthur, Charles 59, 216-219
McCambridge, Mercedes 296
McDaniel, Etta 114-115
McDaniel, Hattie 114
MacDonald, Marie 252-253
MacDonald, Philip 98
McGill, Barney 40, 63
McGrail, Walter 44-47
McGuire, Ann Tucker 223
McGuire, John 198-200
McHugh, Jimmy 204
McKay, George 233, 234
McKay, Scott 252
McKellan, Sir Ian 185
McKenna, Kenneth (variant billing: MacKenna) 55, 72
McKinney, Nina May 249
McLaglen, Victor 27, 146
MacLane, Barton 151-152
MacMahon, Aline 252-253
MacMurray, Fred 168
MacReady, George 246-247, 250-251
McWade, Robert 96
M 16, 99, 222, 283-286
Ma and Pa Kettle (series) 253, 291
Macbeth 292
Mad Doctor, The 216-219
Mad Genius, The 51, 53, 62-64, 150
Mad Ghoul, The 243-245
Mad Love 81
Magic 36, 209
Magician, The 103
Malden, Karl 209
Maltese Falcon, The 151, 279, 283
Maltin, Leonard 216
Man in Black 273
Man in Grey, The 223-224
Man They Could Not Hang, The 176-178, 193, 251
Man Who Changed His Mind, The 158, 160-163

Man Who Knew Too Much, The 266
Man Who Laughs, The 32
Man Who Played God, The 72-73
Man Who Reclaimed His Head, The 13, 17, 120-123, 124
Man Who Wouldn't Die, The 227-228
Man with Nine Lives, The 192-195
Man with Two Faces, The 16, 41, 117-119
Manchurian Candidate, The 18
Mancini, Henry 297-298, 300
Manckiewicz, Joseph 255, 257
Mandrake the Magician 174
Maniac (1934) 209
Maniac (1980) 18, 286
Mann, Bertha 69
Manners, David 101-109, 124-128
Man's Castle 229
Mansfield, Richard 22
Manson, Charles 44
March, Frederic, 24, 127
Marcin, Max 111-112
Marcus, Lee 199
Maree, A. Morgan 277
Margetson, Arthur 155, 159
Margo 235, 237
Mari, George 139
Maria Marten, or the Murder in the Red Barn 148
Marie Antoinette 50
Marion, Paul 259
Mark of the Vampire 16, 129-133
Marnay, Marcelle 144
Marquand, John P. 171
Marsh, Marian 40, 42, 62-64, 136-137
Marshall, Connie 255, 256
Marshall, George 142, 283
Marshall, Herbert 266, 267
Marshall, Tully 65
Martin, Richard 235
Martinez, Nana (see: Woodbury, Joan)
Mary Shelley's Frankenstein 147
Mask of Fu Manchu, The 81-86, 158-159
Mason, James 212, 223-224
Mason, Leroy 227
Massey, Raymond 75-80, 232
Masterson, Whit 291
Mata Hari 96
Matthau, Walter 241
Maugham, W. Somerset 103
Maynard, James 212
Maynard, Ken 114-116
Mayo, Archie, 40-44, 118, 142, 229

Maze, The 52, 74, 212
Mazurki, Mike 251
Meek, Donald 129-133
Melford, George 32-34
Menzies, William Cameron 52-58, 72-73, 211-212, 266
Mercer, Johnny 204
Mercury Theatre of the Air 298
Meredith, Burgess 209
Meredith, Iris 172, 174
Mescall, John 72, 104
Messel, Oliver 273
Metty, Russell 266, 268, 293, 294
Meyer, Louis 21
Meyerinck, Gustav 76
Michael Shayne (series) 227-228
Michaels, Gertrude 82
Middleton, Charles 65, 70-71, 196-197
Mighty Mouse (series) 43
Milani, Chef 241
Milestone, Lewis 138, 252
Miljan, John 284, 285
Miller, Arthur 256
Miller, John C. 207
Miller, Max 93
Miller, Virgil 226
Miller, Walter 114
Mills, Mort 292
Minine, Paul 155
Mirage 241, 275
Missing Head, The 123
Missing Juror, The 17, 250-251
Mr. Moto (series) 226
Mr. Wong (series) 158, 232
Mitchell, Thomas 229, 248-249, 262-263
Mitchell, Yvonne 272-273
Mitchum, Robert 264-265
Mix, Tom 70
Moby Dick 40
Modesty Blaise 285
Moe, G. Ronnie 71
Moffett, Sharyn 265
Monash, Paul 292
Monroe, Vaughn 267
Monster, The (see: Mad Doctor, The)
Monster and the Girl, The 220
Montgomery, Douglass 124
Montgomery, Marshall 37
Montgomery, Robert 98-100, 156-157
Moon of Israel 151
Moontide 16, 229-231
Moore, Eva 75-80

Moore, Matt 27
Moran, Lois 53, 55-56
Moreland, Mantan 57
Morgan, Frank 87-89, 156-157
Morgan, Ira H. "Joe" 35, 37
Morgan, Ralph 217
Morley, Karen 82, 86, 283
Morris, Ernest 212
Morris, Gordon 76
Morris, William 167
Mortal Coils 268
Moss, Frank 87
Moss Rose 89
Most Dangerous Game, The 11, 16, 88
"Mother Goose Land" 170
Motion Picture Producers & Distributors Association (Production Code) 89, 94, 101, 118, 141-142, 145, 184, 185
Mowbray, Alan 48-50
Mudie, Leonard 99-100
Mulford, Clarence E. 138
Mummy, The 76, 82, 107, 158
Mundin, Herbert 73
Muni, Paul 141, 176
Murch, Walter 299
Murder by Invitation 75
Murder by the Clock 15, 44-47, 51, 98, 138, 288
Murder, He Says 168
Murderer Invisible 76
Murder, My Sweet 213
"Murders in the Rue Morgue, The" (as adapted to screen) 208, 209
Murders in the Zoo 17, 89, 90-92
Murnau, F.W. 24, 70, 107
Muse, Dr. Clarence 247
Musuraca, Nicholas 199, 241
My Name Is Julia Ross 260, 279
Myers, Carmel 40
Myers, Harry 173
Myra Breckenridge 234
Mysterious Dr. Fu Manchu, The 82
Mystery of Edwin Drood 124-128
Mystery of Mr. X, The 98-100
Mystery of the Wax Museum, The 150
Mystery Ranch 70-71

-N-

Naish, J. Carrol 65, 123, 261
Naked City 277
Nanook of the North 145
Napier, Alan 249

Naschy, Paul 212
Natwick, Mildred 268, 269
Naughty Marietta 50
Nazi Agent 210
Nebel, Frederick 227
Nebenzal, Seymour 283
Neff, Hildegarde 43
Neilan, Marshall 93
Neill, Roy William 136-137
Neitz, Alvin J. (see: James, Alan)
Nelson, David 308
Nelson, Harriet 308
Nelson, Ozzie 308
Neptune's Daughter 97
Never on Sunday 210
New Arabian Nights, The 156
Newcombe, Warren 84
Newman, Alfred 256
Newman, Emil 225
Newmeyer, Fred 93
Newton, Mary 241
Newton, Robert 147, 274-276
Ney, Richard 266, 267
Nigh, William 93
Night and the City 274
Night Editor 279
Night Has Eyes, The (a.k.a.: *Terror House*) 17, 223-224
Night Key 164-165, 174
Night in Casablanca, A 41
Night Must Fall 16, 122, 154, 252, 254
Night of the Demon 287
Night Train to Munich 275
Nightfall 287-288
Ninotchka 180
Ninth Guest, The 251
No Way Out 255
Noah's Ark 151
Nolan, Lloyd 227-228
None Shall Escape 249
Norris, Edward 141-143
North, Edmund H. 277
Nosferatu 212
Nugent, Elliott 27

-O-

Oberon, Merle 248-249
O'Brien, Dave 174
O'Brien, George 70-71, 278
Obsession 210, 274-276
Ochs, Al 167
Of Mice and Men 210, 252

O'Hara, John 229
O'Neal, Charles 251
O'Neil, Barbara 185
O'Neil, Bob 299
O'Neill, Henry 151
Obsession 17
Oh God! 74
O'Keefe, Dennis 235, 237
Oland, Warner 82-83
Old Dark House, The 17, 75-80, 82, 181
Old Man Rhythm 121
Oliver Twist 272
Olivier, Sir Laurence 185
One More River 124
One Mysterious Night 250
O'Neill, Henry 118, 120
O'Shea, Oscar 211
O'Toole, Peter 43
Ornitz,. Samuel 87, 121
Osborne, Vivienne 255
Ostrow, Lou 236
Otterson, Jack 184-185
Otto, Henry 30-31
Our Gang (series) 169, 209
"Our Wife" 173
Oursler, Fulton 54
Overland with Kit Carson 174
Owen, Arthur E. 180
Owen, Reginald 156-157

-P-

Page, Norvell 171
Paiva, Nestor 172
Palance, Jack 24
Pallette, Eugene 96
Parker, Alan 260
Parker, Cecilia 70-71
Parks, Larry 233, 234
Parma, Tula 235, 237
Parrish, Helen 204
Pascal, Ernest 32
Patrick, Gail 90-92
Patton, Bill 172
Paul, Elliott 252
Pauncefort, George 134
Paxton, Bill 18
Payment Deferred 79
Payne, A.D. 12,
Peck, Gregory 176, 302-305
Penney, Ralph 215
Penthouse 50
Pepper, Barbara 135

Periodicals and Publishers
   American Cinematographer, The 83-84, 178
   American Weekly, The 87
   Boston Miscellany, The 207
   Chicago Tribune 169
   Collier's 81
   Fame 252
   Film Daily, The 211
   Film Quarterly, The 299
   Graham's Magazine 206-207
   Heavy Metal 131
   Hollywood Reporter, The 218
   Kitchen Sink Press 15
   MAD 204
   Motion Picture Exhibitor 170
   New York Times 32, 216, 246
   New York Tribune 207
   New Yorker, The 88
   Popular Publications 170-171, 172
   Saturday Evening Post, The 248
   Showmen's Trade Review 211
   Southern-Fried Homicide 13
   Southwest Heritage 12
   San Diego Sun 93
   Spider, Master of Men, The 170-171
   Variety 72
Pete Smith Specialties (series) 169, 174, 209
Peter Gunn 298
Peters, Susan 270-271
Petrified Forest, The 41, 141
Phantom Creeps, The 172, 180
Phantom Lady 249
Phantom of the Opera, The 42, 79, 122, 124, 190, 244
Phantom of the Rue Morgue 209
Phantom Speaks, The 190
Phillips, Howard 53
Phillips, Jean 220, 221
Pichel, Irving 44-47
Pierce, Herman 148
Pierce, Jack P. 77-78, 125
Plainsman, The 279
Plympton, George 172, 173
Poe, Edgar Allan 15, 16, 102, 131, 187, 206-212, 255, 257, 306, 307
Pogany, Willy 59, 61
Polansky, Roman 241
Polglase, Van Nest 204
"Poor Butterfly" 66
Porlock, Martin (see: MacDonald, Philip)
Powell, William 97

Praskins, Leonard 32
Pratt, Purnell 54
Presley, Elvis 298
Previn, Charles 187
Price, Michael H. 11, 12-18, 249, 287, 309, 310-311
Price, Roger 53
Price, Vincent 15, 147, 183, 184, 186, 208, 212, 249, 255-258, 306-310
Primal Fear 289
Pring, Gerald 180
Prival, Lucien 87
Private Life of Don Juan, The 273
Private Lives of Elizabeth and Essex, The 151
Priestley, J.B. 76, 77
Production Code (see: Motion Picture Producers & Distributors Association)
Prussing, Margaret 127
Pryor, Roger 177, 193
Public Enemy, The 94, 141
Public Hero No. 1 142
Puglia, Frank 233
Pushkin, Alexander 272
Putnam, Nina Wilcox 76
Pybus, Luther Joe 138
Pye, Merrill 99

-Q-

Qualen, John 248-249
Queen of Spades, The 272-273
Quigley, Baby Jane 120
Quine, Richard 270
Quinn, Seabury 171

-R-

Radford, Basil 275
Raffles 59
Raft, George 141
Rage in Heaven 50
Raiders of the Lost Ark 299
Raine, Norman Reilly 283
Rains, Claude 17, 118, 120-123, 124-128, 176, 229-230
Raintree County 275
Raksin, David 225, 227-228
Ramson, Martie 172
Rapaport, David 26
Rasputin and the Empress 82
Rathbone, Basil 183-187, 216-219, 307
Ratoff, Gregory 87-89
Rauh, Stanley 95

"Raven, The" 307
Raven, The 181
Rawhide 283
Rawson, Clayton 227
Ray, Aldo 287-288
Ray, Nicholas 15, 277, 280, 281
Raymond, Gene 264-265
Rebecca 267
Recording Companies
Columbia 203
RCA Victor 280, 298
Red, Eric 288
Red Shoes, The 272
Redman, Frank 204
Reed, Philip 289
Reefer Madness 174
Reid, Carl Benton 279, 280
Reinhardt, Max 107
Relentless 286
Renoir, Jean 24
Reticker, Hugh 152
Return of Chandu, The 173
Return of Fu Manchu, The 82
Return of Frankenstein, The 120, 124
Return of Dr. X, The 150
Return to Oz 299
Revere, Anne 214, 215
Reynolds, Helene 227
Reynolds, Jack 281
Rho, Stella 148
Rhys, Margot 144-146
Richard III, King 183-187, 309-310
Richards, Addison 139, 197
Richards, Frank 202
Ridges, Stanley 188-191
Rio 184
"Rival Dummy, The" 36
Roach, Hal 169
Robbins, Peggy 207
Roberti, Manya 54, 57
Roberts, Allene 270
Robertson, John Stuart 20-26
Robertson, Willard 229
Robins, The (see: Coasters, The)
Robinson, Edward G. 65-66, 117-119, 141, 307
Robinson, George 32, 96-97, 185
Robson, Mark 241
Rockefeller Institute 152
Rockwell, Jack 115
Roddam, Franc 26
Roemheld, Heinz 107, 121

Rogers, Ginger 279
Rogers, Jean 164-165
Rogues Tavern, The 75
Rohmer, Sax 16, 81, 158
Rolf, Erik 246, 247
Romanoff, Mike 280
Romeo and Juliet 40, 273
Romero, César 141-143
Roosevelt, Franklin D. 74
Rope 293
Rosemary's Baby 74, 241
Rosenbloom, Maxie 233, 234
Rosza, Miklos 249
Rota, Nino 275
Roulien, Raoul 229
Route 66 203
Rover Boys (series) 81
Ruben, J. Walter 157
Ruggles, Charlie 90-92
Ruggles of Red Gap 35
Ruric, Peter 103
Russell, Elizabeth 241
Russell, Gail 289
Russell, Rosalind 156-157
Ruthless 107
Ryan, Edmond 180
Ryan, Sheila 225-226

-S-

S O S Coast Guard 179
Sad Sack, The 285
Salt, Waldo 283
Salter, Hans J. 187, 271
San Francisco 50
Sarlabous, Marie Antoinette (see: Bart, Jean)
Satan Met a Lady 283
Sauers, Joseph (see: Sawyer, Joe)
Sawyer, Joe 152
Sayers, Jo Ann 193
Scarface 141
Scarlet Pimpernel, The 273
Scheider, Roy 288
Schenck, Joseph M. 59, 93
Schildkraut, Joseph 210, 260
Schilling, Gus 296
Schmidlin, Rick 130, 299-300
Schneider, Kurt (see: Earles, Harry)
Schneiderman, John 70
Schrayer, Richard 102
Schubert, 107
Scott, Randolph 90-92, 250
Scott, Reginald Maitland Thomas 170-171

Scoundrel, The 216
Screen Directors Playhouse 263
Sea Hawk, The 151
Secret of the Blue Room 79
Secret of the Chateau 79
Secret People, The 273
Secrets of the French Police 17, 87-89
See My Lawyer 111
Selden, Morton 159
Selwyn, Arch 99
Selwyn, Edgar 99-100
Selznick, David O. 87-88, 170, 240
Semels, Harry 172
September Affair, A 269
Seton, Anya 255
Seton, Bruce 148
Seventh Victim, The 17, 239-242, 246, 251
Sh! The Octopus 150
Shades of Grey 168
Shadow, The 174
Shadow of the Eagle, The 174
Shakespeare, Wm. 16, 183-187
Shannon, Harry 295
Shaw, George Bernard 309
Shea, Gloria 114-116
Sheriff, R.C. 77-78
Sherlock Holmes (series) 136, 145, 170, 225, 244
Sherman, Lowell 121
Ship of Fools 26
Shirley of the Circus 184
Shirley Temple's Storybook Theatre 164
Shonteff, Lindsay 36
Show Them No Mercy! 16, 141-143, 283
Shumate, Harold 192
Siegler, Allen G. 172
Sign of the Ram 17, 270-271, 279
Silence, The 111
Silliphant, Stirling 287
Silvers, Phil 168
Simmons, Jean 302, 303
Simms, Ginny 203-205
Simpson, Ivan 100, 157
Sin of Madelon Claudet, The 99
Sinclair, Ronald 185, 186
Singer, Johnny 149
Siodmak, Robert 262-263
Six Who Pass while the Lentils Boil 127
Skelton, Red 174
Skinner, Frank 187
Slaughter, Tod 147-149
Sloane, William 215

Sloman, Edward 44-47
Small, Edward 93, 134
Smith, Art 280
Smith, Wallace 72
Smoking Guns 114-116, 183
So Dark the Night 259-261, 279
Solt, Andrew 277
Son of Dr. Jekyll 24, 157
Son of Frankenstein 180, 181, 184, 185, 187
Sondergaard, Gale 170
Song of the Thin Man 97
Soul of a Monster, The 16, 246-247, 279
Sparkhul, Theodor 221
Specter of the Rose, The 279
Spider, The (1916) 170
Spider, The (1931) 51-58, 170, 211-212
Spider and the Fly, The 170
Spider Returns, The 57, 170-175
Spider Woman Strikes Back, The 170
Spider's Web, The 17, 57, 170-175
Speilberg, Steven 300
Spinell, Joe 18
Spiral Staircase, The 262
Stafford, Jo 267
Stamp, Terence 303
Star, The 220
Stark Love 178
Starrett, Charles 82-86, 174
Steeger, Henry "Harry" 170-171
Steiger, Rod 18
Steiner, Max 88
Stell, Aaron 298
Stephens, Harvey 134-135
Stephenson, Henry 98-100, 265
Sterling, Paul 127
Stevens, Charles 71
Stevenson, Robert 160, 162-163, 267
Stevenson, Robert Louis 20-26, 76, 156-157
Stewart, Elaine 289
Stewart, James 176
Stewart, Martha 279, 280
Stoker, Bram 43
Stolen Life, A 263
Stoller, Mike 65
Stoloff, Morris 172, 173, 261
Stone, George E. 54, 196
Stone, Lewis 82-86, 98-100
Stone, Milburn 244
Stothart, Herbert 131-132
Straight from the Shoulder 220
Strange Confession 123
Strange People 79

Strange, Robert 151-152
Strange Woman, The 107
Stranger, The 293
Stranger on the Prowl 285
Stranger on the Third Floor 198-200, 213
Strangler of the Swamp 211
Stratton, Chester 167-169
Street Angel 229
Streetcar Names Desire, A 268
Strickfaden, Kenneth 84
Strike It Rich 174
String of Pearls, The 148
Stroheim, Erich von 35-39, 93, 104, 107
Stromberg, Hunt 48, 252-254
Struggle, The 154
Stuart, Gloria 75-80, 110, 112
Studios
    All Star 99
    Allied Artists 304
    American International 170
    Chadwick 35
    Chesterfield 79
    Columbia 116, 127, 136, 170, 171, 194, 196-197, 201-202, 213, 214, 232, 233, 246-247, 250-251, 259, 260, 270, 271, 277-282 (also Santana-Columbia)
    Cooper-Schoedsack 145, 166
    Cosmopolitan 81
    Cruze 35, 93-94, 199
    Decla-Bioscop 107
    Disney 163, 170, 209
    Ealing 36
    Edison 172, 174
    Expeditionary 145
    First National (see: Warner Bros.)
    Fleischer 169, 170
    Goldwyn 59-61, 99, 225
    Goodwill 139
    Grand National 171
    Harmon & Ising 209
    Hellinger 277
    Hubley 212
    International (see: Universal)
    MGM 17, 26, 32, 48-50, 53, 81, 82, 84, 99, 107, 122, 124, 131, 132, 156-157, 180, 209, 211, 218, 236, 252, 260
    MGM-British 100, 148
    Majestic Pictures 11, 79
    Mascot 174, 260
    Metropolitan 248
    Monogram 232, 234

October 299
PRC (Producers Releasing Corp.) 228, 291
Pagewood 145
Paramount 21, 51, 53, 91, 127, 138, 140, 168, 170, 197, 216, 220, 275
Pioneer 21
RKO-Radio 17, 135, 185, 198-200, 203, 236, 240, 260, 262, 268, 279
Rank 274-275
Realart 123
Reliance 93, 134
Republic 172, 189, 260, 292
Roach 169
Santana 277-282
Selznick 236
Sound City (Shepperton) 148
Turner Entertainment 17-18, 28, 130, 211
Twickenham 155
UFA 107
United Artists 59, 93-94, 138, 140, 141, 252, 302
Universal Pictures and/or Jewel-Universal and/or Universal-International 11, 15, 32, 42, 51, 91, 96, 98, 101-109, 110, 115-116, 121, 122, 124, 127, 136, 156, 170, 172, 176, 179, 180, 183-187, 225, 231, 240, 244, 246, 262, 268, 289, 291-301
20th Century-Fox, and/or Fox Film Corp. and/or 20th Century Pictures 15, 29-31, 57, 70, 107, 125, 141, 170, 184, 225-226, 227-228, 229, 230, 251, 252, 255, 274, 278
Vitaphone (see: Warner Bros.)
Wanger 87
Warner Bros. and/or First National and/or Vitaphone 15, 17, 51, 118, 134, 141, 150, 167, 168, 169, 232, 277, 278
Weiss Bros. 172
World Film Corp. 127
Sturges, John 271
Submarine 68
Suddenly, Last Summer 255, 273
Suicide Club, The 76, 156-157
Sullivan, Francis L. 127
Summerville, Tom 114
Summers, Jeremy 182
Summers, Walter, 179-182
Sun Never Sets, The 184
Sunrise at Campobello 74

Suspect 262
Sutherland, A. Edward 87, 89, 90-92
Sutherland, Duncan 275
Sutter's Gold 36
Svengali 16, 17, 40-44, 51, 53, 62-64, 110, 117, 150, 297
"Svengali's Cat" 43
Swamp Water 230
Swanson, Gloria 78
Sweeney Todd, the Demon Barber of Fleet Street 147-149
Swell Guy 277
Sylva, Marguerite 241

-T-

Tallichet, Margaret 198-200
Talton, Alice 281
Tamiroff, Akim 292, 295, 298
Tandy, Jessica 268-269
Tap Roots 142
Tarantula 170, 290
Tarzan (series) 218
Tarzan, the Ape Man 50, 84
Tarzan's New York Adventure 144
Tashman, Lilyan 44-47
Tasker, Robert 87
Tattered Dress, The 289-290, 292
Taylor, Estelle 59, 61
Taylor, Ray 172, 173
Technicolor 121
"Tell-Tale Heart, The" 15, 206-212
Tempest, The 74
Terriss, Tom 127
Terror, The 33, 52-53
Testament du Dr. Cordelier, Le 24
Tetzlaff, Ted 216
Texas Chain Saw Massacre, The 75
Tey, Josephine 309-310
That's Right, You're Wrong 203
Thaxter, Phyllis 270
Theatres
    Regina (Beverly Hills) 179-180
These Are the Damned 285
Thesiger, Ernest 75-80
They Drive by Night 277
They Just Had To Get Married 121
Thief of Baghdad, The 216-219
Thimig, Helene 265
Thin Man, The 50, 98, 252
Thirteenth Guest, The 98
39 Steps, The 266-267
This Day and Age 222

Thomas, Frank M. 220
Thornton, Tex 13
Three Live Ghosts 111
Three Stooges (series) 234
Threepenny Opera, The 283
"Thriller" 307
Tierney, Gene 255-257
Tilbury, Zeffie 125, 127
Time without Pity 285
Tiomkin, Dimitri 263
Titanic 79
To Have and Have Not 279
To Kill a Mockingbird 303
Todd, Holbrook N. 211
Tol'able David 94
Toland, Gregg 64, 268
Tone, Franchot 248-249
Tonight or Never 78
Topkapi 210
Torrence, David 82-83
Torrence, Ernest 93-94
Touch of Evil 15, 289, 291-301
Tourneur, Jacques 236, 237, 287
Tourneur, Maurice 236
Tower of London (1939) 136, 176, 183-187
Tower of London (1962) 187
Tracy, Spencer 24, 229
Trader Horn 50
Trilby (see: *Svengali*)
Tristano, Lenny 306
Trouble for Two 17, 156-157
Trowbridge, Charles 176-178, 225
Tschaikowsky, P.I. 107
Turner, George E. 11, 12-18, 29, 194-195, 249, 287, 310-311
Turner, Martin 114-115
Twain, Mark 291
Two Faces of Dr. Jekyll, The 24
Two Ronnies, The 275

-U-

UCLA Film Archives 299
Ulmer, Edgar G. 101-109, 171
Umann, Emil 179-180
Uncivilized 144-146
Under the Rainbow 26
Unforgettable 194
Unger, Gladys 124
Unholy Garden, The 11, 59-61
Unholy Three, The 15, 26-28
Universal Newsreel (series) 102
Unsell, Eve 29

Uptight 210

-V-

Vague, Vera (see: Allen, Barbara)
Valentino, Rudolph 168
Valerie, Joan 225, 226
Vampire Bat, The 11, 79
Van Dyke, W.S. II 50
Van Every, Dale 102
Van Sloan, Edward 68-69, 201-202
Victoria Regina 308
Vignola, Robert G. 170
Vail, Lester 44-47
Varnel, Marcel 53, 72-74
Varney, Bill 299
Veidt, Conrad 24, 32-33
Venturini, Edward 112
Verlorene, Der 285
Verno, Jerry 148
Vidor, Charles 82
Vieller, Bayard 49
Vincent, June 280
Vogel, Paul 211
Vogel, Virgil 298

-W-

Wadsworth, Henry 129-133
Wake of the Red Witch 121
Walbrook, Anton 272-273
Walker, Mark Evan 212
Walker, Stuart 124-128
Walker, Vernon 204
Walking Dead, The 150-153, 174, 226
Wallaby Jim of the Islands 144
Wallace, Edgar 180
Walsh, J.T. 18
Walter, Wilfred 180, 181
Walthall, Henry B 208
Warburton, John 87-89
Ward, Arthur Sarsfield (see: Rohmer, Sax)
Ward, Edward 127
Warde, Shirley 213
Warlock 275
Warner, Jack L. 277, 279
Warren, E. Allyn 84
Warrenton, Gil 112
Warrick, Ruth 252-253
Warwick, Robert 278, 280
Way Out West 173
Wayne, David 283-286
Wayne, John 303
Wayne, Naunton 274-276

Weaver, Dennis 296
Weaver, Marjorie 227
Webb, Jack 285
Webb, Roy 199, 204, 237
Wegener, Paul 107
Weird Science 18, 26
Welles, Orson 15, 64, 253, 268, 285, 289, 291-301, 309
Wellman, William 65-66, 142
Wells, H.G. 76
Wells, Jacqueline 101-109
Werewolf of London 127
Werewolf of Paris, The 130
Whale, James 76-80, 124, 136
What's Happening in Hollywood 184
What's My Line? 285
Whelan, Tim 216, 218
When the Desert Calls 72
While I Live 224
Whip Hand, The 74, 212
Whistler, The (series; all titles on 261) 259, 261
Whitman, Ernest 220, 221
White, Alice 96
White, Stuart Edward 70
Where Love Has Gone 238
Who Is Hope Schuyler? 225-226
Who Killed Aunt Maggie? 190
Wicked Lady, The 223-224
Widmark, Richard 141
Wilcox, Robert 177, 196-197
Wilcoxson, Henry 227
Wild, Wild West, The 26
Wilde, Oscar 251, 306, 309
Wiles, Gordon 55
Willard, John 82
Williams, Charles 224
Williams, D.J. 148
Williams, Earle 29-31
Williams, Emlyn 16, 122, 154-155
Williams, Hugh 180
Williams, Tennessee 268
Wills, Brember 76-80
Wilson, Carey 209
Wilson, Grady L. 13
Wilson, J. Donald 259
Winter, Mrs. T.G. 185
Wisbar, Frank 211
Wisberg, Aubrey 87
Within the Law 99
Wizard, The 76
Wizard of Oz, The 18, 27

Wolfit, Sir Donald 43
Woman in Room 13, The 111
Woman in the Window, The 262
Woman of Distinction, A 97
Woman's Vengeance, A 268-269
Wonder Man 263
Wood, Edward D., Jr. 174, 295
Wood, Sam 134-135, 266-267
Woodbury, Joan 139
Woods, Harry 135
Woolcott, Alexander 117
Woolf, Edgar Allan 82
Woolrich, Cornell 171, 235-238, 261
Wray, Ardel 235, 236
Wray, Fay 11, 15, 59-61, 199
Wright, Will 211
Written on the Wind 292
Wurtzel, Sol 227
Wuthering Heights 16
Wyler, Margaret 15
Wyler, William 15, 199, 283, 302-305
Wylie, Philip 76
Wyndham, Joan 159
Wynn, Keenan 296

-Y-

You Can't Cheat an Honest Man 142
You'll Find Out 203-205, 232
Young and Innocent 266
Young, Bert 173
Young, Clara Kimball 42
Young Guns 303
Young, James 158
Young Lions, The 275
Young, Loretta 65-66
Young, Victor 216
Your True Adventures (series; all titles on 169) 166-169

-Z-

Zahler, Lee 173
Zanuck, Darryl F. 141, 229, 255
Zany, King (see: Chase, Charley)
Ziegfeld Follies 96
Zoo in Budapest 229, 254
Zucco, George 243-245
Zugsmith, Albert 289, 291-301
Zukor, Adolf 21

www.ingramcontent.com/pod-product-compliance
Lightning Source LLC
Chambersburg PA
CBHW071218080526
44587CB00013BA/1419